CONCISE Edition

FOCUS
ON COLLEGE SUCCESS

Constance Staley

University of Colorado, Colorado Springs

WADSWORTH
CENGAGE Learning™

Australia • Brazil • Japan • Korea • Mexico • Singapore • Spain • United Kingdom • United States

FOCUS on College Success, Concise Edition
Constance Staley

Director of College Success: Annie Todd

Development Editor: Marita Sermolins

Associate Media Editor: Emily Ryan

Marketing Manager: Kirsten Stoller

Marketing Communications Manager:
   Beth Rodio

Content Project Manager: Jessica Rasile

Art Director: Linda Helcher

Print Buyer: Susan Carroll

Permissions Manager, Images: Deanna Ettinger

Permissions Manager, Text: Tim Sisler

Production Service/Compositor: Lachina
   Publishing Services

Text Designer: Anne Carter

Cover Designer: George Restrepo

For product information and technology assistance, contact us at
Cengage Learning Academic Resource Center, 1-800-423-0563

For permission to use material from this text or product,
submit all requests online at **www.cengage.com/permissions**
Further permissions questions can be emailed to
permissionrequest@cengage.com

Library of Congress Control Number: 2008931340

ISBN-13: 978-0-495-56954-1

ISBN-10: 0-495-56954-2

Wadsworth Cengage Learning
25 Thomson Place
Boston, MA 02210
USA

Cengage Learning products are represented in Canada by Nelson Education, Ltd.

For your course and learning solutions, visit **academic.cengage.com**

Purchase any of our products at your local college store or at our preferred online store **www.ichapters.com**

Printed in the United States of America
2 3 4 5 6 7 13 12 11 10 09

FOCUS

ON COLLEGE SUCCESS

Constance Staley

University of Colorado, Colorado Springs

BRIEF CONTENTS

CONTENTS

CHAPTER 3:   MAKING USE OF RESOURCES: FINANCES, TECHNOLOGY, AND CAMPUS SUPPORT   49

ACKNOWLEDGMENTS

It's been said that "Achievement is a *we* thing, not a *me* thing, always the product of many heads and hands." Certainly that's true of the monumental effort involved in writing a first edition textbook. There are so many people to thank that this acknowledgements section could be as long as a chapter of *FOCUS on College Success*! However, here I'll at least mention those who have contributed the most, including all the students over the last 30-plus years who have taught me more than I've ever taught them.

Family Let me start at the center of my life. My deepest thanks go to Steve, my Sean-Connery-look-alike husband (How do I put up with it?), who almost forgot what *I* looked like over the last few years. As I *FOCUS*ed away in my attic office day after day and night after night, he brought me too many cups of tea to count. I cherish his devotion. My daughters Shannon and Stephanie helped bring some much-needed balance to my life, and aside from being the most adorable children on the planet, my grandtwins Aidan and Ailie have been a living learning laboratory for me. As little children mastering one new thing after another, they truly have taught me about of the pure joy of learning. And to my beautiful 80-something Mom, who lovingly alternated between urging me to "slow down and relax" and "hurry up and finish," thanks for all your motherly love.

Reviewers The list of reviewers who have contributed their insights and expertise to *FOCUS on College Success* is long. Starting any new edition from scratch requires substantial input. My heartfelt thanks to all of them: Peg Adams, Northern Kentucky University; Josie Adamo, Buffalo State College; Barbara Anderson, Midlands Technical College; Jon Aoki, University of Houston-Downtown; Mercy Azeke, Norfolk State University; Michael Becraft, Austin Peay State University; Lynda Bennett, Blue Mountain Community College; Janet Breaker, Milwaukee Area Technical College; Beverly Brucks, Illinois Central College; Toi Buchanan, Fayetteville Technical Community College; Castell Burton, Valencia Community College; David Campaigne, University of South Florida; Lea Campbell, North Harris Montgomery Community College; Barbara Chavis, Cleveland Community College; Miriam Chiza, North Hennepin Community College; G. Jay Christensen, California State University, Northridge; Regina Vincent Clark, Tennessee State University; Karen Clay, Miami Dade College; Geoff Cohen, University of California, Riverside; Carrie Cokely, Meredith College; Della Colantone, Alderson-Broaddus College; Therese Crary, Highland Community College; Kimberly Cummings, University of Tampa; Allison Cumming-McCann, Springfield College; Janice A. Daly, Florida State University; Vrita H. Delaine, The University of Southern Mississippi; Mark Demark, Alvin Community College; Gigi Derballa, Asheville-Buncombe Technical Community College; Anne Dickens, Lee College; Michael Discello, Pittsburgh Technical Institute; Carmen Etienne, Oakland University; Sally Firmin, Baylor University; Becky Garlick, Blinn College; Sharol Gauthier, University of South Carolina Upstate; Jayne Geissler, East Carolina University; Dee Allen Goedeke, High Point University; Laura Goppold, Central Piedmont Community College; Marie Gore, University of Maryland, Baltimore County; Laurie Grimes, Lorain County Community College; Valerie Hewitt, Remington College; Joseph Jumpeter, Pennsylvania State University, Wilkes-Barre; Page Keller, College of Charleston; Lois Lawson-Briddell, Gloucester County College; Kelly Lee, Orange Coast College; Janet Lindner, Midlands Technical College; Brenda Marina, The University of Akron; Marty Marty, Missouri State University; Claudia McDade, Jacksonville State University; Michelle McDaniel, Middle Tennessee State University; Bridgett McGowen, Prairie View A&M University; Aiesha Miller, The University of Akron; Brian Mitchell, Gibbs College of Boston; Karen Mitchell, Northern Essex Community College; Kelly

Morales, University of Texas-Pan American; Gail Muse, Holmes Community College; Bonnie Porter Pajka, Luzerne County; Community College; Kate Pandolpho, Ocean County College; Stan Parker, Charleston Southern University; James Penven, Virginia Polytechnic Institute and State University; Joni Webb Petschauer, Appalachian State University; Amy Poland, Buena Vista University; Margaret Puckett, North Central State College; Terry Rafter-Carles, Valencia Community College; Melanie Rago, Indiana University; Margaret Rapp, Tyler Junior College; Rebecca Reed, Johnson & Wales University; Virginia Reilly, Ocean County College; Saundra Richardson, University of North Carolina at Pembroke; Chuck Rhodes, Sonoma State University; Jennifer Rockwood, The University of Toledo; Lawrence Rodriguez, Palo Alto College; Bea Rogers, Monmouth University; Keri Rogers, Sam Houston State University; Tara Ross, Keiser College; Patty Santoianni, Sinclair Community College; Sarah Shutt, J. Sargeant Reynolds Community College; Phebe Simmons, Blinn College; Brenda A. Smith, Norfolk State University; Kim Smokowski, Bergen Community College; Marilyn Starkes, Thomas Nelson Community College; Angie Walston, Barton College; Janice Waltz, Harrisburg Area Community College; Jodi Webb, Bowling Green State University; Jill Wilks, Southern Utah University.

Focus Group Participants   The same may be said of all the people who helped react to various versions of the design and responded to my ideas for some new features in a college success textbook: Lea Campbell, North Harris Montgomery Community College; Brenda Marina, The University of Akron; Marty Marty, Missouri State University; Claudia McDade, Jacksonville State University; Brian Mitchell, Gibbs College of Boston; Margaret Puckett, North Central State College; Rebecca Reed, Johnson & Wales University; Bea Rogers, Monmouth University; and Angie Walston, Barton College.

The Wadsworth Team   No book, of course, gets very far without a publisher, and *FOCUS* has had the best publishing team imaginable: the dynamic, highly people-skilled Annie Todd, Director of College Success; the meticulous, multi-talented Marita Sermolins, Development Editor; the energetic, industrious Kirsten Stoller, Marketing Manager; a true professional who combed the first pages and probably did more than I'll ever know, Jessica Rasile, Content Project Manager; the obviously talented and conscientious Art Director, Cate Barr; the artistic voice who came all the way to Colorado for the photo shoot, Sheri Blaney, Senior Permissions Account Manager; and lots of folks I never met, other than on e-mail: Tim Sisler, Text Permissions Researcher; Darren Wright, Photo Permissions Researcher; and Annie Beck, Project Manager at Lachina Publishing Services. I'd like to especially thank Larry Harwood, the master photographer who spent a long, hard weekend clicking photos of the *FOCUS* cast on the University of Colorado at Colorado Springs campus. And heartfelt thanks to Wadsworth's Annie Mitchell and Sean Wakely, who believed in this project from the very start; Sylvia Shepherd, whose creative vision shaped much of this book, and Lauren Larsen, whose wit and wisdom formed the basis for several of the early chapters.

Other Contributors   I'd also particularly like to thank the "*FOCUS* All-Stars," as I call them, my students (and one colleague) who modeled for the photo shoots and starred in the "Inside the *FOCUS* Studio" videos. They followed artistic direction like pros, and they make this book unique. I'd also like to thank my colleagues at UCCS who have helped me develop many of the ideas in this book, whether they know it or not—all the Freshman Seminar faculty past and present, and three key colleagues and friends: Kathy Andrus, Nina Ellis, and Barb Gaddis. I also can't go without thanking the many authors who granted me permission to use their work and four essential scholars who allowed me to use, apply, and extend their instruments throughout the book: Neil Fleming, Brian French, John Bransford, and John Pelley. And thanks to my expert student research assistants, Phil Wilburn and Sarah Snyder, and my best buddy Liz for all her encouraging words. And finally, I'd like to thank Matt McClain, the comedy writer who brought his innovative humor to the learning process through podcast summaries of the chapters and television scripts for the website TV shows. He took the "big ideas" from *FOCUS* chapters and made them memorable to students by using their own best-loved media.

Above all, *FOCUS* has taught me truly to focus. Writing a book takes the same kind of endurance and determination that it takes to get a college degree. My empathy level for my students has, if anything, increased—and I am thankful for all I've learned while writing. It has been a cathartic experience to see what has filled each computer screen as I've tapped, tapped, tapped away. Ultimately, what I have chosen to put into each chapter has told me a great deal about who I am, what I know (and don't), and what I value. There's no doubt: I am a better teacher for having written this book. May all my readers grow through their *FOCUS* experience, too.

MEET THE CAST

Chapter 1

Gloria Gonzales / Debbie

Hometown: Saguache, Colorado

Major: Business with a minor in Communication

Expected Graduation Date: 2010

Lessons Learned: Debbie learned through her first-year seminar course that it takes time and effort to establish great relationships. She got involved in intramural sports, which helped her meet new people and make friends. Although she's doing well now, she wishes she'd studied more her first term.

Toughest First-Year Class: Microeconomics because it was an entirely new subject for her.

Advice to New Students: "Get your priorities straight; college is a great place to be, so get a great start by setting good study habits, and I HIGHLY recommend a planner because you will be surprised at how fast your time can become occupied."

Chapter 2

Tammy Ko / Jessica

Hometown: Manitou Springs, Colorado

Major: Marketing

Expected Graduation Date: 2009

Lessons Learned: Juggling a part-time job while in school, Jessica loved living on campus her first term and meeting new people, but she regretted not talking to other students about which professors and courses to take towards her marketing major. In order to succeed, she says, you've "gotta give it all you've got!"

Toughest First-Year Class: Microeconomics because it wasn't like high school courses that just required memorizing a lot of facts.

Advice to New Students: "Talk to other students to learn about the best professors, and make sure you are studying something that you are interested in."

Chapter 3

Jessica Taylor / Tarren

Background: Like her *FOCUS* Challenge Case character, Tarren also graduated from a private high school and found the transition from high school to college a bit overwhelming. Having lived overseas most of her life, Tarren now calls Colorado Springs home.

Major: English

Expected Graduation Date: 2011

Lessons Learned: "Stay on top of your studies and understand how important teachers are in college and how they can positively influence students."

Toughest First-Year Class: Biology because of heavy reading assignments

Advice to New Students: "Get involved on campus and definitely choose to take a first-year seminar course!"

Free Time: horseback riding, playing tennis, and skiing

Chapter 4

Derek Johnson / Derrick

Hometown: Colorado Springs, Colorado

Major: Communications/Recording Arts

Graduation Date: 2007

Lessons Learned: Even though he's not married and has no children, Derrick and his case study character have much in common—too much to do and too little time! Derrick felt his biggest mistake his first year was not asking enough questions in class. He knows now he should have asked for clarity on content or assignments he didn't understand.

Toughest First-Year Class: English because he and his instructor had differing opinions, but he communicated through the tough spots and earned an "A".

Advice to New Students: "Surround yourself with positive people. As the saying goes, 'you are the company you keep.' I've seen many of my friends drop out because the people they called friends were holding them back from their full potential. Now that I have graduated, I look back at all the people I hold close and know that I wouldn't have made it without them."

Free Time: composing music and producing films

Chapter 5

Annie Miller / Meagan

Hometown: Albuquerque, New Mexico

Major: Nursing

Expected Graduation Date: 2011

Lessons Learned: Megan admits that her biggest mistake her first term was not asking anyone for help with anything. But she enjoyed moving away from home and being more independent, meeting new people, and having a more laid-back academic schedule than her high school schedule had been.

Toughest First-Year Course: Calculus because she was overconfident and didn't study for exams.

Advice to New Students: "Don't give up! College is amazing! Oh, and don't spend all of your money on food."

Free Time: biking, hiking, playing Ultimate Frisbee, and giving campus tours

Chapter 6

Lindsey Collier / Heather

Hometown: Her parents just moved to another state—so where *is* home?

Major: Nursing

Expected Graduation Date: 2010

Lessons Learned: Heather made the mistake of not making academics her first priority, but she learned from her first-year seminar course that she needed to be willing to sacrifice social time for study time.

Advice to New Students: "College isn't like high school—you do actually have to study three times as much for any course. No matter what course it is, study for it. You'll feel much better about receiving high marks than about partying with friends. And get involved on your campus. It's your home away from home, so why not make the most of it?"

Free Time: college Step and Dance Team

Chapter 7
Kevin Baxter / Dave

Hometown: St. Paul, Minnesota

Background: Portraying a student returning to school after fifteen-plus years in the working world, Dave is currently a professor of chemistry at University of Colorado at Colorado Springs.

College Memories: Dave remembers how much he liked the different social environment college provided after graduating from high school.

Toughest First-Year Course: English Composition since writing wasn't exactly his forte.

Advice to New Students: "Study hard, and use your time wisely."

Free Time: woodworking, hiking, and climbing

Chapter 8
Katie Alexander / Christina

Hometown: Colorado Springs, Colorado. Since she went to college in her hometown, Christina really enjoyed the opportunity college provided to meet new people.

Major: Nursing

Expected Graduation Date: 2009

Lessons Learned: Spending her free time with her friends watching movies, going bowling or dancing, and just hanging out, Christina found that like her *FOCUS* Challenge Case character, she, too, would make up excuses to get out of studying and doing her homework. She quickly learned the importance of reading and taking notes. "As weird as it may sound, reading cuts your end study time by more than half. Reading the material ahead of time helps you understand everything so much better."

Advice to New Students: "Stay motivated. College is going to FLY by! If you stay motivated and get good grades, it really will be over before you know it."

Chapter 9
Joe Cloud / Alvin

Hometown: Ganado, Arizona (Navajo Nation)

Major: Business

Expected Graduation Date: 2010

Toughest First-Year Course: Spanish because he came from a place where no other languages are ever spoken.

Lessons Learned: President of the American Indian Science and Engineering Society on campus, Alvin identifies closely with his *FOCUS* Challenge Case character. He, too, is one of a minority of Native Americans in higher education, so a lot of people in his hometown are carefully watching his academic success. Alvin admits his biggest mistake in his first term was not opening up to people—he came to school for class and left without trying to meet new people. But he learned from his mistakes and eventually came to value meeting all sorts of different people through activities on campus.

Advice to New Students: "Learn from *my* mistakes: Be open to try new things, get out of your comfort zone, and be free to be silly—everyone is at some point. You meet a lot of new people that way and it makes your first year the experience of a lifetime."

Chapter 10
Kia Washington / Charmaine

Hometown: Colorado Springs, Colorado

Major: Psychology and Sociology

Graduation Date: 2006 (Charmaine is now working towards a graduate degree in Student Affairs in Higher Education.)

Toughest First-Year Course: General psychology because there was so much to learn in such a short period of time.

Lessons Learned: In her first-year seminar, Charmaine learned how to manage her time more effectively, as well as the necessity of keeping yourself healthy in mind, body, and spirit, something she felt her *FOCUS* Challenge Case character could have benefited from.

Advice to New Students: "Remember to have fun in everything that you do, both academically and otherwise. Take care of yourself first and don't feel as though you have to do everything all the time; sometimes the best parts of life come during moments of down time. This is where you are able to truly reflect on what it is you're doing and remember why you're doing it in the first place!"

Chapter 11

Ethan Cole / Josh

Hometown: Fort Morgan, Colorado

Major: Sociology

Expected Graduation Date: 2008

Lessons Learned: Like his *FOCUS* Challenge Case character, Josh noticed that he, too, didn't always push himself to reach his potential. But he learned through his first-year seminar course that he is responsible for himself and that professors aren't like high school teachers. They will let you fail a class if you don't do what you need to. It's up to you.

Advice to New Students: "Not only did getting involved on campus help me have more fun in school, but it has also helped me academically. It has taught me how to manage my time and has made it so much easier for me to participate with confidence in class. Just make sure you get what you need to do done, and you will enjoy your college experience so much more."

Free Time: "Free time? What's that?! I'm too busy to have free time!" (But he secretly admits he snowboards, plays guitar, draws, and spends time with friends.)

MEET THE AUTHOR

Constance Staley

Hometown: Pittsburgh, Pennsylvania (although she never actually lived there. Instead, she lived all over the world and went to ten schools in twelve years.)

Background: Connie has taught at the University of Colorado at Colorado Springs for more than 30 years after getting a bachelor's degree in education, a master's degree in linguistics, and a Ph.D. in communication.

College Memories: Connie remembers loving her public speaking class as a first-year student and having tons of friends, but being extremely homesick for her family.

Advice to New Students: "Earning a college degree is hard work, takes a long time, and requires a substantial investment of your time, energy, and resources. But it's the best investment you can make in your own future—one you'll never regret."

Free Time: Spending time with her husband, her two daughters, and her boy-girl grandtwins; relaxing at her cabin in the mountains; and traveling around the country to speak to other professors who also care about their first-year students and their success.

INTRODUCTION TO STUDENTS

Dear Reader,

This book is different. It won't coerce, coddle, caution, or coax you. Instead, it will give *you* the tools you need to coach yourself. Ultimately, this book is about you, your college career, and your career beyond college. It's about the future you will create for yourself.

FOCUS on College Success stars a cast of twelve of my own students (and one colleague), like a stage play. One student "actor" is featured in each chapter's opening case study. All thirteen cast members reappear throughout the book, so that you'll get to know them as you read. I've been teaching for more than 30 years now and worked with thousands of students. Each case study is about a real student (with a fictitious name) that I've worked with or a composite of several students. You may find you have some things in common with them. But whether you do or not, I hope they will make this book come to life for you. You'll also be able to meet these "actors" electronically in videos called, "Inside the *FOCUS* Studio," on the book's Online Resource Center.

I love what I do, and I care deeply about students. I hope that comes through to you as a reader. You'll see that I've inserted some of my personality, had a bit of fun at times, and tried to create a new kind of textbook for you. In my view, learning should be engaging, personal, memorable, challenging, and fun.

Most importantly, I know that these next few years hold the key to unlock much of what you want from your life. And from all my years of experience and research, I can tell you straightforwardly that what you read in this book works. It gets results. It can turn you into a better, faster learner. *Really?* you ask. Really! The only thing you have to do is put all the words in this book into action. That's where the challenge comes in.

Getting a college degree takes time, energy, resources, and focus. At times, it may mean shutting down the six windows you have open on your computer, and directing all your attention to one thing in laser-like fashion. It may mean disciplining yourself to dig in and stick with something until you've nailed it. Can you do it? I'm betting you can, or I wouldn't have written this book. Invest yourself fully in what you read here, and then decide to incorporate it into your life. If there's one secret to college success, that's it.

So, you're off! You're about to begin one of the most fascinating, liberating, challenging, and adventure-filled times of your life. I may not be able to meet each one of you personally, but I *can* wish you well, wherever you are. I hope this book helps you on your journey.

Constance Staley

FOCUS ENTRANCE INTERVIEW

Although you may not have experienced life as a new college student for long, we're interested in how you expect to spend your time, what challenges you think you'll face, and your general views of what you think college will be like. Please answer thoughtfully.

INFORMATION ABOUT YOU

Name _____

Student Number _____ Course/Section _____

Instructor _____

Gender _____ Age _____

1. **Ethnic identification:**
   ____ Native American/American Indian   ____ Hispanic
   ____ Caucasian   ____ African American
   ____ Asian or Pacific Islander   ____ Prefer not to answer

2. **Is English your first (native) language?**
   ____ yes   ____ no

3. **Where are you living this term?**
   ____ in campus housing   ____ on my own
   ____ with my immediate family   ____ other (please explain) _____
   ____ with a relative other than my immediate family

4. **Did your parents graduate from college?**
   ____ yes, both   ____ neither
   ____ yes, father only ____ not sure
   ____ yes, mother only

5. **How many credit hours are you taking this term?**
   ____ 6 or fewer   ____ 15–16
   ____ 7–11   ____ 17 or more
   ____ 12–14

6. **Did you start college elsewhere before attending this school?**
   ____ yes   ____ no

7. **In addition to going to college, do you expect to work for pay at a job (or jobs) this term?**
   ____ yes   ____ no

8. **If so, how many hours per week do you expect to work?**
   ____ 1–10   ____ 31–40
   ____ 11–20   ____ 40+
   ____ 21–30

9. **Which of the following describes why you are working for pay this term? (Mark all that apply.)**
   ____ to pay for college tuition   ____ to pay for child care
   ____ to pay for basic expenses that I need (rent, housing, food, etc.)   ____ to pay for textbooks
   ____ to pay for extra expenses that I want (clothes, entertainment, etc.)   ____ to save money for the future
   ____ to buy a car   ____ to see how much I can make
   ____ to support a family   ____ other (please explain) _____

10. **How will you pay for your college expenses? (Check all that apply.)**

____ my own earnings   ____ scholarships and grants

____ my parents' contributions   ____ loans

____ my spouse or partner's contributions   ____ other (please explain) _____

____ my employer's contributions

11. **If you plan to work for pay, where will you work?**

____ on campus   ____ off campus   ____ at more than one job

12. **If you are entering college soon after completing high school, on average, how many total hours per week did you spend studying outside of class in high school?**

____ 0–5	____ 26–30
____ 6–10	____ 31–35
____ 11–15	____ 36–40
____ 16–20	____ 40+
____ 21–25	____ I am a returning student and attended high school some time ago.

13. **What was your high school grade point average?**

____ A+	____ C+
____ A	____ C
____ A−	____ C−
____ B+	____ D or lower
____ B	____ I don't remember.
____ B−	

INFORMATION ABOUT YOUR COLLEGE EXPECTATIONS

14. **How do you expect to learn best in college? (Check all that apply.)**

____ by looking at charts, maps, graphs   ____ by reading books

____ by looking at color-coded information   ____ by writing papers

____ by looking at symbols and graphics   ____ by taking notes

____ by listening to instructors' lectures   ____ by going on field trips

____ by listening to other students during an in-class discussion   ____ by engaging in activities

____ by talking about course content with friends or roommates   ____ by actually doing things

15. **For each of the following pairs of descriptors, which set sounds most like you? (Please choose between the two options on each line and place a checkmark by your choice.)**

____ Extraverted and outgoing   or   ____ Introverted and quiet

____ Detail-oriented and practical   or   ____ Big-picture and future-oriented

____ Rational and truthful   or   ____ People-oriented and tactful

____ Organized and self-disciplined   or   ____ Spontaneous and flexible

16. ***FOCUS* is about 11 different aspects of college life. Which are you most interested in? Which may contain information you expect to find most challenging to apply in your own life? (Check all that apply.)**

Most interested in	Most challenging to apply to myself		Most interested in	Most challenging to apply to myself	
____	____	Building dreams, setting goals	____	____	Engaging, listening, and note-taking in class
____	____	Learning to learn	____	____	Developing your memory
____	____	Using resources: finances, technology, and campus support	____	____	Reading and studying
____	____	Managing time and energy	____	____	Taking tests
____	____	Thinking critically and creatively	____	____	Building relationships
			____	____	Choosing a major and career

17. **Which one of your current classes do you expect to find most challenging this term and why?**

Which class? (course title *or* department and course number) _____

Why? _____

Do you expect to succeed in this course? ____ yes ____ no

Perhaps (please explain): _____

18. **How many total hours per week do you expect to spend outside of class studying for your college courses this term?**

____ 0–5   ____ 26–30

____ 6–10   ____ 31–35

____ 11–15   ____ 36–40

____ 16–20   ____ 40+

____ 21–25

19. **Which of the following on-campus resources do you plan to use once or more this term? (Please check all that apply.)**

____ library

____ campus learning centers (whatever is available on your campus, such as a Writing Center, Math Learning Center, etc.)

____ computer labs

____ the Student Success Center or New Student Center, if one is available

____ the Counseling Center, if one is available

____ professors' office hours for individual meetings/conferences/help

____ student clubs or organizations

____ none

20. **For the following sets of opposite descriptive phrases, put a checkmark on the line between the two that best represent your response.**

I expect my first term of college to:

challenge me academically	____ ____ ____ ____ ____	be easy
be very different from high school	____ ____ ____ ____ ____	be a lot like high school
be exciting	____ ____ ____ ____ ____	be dull
be interesting	____ ____ ____ ____ ____	be uninteresting
motivate me to continue	____ ____ ____ ____ ____	discourage me
be fun	____ ____ ____ ____ ____	be boring
help me feel a part of this campus	____ ____ ____ ____ ____	make me feel alienated

21. **Please mark your *top three areas of concern* relating to your first term of college by placing 1, 2, and 3 next to the items you choose.**

____ I might not fit in.

____ I might have difficulty making friends.

____ I might not be academically successful.

____ My performance might disappoint my family.

____ My personal life might interfere with my studies.

____ My studies might interfere with my personal life.

____ I might have financial difficulties.

____ My job might interfere with my studies.

____ My studies might interfere with my job.

____ My social life might interfere with my studies.

____ My studies might interfere with my social life.

____ My professors might not care about me as an individual.

____ I might not finish my degree.

____ I might miss the company of my friends.

____ I might miss the company of my family.

____ I might not manage my time well.

____ I might be bored in my classes.

____ I might feel intimidated by my professors.

____ I might feel overwhelmed by all I have to do.

____ other (please explain) _____

22. **Broadly speaking, which area do you expect to major in?**

____ Arts & Sciences   ____ Nursing/Health Sciences

____ Education   ____ Business

____ Engineering   ____ other (please explain) _____

23. **How certain are you now of a chosen major? (1 = totally sure, 5 = totally unsure)** ____

24. **How certain are you now that you will complete your degree? (1 = totally sure, 5 = totally unsure)** ____

25. **How certain are you now that you will complete your degree at this school? (1 = totally sure, 5 = totally unsure)** ____

26. **How certain are you now of your intended career choice? (1 = totally sure, 5 = totally unsure)** ____

27. **How certain are you now about whether you'll obtain an advanced degree after you finish college? (1 = totally sure, 5 = totally unsure)** ____

28. **What do you expect your grade point average to be at the end of your first term of college?**

    ____ A+   ____ B   ____ C

    ____ A   ____ B−   ____ C−

    ____ A−   ____ C+   ____ D or lower

    ____ B+

29. **All college students develop expectations of what college will be like from various sources. How did you develop your expectations of what college might be like? (Mark your top three information sources with 1, 2, and 3.)**

    ____ TV and movies

    ____ friends/siblings who have already gone to college

    ____ discussions with teachers/counselors in high school

    ____ information I received from colleges in the mail

    ____ talks with my parents

    ____ talks with my friends who are also now freshmen

    ____ the Internet

    ____ other (please explain) _____

30. **How confident are you in yourself in each of the following areas? (1 = very confident, 5 = not at all confident)**

    ____ overall academic ability

    ____ mathematical skills

    ____ leadership ability

    ____ reading skills

    ____ public speaking skills

    ____ study skills

    ____ technology skills

    ____ physical well being

    ____ writing skills

    ____ social skills

    ____ emotional well being

    ____ teamwork skills

31. **Why did you take the course for which you are using this textbook? (Mark your top three reasons with 1, 2, and 3.)**

    ____ It was required.

    ____ It sounded interesting.

    ____ I thought it would help make my transition to college easier.

    ____ I thought it would help me learn about the campus.

    ____ I thought it would help me make friends.

    ____ I thought it would help me academically.

    ____ My parent(s) or other family member(s) thought it was a good idea.

    ____ My advisor recommended it.

    ____ A high school teacher/counselor recommended it.

    ____ The information I received in campus mailings convinced me.

    ____ The materials I received at freshman orientation convinced me.

    ____ A friend/sibling who'd taken this course recommended it.

    ____ other (please explain) _____

32. **What is the most important reason you decided to attend this school? (Check one)**

    ____ Recommendation of friend(s) who attended here

    ____ Reasonable cost

    ____ Reputation of the school

    ____ Location of the school

    ____ Availability of academic programs I'm interested in

    ____ Financial aid I was offered

    ____ Recommendation of high school teachers/counselors

    ____ Campus website

    ____ other (please explain) _____

33. **Was this school your first choice among the colleges you considered?** ____ yes ____ no

34. **Why did you decide to go to college? (Check all that apply)**

    ____ Because I want to build a better life for myself.

    ____ Because I want to build a better life for my family.

    ____ Because I want to be very well off financially in the future.

    ____ Because I need a college education to achieve my dreams.

    ____ Because my friends were going to college.

    ____ Because my family encouraged me to go.

    ____ Because it was expected of me.

    ____ Because I was recruited for athletics.

    ____ Because I want to continue learning.

    ____ Because the career I am pursuing requires a degree.

    ____ Because I was unsure of what I might do instead.

    ____ other (please explain) _____

35. **Looking ahead, how satisfied do you expect to be with your decision to attend this school?**

___ very satisfied   ___ somewhat dissatisfied

___ satisfied   ___ very dissatisfied

___ not sure

36. **What are you most looking forward to in college?** _____

_____

37. **How would you describe the best outcomes you hope for at the end of this term? Why are they important to you?** _____

_____

38. **Do you expect to achieve these outcomes? Why or why not?** _____

_____

1 Building Dreams, Setting Goals

YOU'RE ABOUT TO DISCOVER...

- How this book will help you learn

- What motivates you

- How your attitude can sabotage you

- Why you should distinguish between dreams and goals

- How to develop goals that work

- What it takes to succeed in college

R E A D I N E S S   C H E C K

Before beginning this chapter, take a moment to answer these questions. Your answers will help you assess how ready you are to focus.

1 = not very/not much/very little/low   10 = very/a lot/very much/high

Based on reading the "You're about to discover..." list and skimming this chapter, how much do you think you probably already know about the subject matter?

    1   2   3   4   5   6   7   8   9   10

How much do you think this information might affect your college success?

    1   2   3   4   5   6   7   8   9   10

How much do you think this information might affect your career success after college?

    1   2   3   4   5   6   7   8   9   10

In general, how motivated are you to learn the material in this chapter?

    1   2   3   4   5   6   7   8   9   10

How ready are you to focus on this chapter—physically, intellectually, and emotionally? Circle a number for each aspect of your readiness to focus.

    1   2   3   4   5   6   7   8   9   10

If any of your answers is below a 5, consider addressing the issue before reading. For example, if you're feeling scattered, take a few moments to settle down and focus.

Finally, how long do you think it will take you to complete this chapter? _____ Hour(s) _____ Minutes

Gloria Gonzales

It was her first day of college. As Gloria Gonzales walked to her first class, "College Success," she had mixed feelings: excitement, anticipation, anxiety, and apprehension. She wondered if she'd meet any interesting people, if she'd like her instructor, and if she'd learn anything important in this class. After all, she'd gotten good grades in high school without even trying hard. If she just put in some effort, she thought, she'd be successful in college, too. How can you study something like "College Success" for a whole term? she asked herself.

To be honest, Gloria thought she probably already knew most of what there was to learn in this course, and if she didn't, so what? She knew what she had to do to get good grades—everyone does—but she didn't always choose to do it, that's all. School was part of her life, but it wasn't always her top priority. At least this course would probably be easier than her math course or her composition course with all that writing.

Gloria wasn't the first person in her family to go to college. Her sister had attempted it, but she'd dropped out after her first term and gotten a job. "College, who needs it?" she'd exclaimed. "I want to start earning good money right away, not years from now!" There were times when Gloria thought her sister might be right. Her sister certainly seemed able to afford some of the things Gloria had always wanted herself. Was college really going to be worth all the time, effort, and expense? But everyone she knew was going to college; it was the right thing to do after high school, and everyone expected it of her.

Gloria's family didn't have much money. They were sacrificing to help finance her college education. She'd better perform, they'd said. They'd told her point-blank that her sister had set a bad example, and that her first-term grades had better not include anything lower than a B. Frankly, Gloria was beginning to feel a twinge of performance pressure. Of all the children in her family, her sister had always been considered the smartest, and she'd given up after only one term. If her sister couldn't do it, how could Gloria? If she were to succeed, exactly what would it take?

Despite her worries as she walked down the hallway toward the classroom, Gloria was sure of one thing: She looked good today—really good. Her sister's skirt fit perfectly, the new red shirt was definitely her color, and thankfully it was a good hair day. Gloria had always been able to make heads turn.

Beneath it all, Gloria knew what she wanted, anyway. She was going into the fashion industry. She'd dreamed of that since she was ten years old. She wasn't sure exactly what she'd need to do to make

it, but she'd worked in a clothing store at the mall all through high school, and she was good at it. In fact, the store kept trying to give her more hours because she had such exceptional customer service skills. She thought she'd probably just work her college courses around her thirty-five hours a week there.

Gloria's parents wanted her to major in engineering because they thought it would be a lucrative and stable profession. They were always clipping articles about engineering jobs from the newspaper and giving them to her, but she kept telling them she had no interest. "There'll always be good jobs for engineers," they said. She'd heard it so many times that her usual response now was "Yeah, whatever. . . ." While they talked engineering, she dreamed of becoming a famous fashion designer with her own line of clothing. She was going to call it "Gloria." Her parents had named her after their favorite rock-and-roll song of all time, "G-L-O-R-I-A." Imagine—her own clothing label with her name on it!

As she reached for the classroom doorknob, Gloria couldn't help wondering about the two questions at the forefront of her mind: "What will college really be like?" and "Will I be successful?" She took a deep breath as she opened the classroom door. *This is it*, she thought. Somehow, she felt as if she were outside herself, watching on the big screen—replete with Panavision and DTS sound. *This is real; this is me, starring in my own movie*, she said to herself. And even though it felt good, Gloria had to wonder about the ending. All she could do was hope for the best.

WHAT DO **YOU** THINK?

Now that you've read about Gloria Gonzales, answer the following questions. You may not know all the answers yet, but you'll find out what you know and what you stand to gain by reading this chapter.

1. Describe Gloria's motivation to succeed in college. Is she sufficiently motivated to succeed?
2. Describe Gloria's beliefs about her intelligence. Does she think college is mostly about effort or about ability? Is Gloria a *learner* or a *performer*?
3. Is Gloria's vision of becoming a famous fashion designer a goal or a dream? Why?
4. Identify three things (attitudes, beliefs, fears, and so on) that do not show focus and might cause Gloria to make poor life management choices.
5. Identify three things that do show focus and might help Gloria make good life management choices.
6. What elements of Gloria's situation are similar to your own college experience thus far?
7. Gloria's parents' definition of success in school meant getting good grades. Do you agree with this definition? Why or why not? Could equating good grades with success actually hinder Gloria's ability to succeed? If so, how?

Who Are You?
And What Do You Want?

Imagine this voicemail greeting: "Hi. At the tone, please answer two of life's most important questions. Who are you? And what do you want?" Beep. Can you answer these questions right now? How much do you really know about yourself and what you want from this life of yours?

Don't worry. These aren't trick questions and there are no wrong answers. But there are some answers that are more right for you than others. College is a great time to think about who you are and what you want. In addition to learning about biology or history or business—whatever you choose for a major—college will be a time to learn about yourself: your motivation, values, dreams, and goals. College is a time when you'll make some of the most important choices of your life. Which major will you choose? Which career will you aim for? How many lifelong friends will you make? From this point on, it's up to you. Have you ever heard this phrase with ten two-letter words: "If it is to be, it is up to me"? It's true.

Think about it: a college education is one of the best investments you can make. Once you've earned a college degree, it's yours forever. Someone can steal your car or walk away with your cell phone, but once you've earned a college degree, no one can ever take it from you. Your choice to be a college graduate will pay off in many ways. So even if you aren't sure exactly how you want to spend the rest of your life right now, you can't go wrong by investing in your future.

This book starts with the big picture: your life. It's about managing your life, being fully invested in what you're doing, and using your abilities to their utmost. Notice the phrase "managing your life"—not *controlling* your life. Let's face it: many things in life are beyond our control. But you can manage your life by making smart choices, setting realistic goals, monitoring your time and energy, motivating yourself, and ultimately creating your own future. As the title of this book states boldly, it's about focus.

> **"What is important is to keep learning, to enjoy challenge, and to tolerate ambiguity. In the end there are no certain answers."**
>
> **Martina Horner, former President of Radcliffe College**

For many of us, focusing is a challenge. We work too many hours, crowd our lives with obligations, and rush from one thing to the next. We're good at multitasking. We can surf the Internet, listen to a new CD, watch a DVD, and read this chapter—all at the same time! While we've become skilled at multitasking, we may have sacrificed some of the self-discipline required for in-depth study. Multitasking may be a great skill to have when you're a corporate CEO, but learning to focus is what most college students need. In fact, recent research indicates that multitasking hurts your brain's ability to learn, and that what you learn while you're distracted by other things is harder to use and recall.[1]

Left: FogStock LLC/Index Open. Right: PhotoObjects.net/Jupiter Images

Of course, some people achieve success without a college degree, but by and large, they're the exception. Even Steven Spielberg, self-made billionaire in the film industry and winner of Academy Awards for *Schindler's List* and *Saving Private Ryan*, felt the need to finish the college degree he had started more than thirty years before. "I wanted to accomplish this for many years as a 'thank you' to my parents for giving me the opportunity for an education and a career, and as a personal note for my own family—and young people everywhere—about the importance of achieving their college education goals," he said. "But I hope they get there quicker than I did. Completing the requirements for my degree 33 years after finishing my principal education marks my longest post-production schedule."[2]

If you read this book carefully and follow its advice, it will help you become the best student you can possibly be. It will give you practical tools to help you manage your life. It will take you beyond college into your career. And most of all, it will encourage you to become a true scholar. That is this book's challenge to you as you begin your college career.

EXERCISE 1.1 We'd Like to Get to Know You...

Take a few minutes to finish the following statements. Think about what each sentence says about you. Use your responses to introduce yourself to the class or form pairs, talk over your responses together, and use your partner's answers to introduce him or her to the class.

1. I'm happiest when _____.

2. I'm disappointed when _____.

3. If I had an extra $100, I'd _____.

4. The thing I'm most proud of is _____.

5. Once people get to know me, they're probably surprised to find I'm _____ _____.

6. My family wants me to _____.

7. I'd really like to become _____.

8. My friends enjoy me because _____.

9. I've been known to consume large quantities of _____.

10. I'd rather be _____ than _____.

11. When I'm under pressure, _____.

12. My best quality is _____.

13. My worst quality is _____.

14. The academic skill I'd most like to develop is _____.

15. One thing I'd like to figure out about myself is _____.

Spending Time "in the System"

CHALLENGE → REACTION

Challenge: How do people learn?

Reaction: _____

Spending time "in the system"? No, being in college isn't like being in jail—far from it. Many people reflect back on their college days as one of the most enjoyable, active, and interesting times of their lives.

"The system" is the approach used in this book to structure productive learning: the Challenge → Reaction → Insight → Action system. It is based on the work of Dr. John Bransford and his colleagues, who together wrote an influential book called *How People Learn* (2000).

Figure 1.1 summarizes how learning requires focus, and focus involves the four steps in this system. This book asks you to write and discuss things along the way: your reactions, your insights, and the actions you plan to take. This book's goal for you is *transformative learning*: "a process of examining, questioning, validating, and revising [your] perceptions."[3] What you'll learn by reading it has the potential to *transform*, or *change* you, so that you're ready to meet the many challenges that await you in college and in life. Here's a step-by-step explanation of the learning system used in this book.

STEP 1: Accept the *FOCUS* challenge. Every time you study a new subject or take a new course, you are challenged, right? Within each chapter of this book, you'll be presented with challenges, beginning with a case study about a college student—perhaps someone like you or a friend—who is experiencing something new and difficult. Research shows that people can learn more

Figure 1.1

How People Learn

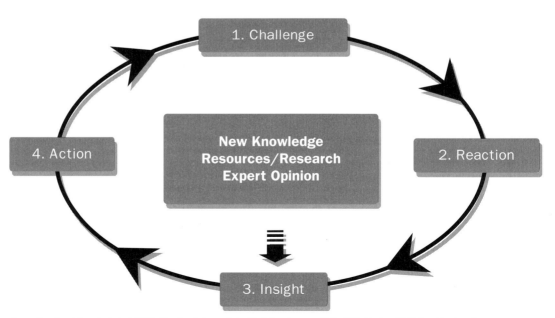

Source: Based on J. Bransford, et al. (2000). *How People Learn: Brain, Mind, Experience, and School.* Washington, DC: National Academy Press.

from examples of things going wrong than they can from examples of things going smoothly. You'll be presented with additional challenges related to the chapter's content to pique your curiosity, motivate you to keep reading, and start a learning chain reaction. Don't skip over this step; it's an important part of the learning process. Challenge yourself!

STEP 2: React to the challenge. Whenever you're learning something new, the best place to start is by identifying what you think you already know—your gut reaction. You're a novice to any new field you're studying, not an expert, but you bring with you to the learning process a set of preconceptions, assumptions, sometimes biases or misperceptions, and of course, all your previous experiences. Your reaction to each challenge will tell you what you think you already know. By the end of the chapter, you'll know more about all the challenges you've encountered throughout your reading. The goal of this book is to help you become a deep learner, as opposed to skimming the surface and simply rushing on to the next assignment and the next course—as many college students do. It will ask you to pause, take stock, focus, and think.

STEP 3: Use new knowledge to gain insights. After your initial reaction, you must pay attention to your inner voice—insights you've gained from new knowledge. "Insight → Action" activities help you keep track of them. Let's say, that you read later in this chapter about goal setting. When you first thought about it, the whole idea of setting goals seemed simple, but after reading about it, you decide you really hadn't thought about it very deeply and had only vague notions about setting your own goals. The difference between step 2 (whatever reaction you

"Surround yourself with people who take their work seriously, but not themselves, those who work hard and play hard."

Colin Powell, former U.S. Secretary of State

provided to the challenge) and step 3 (the insights you've gained) demonstrates that learning is taking place.

STEP 4: Use your insights to propel you toward action. Insights have no impact unless they lead to change. Decide how an insight affects your existing beliefs, how it changes them, and therefore, what you've learned. Your insights may lead you to change your behavior, develop an informed opinion, or make choices about your education, your job, your family, or your life. The bottom line is: You must use your insights to take action. Think of this comparison. One day you feel sluggish, you notice that your clothes are tight, and you are suddenly aware that you're out of shape. You realize that you must make healthier food choices and exercise more. But if you don't take action, it won't happen. To become real, new knowledge must lead to personal insights that result in action.

Each step in this four-part system is important. For example, if you skip step 2, *react to the challenge*, by identifying what you *think* you know, you may assume you already know all the new information you're reading or hearing. You may think, "Sure, of course, that makes sense. I already knew that," when you really didn't. In truth, the French philosopher Voltaire was right: "Common sense is not so common." Realizing there's a gap between steps 2 and 3—what you thought you knew and the insights you've gained from new knowledge—is important. And actually putting the insights you gain into real, live, honest-to-goodness action is vital.

As you work through this book, the Challenge → Reaction → Insight → Action system will continue cycling back to step 1, presenting you with new challenges. If you follow the system built into this book and integrate it into your other academic pursuits, you can become a lifelong learner. Thinking in terms of the learning cycle will become ingrained.

INSIGHT ⮕ ACTION

1. What do you think about the Challenge → Reaction → Insight → Action system? Does it make sense? Do you understand how it works? Write a few paragraphs describing it in your own words.

2. Are you committed to using it throughout this book to validate its effectiveness? If so, write down exactly what will be required of you.

How Motivated *Are* You and *How* Are You Motivated?

CHALLENGE ⮕ REACTION

How intrinsically motivated are you? Read each of the following statements and circle the number beside each statement that most accurately represents your views about yourself.

	Completely Not True	Somewhat Not True	Neutral	Somewhat True	Completely True
1. I have academic goals.	1	2	3	4	5
2. I am confident I can complete my degree.	1	2	3	4	5
3. I determine my career goals.	1	2	3	4	5
4. I enjoy solving challenging, difficult problems.	1	2	3	4	5
5. I work on an assignment until I understand it.	1	2	3	4	5
6. I am confident I will graduate from college.	1	2	3	4	5
7. I determine the quality of my academic work.	1	2	3	4	5
8. I am pursuing a college degree because I value education.	1	2	3	4	5
9. I feel good knowing that I determine how my academic career develops.	1	2	3	4	5
10. I have high standards for academic work.	1	2	3	4	5
11. Staying in college is my decision.	1	2	3	4	5
12. I study because I like to learn new things.	1	2	3	4	5
13. I enjoy doing outside readings in connection to my future coursework.	1	2	3	4	5
14. I am intrigued by the different topics introduced in my courses.	1	2	3	4	5
15. I study because I am curious.	1	2	3	4	5
16. I look forward to going to class.	1	2	3	4	5
17. I am excited to take more courses within my major.	1	2	3	4	5
18. I enjoy learning more within my field of study.	1	2	3	4	5
19. I like to find answers to questions about material I am learning.	1	2	3	4	5
20. I enjoy studying.	1	2	3	4	5
21. I have pictured myself in a profession after college.	1	2	3	4	5

	Completely Not True	Somewhat Not True	Neutral	Somewhat True	Completely True
22. I am excited about the job opportunities I will have when I graduate.	1	2	3	4	5
23. I have pictured myself being successful in my chosen profession.	1	2	3	4	5
24. I believe I will make a substantial contribution to my chosen profession.	1	2	3	4	5
25. I feel good knowing I will be a member of the professional community in my area of study.	1	2	3	4	5

Total each column, then add your scores across. _____ + _____ + _____ + _____ + _____ =

_____ OVERALL SCORE

Continue reading to find out what your overall score means.

When it comes to getting a college education, where does motivation come into the picture? In general, motivation is your desire to engage and put forth effort, even when the going gets rough. The word *motivation* comes from Medieval Latin, *motivus*, meaning "moving or impelling." What moves you to learn? There are many ways to define motivation, and different people are motivated by different things.

How motivated would you be to learn something difficult, such as a new language, one you'd never studied before? Let's say that you were offered a chance to learn Finnish, a challenging language that is not related to English. For example, in Finnish *Kiitoksia oikein paljon* means "thank you very much." Finnish would be a challenge to learn. To determine your level of motivation, it would help to know your attitude toward Finland and Finnish people, whether you needed to learn Finnish for some reason, how you felt about learning it, if you thought you could learn it successfully, if you were reinforced in some way for learning it, and just how stimulating you found the learning process to be.[4] In other words, your motivation level depends on many factors, right?

You'd probably be more motivated to learn Finnish if these sorts of things were part of the picture: (a) you were going to visit relatives in Finland and were excited about it, (b) you'd always excelled at learning foreign languages and you expected to learn this one easily, (c) your boss was planning to transfer you to Helsinki as part of a big promotion, or (d) you enjoyed your Finnish language class, thought the instructor was a gifted teacher, and found the other students to be as motivated as you were. So, whose job is it to motivate you? Your instructor's? Your parents'? This book's? Yours? *Can* anyone else besides you motivate you? This book will ask you: how motivated *are* you to succeed in college? And *how* are you motivated?

> "You are never given a wish without the power to make it come true. You may have to work for it, however."
>
> **Richard Bach, from *Illusions***

To assess your own motivation, it's important to understand the difference between *extrinsic* and *intrinsic* motivation. People who are *extrinsically*, or externally, motivated learn in order to get a grade, earn credits, or complete a requirement, for example. They are motivated by things outside themselves. You could be motivated to learn Finnish to earn three credits, or to get an A, or to meet a foreign language requirement. People who are *intrinsically*, or internally, motivated learn because they're curious, fascinated, challenged, or because they truly want to master a subject. They are motivated from within. You could be motivated to learn Finnish for the challenge, because you're curious about it, or because you find it fascinating. Let's be realistic, however. Extrinsic motivation is real and important. You need a particular number of credit hours to graduate. You'd rather get A's than F's. But how intrinsically motivated you are in college will have a great deal to do with just how successful you are. The motivation to become truly educated must come from within you.

You completed the Academic Intrinsic Motivation Scale (AIMS) in the previous "Challenge → Reaction," which is designed to measure your intrinsic, or internal, motivation to succeed in college in terms of these four C-Factors:

1. Curiosity. Do you want to acquire new knowledge? Are you truly interested in what you're learning? Do you ask questions? Do you allow your curiosity to propel your learning?

2. Control. Do you think the academic investment you make will lead to successful outcomes? Do you believe you can control how successful you'll be?

3. Career outlook. Are you goal oriented? Are you future oriented? Can you imagine yourself graduating and getting a job you want?

4. Challenge. Does your college coursework challenge you appropriately? Too much challenge can cause you to become frustrated and give up. Not enough challenge can cause you to lose interest.[5]

If your overall score on the AIMS was 100–125, you're intrinsically motivated at a high level. If you scored between 75 and 99, you're intrinsically motivated at a moderate level, but increasing your intrinsic motivation may help you achieve more. If you scored below 75, a lack of intrinsic motivation could interfere with your college success. If you're intrinsically motivated, you'll accept challenges, react to them by identifying what you already know, seek insights from new knowledge, and take action based on what you've learned.

Like the Challenge → Reaction → Insight → Action system, the Academic Intrinsic Motivation Scale's C-Factors reappear throughout the book to boost your intrinsic motivation:

C CULTIVATE Your Curiosity Each chapter includes a short article on what is required for college success. You'll read cutting-edge information that may pique your curiosity and lead you to consider exploring the original source or related material on your own.

C CONTROL Your Learning You are encouraged throughout this book to apply the content covered to your most challenging class this term and to take charge of your own learning, which is vital to college success.

C CREATE A Career Outlook   Each chapter includes a "Focus on Careers" interview with a professional. As you read them, think about the interviewees' stories, and ask yourself whether you have the interest and motivation required to get where they are. Following the interview, you'll read some quick facts in a section called "Create a Career Outlook" to see how this career might fit you.

C CHALLENGE Yourself Quizzes   In general, if a course is too challenging, you may be tempted to give up. If it's too easy, you may lose interest. Adjusting the level of challenge to one that's right for you is key to keeping yourself motivated to learn. Online quizzes for each chapter will challenge you so that you can work at your best. For more practice online, go to http://www .cengage.com/colsuccess/staleyconcise to take the Challenge Yourself online quizzes.

INSIGHT ⟶ ACTION

1. Describe a time when you succeeded in learning something and one in which you failed to learn something. What was the learning experience like? Were you extrinsically or intrinsically motivated? Why?

2. What types of things fascinate you and fire up your intrinsic motivation? What actions can you take to help you think more deliberately about your motivation and how it affects your learning?

EXERCISE 1.2 The Ideal Student

Create your own personal top-ten list of the characteristics (attitudes and actions) of an ideal student. Bring your completed list to your next class session where everyone can read their lists, and begin to add, delete, merge, and create a master list to which everyone can subscribe. Put your initials next to each of the ten items on the master list that you promise to do throughout the term. Your personal top-ten list, which your instructor may discuss with you individually at a later time, will become your learning contract for the course.

FOCUS ON CAREERS: Eric Sween, Psychologist

Courtesy of Eric Sween

Q1: What do you do in your work?
My specialization is in the psychological field known as narrative therapy—in other words, how people make meaning of the events in their lives. In my private practice I see both individuals and couples. People come into therapy for a wide variety of reasons, for example, when they feel stuck with something in their lives—some with unemployment, or relationships, or divorce. My responsibilities include listening, understanding people's perspectives, and helping them set and reach their goals. I especially value working with people who are at some sort of turning point in their lives.

Q2: What are the three most important skills you need to do well in this career?
First, a therapist needs to be able to listen really well and appreciate another person's perspective. Second, a therapist must be genuinely curious about people and try to understand what is most meaningful to them. And finally, it's important to be flexible and tailor what you do with each person you are working with. Some people need problem solving and concrete steps. Some need to be really heard and empathized with. And some need information and a connection to additional resources. The key is to know the difference in what clients need in order to reach their goals.

Give Yourself an Attitude Adjustment

There's a difference of opinion on the subject of attitude. Some people say attitude is not all that important. Attitude-schmattitude, they say. Others say that *attitude* is more important than *aptitude*. What do you think?

In research studies conducted by Rick Snyder at the University of Kansas, students who scored high on a measure of hope got higher grades. Snyder explained that students with high hopes set themselves higher goals and know how to work hard to attain them.

Quick quiz. How many times a day do you catch yourself saying "Whatever…," and rolling your eyes? Whatever-ness—an attitude of cynicism, apathy, disdain, or impatience—takes a lot less effort than optimism, respect, kindness, or any other positive response. Whether you realize it or not, whatevers chip away at your motivation, and they can contribute to self-sabotaging your opportunities to succeed in life. When it comes to your college education, one good thing you can do for yourself is to purge the word *whatever* from your vocabulary. Your education is much too important for whatevers—and so are you.

> **"A positive attitude is your most priceless possession, one of your most valuable assets. To a great extent, it determines the overall quality of your life."**
>
> **Keith Harrell, from**
> ***Attitude Is Everything***

Six Ways to Adjust Your Attitude

The good thing about attitude is that you can change it yourself. As you think about benefits of fine-tuning your attitude, keep these six recommendations in mind:

1. Know that you always have choices. Regardless of circumstances—your income, your background, or your prior academic record—you always have a choice, even if it's limited to how you choose to perceive your current situation.

2. Take responsibility for your own outcomes. Coach Vince Lombardi used to have his players look in a mirror before every game and ask themselves, "Am I

C CREATE a Career Outlook

PSYCHOLOGIST
Have you ever considered a career as a psychologist or counselor?

Facts to Consider[6]
Academic preparation required: a master's or doctoral degree

Future workforce demand: growth projected at a faster rate than the average job category through 2014, particularly for highly trained specialists

Work environment: Four of ten psychologists are self-employed; the rest work in clinics, hospitals, schools, nonprofit agencies, or industrial settings.

Essential skills: listening, communicating, analyzing, rapport building (for clinical psychologists), and research and statistical skills (for experimental psychologists)

Questions to Ponder
1. Do you have (or could you acquire) the skills this career requires?
2. Are you interested in a career like this? Why or why not?

For more career activities online, go to http://www.cengage.com/colsuccess/staleyconcise to do the Team Career exercises.

Q3: What advice would you give college students who are interested in exploring a career in psychology or psychotherapy?
If you are interested in any career that involves psychology, spend time with people. People are endlessly interesting. Talk to people who are different than you. See if you can understand another person's worldview so that it really makes sense to you. If you enjoy doing these things, then you might enjoy a career similar to the one I've chosen.

looking at the person who is helping me win or the one who is holding me back?" Blaming others simply diminishes your own power to work toward constructive responses to challenges.

3. **Choose your words carefully.** "Can't" and "won't" are two of the biggest inhibitors to a healthy attitude. Also pay attention to how you describe things. Is the cup half empty or half full? State things in the positive rather than the negative (for example, "stay healthy" rather than "don't get sick"). Language is a reflection of attitude.

4. **Fill your mind with messages about the attitude you want to have.** The old adage, "garbage in, garbage out," applies to attitudes as well. There are numerous books, CDs, and films that offer positive, motivating messages. Paying attention to role models whose traits you admire is also a great way to bolster your outlook.

5. **Convert learning points into turning points.** Have you ever watched someone do something so badly that you've said to yourself, "I'm never going to do that! I'm going to do it differently!"? You can also choose to learn from your own mistakes and setbacks. They all offer some sort of lesson—be it greater clarity, personal growth, or a new vision—even if it takes a bit of distance from the event to see what you can learn.

6. **Acknowledge your blessings.** Taking time at the end of each day to recognize and feel gratitude for the blessings in your life—no matter how large or small—is a great way to amplify a positive attitude.

Box 1.1 Statements That Ought to Be Outlawed in College . . . and Why

Since words reflect attitudes (and help shape them), listen for statements like these escaping from your mouth. They can negatively affect your attitude and therefore your learning:

- "I thought college classes would be more interesting than they are." *Interesting* is in the mind of the beholder.

- "I didn't learn a thing in that class." Actively search for what you can take away from a class, even if it didn't quite meet your expectations.

- "The textbook is really dull. Why bother reading it?" Reading may not be your favorite pastime, but you may learn more from a textbook than you can predict.

- "The professor is soooo-o-o boring." In life, we all interact with all types of personalities, so begin to appreciate differences in communication styles now.

- "Why do I have to take this required course? What's the point?" The point is to broaden your horizons, expand your skills as a critical thinker, and become a lifelong scholar.

Care enough to give yourself every opportunity to do your best. And, yes, every class, every situation in life, is an opportunity. You're worth it.[7]

EXERCISE 1.3 Your Academic Autobiography

Write a three-page academic autobiography describing your preparation for college. Describe the quality of your primary, middle, and high school learning experiences. Did they prepare you for what you're experiencing now in college? What do you think will be your strengths and weaknesses as a college student? Look back at your academic self throughout your schooling and look ahead to the kind of student you're planning to be in college, then write your academic autobiography. Or as an alternative, create a presentation answering these questions for your classmates.

Ability versus Effort: What's More Important?

Successful people have several things in common: they love learning, seek challenges, value effort, and persevere even when things become difficult.[8] They demonstrate both ability and effort. These two things are the basic requirements for success. College is about both.

Think about some of the possible combinations of ability and effort. If you have high ability and exert great effort, you'll most likely succeed. If you have high ability and exert little effort, and still succeed, you've just proved how smart you must be! But if you have high ability and exert little effort and fail, you can always claim you didn't have the time to invest or you didn't care, right? You can always maintain that you could have done well if you'd tried harder: "I could have been another J. K. Rowling; I'm a great writer." If you had really tried for that kind of success, you wouldn't have been able to say that. That's a dangerous strategy, one that's called "self-handicapping."[9] Some college students consciously or unconsciously apply this strategy. They exert little effort, perhaps because they have no confidence in themselves or because they fear failure, and then they rationalize when they don't do well.

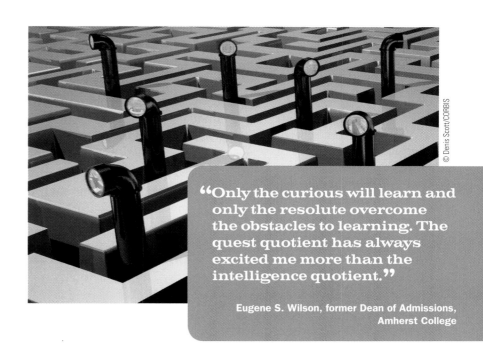

© Denis Scott/CORBIS

"Only the curious will learn and only the resolute overcome the obstacles to learning. The quest quotient has always excited me more than the intelligence quotient."

Eugene S. Wilson, former Dean of Admissions, Amherst College

CHALLENGE ⮕ REACTION

What is intelligence? Are people born with a certain amount? Or can it be cultivated through learning? Using the following scale, indicate the extent to which you agree or disagree with each of the following statements by writing the number that corresponds to your opinion in the space next to each statement. There are no right or wrong answers.

Theories of Intelligence Scale

1	2	3	4	5	6
Strongly Agree	Mostly Agree	Agree	Disagree	Mostly Disagree	Strongly Disagree

_____ 1. You have a certain amount of intelligence, and you can't really do much to change it.

_____ 2. You can learn new things, but you can't really change your basic intelligence.

_____ 3. You can always substantially change how intelligent you are.

_____ 4. No matter how much intelligence you have, you can always change it quite a bit.

Research shows that what you *believe* about your own intelligence—your *mindset*—can make a difference in how successful you'll be in college. At first glance this statement seems absurd. After all, you're either smart or you're not, right? Wrong.

The scaled questions demonstrate that there are two basic ways to define intelligence. Some of us are *performers*, who agree with statements 1 and 2, while others of us are *learners*, who agree more with statements 3 and 4. *Performers* believe that intelligence is a fixed trait that cannot be changed. From the moment you're born, you have a certain amount of intelligence that's been allotted to you, and that's that. *Learners*, on the other hand, believe you can grow your intelligence if you capitalize on opportunities to learn. Whenever you tackle a tough challenge, you learn from it. The more you learn, the more intelligent you can become. Understanding which view of intelligence you endorse will make a difference in how you approach your college classes, as well as the outcomes—both positive and negative—that you'll achieve.

Students who are taught the value of a learning mindset over a performance mindset can actually achieve more than students who don't.[10] In one study, college students' views of intelligence predicted the goals students valued in college. *Performers* were more likely to want to give up in challenging situations; learners wanted to try harder. Over their years at the university, *performers*, who had originally entered with higher SAT scores, did not perform better than *learners*, and they had lower self-esteem.[11] In one study that measured the electrical activity in college

C CONTROL Your Learning

YOUR TOUGHEST CLASS

Think about all the courses you're enrolled in this term. Use the following matrix to analyze your C-Factors for these courses. Describe each course in terms of its *challenge* level, your *curiosity* about the subject, how much *control* you believe you have to succeed, and the way each class impacts your *career outlook*. Once you've determined the levels of challenge, curiosity, control, and career outlook you perceive in your courses, remember that it's *your* responsibility to adjust them.

- Which classes will be your most challenging this term?
- What is the relationship between the four C-Factors and your intrinsic motivation to learn in each course?
- What can you do to increase your intrinsic motivation and become more successful?

Course Title	Challenge	Curiosity	Control	Career Outlook	Adjustments Required
Composition	Very High: never been good at writing	Very Low: had a discouraging teacher in H.S.	Moderate: probably higher than it feels to me	Will need to know how to write in any job	Need to spend more time pre-writing and going to the campus Writing Center for help

students' brains as they performed a difficult task, brain activity showed that *performers* cared most about whether their answers were right or wrong, while *learners* were interested in follow-up information they could learn from.[12] Yet another study showed that *learners* are more likely to buckle down academically, even when they feel depressed.[13] It's clear: believing you're a *learner* provides advantages in motivation, achievement, enjoyment, and commitment.

Regardless of what you believe about your precise intelligence level, the fact is this: *intelligence can be cultivated through learning.* And people's theories about their intelligence levels can be shifted.

INSIGHT ⇒ ACTION

1. Think of a time in your past when you faced a challenge in school—either with academics or co-curricular activities—that overwhelmed you to the point where you chose not to see the challenge through. Describe the challenge and how you avoided it. How might that experience have ended differently for you if you had adopted a learning perspective toward it? What would you have gained by mastering the challenge?

2. What actions can you take to become more of a *learner* and less of a *performer*, particularly in your most challenging class this term?

What Drives You?
Values, Dreams, and Goals

CHALLENGE ⇒ REACTION

What are your core values? Review the following list and check off the items that you value. Don't spend too much time thinking about each one; just go with your initial gut reaction. For each item, ask yourself "Is this something that's important to me?"

_____ Health	_____ Wealth	_____ Financial wealth
_____ Fitness/Physical strength	_____ Independence	_____ Commitment
_____ Loyalty	_____ Honesty	_____ Compassion
_____ Academic achievement	_____ Children	_____ Leisure time
_____ Success	_____ Leadership	_____ Balance
_____ Happiness	_____ Family	_____ Friendship
_____ Social life	_____ Marriage/Partnership	_____ Recognition
_____ Athletics	_____ Spirituality	_____ Status
_____ Creativity	_____ Variety	_____ Wisdom
_____ Meaningful work	_____ Challenge	_____ Time spent alone
_____ Adventure	_____ Personal growth	_____ Other (list here)

Now review all of the items you checked off and circle the five that are most important to you at this point in your life. Then rank them by putting a number next to each of the five circled values with number one as your top priority. Finally, take stock. Is this the person you want to be? Is there anything about your values that you would like to change? If so, what's keeping you from making this change?

Before tackling the big questions about what you want to create with your life, it's important to first take a close look in the mirror. Who are you? What makes you tick? What do you value? What are your goals? Where will your dreams take you?

Values at the Core

What do you value in life? By taking time to examine your personal values, managing your life will become easier and make more sense. Values can be intangible concepts such as love or respect, or tangible things such as family or money, and understanding how they motivate you isn't as simple as it might seem. Values can change as you go through life. For example, if you're single now, you may value the freedom to meet a variety of potential romantic partners. Later, however, you may want a committed relationship because you value companionship and stability more than you used to. For this reason, it's important to reassess your values from time to time and reprioritize them.

Another complicating factor is that values can conflict with one another. Suppose that you value honesty and kindness, and you are at a party and a friend asks you what you think of her new hair color. You honestly think it's hideous, but telling her so would hurt her feelings, thus violating your value of being kind. How do you respond? That would depend on which value is a higher priority for you. You have to make an on-the-spot decision about which value to tap. Once you define your values, however, they can serve as guideposts in helping you make choices every day—everything from the insignificant day-to-day choices to more significant ones such as which major to pursue in college.

In the Challenge → Reaction → Insight → Action system, knowing your values in life is key to understanding your reaction. Once you've defined your values, you can use them in your daily life to guide your actions. For example, if academic achievement is one of your top values, the next time you have the urge to cut class, consider the impact that choice would have on your value system. There is a great inner satisfaction that comes from living a life tied to core values.

Dreams versus Goals

Do you agree or disagree with this statement: "I can be anything I want to be"? If you are like most students, people have probably told you this frequently. Your parents and teachers all want you to have positive self-esteem, and certainly there are many career options available today. But is it true? Can you be *anything* you want to be? What's the difference between a dream and a goal?

As a college student, you may dream of being a famous doctor or a famous athlete or just plain famous. That's the beauty of dreams—you can imagine yourself in any career, any circumstances. When you're dreaming, you don't even have to play by the rules of reality. Dreams are fantasy-based—*you* in a perfect world. But when it's time to come back to reality, you discover that there are, in fact, rules. You may have dreamed of becoming a top-earning NBA player or a top fashion model when you were a child, but you have grown up to be the same height as Uncle Al or Aunt Sue—and that's not tall enough.

Dreams alone are not enough when it comes to "creating the future." As professional life coach Diana Robinson says, "A dream is a goal without legs." And without legs, that goal is going nowhere. Dreaming is the first step to creating the future you want, but making dreams come true requires planning and hard work. Gloria Gonzales wanted to become a fashion designer because she liked clothes and people always told her she looked good. As she continues through college, however, she will come to understand the nuts and bolts of the fashion design business. The fashion industry might be challenging to break into, but that doesn't mean she should abandon her dream. She must find a reality-based path to help her turn her dreams into goals. Just dreaming isn't enough.

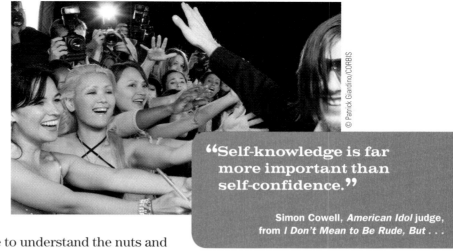

© Patrick Giardino/CORBIS

"**Self-knowledge is far more important than self-confidence.**"

Simon Cowell, *American Idol* judge, from *I Don't Mean to Be Rude, But . . .*

Dreams are exciting; you can let your imagination run wild. Goals are real; you must work out how to actually achieve your dreams. Goal setting is an important part of the life management skills this book will help you develop. Your goals may not seem at all clear to you right now, but the important thing is to learn that there's a right way and a wrong way to go about goal setting. The best way to ensure that the goals you set will serve you well is to make sure you *FOCUS*. Here's a brief overview of what that means.

F **Fit.** Your goal must fit your values, your character, and who you are as a person. Goals that conflict with any of these things will not only be difficult to accomplish, but they just won't work. If your goal is to become a writer for a travel magazine because you love adventure, but you haven't conquered your fear of flying, you're in trouble.

O **Ownership.** Own your goals: see it, taste it, want it! It must be your goal, not someone else's goal for you. Ask yourself: Does the thought of achieving this goal get me fired up? Do I genuinely own this goal or do I feel I ought to have this goal because it sounds good or pleases someone else?

C **Concreteness.** For any goal to be effective, it must be real. In other words, you must be able to describe your goal—and its ultimate outcome—in complete and specific detail, including your deadline for accomplishing it. "To run a mile in less than six minutes by March 4th" is much more concrete than "to eventually run faster." The more concrete, the better.

U **Usefulness.** Goals must be useful. They must serve a purpose, and that purpose should be tied to your long-term vision of the person you want to become. For example, if you want to work for an international corporation some day, it would be useful to begin studying a foreign language now.

S **Stretch.** In the business world, people talk about stretch goals. These are goals that require employees to stretch beyond their predictable limits to achieve something more challenging. Goals must be based in reality, but also offer you a chance to grow beyond the person you currently are.

Goals should be set for different time frames in your life to include both short- and long-term goals. Once your long-term goals are set (though they may shift over time as *you* shift over time), you will then want to set some short-term goals, which act as intermediate steps to achieving your long-term goals.

Long-Term Goals What do I want to accomplish…	Short-Term Goals What do I want to accomplish…
In my lifetime?	This year?
In the next twenty years?	This month?
In the next ten years?	This week?
In the next three to five years?	Today?

INSIGHT ⊖ ACTION

1. Briefly describe one of your dreams for the future. Now list several goals that, when accomplished, would help you create the dream you listed. First think of long-term goals, followed by short-term goals. Next to each goal, write the time frame (that is, 10 years, 3–5 years, within 1 year, within a month, and so on).

2. Select one of the goals you listed. Run it through a quick check to ensure that it's a FOCUS goal. Circle the appropriate answer:

– Does this goal **fit** me?	Yes No
– Do I really want this goal? Do I **own** it?	Yes No
– Does my goal have **concrete** details and deadlines?	Yes No
– Is this goal **useful** to me? Does it serve a purpose?	Yes No
– Does this goal **stretch** me? Is it challenging, yet achievable?	Yes No

If you answered "no" to any of the previous questions, your goal needs to be more *FOCUS*ed.

3. Pick one of the short-term goals from your list in question 1. What could you do today to work toward accomplishing that goal? List one to three to-do items.

4. Pick one of the items on your to-do list from question 3 and do it now. It may be something seemingly insignificant, or you may be tempted to tell yourself that you could easily do it tomorrow. But doing it today—*now*—will not only put you one step closer to your dream, but it will help you accomplish something concrete.

Digital Vision/Getty Images

"What you get by achieving your goals is not as important as what you become by achieving your goals."

Zig Ziglar, Motivational speaker, writer, and trainer

KNOW THYSELF!
HOW HARD CAN THAT BE?

Knowing yourself doesn't sound like much of a challenge, does it? After all, you've lived with yourself for a long time. You know every freckle, every dimple, every quirk. Or do you?

Socrates advised many centuries ago, "Know thyself." But David Dunning, professor of psychology at Cornell University and author of *Self-Insight: Roadblocks and Detours on the Path to Knowing Thyself* (2005), says that most of us really don't know ourselves as well as we think we do. In fact, when we're asked to predict how well we'll do at something, and that prediction is compared to our actual performance afterward, most of us are off base. In one study, college students were given a pop quiz to test their logical reasoning skills. After they finished, they were asked to compare their performance with that of their peers, and to predict the number of items they got right.

Dunning and his research colleague, Justin Kruger, split the test-takers into four quarters: students who performed in the bottom quarter, the second, third, and top quarter. Then they compared how students actually performed with how well they thought they'd done.

In general, students who thought they did best often performed in the bottom quarter, and students with the highest scores sometimes underestimated their performance. Take a look at Figure 1.2, which summarizes the typical pattern uncovered in Dunning's research to date. In particular, compare participants in the bottom quarter with those in the top one, and you'll see that the participants who did the worst were the ones who were the most optimistic!

If Dunning's research is right, why is this so? Why aren't we all right on the mark? Specifically, why can't people tell when they're not doing a good job? One hypothesis Dunning offers is that people can't be expected to recognize when they're not performing adequately. Because they *don't* know how to do what they're doing (and therefore they aren't doing it well),

they're simply not in a position to know. The skills they need in order to *do* a good job are the exact same skills they need to *recognize* whether they are doing a good job. So they hope for the best. And while optimism isn't a bad thing—in fact, it's generally a good thing—realism is critical, too, in college and in life.

That's why it's important to seek input from your instructors about the quality of your work. Assessing it is their job! Work with other students so that you can observe their skill levels compared with your own. Learn from self-assessment instruments. Use your classes as an opportunity to gather all the self-knowledge you can. Rather than simply hoping for the best, do all you can to get to know yourself better and give college your best shot.

Figure 1.2

Typical Relationship Found Between Perceived and Actual Performance

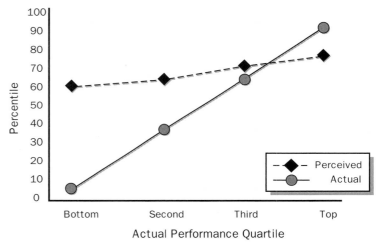

Source: D. Dunning. (2005). *Self-Insight: Roadblocks and Detours on the Path to Knowing Thyself.* New York: Psychology Press, p. 18.

College Success: You Make the Call

What does it mean to succeed? Actually, success is difficult to define, and different people define success differently. Right now in college, you may think of success in terms of your future income. But is success simply about material wealth? Is it about fame? Status?

According to motivational author Robert Collier, "Success is the sum of small efforts, repeated day in and day out." Perhaps to you, success is somewhere off in the distant future, and it happens more or less suddenly, like winning the lottery. Actually, success begins right now. You should be the one to define what success will look like in your life, but generally, success is *setting out to do something that's personally meaningful, and then being fully engaged while doing it.* It's that simple.

In order to understand your own definition of success in college, first you need to ask yourself why you're here. Why *did* you come—or return—to college, anyway? Do you want to develop into a more interesting, well-rounded, educated human being? Are you working toward a degree that leads to a specific career? Do you have children and want an education in order give them a better life? Did your mom or dad tell you that college wasn't optional?

We will assume that part of your definition of succeeding in college includes *graduating* from college. This book provides you with an honest look at what that takes, including numerous opportunities to assess yourself in these areas. It also offers an array of tools you can use throughout your college career and in your life beyond college.

Graduating from College: What It Takes

CHALLENGE ⮕ REACTION

Many factors (besides grades and entrance test scores) impact your success in college. Read this list and ask yourself how you measure up in each of these areas. Mark an honest response from 1 to 7. If you're just beginning college and you're unsure about how you'll do, use your habits in the past to gauge your responses.

1	2	3	4	5	6	7
NO!	NO	No	Maybe/Sometimes	Yes	YES	YES!

_____ **Ability to adapt.** Are you the type of person who thrives in new environments? Do you enjoy meeting new classmates, new professors, and new counselors? In general, do you like—and do well—with change?

_____ **Attitude.** Do you have a positive attitude toward your education? Do you want to be here? Are you motivated to learn and grow? Are you willing to do the hard work involved in earning a college degree? Are you respectful of your instructors, your fellow students, and yourself?

_____ **Maturity.** Are you emotionally mature? Are you willing to display the level of maturity required to manage your college education over time and earn a degree?

_____ **Class attendance.** Do you have a good track record of attending class in the past? Are you willing to commit to attending each of your college classes regularly, regardless of whether or not you actually *feel* like attending on a particular day? Did you know that class attendance is a major predictor of college success?

_____ **Study habits.** Do you spend enough time studying? Do you study until you understand the material or do you simply study until you're out of time or need to move on to the next thing? Are you willing to make the necessary commitment to time spent studying?

_____ **Note-taking skills.** Note-taking is not an ability we're born with. It's a skill that must be learned, and it can be taught to just about anyone. How complete and comprehensive are your notes? Do you work with them *after* class (color-coding, retyping, and so on)? Do you work with your notes so that they're useful aids at exam time?

_____ **Academic support services.** Do you know what resources are available on campus to help you with academic issues? Have you visited any offices that provide support services on your campus to familiarize yourself with them? Are you willing to use a tutor to help with a particular course if it should overwhelm you?

_____ **Personal support system.** How strong is your personal support system? Who cares about your success in college? Do you have family, siblings, and friends who support you, encourage you, and ask how you're doing? How often do you see or e-mail these people? How willing are you to make friends on campus who also value academic success?

_____ **Faculty connections.** Do you plan to interact with your instructors? Are you interested in knowing more about your instructors, their backgrounds, and their academic interests beyond the particular class you're taking with them? Are you willing to visit your instructors during their office hours if you are having difficulty with a class? Would you consider finding a mentor among your instructors?

_____ **Campus connection.** Are you connected to people and events on your campus? Are you involved in any co-curricular activities in which you interact with others? Do you plan to participate in or attend on-campus events? Sometimes students unknowingly fall prey to the PCP (parking lot, class, parking lot) syndrome. They're only on campus for their classes, and as soon as they get out of class, they're outta there. Believe it or not, connecting to your campus, other students, and your instructors is critical to your success.

_____ **Time management skills.** Are you capable of managing your time effectively so that the important things—not necessarily just the urgent or exciting, fun things—get completed? Have you ever purposefully learned a system of time management? Are you willing to learn these skills? Do you understand that *time* management is really about *energy* management?

_____ **Money management skills.** How good are you at managing your money? Are you currently debt-free aside from any student loans required to attend college? Some students fall into the trap of using their school loans or grants to pay off credit card debt. Or they work far too many hours, which takes time away from their studies and makes academic success difficult to achieve. While managing your money isn't an academic skill, per se, not knowing how to do it can substantially impact your college career.

Now add up your scores on each item for a final tally. While this list isn't exhaustive, these factors are vital to college success. If your score was 60 or higher, you're in good shape. If not, take a close look at the areas that could affect your college success, read more about them in this book, and develop insights that lead to more effective action.

Some students think obtaining a college degree is merely a financial transaction. Not so. There's much more to it than that. A college education requires you to invest your ability, your intellect, your drive, your effort—and yourself.

Did you notice that none of the things listed in the "Challenge → Reaction" are innate talents that you're simply born with? That's the good news. All of these factors that support your goal of graduating from college are things you can become better at if you are committed to doing so. And in making commitments to improving these factors *now*, you are making a commitment to graduate from college *later*.

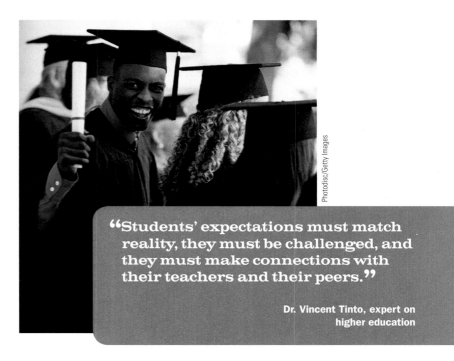

Photodisc/Getty Images

"Students' expectations must match reality, they must be challenged, and they must make connections with their teachers and their peers."

Dr. Vincent Tinto, **expert on higher education**

The Bad News: Obstacles along the Way

Getting accepted to college is a good thing! You should feel proud. But realistically, the distance between getting accepted to college and graduating from college is considerable, and the journey can be both exhilarating and discouraging at times. Of all the college students who began as first-year students in 1992, only two-thirds had graduated eight years later.[14]

Risk factors include working more than thirty hours per week, going to school part-time, being a single parent or having children at home, and being a first-generation college student.[15] The important thing to keep in mind as you think about risk factors is that they alone cannot determine your ultimate level of success. Don't throw in the towel now if you had a child at age sixteen or are working thirty-five hours per week off campus. These factors are presented merely as information to assist you on your journey. They are simply *predictors*—not *determiners*. Only you can determine your outcomes in life, and that includes your success in college.

It's worth taking a close look at these success inhibitors now, rather than becoming a statistic yourself later. Your effort, attitude, and willingness to get any help you need to succeed are all vital. Henry Ford was right: "Whether you think you can or you can't, you're right."

The Good News: Benefits at the End of the Road

Regardless of how you choose to define success as it pertains to your college experience, it's a fact that there are plenty of benefits to graduating from a college or university. Here's a quick look at some of them:

1. Higher Earning Potential. On average, college graduates earn twice as much income as their peers with only a high school diploma (see Figure 1.3).[16]

2. Lower Unemployment Rates. College graduates are more employable than their non-degreed peers. This is especially helpful during cyclic downturns in the economy, when many people—even talented and committed employees—find themselves out of work.

3. Wisdom. College students have the opportunity to gain understanding about a broad array of topics—politics, sociology, and current affairs to name a few. A well-educated person knows Sigmund Freud's contribution to psychological theory, Charles Darwin's contribution to evolutionary theory, and Adam Smith's contribution to economic theory. But beyond theories, facts,

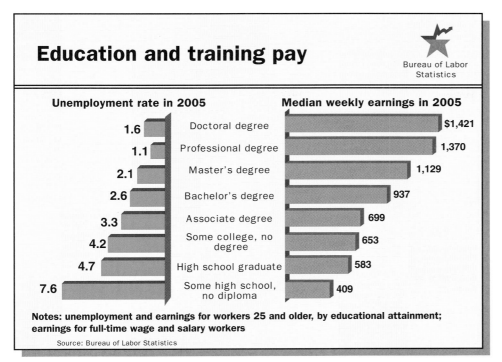

Figure 1.3

Education, Earnings, and Employment: The Quantifiable Value of a College Degree

Education and training pay

Bureau of Labor Statistics

Unemployment rate in 2005		Median weekly earnings in 2005
1.6	Doctoral degree	$1,421
1.1	Professional degree	1,370
2.1	Master's degree	1,129
2.6	Bachelor's degree	937
3.3	Associate degree	699
4.2	Some college, no degree	653
4.7	High school graduate	583
7.6	Some high school, no diploma	409

Notes: unemployment and earnings for workers 25 and older, by educational attainment; earnings for full-time wage and salary workers

Source: Bureau of Labor Statistics

Source: Education and Training Pay. (2005) U.S Bureau of Labor Statistics. Available: http://www.bls.gov/emp/emped05.pdf

and dates, a well-educated person knows how to think critically, contribute to society, and manage his or her life.

4. Insight. College students have the opportunity to understand themselves better as they participate in the academic, social, and co-curricular opportunities of higher education.

5. True Scholarship. College students have the opportunity to become lifelong learners. True scholarship is not about making the grade. It's about becoming the best student-learner you can be—inside or outside of the classroom.

6. Lifelong Friendships. Many college graduates report that some of their strongest lifelong relationships were formed during their time at college. Choosing to attend college and choosing a specific major puts you in touch with a network of people who share your specific interests.

This Course Has a Proven Track Record

If you're reading this book, there's a good chance you're enrolled in a first-year seminar course. It may be called "Freshman Seminar," "First-Year Forum," "University 101," "First-Year Experience," "College Success," "A Learning Community," or any of a host of other names. These courses are designed to introduce you to college life, familiarize you with your own campus, and help you refine your academic skills. Do they work? According to experts,

> **"Ability is what you're capable of doing. Motivation determines what you do. Attitude determines how well you do it."**
>
> **Lou Holtz, former college football coach and ESPN sports analyst**

"In short, the weight of evidence indicates that FYS [first-year seminar] participation has statistically significant and substantial, positive effects on a student's successful transition to college. . . . And on a considerable array of other college experiences known to be related directly and indirectly to bachelor's degree completion."[17] In general, students who participate in first-year seminars complete more credit hours, adjust to college more quickly, become more involved in campus life, view themselves and their skills more accurately, enjoy and appreciate their college experience, and ultimately, graduate. That's what this course is about. Now it's up to you!

C CHALLENGE Yourself Quizzes   For more practice online, go to http://www.cengage .com/colsuccess/staleyconcise to take the Challenge Yourself online quizzes.

 NOW WHAT DO YOU THINK?

At the beginning of this chapter, Gloria Gonzales, an excited but anxious student, was about to begin her college career. Now after reading this chapter, would you respond differently to any of the questions you answered about the "FOCUS Challenge Case"?

R E A L I T Y   C H E C K

On a scale of 1 to 10, answer these questions now that you've completed this chapter.

1 = not very/not much/very little/low   10 = very/a lot/very much/high

In hindsight, how much did you *really* know about this subject matter before reading the chapter?

1   2   3   4   5   6   7   8   9   10

How much do you think this information might affect your college success?

1   2   3   4   5   6   7   8   9   10

How much do you think this information might affect your career success after college?

1   2   3   4   5   6   7   8   9   10

How long did it actually take you to complete this chapter (both the reading and writing tasks)? _____ Hour(s) _____ Minutes

Compare these answers to your answers from the "Readiness Check" at the beginning of this chapter. How might the gaps between what you thought before starting the chapter and what you now think affect how you approach the next chapter?

 To download mp3 format audio summaries of this chapter, go to http://www.cengage.com/colsuccess/staleyconcise.

2 Learning about Learning

YOU'RE ABOUT TO DISCOVER...

- How learning changes your brain

- How people are intelligent in different ways

- How you learn through your senses

- How to become a more efficient and effective learner

READINESS CHECK

Before beginning this chapter, take a moment to answer these questions. Your answers will help you assess how ready you are to focus.

1 = not very/not much/very little/low   10 = very/a lot/very much/high

Based on reading the "You're about to discover..." list and skimming this chapter, how much do you think you probably already know about the subject matter?

1   2   3   4   5   6   7   8   9   10

How much do you think this information might affect your college success?

1   2   3   4   5   6   7   8   9   10

How much do you think this information might affect your career success after college?

1   2   3   4   5   6   7   8   9   10

In general, how motivated are you to learn the material in this chapter?

1   2   3   4   5   6   7   8   9   10

How ready are you to focus on this chapter—physically, intellectually, and emotionally? Circle a number for each aspect of your readiness to focus.

1   2   3   4   5   6   7   8   9   10

If any of your answers are below a 5, consider addressing the issue before reading. For example, if you're feeling scattered, take a few moments to settle down and focus.

Finally, how long do you think it will take you to complete this chapter? _____ Hour(s) _____ Minutes

Tammy Ko

"How depressing!" Tammy Ko whispered under her breath as she walked out of her "Introduction to Criminology" class on a dark, rainy Thursday afternoon. *What's with him, anyway?* she asked herself pointedly about the professor.

Tammy was a first-semester student at a large state campus several hours from her tiny hometown, where she'd been a popular student. If you leafed through her high school yearbook, you'd see Tammy's picture on nearly every page. There Tammy had been a big fish in a small pond, but now it was the other way around.

Even though she found college life at the large state university overwhelming, Tammy was excited about her major, forensic chemistry. The crime shows on TV were her favorites. She watched them all each week. She rationalized how much time it took by thinking of it as career development. The fun was picturing herself as an investigator solving headline cases: "Man Slain, Found in City Park" or "Modern Day 'Jack the Ripper' Terrorizes Las Vegas." She could envision herself hunched over laboratory equipment, testing intently for fibers or DNA, and actually breaking the case.

When she registered for classes, her academic advisor had told her that taking an "Introduction to Criminology" course from the sociology department would be a good idea. "It'll teach you how to think," he'd said, "and it'll give you the background you need to understand the criminal mind. At the end of this class," he said, "you'll know if you really want to pursue a career in forensics." *Maybe it would teach me how to think,* Tammy thought to herself now that the term was underway, *if only I could understand the professor. Forget understanding the criminal mind—I'd just like a glimpse into his!*

Professor Caldwell was quiet and reserved, and he seemed a bit out of touch. He dressed as if he hadn't bought a new article of clothing in as many years as he'd been at the university. In class, he was very articulate, knowledgeable, and organized with his handouts neatly piled on the desk, and he covered each day's material methodically, point by point. Tammy wished he'd venture from his notes occasionally to explore fascinating, related tangents. Tammy had always preferred teachers who created exciting things to do in class over teachers who went completely by the book.

Tammy's biggest complaint about Professor Caldwell was that he only talked about *theories* of criminology. When was he ever going to get to the hands-on part of the course? She couldn't help thinking, *When will we stop talking about theories and start working on real cases—like the ones on all those TV shows?*

To make matters worse, learning from lectures was not Tammy's strong suit. She hadn't done well on the first exam because she'd had to resort to memorizing things that didn't make much sense to her, and her D grade showed it. The exam consisted of one question: "Compare and contrast two theories of criminology discussed in class thus far." Tammy hated essay tests. She was at her best on tests with right or wrong answers, like true-false or multiple-choice questions. Making sense out of spoken words that go by very quickly during a lecture and trying to psych out professors' preferred answers on essay tests were challenges to her.

But her "Introduction to Criminology" class was far from hands-on. In fact, Tammy had noticed that many of her teachers preferred talking about things to doing things. They seemed to take more interest in theories than in the real world. *Too bad*, she thought, *the real world is where exciting things happen.* Although she hated to admit it, sometimes Tammy couldn't wait for college to be over so that she could begin her career in the real world. A few of Tammy's friends had taken Professor Caldwell's classes. "Just try and memorize the stuff; that's all you can do," they'd advised her. Regardless of what they happened to be talking about, somehow the conversation always came around to Professor Caldwell and how impossible it was to learn in his classes.

WHAT DO **YOU** THINK?

Now that you've read about Tammy Ko, answer the following questions. You may not know all the answers yet, but you'll find out what you know and what you stand to gain by reading this chapter.

1. Why is Tammy having difficulty learning in her "Introduction to Criminology" class?
2. Is Tammy smart? If so, in what ways? What is she particularly good at?
3. What sensory modality does Tammy prefer for taking in information?
4. How would you describe Professor Caldwell's teaching style?
5. What are the differences between Professor Caldwell's teaching style and Tammy's learning style? How do these differences impact Tammy's learning?
6. What should Tammy do to become a better learner in Professor Caldwell's class?

> **"O! this learning, what a thing it is."**
>
> **William Shakespeare**

Go to the Head of the Class: Learning and the Brain

CHALLENGE → REACTION

Challenge: What is learning?

Reaction: The following statements represent common student views on learning. Think about each statement, and mark it **true** or **false** based on your honest opinion.

_____ 1. Learning is often hard work and really not all that enjoyable.

_____ 2. Memorization and learning are basically the same thing.

_____ 3. The learning done in school is often gone in a few weeks or months.

_____ 4. In college, most learning takes place in class.

_____ 5. Learning is usually the result of listening to an instructor lecture or reading a textbook.

_____ 6. The best way to learn is by working alone.

_____ 7. Most students know intuitively how they learn best.

_____ 8. Teachers control what students learn.

_____ 9. Learning only deals with subjects taught in school.

_____ 10. The learning pace is controlled by the slowest learner in the class.

You probably noticed that many of these statements attempt to put learning in a negative light. How many did you mark true? This chapter will help you understand more about learning as a process and about yourself as a learner. As you read, your goal should be to use the insights you gain to become a better learner.

Let's start our exploration of the learning process close to home—in our own heads. What's going on up there, anyway? While your hands are busy manipulating test tubes in chemistry lab, or your eyes are watching your psychology professor's PowerPoint presentation, what's your brain up to? The answer? Plenty.

Use It or Lose It

The human brain consists of a complex web of connections between neurons. This web grows in complexity as it incorporates new knowledge. But if the connections are not reinforced frequently, they degenerate. As you learn new things, you work to hardwire these connections, making them less susceptible to degeneration. When your professors repeat portions of the previous week's lecture or assign follow-up homework to practice material covered in class, they're helping you to form connections between neurons through repeated use—or, in other words, to learn. Repetition is vital to learning. You must use and reuse information in order to hardwire it.

American humorist Will Rogers once said, "You know, you've got to exercise your *brain* just like your muscles." He was right. Giving your brain the exercise it needs—now and in your years after college—will help you form connections between neurons that, if you keep using them, will last a lifetime. From a biological point of view, that's what being a lifelong learner means. The age-old advice "use it or lose it" is true when it comes to learning.

Ask Questions and Hardwire Your Connections

Your professors have been studying their disciplines for years, perhaps decades. They have developed extensive hardwired connections between their brain neurons. They are *experts*.

By contrast, you are a *novice* to whatever discipline you're studying. You've not yet developed the brain circuitry that your professors have developed. This realization points to a potential problem. Sometimes professors are so familiar with what they already know from years of traveling the same neuron paths that what you're learning for the first time seems obvious to them. Without even realizing it, they can expect what is familiar to them to be obvious to you. Think of how challenging it is when you try to teach something that you understand thoroughly to another person who doesn't, like teaching someone who has never used a computer before how to upload an assignment.

> **"Learning is not so much an additive process, with new learning simply piling up on top of existing knowledge, as it is an active, dynamic process in which the connections are constantly changing and the structure reformatted."**
>
> **K. Patricia Cross, Professor Emerita of Higher Education, University of California, Berkeley**

Since you're a novice, you may not understand everything your professors say. Ask questions, check, clarify, probe, and persist until you do understand. Sometimes your confusion is not due to a lack of knowledge, but a lack of the *correct* knowledge. For example, you may study for a test by doing only one thing—reading and re-reading the textbook. Actually, it's important to be familiar with an array of study tools and choose the ones that work best for you.

Think of it this way. Some of the neural connections you brought with you to college are positive and useful, and some are counter-productive. When you learn, you not only add new connections, but you rewire some old connections. While you're in college, you're under construction![1]

Take Charge and Create the Best Conditions for Learning

Throughout this discussion, we've been talking about internal processes in your brain. *Your* brain, not anyone else's. The bottom line is this: Learning must be *internally initiated*—by you. It can only be *externally encouraged*—by someone else. You're in charge of your own learning. Learning changes your brain.

Let's look at food as an analogy: If learning is a process that is as biological as digestion, then no one can learn for you, in the same way that no one can eat for you. The food in the refrigerator doesn't do you a bit of good unless you walk over, open the door, remove the object of your desire, and devour it. It's there for the taking, but you must make that happen. To carry the analogy further, you eat on a daily basis, right? "No thanks, I ate last week" is a senseless statement. Learning does for your brain what food does for your body. Nourish yourself!

Brain researchers tell us the best state for learning has ten conditions.

1. You're intrinsically motivated (from within yourself) to learn material that is appropriately challenging.

> *Examine where your motivation to learn comes from.* Are you *internally* motivated because you're curious about the subject and want to learn about it or externally motivated to get an A or avoid an F? Can you generate your own internal motivation? This book has built-in reminders to boost your intrinsic motivation. Use them to your advantage as a learner.

> *Adjust the level of challenge yourself.* If you're too challenged in a class, you become anxious. Make sure you're keeping up with the workload and that you've completed the prerequisites. In many disciplines, you must know the fundamentals before tackling more advanced concepts. If you're not challenged enough, you can become bored and disengaged. Your professor will provide the baseline challenge for everyone in the class. But it's up to you to fine-tune that challenge for yourself. Get extra help if you aren't quite up to the task or bump up the challenge a notch or two if you're ahead of the game so that you're continually motivated to learn.

2. You're appropriately stressed, but generally relaxed.

> *Assess your stress.* According to researchers, you learn best in a state of *relaxed alertness*, a state of high challenge and low threat.[2] While relaxed alertness may sound like an oxymoron, it can be achieved. No stress at all is what you'd find in a no-brainer course. Some stress is useful; it helps engage you in learning. How stressed are you—and why—

C CULTIVATE Your Curiosity

CAN YOU BUILD A BETTER BRAIN?

Don't look now, but you're a very busy person! If you were watching a movie of your life at this moment, what would the scene look like? A cell phone in your hand, a website open on your computer screen, your iPod plugged in, the TV lit up, and this book propped in your lap? So much to do, so little time! There's no way to squeeze more than twenty-four hours into a day. All we can hope for is that some scientist somewhere will develop a way to get a bigger, better brain! But let's face it: brain enhancement surgery won't be available any time soon.

Even so, scientists have been busy recently learning more about this heady organ of ours. Now in new and fascinating ways, the sciences of biology and psychology are joining hands to study the human brain.[3]

What's the secret to a healthy brain? When we think of fitness, most of us think from the neck down—strong abs, bulging pecs, and tight glutes. But brain health tops them all. New evidence shows that physical exercise helps our brains shrug off damage, reinforce old neural networks, and forge new ones. Denser neural networks help us process information better, store it, and ultimately result in a smarter brain!

Current research focuses on a protein called BDNF, for brain-derived neurotrophic factor. BDNF, which helps nerve cells in our brains grow and connect, is important for development in the womb, but it's also important in adult brains. Simply put: it helps us learn. According to researchers, rats that eat a high-calorie, fast-food diet and have a couch-potato lifestyle have less BDNF in their brains. Omega-3 fatty acids found in fish normalize BDNF levels and counteract learning disabilities in rats with brain injuries. Scientists are working to see if the same thing may be true for humans.[4]

"Exercise your brain. Nourish it well. And the earlier you start the better," scientists tell us.[5] New research indicates that the goal should be to store up a cognitive reserve. And just how do we do that? Education! People who are less educated have twice the risk of getting Alzheimer's disease in later life, and people who are less educated and have ho-hum, nonchallenging jobs have three to four times the risk. According to researchers, "College seems to pay off well into retirement."[6] It *can* help you build a better brain!

when you get to class? Are you overstressed because you've rushed from your last class, cruised the parking lot for half an hour to find a good spot, or because you haven't done the reading and hope you won't be called on? Prepare for class so that you're ready to jump in. Or instead of too much stress, are you understressed because you don't value the course material? Consider how the information can be useful to you—perhaps in ways you've never even thought of. Here's the vital question to ask yourself: How much stress do I need in order to trigger my best effort?

> *Attend to your overall physical state.* Are you taking care of your physical needs so that you can stay alert, keep up with the lecture, and participate in the discussion?

3. You enter into a state researchers call "flow" when you're so totally absorbed in what you're doing that you lose track of everything else.[7]

> *Identify the kinds of learning situations that help you "flow."* Do you get fully engaged by hands-on activities? Do you find that certain courses naturally capture your attention such that you're surprised when it's time for class to end? Understanding your own preferences and style as a learner are key here.

> *Think about what you can do as a learner to get yourself there.* Not all classes or subjects will naturally induce a flow state in you. Nevertheless, ask yourself what *you* can do to focus on learning and exclude distractions. How can you become more engrossed in what you're learning?

4. You're curious about what you're learning, and you look forward to learning it.

> *Get ready to learn by looking back and by looking ahead.* When you're about to cross the street, you must look both ways, right? Keep that image in mind because that's what you should do before each class. What did class consist of last time? Can you predict what it will consist of next time?

> *Focus on substance, not style.* Part of Tammy's bias against Professor Caldwell focused on his appearance. Despite society's obsession with attractiveness, grooming, and fashion, a student's job is to ask: What can I learn from this person? Passing judgment on physical appearance just encourages you to play the blame game and derails your learning.

5. You're slightly confused, but only for a short time.[8]

> *Use confusion as a motivator.* You may not be getting the lecture's main points because you don't understand new terms used along the way. Look them up early on in the learning process. Ask yourself what background information would help things click—and find out the answers to those questions.

"When we come to know something, we have performed an act that is as biological as when we digest something."

Henry Plotkin, *Darwin Machines and the Nature of Knowledge* (1994)

> *Ask questions!* To your professor, questions indicate *interest*, not *idiocy*. Don't be afraid to probe more deeply into the material. As they say, "The only stupid question is the one you don't ask."

6. You search for personal meaning and patterns.

> *Ask yourself: What's in it for me?* Why is knowing this important? How can I use this information in the future? Instead of dismissing material that appears unrelated to your life, try figuring out how it *could* relate. You may be surprised!

> *Think about how courses relate to one another.* How does this new knowledge align with other things you're learning in other courses? Does sociology have anything to do with history? Psychology with economics?

7. Your emotions are involved, not just your mind.

> *Evaluate your attitudes and feelings.* Do you like the subject matter? Do you admire the teacher? Remember your high school teacher, Mr. Brown, whose class you just couldn't stand? Not every class will be your favorite. That's natural. But if a class turns you off as a learner, instead of allowing your emotions to take over, ask why and whether your feelings are in your best interest.

> *Make a deliberate decision to change negative feelings.* Fortunately, feelings can be changed. Hating a course or disliking a professor can only build resentment and threaten your success. It's possible to do a one-eighty and transform your negative emotions into positive energy.

8. You realize that as a learner you use what you already know in constructing new knowledge.[9]

> *Remember that passive learning is an oxymoron.* When it comes to learning, you are the construction foreman, building on what you already know to construct new knowledge. You're not just memorizing facts someone else wants you to learn. You're a full partner in the learning process!

> *Remind yourself that constructing knowledge takes work.* No one ever built a house by simply sitting back or just hanging out. Builders work hard, but in the end, they have something to show for their efforts. In your college courses, you must identify what you already know and blend new knowledge into the framework you've built in your mind. By constructing new knowledge, you are building yourself into a more sophisticated, more polished, and most certainly, a more educated person.

"Personal participation is the universal principle of knowing."

Michael Polanyi, Hungarian-British scholar
(1891–1976)

9. **You understand that learning is both conscious and unconscious.**

> *Watch where your mind goes when it's off duty.* Does learning take place when you're not deliberately trying to learn? Some of what you learn will be immediately obvious to you, and some will dawn on you after class is over, while you're in the shower, or eating lunch, or falling asleep at night, for example. Pay attention to your indirect learning and move it into your line of vision.

> *Remember that both kinds of learning are important.* Both conscious learning and unconscious learning count. There are no rules about when and where learning can occur. Capitalize on both.

> **"It is what we think we know already that often prevents us from learning."**
>
> **Claude Bernard, French physiologist (1813–1878)**

10. **You're given a degree of choice in terms of what you learn, how you do it, and feedback on how you're doing.**

> *Make the most of the choices you're given.* College isn't a free-for-all in which you can take any classes you like toward earning a degree. However, which electives you choose will be up to you. Or in a particular course, if your instructor allows you to write a paper or shoot a video, choose the option that will be more motivating for you. When you receive an assignment, select a topic that fires you up. It's easier to generate energy to put toward choices you've made yourself.

> *Use feedback to improve, and if feedback is not given, ask for it.* It's possible to get really good at doing something the wrong way. Take a golf swing or a swimming stroke, for example. Without someone intervening to give you feedback, it may be difficult to know how to improve. Your instructors will most likely write comments on your assignments to explain their grades. Assessing your work is their job; it's what they must do to help you improve. Take their suggestions to heart and try them out.

All of us are already good learners in some situations. Let's say you're drawn to technology, for example. You're totally engrossed in computers and eagerly learn everything you can from books, classes, and online sources—and you sometimes totally lose yourself in a flow state as you're learning. No one has to force you to practice your technology skills or pick up an issue of *Wired* or *PC World.* You do it because you want to. In this case, you're self-motivated and therefore learning is easy. This chapter provides several different tools to help you understand your own personal profile as a learner so that you can try to learn at your best in *all* situations.

YOUR TOP-TEN LIST

Reflect on yourself as a learner in each of the classes you're enrolled in this term. How optimal are the conditions for learning? How can you adjust the learning environment *yourself* to optimize it? Label the classes you're taking this term, and put checkmarks next to the conditions that are present in each class. Reflect on why you chose to mark these items (or didn't) in each class.

Ten Conditions for Optimal Learning

COURSE NAMES	Class 1:	Class 2:	Class 3:	Class 4:	Class 5:
1. You're intrinsically motivated to learn material that is appropriately challenging.	☐	☐	☐	☐	☐
2. You're appropriately stressed, but generally relaxed.	☐	☐	☐	☐	☐
3. You enter into a state researchers call flow.	☐	☐	☐	☐	☐
4. You're curious about what you're learning, and you look forward to learning it.	☐	☐	☐	☐	☐
5. You're slightly confused, but only for a short time.	☐	☐	☐	☐	☐
6. You search for personal meaning and patterns.	☐	☐	☐	☐	☐
7. Your emotions are involved, not just your mind.	☐	☐	☐	☐	☐
8. You realize that as a learner you use what you already know in constructing new knowledge.	☐	☐	☐	☐	☐
9. You understand that learning is both conscious and unconscious.	☐	☐	☐	☐	☐
10. You're given a degree of choice in terms of what you learn, how you do it, and feedback on how you're doing.	☐	☐	☐	☐	☐

Which course has the most checkmarks? Is this the course that you find easiest? The most engaging? Which course has the least number of checkmarks? Is this the course that you find the most difficult? The least interesting? Considering these ten optimal conditions for learning, what specific actions can you take to enhance your learning in your most challenging class?

Multiple Intelligences: *How* Are You Smart?

CHALLENGE ⟳ REACTION

Challenge: Are people smart in different ways? How so?

Reaction: On each line, put checkmarks next to all the statements that best describe you.

Linguistic Intelligence: **The capacity to use language to express what's on your mind and understand others ("word smart")**

_____ I'm a good storyteller.

_____ I enjoy word games, puns, and tongue twisters.

_____ I'd rather listen to the radio than watch TV.

_____ I've recently written something I'm proud of.

_____ I can hear words in my head before I say or write them.

_____ When riding in the car, I sometimes pay more attention to words on billboards than I do to the scenery.

_____ In high school, I did better in English, history, or social studies than I did in math and science.

_____ I enjoy reading.

Logical-Mathematical Intelligence: **The capacity to understand cause/effect relationships and to manipulate numbers ("number/reasoning smart")**

_____ I can easily do math in my head.

_____ I enjoy brainteasers or puzzles.

_____ I like it when things can be counted or analyzed.

_____ I can easily find logical flaws in what others do or say.

_____ I think most things have rational explanations.

_____ Math and science were my favorite subjects in high school.

_____ I like to put things into categories.

_____ I'm interested in new scientific advances.

Spatial Intelligence: **The capacity to represent the world visually or graphically ("picture smart")**

_____ I like to take pictures of what I see around me.

_____ I'm sensitive to colors.

_____ My dreams at night are vivid.

_____ I like to doodle or draw.

_____ I'm good at navigating with a map.

_____ I can picture what something will look like before it's finished.

_____ In school, I preferred geometry to algebra.

_____ I often make my point by drawing a picture or diagram.

Bodily-Kinesthetic Intelligence: **The capacity to use your whole body or parts of it to solve a problem, make something, or put on a production ("body smart")**

_____ I regularly engage in sports or physical activities.

_____ I get fidgety when asked to sit for long periods of time.

_____ I get some of my best ideas while I'm engaged in a physical activity.

_____ I need to practice a skill in order to learn it, rather than just reading or watching a video about it.

_____ I enjoy being a daredevil.

_____ I'm a well-coordinated person.

_____ I like to think through things while I'm doing something else like running or walking.

_____ I like to spend my free time outdoors.

Musical Intelligence: **The capacity to think in music, hear patterns and recognize, remember, and perhaps manipulate them ("music smart")**

_____ I can tell when a musical note is flat or sharp.

_____ I play a musical instrument.

_____ I often hear music playing in my head.

_____ I can listen to a piece of music once or twice, and then sing it back accurately.

_____ I often sing or hum while working.

(continued)

_____ I like music playing while I'm doing things.

_____ I'm good at keeping time to a piece of music.

_____ I consider music an important part of my life.

Interpersonal Intelligence: The capacity to understand other people ("people smart")

_____ I prefer group activities to solo activities.

_____ Others think of me as a leader.

_____ I enjoy the challenge of teaching others something I like to do.

_____ I like to get involved in social activities at school, church, or work.

_____ If I have a problem, I'm more likely to get help than tough it out alone.

_____ I feel comfortable in a crowd of people.

_____ I have several close friends.

_____ I'm the sort of person others come to for advice about their problems.

Intrapersonal Intelligence: The capacity to understand yourself, who you are, and what you can do ("self-smart")

_____ I like to spend time alone thinking about important questions in life.

_____ I have invested time in learning more about myself.

_____ I consider myself to be independent minded.

_____ I keep a journal of my inner thoughts.

_____ I'd rather spend a weekend alone than at a place with a lot of other people around.

_____ I've thought seriously about starting a business of my own.

_____ I'm realistic about my own strengths and weaknesses.

_____ I have goals for my life that I'm working on.

Naturalistic Intelligence: The capacity to discriminate between living things and show sensitivity toward the natural world ("nature smart")

_____ Environmental problems bother me.

_____ In school, I always enjoyed field trips to places in nature or away from class.

_____ I enjoy studying nature, plants, or animals.

_____ I've always done well on projects involving living systems.

_____ I enjoy pets.

_____ I notice signs of wildlife when I'm on a walk or hike.

_____ I can recognize types of plants, trees, rocks, birds, and so on.

_____ I enjoy learning about environmental issues.

Which intelligences have the most checkmarks? Although this is an informal instrument, it can help you think about the concept of multiple intelligences, or MI. _How_ are you smart?

Based on Armstrong, T. (1994). _Multiple intelligences in the classroom._ Alexandria, VA: Association for Supervision and Curriculum Development, pp. 18–20.

Have you ever noticed that people are smart in different ways? Consider the musical genius of Mozart, who published his first piano pieces at the age of five. Or think about Tiger Woods, who watched his father hit golf balls and mimicked his dad's swing while still in his crib. Not many of us are as musically gifted as Mozart or as physically gifted as Tiger Woods, but we all have strengths. You may earn top grades in math, and not-so-top grades in English, and your best friend's grades may be just the opposite.

According to Harvard psychologist Howard Gardner, people can be smart in at least eight different ways. Most schools focus on particular types of intelligence, linguistic and logical-mathematical intelligence, reflecting the three R's: reading, writing, and 'rithmetic. But Gardner claims intelligence is actually multifaceted. It can't be measured by traditional one-dimensional standardized IQ tests and represented by a three-digit number: 100 (average), 130+ (gifted), or 150+ (genius). Gardner defines intelligence as "the ability to find and solve problems and create products of value in one or more cultural setting."[10]

So instead of asking the traditional question "How smart are you?" a better question is "How are you smart?" The idea is to find out *how*, and then apply this understanding of yourself to your academic work in order to achieve your best results.

Translate Content into Your Own Intelligences

Do you sometimes wonder why you can't remember things for exams? Some learning experts believe that memory is intelligence-specific. You may have a good memory for people's faces but a bad memory for their names. You may be able to remember the words of a country-western hit but not the dance steps that go with it. The Theory of Multiple Intelligences may explain why.[11]

Examine your own behaviors in class. If your instructors use their linguistic intelligence to teach, as many do, and your intelligences lie elsewhere, can you observe telltale signs of your frustration? Instead of zeroing in on the lecture, do you fidget (bodily-kinesthetic), doodle (spatial), or socialize (interpersonal)? You may need to translate the information into your own personal intelligences, just as you would if your professor speaks French and you speak English. This strategy might have worked for Tammy Ko from the "FOCUS Challenge Case." Professor Caldwell's most developed intelligence is linguistic, whereas Tammy's are bodily-kinesthetic (manipulating test tubes) and interpersonal (interacting with people). Tammy's learning problems are partially due to a case of mismatched intelligences between Professor Caldwell and herself.

Let's say one of your courses this term is "Introduction to Economics," and the current course topic is the Law of Supply and Demand. Basically, "the theory of supply and demand describes how prices vary as a result of a balance between product availability at each price (supply) and the desires of those with purchasing power at each price (demand)."[12] To understand this law, you could read the textbook (linguistic); study mathematical formulas (logical-mathematical); examine charts and graphs (spatial); observe the Law of Supply and Demand in the natural world, through the fluctuating price of gasoline, for example (naturalist); look at the way the Law of Supply and Demand is expressed in your own body, using food as a metaphor (bodily-kinesthetic); reflect on how and when you might be able to afford something you desperately want, like a certain model of car (intrapersonal); or write (or find) a song that helps you understand the law (musical). You needn't try all eight ways, but it's intriguing to speculate about various ways to learn that may work for you, rather than assuming you're doomed because your intelligences don't match your instructor's.

Use Intelligence-Oriented Study Techniques

What if your strongest intelligence is different from the one through which course material is presented? What can you do about it? Take a look at the following techniques for studying using different intelligences. Tweaking the *way* you study may make a world of difference.

Linguistic --→	1. Rewrite your class notes. 2. Record yourself reading through your class notes and play it as you study. 3. Read the textbook chapter aloud.
Logical Mathematical --→	1. Create hypothetical conceptual problems to solve. 2. Organize chapter or lecture notes into a logical flow. 3. Analyze how the textbook chapter is organized and why.
Spatial --→	1. Draw a map that demonstrates your thinking on course material. 2. Illustrate your notes by drawing diagrams and charts. 3. Mark up your textbook to show relationships between concepts.
Bodily–Kinesthetic --→	1. Study course material while engaged in physical activity. 2. Practice skills introduced in class or in the text. 3. Act out a scene based on chapter content.
Musical --→	1. Create musical memory devices by putting words into well-known melodies. 2. Listen to music while you're studying. 3. Sing or hum as you work.
Interpersonal --→	1. Discuss course material with your classmates in class. 2. Organize a study group that meets regularly. 3. Meet a classmate before or after class for coffee and course conversation.
Intrapersonal --→	1. Keep a journal to track your personal reactions to course material. 2. Study alone and engage in internal dialogue about course content. 3. Coach yourself on how to best study for a challenging class.
Naturalistic --→	1. Search for applications of course content in the natural world. 2. Study outside (if weather permits and you can resist distractions). 3. Go to a physical location that exemplifies course material (for example, a park for your geology course).

Develop Your Weaker Intelligences

It's important to cultivate your weaker intelligences. Why? Because life isn't geared to one kind of intelligence. It's complex. A photo journalist for *National Geographic*, for example, might need linguistic intelligence, spatial intelligence, interpersonal intelligence, and naturalist intelligence. Being well-rounded, as the expression goes, is truly a good thing. Artist Pablo Picasso once said, "I am always doing that which I cannot do, in order that I may learn how to do it."

Use your multiple intelligences to multiply your success. Remember that no one is naturally intelligent in all eight areas. Each individual is a unique blend of intelligences. But the Theory of Multiple Intelligences claims that we all have the capacity to develop all of our eight intelligences further. That's good news!

INSIGHT ➔ ACTION

1. What are your most developed intelligences? Describe a situation in which you excelled as a learner and how the Theory of Multiple Intelligences helps explain your success.

2. Now do the opposite. Describe a situation in which you did not excel as a learner and how the Theory of Multiple Intelligences helps explain your difficulty.

3. Which of your intelligences would you like to develop further? Why? What actions can you take to do so?

How Do You Perceive and Process Information?

CHALLENGE ➔ REACTION

Challenge: You've lived with yourself for many years now, but how well do you know yourself as a learner?

Reaction: List as many descriptive phrases about your learning preferences as you can. For example, you might write, "I learn best when I listen to an instructor lecture" or "I learn best when I make color-coded binders for each class." Use this activity to discover some specifics about your learning style.

Style—we all have it, right? What's yours? Baggy jeans and a T-shirt? Sandals, even in the middle of winter? A signature hairdo that defies gravity? When it comes to appearance, you have your own style. You know it, and so does everyone who knows you.

Think about how your mind works. For example, how do you decide what to wear in the morning? Do you turn on the radio or TV for the weather forecast? Stick your head out the front door? Ask someone else's opinion? Throw on whatever happens to be clean? We all have different styles, don't we?

So what's a learning style? A learning style is defined as your "characteristic and preferred way of gathering, interpreting, organizing, and thinking about information."[13]

Here's one way of looking at things. The way you perceive information and the way you process it—your perceiving/processing preferences—are based in part on your senses. Which sensory modalities do you prefer to use to take

> **"Learning how to learn is life's most important skill."**
>
> **Tony Buzan, memory expert**

in information—your eyes (visual-graphic or visual-words), your ears (aural), or all your senses using your whole body (kinesthetic)? Which type of information sinks in best? Which type of information do you most trust to be accurate?

To further understand your preferred sensory channel, let's take this hypothetical example. Assume a rich relative you didn't even know you had leaves you some money, and you decide to use it to buy a new car. You must first answer many questions: What kind of car do you want to buy—an SUV, a sedan, a sports car, a van, or a truck? What are the differences between various makes and models? How do prices, comfort, and safety compare? Who provides the best warranty? Which car do consumers rate highest? How would you go about learning the answers to all these questions?

 Visual. Some of us would **look**. We'd study charts and graphs comparing cars, mileage, fuel tank capacity, maintenance costs, and customer satisfaction. We learn through symbolic representations that explain what could have been said in normal text format.

 Aural. Some of us would **listen**. We'd ask all our friends what kind of cars they drive and what they've heard about cars from other people. We'd pay attention as showroom salespeople describe the features of various cars. We learn through sounds by listening.

 Read/Write. Some of us would **read** or **write**. We'd buy a copy of *Consumer Reports* annual edition on automobiles, or copies of magazines such as *Car and Driver* or *Road and Track*, and write lists of each car's pros and cons. We learn through words by reading and writing.

 Kinesthetic. Some of us would want to **do it**. We'd go to the showroom and test drive a few cars to physically try them out. We learn through experience when all our sensory modalities are activated.

What would you do? Eventually, as you're deciding which vehicle to buy, you might do all these things, and do them more than once. But learning style theory says we all have preferences in terms of how we perceive and process information.

EXERCISE 2.1 VARK Learning Styles Assessment

Choose the answer which best explains your preference and circle the letter. Please select more than one response if a single answer does not match your perception. Leave blank any question that does not apply.

1. You are helping someone who wants to go downtown, find your airport or locate the bus station. You would:
   a) draw or give her a map.
   b) tell her the directions.
   c) write down the directions (without a map).
   d) go with her.

2. You are not sure whether a word should be spelled "dependent" or "dependant." You would:
   a) see the word in your mind and choose by the way different versions look.
   b) think about how each word sounds and choose one.

c)   find it in a dictionary.
   d)   write both words on paper and choose one.

3. You are planning a group vacation. You want some feedback from your friends about your plans. You would:
   a)   use a map or website to show them the places.
   b)   phone, text or email them.
   c)   give them a copy of the printed itinerary.
   d)   describe some of the highlights.

4. You are going to cook something as a special treat for your family. You would:
   a)   look through the cookbook for ideas from the pictures.
   b)   ask friends for suggestions.
   c)   use a cookbook where you know there is a good recipe.
   d)   cook something you know without the need for instructions.

5. A group of tourists want to learn about the parks or wildlife reserves in your area. You would:
   a)   show them internet pictures, photographs or picture books.
   b)   talk about, or arrange a talk for them, about parks or wildlife reserves.
   c)   give them a book or pamphlets about the parks or wildlife reserves.
   d)   take them to a park or wildlife reserve and walk with them.

6. You are about to purchase a digital camera or cell phone. Other than price, what would most influence your decision?
   a)   Its attractive design that looks good.
   b)   The salesperson telling me about its features.
   c)   Reading the details about its features.
   d)   Trying or testing it.

7. Remember a time when you learned how to do something new. Try to avoid choosing a physical skill, like riding a bike. You learned best by:
   a)   diagrams and charts—visual clues.
   b)   listening to somebody explaining it and asking questions.
   c)   written instructions—e.g. a manual or textbook.
   d)   watching a demonstration.

8. You have a problem with your knee. You would prefer that the doctor:
   a)   showed you a diagram of what was wrong.
   b)   described what was wrong.
   c)   gave you a pamphlet to read about it.
   d)   used a plastic model of a knee to show what was wrong.

9. You want to learn a new software program, skill or game on a computer. You would:
   a)   follow the diagrams in the book that came with it.
   b)   talk with people who know about the program.
   c)   read the written instructions that came with the program.
   d)   use the controls or keyboard and try things out.

10. I like websites that have:
   a)   interesting design and visual features.
   b)   audio channels where I can hear music, radio programs or interviews.
   c)   interesting written descriptions, lists and explanations.
   d)   things I can click on or try out.

11. Other than price, what would most influence your decision to buy a new non-fiction book?
   a)   The cover looks appealing.
   b)   A friend talks about it and recommends it.
   c)   You'd quickly read parts of it.
   d)   It contains real-life stories, experiences and examples.

12. You are using a book, CD or website to learn how to take photos with your new digital camera. You would like to have:
   a)   diagrams showing the camera and what each part does.
   b)   a chance to ask questions and talk about the camera and its features.

(continued)

c) clear written instructions with lists and bullet points about what to do.
d) many examples of good and poor photos and how to improve them.

13. Do you prefer a teacher or a presenter who uses:
a) diagrams, charts or graphs?
b) question and answer, talk, group discussion or guest speakers?
c) handouts, books or readings?
d) demonstrations, models, fieldtrips, role plays or practical exercises?

14. You have finished a competition or test and would like some feedback. You would like to have feedback:
a) using graphs showing what you had achieved.
b) from somebody who talks it through with you.
c) in a written format, describing your results.
d) using examples from what you have done.

15. You are going to choose food at a restaurant or cafe. You would:
a) look at what others are eating or look at pictures of each dish.
b) ask the server or friends to recommend choices.
c) choose from the written descriptions in the menu.
d) choose something that you have had there before.

16. You have to give an important speech at a conference or special occasion. You would:
a) make diagrams or create graphs to help explain things.
b) write a few key words and practice your speech over and over.
c) write out your speech and learn from reading it over several times.
d) gather many examples and stories to make the talk real and practical.

Source: N. Fleming. (2001–2007). *VARK, a Guide to Learning Styles*. Version 7.0. Available at http://www.vark-learn.com/english/page.asp?p=questionnaire. Adapted and used with permission from Neil Fleming.

Scoring the VARK

Let's tabulate your results.

Count your choices in each of the four VARK categories.	(a)	(b)	(c)	(d)
	Visual	Aural	Read/Write	Kinesthetic

FOCUS ON CAREERS: Neil Fleming, University Professor, Creator of the VARK

Courtesy of Neil Fleming

Q1: What's it like to be a college teacher? What are the pros and cons of the profession?
Although I write and speak widely, teaching is my favorite job because you get to talk with so many interesting people (students) and you sometimes make a difference in their lives. There are those great moments when you see that a student has "gotten it." Those "Aha!" moments are priceless. You also get to learn new things with your students so you stay a learner for life and never "mature"! The bad days are those when you realize that you have "missed" some students or that they have somehow lost interest in you and what you teach.

Q2: What is your understanding of how learning happens?
I think learning happens when students accept, adjust, and alter the "scripts" they carry in their heads. "Scripts" are the outcome of neural pathways in our brain. Those pathways can be clear and unobstructed, open and inviting, sheathed and insulated against change, or overgrown and in danger of being lost.

We all learn in particular ways. Sometimes those ways serve us well. We need to understand what those ways are and cultivate them. But other times our learning preferences don't serve us well because of the particular material we're trying to learn. It's sort of like trying to build a house without the right tools. It's just not going to work, or at the very least, it's going to be a struggle. In those cases, we need to adjust our learning to fit the content and the situation.

In general, I know students have learned something well when they can teach it to someone else.

Now that you've calculated your scores, do they match your perceptions of yourself as a learner? Could you have predicted them? The VARK's creators believe that *you* are best qualified to verify and interpret your own results.[14]

Using Your Sensory Preferences

Knowing your preferences can help you in your academic coursework. If your highest score (by 4 or 5 points) is in one of the four VARK modalities, that particular learning modality is your preferred one.[15] If your scores are more or less even between several or all four modalities, these scores mean that you don't have a strong preference for any single modality. A lower score in a preference simply means that you are more comfortable using other styles. If your VARK results contain a zero in a particular learning modality, you may realize that you do indeed dislike this mode or find it unhelpful. You might want to reflect on why you omit this learning modality. To learn more about your results and suggestions for applying them, see Figure 2.1 for your preferred modality.

Most college classes emphasize reading and writing; however, if your lowest score is in the read/write modality, don't assume you're academically doomed. VARK can help you discover alternative, more productive ways to learn the same course material. You may learn to adapt naturally to a particular instructor or discipline's preferences, using a visual modality in your economics class to interpret graphs and a kinesthetic modality in your chemistry lab to conduct experiments.

However, you may also find that you need to deliberately and strategically re-route your learning methods in some of your classes, and knowing your VARK preferences can help you do that. Learning to capitalize on your preferences and translate challenging course material into your preferred modality may serve you

C CREATE a Career Outlook

COLLEGE PROFESSOR
Have you ever considered a career as a college professor?

Facts to Consider[16]

Academic preparation required: A master's degree, or more often, a doctoral degree is required, although in some fields highly cultivated expertise or practical experience is sufficient.

Future workforce demand: Prospects for new jobs will be good in the future, although many openings will be for part-time teachers.

Work environment: College professors have flexible schedules, teach a wide variety of subjects (usually related within one field), and conduct research.

Essential skills: reading; writing; communicating with individual students, to a classroom of students, or in work-related committees; collecting and analyzing data; using technology to teach, communicate, and present information

Questions to Ponder
1. Do you have (or could you acquire) the skills this career requires?
2. Are you interested in a career like this? Why or why not?

For more career activities online, go to http://www.cengage.com/colsuccess/staleyconcise to do the Team Career exercises.

Q3: In your opinion, are most students today visual, aural, read/write, or kinesthetic learners?
The VARK data I've collected indicate that the most common preference for students is kinesthetic, that is, they want to experience the learning or have the teacher relate the learning to things that they know, have seen, or can do. The plain truth is that the teacher who can provide links to the reality of students is going to reach more students.

Q4: How can students who want to go into the teaching profession best prepare themselves?
If students want to become teachers at any level, they must understand how people learn, and they must devote themselves to helping people do it. In my view, it's the best profession in the world. If students want a fulfilling career, a career in which they have the potential to bring forth lasting, and sometimes life-altering, change, they should consider teaching.

Figure 2.1

Visual, Aural, Read/Write, and Kinesthetic Learning Strategies

VISUAL

General Strategies

Draw maps.
Create charts.
Develop graphs.
Use symbols.
Draw diagrams.
Underline text.
Make flowcharts.
Use highlighters.
Write with different colors.
Draw pictures.
Use word imagery.
Use spatial arrangements.
Pay attention to teachers who are dramatic and dynamic.

Study Strategies

Convert your lecture notes to a visual format.
Study the placement of items, colors, and shapes in your textbook.
Put complex concepts into flowcharts or graphs.
Redraw ideas you create from memory.

Exam Strategies

Practice turning your visuals back into words.
Practice writing out exam answers.
Recall the pictures you made of the pages you studied.
Use diagrams to answer exam questions, if your instructor will allow it.

AURAL

General Strategies

Discuss topics with other students.
Use a tape recorder so you can listen more than once.
Attend as many class lectures as you can.
Leave space in your lecture notes for later recall and filling in.
Join a study group.
Find ways to talk about and listen to conversations about the material.
Describe the material to a student who wasn't there.
Make a point of remembering examples, stories, and jokes—things people use to explain things.
Tune in to your teacher's voice.

Study Strategies

Read your notes aloud.
Explain your notes to another auditory learner.
Ask others to "hear" your understanding of the material.
Talk about your learning to others or to yourself.
Record your notes onto tapes or CDs or listen to your instructors' podcasts.
Realize that your lecture notes may be incomplete. You may have become so involved in listening that you stopped writing. Fill your notes in later by talking with other students or getting material from the textbook.

Exam Strategies

Practice by speaking your answers aloud.
Listen to your own voice as you answer questions.
Opt for an oral exam if allowed.
Imagine you are talking with the teacher as you answer questions.

READ/WRITE

General Strategies

Make lists.
Take lecture notes (almost verbatim).
Journal about what you're learning.
Pay attention to headings.
Read textbooks thoroughly.
Compile/read glossaries.
Write out definitions.
Read/find quotations.
Look up words in the dictionary.
Pay attention to printed handouts.
Read outside library materials.
Read websites and web pages.
Read manuals (for computers or labs).
Listen to teachers and students who are articulate.

Study Strategies

Write out your lecture notes again and again.
Read your notes (silently) again and again.
Put ideas and principles into different words.
Translate diagrams, graphs, etc., into text.
Rearrange words and "play" with wording.
Turn diagrams and charts into words.

Exam Strategies

Write out potential exam answers.
Practice creating and taking exams.
Type out your answers to potential test questions.
Organize your notes into lists or bullets.
Write practice paragraphs, particularly beginnings and endings.

KINESTHETIC

General Strategies

Go on field trips.
Find real examples of abstract concepts.
Apply information.
View exhibits, samples, and photos.
Use hands-on approaches—computers, for example.
Take advantage of labs.
Engage in service-learning related to the course.
Listen to teachers who give real-life examples.
Don't forget that you need to do things in order to remember them.
Use all your senses.

Study Strategies

Recall experiments, field trips, etc.
Remember the real things that happened.
Talk over your notes with another "K" person.
Use photos and pictures that make ideas come to life.
Go back to the lab, your manual, or your notes that include real examples.
Remember that your lecture notes will have gaps if topics weren't concrete or relevant for you.
Use case studies to help you learn abstract principles.

Exam Strategies

Role-play the exam situation in your room (or the actual classroom).
Put plenty of examples into your answers.
Write practice answers and sample paragraphs.
Give yourself practice tests.

well. Remember these suggestions about the VARK, and try them out to see if they improve your academic results.

1. VARK preferences are not necessarily strengths. However, VARK is an excellent vehicle to help you reflect on how you learn and begin to reinforce the productive strategies you're already using or select ones that might work better.

2. If you have a strong preference for a particular modality, practice multiple suggestions listed in Figure 2.1 for that particular modality. Reinforce your learning through redundancy.

3. An estimated 55 to 65 percent of people are multimodal. In a typical classroom of 30 students (based on VARK data):

   - 17 students would be multimodal,
   - 1 student would be visual,
   - 1 student would be aural,
   - 5 students would be read/write,
   - 6 students would be kinesthetic,

   and the teacher would most likely have a strong read/write preference![17]

4. If you are multimodal, as most of us are, it may be necessary to use all your modalities to boost your confidence in your learning. Practice the suggestions for all of your preferred modalities.

5. While in an ideal world, it would be good to try to strengthen lesser preferences, you may wish to save that goal for later in life. Fleming's students eventually convinced him that college isn't the place to experiment. Academic results are important, and often scholarships and graduate school acceptance hang in the balance. You, too, may decide it's better to try to strengthen existing preferences now and work on expanding your repertoire later. This book will give you an opportunity to practice your VARK learning preferences—whatever they are—in each chapter.

INSIGHT ⟶ ACTION

Go back to the earliest days of your schooling and identify three peak learning experiences—times when you were most engaged as a learner. Perhaps during these learning peaks you were operating in "flow" mode. You were so engrossed in what you were learning that you lost track of everything around you and how long you had been working. After you've identified these experiences, list the primary VARK modality or modalities that you were using at the time. Does your list match your results on the VARK instrument? Were you using your most preferred modality? List some specific ways you can translate tasks in your most challenging classes into your VARK preferences.

Ultimately, learning at your best is up to you. Each chapter of this book will remind you of your VARK preferences with special activities to reinforce your sensory modalities.

Gaining the insights provided in this chapter and acting on them have the potential to greatly affect your college success. Understand yourself, capitalize on your preferences, build on them, focus, and learn!

EXERCISE 2.2 VARK Activity

Complete the recommended activity for your preferred VARK learning modality. If you are multimodal, select more than one activity. Your instructor may ask you to (a) give an oral report on your results in class, (b) send your results to him or her via e-mail, (c) post them online, or (d) contribute to a class chat.

 Visual: Think about a particular course or exam you studied for in the past. Create a personal chart that compares the learning strategies for each of the four VARK modalities you used and the degree of success you had using each one.

 Aural: Interview another student who is a member of a campus honor society. Which VARK strategies does this student use and why? Determine whether these strategies would work for you.

 Read/Write: Write a one-page summary of what you have learned about yourself as a result of reading this chapter.

 Kinesthetic: If your campus has a learning center, visit it to gather additional information about your learning style. Apply what you have learned to create a plan to prepare for your next exam.

C CHALLENGE Yourself Quizzes For more practice online, go to http://www.cengage.com/colsuccess/staleyconcise to take the Challenge Yourself online quizzes.

 NOW WHAT DO YOU THINK?

At the beginning of this chapter, Tammy Ko, a frustrated and disgruntled student, faced a challenge. Now after reading this chapter, would you respond differently to any of the questions you answered about the "FOCUS Challenge Case"?

R E A L I T Y   C H E C K

On a scale of 1 to 10, answer these questions now that you've completed this chapter.

1 = not very/not much/very little/low   10 = very/a lot/very much/high

In hindsight, how much did you *really* know about this subject matter before reading the chapter?

   1   2   3   4   5   6   7   8   9   10

How much do you think this information might affect your career success after college?

   1   2   3   4   5   6   7   8   9   10

How much do you think this information might affect your college success?

   1   2   3   4   5   6   7   8   9   10

How long did it actually take you to complete this chapter (both the reading and writing tasks)? _____ Hour(s) _____ Minutes

Compare these answers to your answers from the "Readiness Check" at the beginning of this chapter. How might the gaps between what you thought before starting the chapter and what you now think affect how you approach the next chapter?

 To download mp3 format audio summaries of this chapter, go to http://www.cengage.com/colsuccess/staleyconcise.

3 Making Use of Resources: Finances, Technology, and Campus Support

READINESS CHECK

Before beginning this chapter, take a moment to answer these questions. Your answers will help you assess how ready you are to focus.

1 = not very/not much/very little/low   10 = very/a lot/very much/high

Based on reading the "You're about to discover…" list and skimming this chapter, how much do you think you probably already know about the subject matter?

1 2 3 4 5 6 7 8 9 10

How much do you think this information might affect your college success?

1 2 3 4 5 6 7 8 9 10

How much do you think this information might affect your career success after college?

1 2 3 4 5 6 7 8 9 10

In general, how motivated are you to learn the material in this chapter?

1 2 3 4 5 6 7 8 9 10

How ready are you to focus on this chapter—physically, intellectually, and emotionally? Circle a number for each aspect of your readiness to focus.

1 2 3 4 5 6 7 8 9 10

If any of your answers are below a 5, consider addressing the issue before reading. For example, if you're feeling scattered, take a few moments to settle down and focus.

Finally, how long do you think it will take you to complete this chapter? _____ Hour(s) _____ Minutes

Jessica Taylor

Jessica Taylor could still remember

the day she'd gotten her college acceptance letter. It began, "It is my distinct pleasure to tell you that you have been accepted …." Accepted by her first choice school! How fortunate could she be?

Before she left for college everything was going Jessica's way. She'd felt ready to leave her family, her small private high school, the suburbs, and ready to be on her own.

Even though she didn't think about it much, Jessica had led a relatively privileged life. She'd gone to a select, private college prep high school, called The Oaks, in the suburbs where the teachers always reminded the students that they were being groomed for college.

Jessica had struggled with an eating disorder in high school, but thanks to her parents, her teachers, and a wonderful counselor, she'd managed to get a handle on it. Her counselor had told her that the actual percentage of people with diagnosed eating disorders is low, but she also knew that lots of girls have symptoms at one time or another. In fact, she wondered if her new college roommate, Angela, who skipped most meals in the dining hall and whose size 2 jeans bagged on her, might be one of them. Anyway, Jessica was doing well now, and she had things in perspective. But she was going to find the Counseling Center on campus, just in case she needed it. She didn't know exactly where it was. In fact, she didn't know where a lot of things were. The campus seemed huge to her.

The best thing that had happened to Jessica in college was her new circle of friends. She met them in her First-Year Seminar class, and then she noticed many of them in her other Learning Community classes and even in her residence hall. They'd all go to "The Village" close to campus, browse through the boutiques, get manicures, and have lunch. It was a good thing she'd applied for four credit cards during the campus promos. Sometimes she had to put her purchases on more than one card so that she wouldn't exceed her limit. Her male friends spent a lot of money, too, on computer games, and they stayed up half the night playing them. She'd heard that college was supposed to be fun, and she could see why.

But, Jessica's spending was getting out of control. Over time there were gas for trips to see her boyfriend, Collin, groceries she kept in her room since she didn't like the residence hall

food, cell phone bills—you name it. She and her parents had never talked about budgeting and spending money before she'd left home. Her family wasn't independently wealthy, but they were comfortable. They'd opened a bank account for her, put a fairly generous amount in it, and told her to ration it out for the term.

But when her first credit card statement arrived, she was flabbergasted. This one bill alone would wipe her out! *Should I ask my parents for more?* she thought. *Or should I just make the minimum payment for now and plan to cut down on my spending?* Her parents had advised her not to get a job in college. "Just concentrate on your studies, Jessica," they'd said.

Also, she'd received a worrisome instant message that morning from Collin which hinted that he'd met somebody at his school he wanted to get to know better. They'd had an agreement to keep their long-distance relationship going while they were in college, but now it seemed that he was going back on his word. She hadn't met anyone at college who came close to Collin in looks or personality. The thought that they might not be together was devastating.

Besides the worry about her finances and Collin, Jessica found out she'd earned a C- on her first history test. Everything had gotten off to such a good start, but now it all seemed beyond her control. Depressed and anxious for the first time since she'd left home, Jessica skipped not only breakfast, but lunch and dinner, too. At least eating was one thing she *could* control. She didn't know where to turn. Maybe college would be more overwhelming than she'd first thought. Maybe her worst fears would come true after all. Maybe she couldn't fool everyone into thinking she was the totally together person she wasn't sure she really was.

WHAT DO YOU THINK?

Now that you've read about Jessica Taylor, answer the following questions. You may not know all the answers yet, but you'll find out what you know and what you stand to gain by reading this chapter.

1. What potential problems could affect Jessica's success in college? List all the problems you can identify and their possible impact.

2. What, in particular, is Jessica doing wrong with her finances?

3. Identify three money management techniques that Jessica should begin to use immediately.

4. What specific campus resources that might help Jessica are available at your school?

Resources for College Success

CHALLENGE ⟳ REACTION

Challenge: What types of campus resources can help college students become academically successful?

Reaction: _____

Do you know this student? After his first year of college, James got a summer job in the brutally hot warehouse for the new superstore in his town. He moved huge boxes of paper towels, giant bags of dog food, and everything else you could think of across the floor. Actually, he discovered it felt good to take home a fairly substantial paycheck. He didn't mind the hard work, and it wasn't long until the bonuses gave him more earning power than his parents. Secretly, he enjoyed his job more than he'd enjoyed college, and he didn't want the summer to end. So instead of quitting his job, he quit college. James joined one of the fastest growing groups in America, along with one in three other Americans in their mid-twenties today. He became a college dropout. Ten years and three kids later, he still hopes to return, but it just never seems to work out. It's the only decision he's made in his life that he regrets.[1]

Could James have been successful in college? Most likely he could have been, but he didn't take to college right away, for whatever reasons, so he went for short-term *gains* over long-term *goals*. If he's ever laid off and seeking new employment, he may find himself unable to get hired into a job he really wants.

If you run into roadblocks, remember that many different support systems are in place for you in college. You just need to know what they are and take advantage of them. If you need financial help, there's an Office of Financial Aid or an Office of Campus Employment—perhaps known by another title, but a unit performing the same functions. If you need technology assistance, visit the Campus Technology Helpdesk online, call their hotline, or just walk in and ask your question. And the Campus Counseling Center is there to help with adjustment issues, self-esteem problems, eating disorders, or whatever you need. Most campuses today go to great lengths to help you succeed because they don't want you to become another "James." They want you to stay in college and succeed.

Unfortunately, many first-year students allow their coursework to slip a bit, miss a class here or there, get behind on assignments, and gradually begin to slack off. Once that happens, they never catch up. They never have time to use the campus learning center or writing center or counseling center, when all those helping hands are there for the taking. Is the answer to quit college as James did? If *you* ran into difficulties and dropped out as he did, is that something you'd eventually regret, too?

Hot Ideas/IndexOpen

"Fame is a vapor, popularity is an accident, money takes wings, those who cheer you today may curse you tomorrow. The only thing that endures is character."

Horace Greeley, American newspaper editor and politician (1811–1872)

This chapter will explore three types of resources—finances, technology, and campus support—in some detail so that you can make smart decisions during your time in college.

INSIGHT ⊖ ACTION

1. Are there any potential reasons why you'd consider dropping out of college?

2. Why would these factors influence you? Do you expect them to? What hangs in the balance?

Exercise 3.1 *Picture* Success!

As a group of two to four students, purchase a disposable camera. (Or your instructor may provide you with a digital camera, checked out from your campus media center.) Go on a scouting expedition and take pictures of all the things you'll need in order to be successful in college. Your pictures may be of campus support centers, people, other students—whatever you find that will contribute directly to your academic success. Bring your pictures to class and present them to your classmates, explaining the reasons why you chose to include each picture. If your pictures are digital, put them into a PowerPoint presentation to show your classmates.

Financial Resources: Managing Your Money

CHALLENGE ⊖ REACTION

Challenge: How good are you at managing your finances?

Reaction: Fill out this ten-question survey to get an indication of how financially savvy you are.

	Always true of me	Sometimes true of me	Never true of me
1. At any given moment in time, I know the balance in my checkbook.			
2. I use my credit card for particular types of purchases only, such as gas or food.			
3. I pay off my credit card bills in full every month.			
4. I know the interest rate on my credit card.			
5. I resist impulse buying and only spend when I need things.			
6. I have a budget and I follow it.			
7. I put money aside to save each month.			
8. When I get a pay raise, I increase the proportion of money I save.			
9. I keep track of my spending on a daily or weekly basis.			
10. I don't allow myself to get pressured by others into buying things I don't really need.			

Look over your responses. If you have more checks in the "Never true of me" column than you do in either of the two others, you may be able to put the information you're about to read in this chapter to good use!

Let's face it: money is important. Even though they say money can't buy happiness, plenty of folks would like to test the hypothesis! In one recent national study, nearly three-quarters of first-year students said they think it's essential or very important to be "very well-off financially," and in another study, 80 percent of 18- to 25-year-olds in America cited getting rich as a top goal for this generation of students.[2] How do you feel about that? Studies show that working too many hours for pay increases your chances of dropping out of college.[3] Many students find themselves working more to pay off major credit card debt, which takes time away from their studies, or taking a semester off from college to work to pay off their credit cards and never coming back: "Finances are the most common reason college students give for dropping out."[4] While there's evidence that working a moderate amount can help you polish your time and energy management skills, the real secret to financial success in college can be reduced to one word: *budget*.

The Ins and Outs of Money Management

Early in your first term, if not before, build a realistic, working budget. Okay, creating a budget may sound like drudgery, but it is important. According to one study, only 44 percent of college students clearly understood the term *budget*.[5] Many students never bother to create a budget—and plenty of those who do don't actually use it![6]

A budget is simply an itemized estimate of income and expenses that helps you develop a personal spending plan. When you break down your *money in* versus *money out*, you see reality in black and white, and you may be surprised by comparing the two totals. You may also realize that you need to put the skids on your unplanned spending. Complete Exercise 3.2 to help you develop a budget of your own.

Exercise 3.2 Your Monthly Budget

Part A: Monthly Income

Loans, grants, scholarships	$_____
Support from parents, other family members, spouse, etc.	$_____
Paycheck	$_____
Cash on hand	$_____
Other	$_____
Total	**$_____**

How much income do you expect to make per month? Make sure you figure in everything.

Next, begin recording your monthly expenditures. Start with fixed costs that remain the same from month to month, such as rent or a car payment. Do you pay tuition in installments, or is all your tuition due by a certain date? It may help to collect actual receipts or credit card bills and have them in front of you as you work. Once you begin recording, you may be surprised to find out exactly where your money goes.

Part B: Monthly Expenses

Tuition	$_____
Room or rent/mortgage	$_____
Board or food (groceries)	$_____
Books, supplies for school	$_____
Transportation, car payment, etc.	$_____
Computer/electronics (printer cartridges, Internet, etc.)	$_____
Travel (trips home, vacations, etc.)	$_____
Entertainment (movies, music CDs, DVDs, eating out)	$_____
Utilities (phone, electricity, heat, water, garbage removal, etc.)	$_____
Personal items (haircut/color, cosmetics, gym membership, etc.)	$_____
Credit card payments	$_____
Cash withdrawals	$_____
Other (child care, vet visits, etc.)	$_____
Total	**$_____**
Money IN from Part A	**$_____**
(Minus) Money OUT from Part B	**$_____**
Amount remaining to save or invest	**$_____**

Look over your expenses. Obviously, if your expenditure total is larger than your income, it's time to reevaluate and come up with a budget you can actually live with. Your school may offer a "managing your money" workshop through its learning center. Check out library materials or explore credible websites on this subject to learn all you can. After you get a handle on your current financial situation, it's even a good idea to start to save and invest whatever you can afford on a monthly basis.

Exercise 3.3 Create a Spending Log

How much money do you spend on an average day? Take a look at this student's spending log, then complete one for yourself. Choose one entire day that is representative of your spending, and use this chart to keep track of how you spend money. Write down everything from seemingly small, insignificant items to major purchases, and explain why you made that purchase. Your log may look something like this student's:

TIME	ITEM	LOCATION	AMOUNT	REASON
8 a.m.–9 a.m.	coffee and bagel	campus coffee cart	$ 3.50	overslept!
9 a.m.–10 a.m.	typing paper	bookstore	$ 2.50	history paper due
10 a.m.–11 a.m.	gas fill-up	convenience store	$35.00	running on fumes!
11 a.m.–12 p.m.	burger and fries	fast-food restaurant	$ 6.00	lunch on the run
12 p.m.–1 p.m.	toiletries, etc.	drugstore	$18.00	ran out
1 p.m.–2 p.m.	bottled water	bookstore	$ 2.50	forgot to bring
2 p.m.–3 p.m.	notebook, supplies	bookstore	$12.00	book bag stolen
3 p.m.–4 p.m.	STUDY TIME			
4 p.m.–5 p.m.	STUDY TIME			

(continued)

5 p.m.–6 p.m.	pizza	nearby pizza place	$12.50	met friends
6 p.m.–7 p.m.	soft drink	bookstore	$ 1.50	bring to library
7 p.m.–8 p.m.	candy bar	vending machine	$ 1.50	munchies!
8 p.m.–9 p.m.	laundry	campus laundromat	$ 5.00	out of clean clothes
9 p.m.–10 p.m.		STUDY TIME		
10 p.m.–11 p.m.		STUDY TIME		
11 p.m.–12 a.m.		weekend movie, online tickets, DVDs, CDs	$129.00	friends' recommendations
		cell phone upgrade	$20.00	need plan w/ more minutes

This student has spent $249 today without doing anything special! When you analyze his expenditures, you can find patterns. He seems to (1) spend money at the campus bookstore throughout the day, (2) spend relatively large amounts of money online, (3) be particularly vulnerable late at night, and (4) spend money grabbing food on the run. These are patterns he should be aware of if he wants to control his spending. He could pack food from home to save a significant amount of money, for example. Now create your own chart.

TIME	ITEM	LOCATION	AMOUNT	REASON
8 a.m.–9 a.m.				
9 a.m.–10 a.m.				
10 a.m.–11 a.m.				
11 a.m.–12 p.m.				
12 p.m.–1 p.m.				
1 p.m.–2 p.m.				
2 p.m.–3 p.m.				
3 p.m.–4 p.m.				
4 p.m.–5 p.m.				
5 p.m.–6 p.m.				
6 p.m.–7 p.m.				
7 p.m.–8 p.m.				
8 p.m.–9 p.m.				
9 p.m.–10 p.m.				
10 p.m.–11 p.m.				

The Perils of Plastic

CHALLENGE ➔ REACTION

Challenge: What are the pros and cons of using credit cards over cash?

Reaction: _____

College tuition is expensive, and so are housing, transportation, computers, cell phones, books, and food. College costs are spiraling upward, but not just because of tuition increases. Graduates often place the blame for their financial woes on the almighty credit card they signed up for that very first day of college. They stopped at a booth on campus, snapped up the credit card offer with zero percent interest (for the first month only, it turns out), and got a free T-shirt (that ended up costing a lot because of a hefty annual fee).

College students are offered an average of eight credit cards during the first week of school, and the average college student still carries four credit cards and has an average outstanding balance of $2,169.[7]

In fact, some students collect credit cards like your Grandmother collects pictures of you—and max them all out! Two-thirds of undergraduates make the minimum payment each month, and 11 percent say they can't even do that.[8] Everything bought on long-term credit costs more than it would if you paid cash. Eventually, monthly finance charges on credit cards can mount higher than the expenditures themselves. In one study, university administrators stated that they lose more students to credit card debt than to academic failure.[9] Here are two interesting financial facts about plastic you may not know:

"As a child, a library card takes you to exotic, faraway places. When you're grown up, a credit card does it."

Sam Ewing, professional writer

> Graduating with an out-of-control credit card balance can make your life difficult for years to come. Typically, a bad credit rating sticks with you for seven years. It may be difficult to get a loan or finance a big purchase until that time is over. If you're able to secure a loan, interest rates may be higher because of the black marks on your record. After you complete your college degree, you may want to get married, buy a car, or invest in a house. Look at these potentially shocking figures:

The average cost of a wedding = $27,690[10]
The average price of a new car = $28,000[11]
The average price of a new house = $264,540[12]

Your ability to get a job or go to graduate school may be hurt by a bad credit rating. Employers, even medical schools, often run routine credit checks on applicants. Although the future may seem a long way off now, it's important to evaluate your short-term spending habits in terms of your long-term goals.

> Graduating with a good credit rating helps. Despite all the warnings you're reading in this chapter, you don't have to avoid paying by credit altogether. Establishing a good credit rating while you're in college can benefit you enormously if you play your cards right. Eventually, if you build up your good credit by spending responsibly and paying your bills on time and in full, if possible, you'll be the beneficiary of your own financial wisdom when you do want to invest in a big-ticket item later.

Box 3.1 Financial Aid: Top-Ten FAQs

Most students need financial help of some kind to earn a college degree. Here is some information to help you navigate your way financially.[13]

1. **Who qualifies for financial aid?** You may not think you qualify for financial aid, but it's a good idea to apply anyway. You won't know until you try, and some types of aid are based on criteria other than need.

2. **What does FAFSA stand for? And where do I get a copy?** FAFSA stands for Free Application for Federal Student Aid, and you can get a copy from your campus Financial Aid office, or public library, by calling 1-800-4-FED-AID, or by going to www.fafsa.ed.gov and fill out the FAFSA online.

3. **What types of financial aid exist?** You can receive financial aid in the form of scholarships, fellowships, loans, grants, or work-study awards. Generally, scholarships and fellowships are for students with special academic, artistic, or athletic abilities; students with interests in specialized fields; students from particular parts of the country; or students from underrepresented populations. Typically, you don't repay them. Loans and grants come in a variety of forms and from several possible sources, either government or private. Typically, loans must be repaid. In addition, if you qualify for a need-based work-study job on or off campus, you can earn an hourly wage to help pay for school.

4. **When should I apply?** You can apply for financial aid any time after January 1 of the year you intend to go to college (because tax information from the previous year is required), but you must be accepted and enrolled to receive funds.

5. **Do I have to reapply every year?** Yes. Your financial situation can change over time. Your brothers or sisters may start college while you're in school, for example, which can change your family's status.

6. **How can I keep my financial aid over my college years?** Assuming your financial situation remains fairly similar from year to year, you must demonstrate that you're making progress toward a degree in terms of credits and a minimum GPA.

7. **Who's responsible for paying back my loans?** You are. Others can help you, but ultimately the responsibility is yours and yours alone. If your parents forget to make a payment or don't pay a bill on time, you will be held responsible.

8. **If I leave school for a time, do I have to start repaying my loans right away?** Most loans have a grace period of six or nine months before you must begin repayment. You can request an extension if you "stop out," but you must do so before the grace period ends.

9. **If I get an outside scholarship, should I report it to the Financial Aid office on campus?** Yes. They'll adjust your financial aid package accordingly, but those are the rules.

10. **Where can I find out more?** Your best source of information is in the Office of Financial Aid right on your own campus. Or call the Federal Student Aid Information Center at 1-800-433-3243 and ask for a free copy of *The Student Guide: Financial Aid* from the U.S. Department of Education.

INSIGHT → ACTION

1. Look back at your spending log and identify your particular weaknesses. What are they? Why do you find buying these things so compelling?

2. What actions can you take to prevent people and circumstances from adversely affecting your spending habits? Describe specific steps you plan to take.

Getting "Fiscally Fit": Suggestions to Curb Your Credit Card Spending

Here are some financial recommendations worth serious consideration. While some of them may seem obvious, *knowing about* and *doing* are two different things.

1. Leave home without it. Don't routinely take your credit card with you. Use cash and save your credit card for true emergencies. Do you really want to risk paying interest on today's ice cream cone years from now? Use your credit card for essential items only, like gas or groceries.

2. **Don't spend money you don't have.** Only charge what you can pay for each month. Remember that procrastination doesn't just apply to time; it applies to money, too. A spring break trip that costs $1,000 will take 12 years of minimal payments to pay off at an 18 percent interest rate. And that $1,000 trip will eventually cost you $2,115! You may assume that you'll pay off all your credit card bills when you graduate and get a good job. But it's hard to get ahead when a quarter or more of your take-home salary is hijacked off the top to pay off your debt.

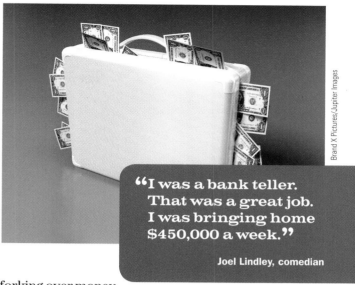

> **"I was a bank teller. That was a great job. I was bringing home $450,000 a week."**
>
> **Joel Lindley, comedian**

3. **Distinguish between *needs* and *wants*.** You may think you need particular items in order to be socially accepted (spending money just like everyone else), optimally satisfied (buying alternative food because campus food isn't to your liking), or physically attractive (forking over money for pricey manicures). Here's a rule of thumb: If charging something simply helps you move from "acceptable" to "amazing," it's not an emergency. Do you really need a mocha latté every day? A regular old cup of coffee a day sets you back $500 a year!

4. **Understand how credit works.** It's important to know the basics. In one study, 71 percent of college students had no idea how much interest they were paying on their credit card bills.[14] Here are some terms you need to know:

   > **Credit reports.** Your financial history is maintained by one of several credit-reporting agencies: Equifax, Experian, and TransUnion. Banks and stores submit your "grades" that together create your financial transcript. Your financial grades are based on factors like these: (1) how many credit cards you owe money on, (2) how much money you owe, and (3) how many late payments you make. Bad grades on your credit report can make your life difficult later.

   > **Fees.** Credit card companies charge you in three ways: annual fees (a fee you must pay every year to use the card), finance charges (a charge for "loaning" you the money you can't pay back when your bill is due), and late fees (for missing a monthly payment deadline). The fine print is worth reading. Student credit card interest rates and late fees can be substantially higher than those for working adults. Look closely at how long the grace period is, what late fees you'll be charged, and how much it'll cost you if you go over your charging limit.

   > **The fine print.** How can you learn more? Read your credit card contract carefully. For example, with some cards, you start paying interest the moment you charge something.

5. **Use a debit card instead of a credit card.** A debit card will help you track of your spending. You must first establish a checking account at a bank, and then each time you use your debit card for a purchase, the amount you spend will be instantly deducted. Instead of waiting for your credit card statement to arrive to find out your financial state of affairs, you can keep track continually.

© Tom & Dee Ann McCarthy/CORBIS

"I've got all the money I'll ever need, if I die by four o'clock."

Henny Youngman, comedian

6. **Don't use your college grants or loans to pay off your credit card.** This is truly a losing proposition that can cause you to sink deeper and deeper into debt. Normal daily consumer expenditures like groceries, meals out, and gas are viewed as bad debt if they get out of control. College tuition and mortgages—things that improve you in the long run, on the other hand, are considered good debt as long as you don't default on them. Defaulting on (or not paying back) a college loan has serious consequences. The Internal Revenue Service can withhold your U.S. personal income tax refund and apply it to the amount you owe, or your employer may be asked to deduct payments from your paycheck. If you return to school, you won't be entitled to additional federal student aid.[15] Typically, depending on the type of loan you have, if you're attending school at least half time, you have six to nine months after you graduate, leave school, or drop below half-time status before you must begin repaying your loan. Check with your funding agency or campus loan office for information that applies directly to you.[16]

7. **If you're already in credit card trouble, ask for help.** Talk to your parents, an older brother or sister, an adult you trust, or someone who can help you figure out what to do. Formulate a realistic plan to reduce your debt. Better yet, don't get yourself in financial trouble in the first place.

INSIGHT ⟶ ACTION

1. Describe a situation in which you spent more than you realized. What was it about the situation that may have contributed to your willingness to do that?

2. Of the suggestions to become more "fiscally fit" described in this section, which ones, specifically, will you act on? How will you accomplish your goals?

Technology Resources: E-Learning versus C-Learning

CHALLENGE ⟶ REACTION

Challenge: List five potential disadvantages to e-learning and five potential solutions to deal with them.

Reaction: _____   _____
_____   _____
_____   _____
_____   _____
_____   _____

What do an American soldier in Afghanistan, a single mother of twin toddlers in California, and a victim of cerebral palsy in New York have in common? All three are taking the same online course in psychology. Instead of c-learning (traditionally, in the classroom), they're engaging in *distance education* or e-learning (electronically, online).

What are the differences between e-learning and c-learning? E-learning is sometimes defined as structured learning that takes place without a teacher at the front of the room. If you're an independent, self-motivated learner, e-learning can be a great way to learn because you are in control.

> You control *when* you learn. Instead of that dreaded 8:00 a.m. class—the only section that's open when you register—you can schedule your e-learning when it's convenient for you.

> You control *how* you learn. If you are an introvert, e-learning may work well for you. You can work thoughtfully online and take all the time you need to reflect. If you are outgoing, however, you may become frustrated by the lack of warm bodies around. Jumping into threaded discussions and chatting online may satisfy some of those needs. If you're a kinesthetic learner, the keyboard action may suit you well.

> You control how fast you learn. You know for a fact that students learn at different rates. With e-learning, you don't have to feel you're slowing down the class if you continue a line of questioning or worry about getting left in the dust if everyone else is way ahead of you.

E-learning can be a very effective way to learn, but it does require some adjustments. Here are some suggestions for making the best of your e-learning opportunities.

1. Work to obtain course material. Instead of listening to your professor lecture at the front of the room, you will have to obtain information by downloading files or by reading lecture notes yourself.

2. Communicate your needs to your professor. Your professor won't be able to see your quizzical looks when you don't understand something. Instead of wishing she'd somehow notice or hoping for the best, you'll need to take direct action by e-mailing her, for example.

3. Stay in touch with other students in the course. Use e-mail to communicate with your cyber-classmates to build an online learning community. They may be able to clarify an assignment or coach you through a tough spot.

4. Take notes. When you're sitting through a lecture, you handwrite notes to review later. If you're reading lecture notes online, open a word processing application and toggle back and forth for note-taking purposes.

5. Keep your antivirus program up to date. When you upload assignment files, you run the risk of infecting your professor's computer with whatever viruses your computer may have. Make sure your antivirus software is up to date to keep that embarrassing accident from happening.

> **"The illiterate of the 21st century will not be those who cannot read and write, but those who cannot learn, unlearn, and relearn."**
>
> **Alvin Toffler, American writer and futurist**

6. **Create a positive learning environment.** Since you'll most likely to do your e-learning in your own personal space, make sure the environment is conducive to learning. If your computer is next to the TV, it may take super-human self-control to stay focused on your e-course. Do your work in a computer lab, or if you have a laptop, find a spot that's calm, well lit, and quiet.

7. **Use each login session as an opportunity to review.** It's natural—and preferable—to begin each online session by reviewing what you did or how much progress you made last time.

8. **Call on your time management skills.** If your e-course is self-paced, you'll need to plan ahead, schedule due dates, and above all, discipline yourself to make continual progress. If you're sharing a computer with other family members, you'll need to negotiate a master schedule. Remember that you may need to be online at particular times to engage in class chats or discussions.[17]

College Students and the Net: The Good, the Bad, and the Ugly

CHALLENGE ➔ REACTION

Challenge: What do you see as the best and worst aspects of using the Internet to help you learn in college?

Reaction: _____

The Good. College students are the leading consumers of digital technology in the United States.[18] In one study, 79 percent of college students reported that the Internet has had a positive impact on their college academic experience.[19] For many of us, the Internet is how we get our news, our research, our entertainment, and our communication. When it comes to all the potential benefits of the Internet, think about advantages like these:

FOCUS ON CAREERS: John M. Hearn, Jr., IT Systems Analyst

Courtesy of John M. Hearn Jr.

Q1: What do you do on a day-to-day basis in your job? What are your greatest challenges?
My department at Sanofi-Aventis Pharmaceuticals is responsible for engineering and maintaining the Common Desktop Solution for approximately 80,000 users. We analyze new technologies and evaluate whether and how they can benefit from that solution. But we are a pharmaceutical company, not a computer company, so we are supporting our employees as they do *their* jobs, primarily. On a day-to-day basis, my greatest challenges are not technical. Instead, they involve managing time and ideas and working with others as a team member.

Q2: Why did you decide on a high-tech career?
I have always been drawn to technology, and it has always come fairly easily to me. Problem solving and logic have always been strengths for me,

and although I would have loved to have been a rock-star, I decided to go with a career for which success was more certain. If you decide on a career that's likely to lead to success, instead of one that may be a constant struggle, it's bound to provide you with more happiness.

Q3: Is the job you have now your dream job?
I'm a fairly recent college graduate, so the honest answer to that question is no. Very few people land their dream jobs right out of college. By the time I graduated, the economic picture had changed somewhat. But fortunately, I could rely on connections I had made during an internship in college to find a job. Employers are always interested in experience in addition to classes and grades. Internships help you gain experience that's hard to get on your own. My advice is: Never lose sight of your dream job, but always remember that you have to "grow" into it.

> **Currency.** While some of the information posted on the Internet is not particularly up to date, it is possible to access real-time information sources online. This is especially important when timing is everything—during a crisis or a national emergency, for example. Reports, articles, and studies that might take months to publish in conventional ways are available on the web as soon as they're written.

> **Availability.** The Internet never sleeps. If you can't sleep at 2:00 a.m., the Internet can keep you company. It can be a good friend to have. Unlike your real instructor who teaches other classes besides yours and attends marathon meetings, Professor Google is always in.

> **Scope.** You can find out virtually anything you want to know on the Internet. You can get the recipe for multiple versions of the world's best chocolate chip cookie, find legal assistance if someone sideswipes your new set of wheels, and get medical advice on everything from Athlete's Foot to Zits. (Of course, real human beings are usually a better option for serious questions.)

> **Interactivity.** Unlike other media, the Internet lets you talk back—at least more quickly. You can write a letter to the editor of a newspaper and wait for a reply. The Internet lets you communicate instantaneously and incessantly.

> **Affordability.** As of January 2007, there were 11,093,529,692 Internet users worldwide; 210 million Americans are on the Net today.[20] After your initial investment in a computer, and your monthly access fee, you get a great deal for your money.

Q4: Beyond a college degree in a technical field, what other personal or personality characteristics are required for success?

To thrive in this highly competitive job market, it's important to be *proactive*, rather than *reactive*. Don't *wait* for things to happen—*make* them happen! Here's an example of what I mean. Many students continue on to college because they believe it's natural, or necessary, or because someone else wants them to. They *react* to what's expected. But when they finish college, there is no natural next step. They must create their own next step. If you decide to enter the world of IT, develop your own career path. Be *proactive*. But make sure that your path is flexible enough to adapt to the volatile world of technology.

C CREATE a Career Outlook

COMPUTER SCIENTIST

Have you ever considered a high-tech career as a computer professional?

Facts to Consider[21]

Academic preparation required: a wide range, from an associate's to a doctoral degree; however, a bachelor's degree is required for most jobs

Future workforce demand: Rapid growth is expected, with over 450,000 new jobs projected between 2004 and 2014. The rapidly growing and changing world of technology has generated a variety of career paths—computer scientists, database administrators, network systems analysts, computer programmers, technology trainers, software engineers, e-commerce specialists, and so forth.

Work environment: Most workers in this career field work in quiet, clean offices; however, increasingly, employees telecommute at least part of the time. Many work more than a standard forty-hour week.

Essential skills: technical, logical thinking, focusing, communication, analytical, problem-solving, and teamwork skills

Questions to Ponder

1. Do you have (or could you acquire) the skills this career requires?
2. Are you interested in a career like this? Why or why not?

For more career activities online, go to http://www.cengage.com/colsuccess/staleyconcise to do the Team Career exercises.

"**For a list of all the ways technology has failed to improve the quality of life, please press three.**"

Alice Kahn, technology author

The Bad. Too much of a good thing—anything—can be bad. When anything becomes that central to our lives, it carries risks. Here are some Internet dangers worth contemplating:

> Inaccuracy. Often we take information presented to us at face value. The usual checks and balances to verify information on the Internet aren't always in place. Of course, online scholarly journals subject their published studies to peer review, and they only publish valid research online, but on many sites, the responsibility for verifying information rests with you—the information consumer. "Bob's Statistics Home Page" and the U.S. Census Bureau's website aren't equally valid.

> Complacency. It's easy to allow the convenience of the Internet to turn intellectual *curiosity* into intellectual *complacency*. Why bother doing hours of library research on the topic for your paper when others have already been there, done that, and published it on the Internet? If today's new definition of knowledge really has shifted, as experts say, from "being able to remember and repeat information to being able to find and use it," why not *find* information on the Internet and *use* it?

The ultimate use, some students think, is downloading someone else's paper.[22] What's wrong with that? Besides the issue of plagarism, however, remember that the *how* of learning is as important as the *what*. If all you ever did was cut, paste, and download, you wouldn't learn how to do research yourself. You may never have to give your boss a five-page paper on the poetry of Wordsworth, but you may need to give her a five-page summary of your progress on the Jones Project. Work-related assignments require critical thinking, research, and writing. No one's researched that particular topic before. You'll have to do it yourself, and your job *now* is to make sure you develop the skills to do your job *in the future*.

> Reductionism. Being able to find the answer to almost everything in a matter of seconds can give us the false impression that what we find so readily is enough. Using the Internet as your sole source of information can lure you into surface, rather than deep, learning. When information is reduced to screen shots, soundbites, and video clips, it's easy to become a "reductionist," someone who shrinks things into quick bytes. Many questions don't have quick answers, and many problems don't have simple solutions.[23]

The Ugly. The Internet can be used in perverse ways. Take a look at one student's social networking page in Figure 3.1 and see if you can see where things are headed.

Like the hypothetical Victoria Tymmyns featured in Figure 3.1, some students publish inappropriate or confidential information on their Facebook and MySpace accounts with dangerous consequences. Victoria has posted her address, phone numbers, and moment-by-moment whereabouts, and you can see that she's now being stalked by a predator. It's also true that what some students post in a moment of frivolity can later cost them a job opportunity. (Employers regularly check these sources for insider information on applicants.) News

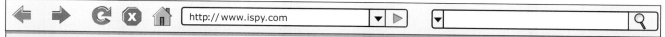

ISpy.com   RMSU

[View More Photos of Me](#)

Status   edit

Doin' shots at Annie Oakley's!

RMSU Friends

425   friends at RMSU   See All

Seymore Bonz   N.O. Body

Friends in Other Networks

Cal (12)
UF (40)
CMU (6)
KSCC (7)
RMSU (425)

Basic Info [edit]

Name:	Victoria Tymmyns
Looking For:	A Good Time
Residence:	Pine Valley 456
Birthday:	June 12, 1990

Contact Info [edit]

Email:	VicTym@rmsu.edu
AIM Screenname	VicTym
Mobile:	719.111.1112
Current Address:	123 Fake St. Great Bluffs, CO 80900

Personal Info [edit]

Activities:	Drinkin' at "Annie Oakley's" every Fri. night Karaoke at "All That Jazz" every Sat. night.
Favorite Music:	Black Flag, NIN, DK, the Clash
Favorite Movies	Shrek, Dracula

Work Info [edit]

Company:	Common Grounds on Corner Mountview
Schedule:	Work M – F 7AM –2PM

The Wall [edit]

 N.O. Body wrote: at 11:00am August 1, 2008
Saw u dancing at Annie Oakley's!! Whatta hottie! We should meet.

 N.O. Body wrote: at 1:00pm August 1, 2008
Aw come on! U know u want to meet me!

 N.O. Body wrote: at 3:02pm August 1, 2008
Still no response? What 's up? Do u wanna play or not?

 Seymore Bonz wrote: at 4:27pm August 1, 2008
R we still hookin up w/the gang at Annie Oakley's tonight?
Meet you guys at the front door at 10.

 N.O. Body wrote: at 5:20pm August 1, 2008
Sounds fun. Maybe I'ii see u there.

 Bay-Bee Face wrote: at 10:17pm August 2, 2008
Can you believe how we much we rocked last night? What was the deal with that guy
who kept staring at us? He gave me the creeps!! You switched shifts w/Mary right?
Working at 4?

 N.O. Body wrote: at 12:39pm August 2, 2008
Gee, BTW u were dressed, I just assumed u liked being stared at… U looked really
cute at work.

 N.O. Body wrote: at 2:21pm August 3, 2008
What's the matter sweetheart? U looked unhappy to see me at work today. Why
didn't u talk to me? BTW, nice house u got. Who knew you lived in such a nice neighborhood.

 N.O. Body wrote: at 12:57pm August 5, 2008
Nice dog u have. Ur parents must be outta town—no one's been home all night.

 N.O. Body wrote: at 7:26pm August 5, 2008
U never showed up for ur shift today. I waited all day for u. Saw your friends.
They said somebody poisoned your dog. That's a shame—such a yappy
little thing. I hate stuck-up women. Guess I'll just have to find u in person…

Figure 3.1

Fictional Ispy.com page

Companion, M. (2006). Victoria Tymmyns Ispy.com. Used with permission.

headlines sometimes report the dangers of Internet romances gone wrong. Researchers point out that almost half of U.S. children between ages 10 and 17 reported viewing pornography on the Internet over the past year; 80 percent say they stumbled on it accidentally by misspelling a word or while searching for unrelated content.[24] And some people are so addicted to the Net that they replace their uneventful real lives with seemingly exciting online ones.

What does all this have to do with you? Everything! It's important to remember that the Internet itself is neutral. It can be used constructively or destructively, based on the choices you make. It can be an exciting, invigorating, essential part of your college experience. Use it wisely!

Exercise 3.4 Technology Project: Group Ad

Working with two or three classmates and using PowerPoint, create a television ad (as professional-looking as possible) for the course for which you're using this book. Use text, images, and music. The advertisement shouldn't be long—two or three minutes, or the length of the song you use—but it should describe what the course is about and why other students should take it. Be as creative as you like! Once you've created your presentation, play your ad for the class. As an alternative, create a group ad for a campus resource—a campus support center, for example, or a student organization.

Library Resources

CHALLENGE → REACTION

Challenge: What does the term *information literacy* mean? By your definition, are you information literate?

Reaction: _____

 CULTIVATE Your Curiosity

CHOOSE TO CHOOSE!

Have you ever thought about how many dozens, if not hundreds, of choices you make each day? From the second you wake up, you're making decisions, even about the simplest things, like whether to order a cappuccino or a latté; decaf, half-caf, or high-octane; nonfat, two-percent, or the real deal.

Psychologist and professor Barry Schwartz, in his book, *The Paradox of Choice: Why More Is Less* (2004), believes that making non-stop choices can actually lead us to "invest time, energy, and no small amount of self-doubt, and dread." Choosing a new cell phone plan can take some people weeks while they research models of cell phones, minutes available, quotas of text messages, and Internet access, not to mention the fine print. Simply put: Being flooded with choices, while it feels luxurious, can be stressful and even unrewarding. Paralysis, anxiety, and stress rather than happiness, satisfaction, and perfection can be the result of too much "more."

Some of us, Schwartz says, are "maximizers"; we don't rest until we find the best. Others of us are "satisficers"; we're satisfied with what's good enough, based on our most important criteria. Of course, we all do some "maximizing" and some "satisficing," but generally, which are you?

Here are Schwartz's recommendations to lower our stress levels in a society where more can actually give us less, especially in terms of quality of life:

1. **Choose to choose**. Some decisions are worth lengthy deliberation; others aren't. Be conscious of the choices you make and whether they're worth the return on your investment. "Maximize" when it counts and "satisfice" when it doesn't.

2. **Remember that there's always greener grass somewhere**. Someone will always have a better job than you do, a nicer apartment, or a more attractive romantic partner. Regret or envy can eat away at you, and second-guessing can bring unsettling dissatisfaction.

3. **Regret less and appreciate more**. While green grass does abound, so do sandpits and bumpy roads. That's an important realization, too! Value the good things you already have going for you.

4. **Build bridges, not walls**. Think about the ways in which the dozens of choices you've already made as a new college student give you your own unique profile or "choice-print": where you live, which classes you take, clubs you join, meal plan you select, campus events you attend, your small circle of friends, and on and on. Remember that, and make conscious choices that will best help you succeed.[25]

You've heard it since you were a child: "The library is your friend." As a young child, it was exciting to go to the library, choose a book, check it out with your own library card, and bring it home to read. In college, the library is more than just a friend. It should become your best friend! Beyond Googling to find research for your assignments, learn your way around the actual, physical, non-cyber library on your campus. The library has many resources you won't find online, including real, honest-to-goodness librarians. Asking a reference librarian for help can save you hours of unproductive digging on your own.

One skill that is central to your college success is information literacy. Assume you are asked to write a five-page paper on *information literacy* for one of your classes. Where would you start? You know what literacy is, and you know what information is, but what is information literacy? Many experts would say it's *the* key to college success. If your reaction to this challenge was to go online, you're probably not alone. The first thing many students would do is Google the term. If you did that, you would get over fifty million hits. That's not much help—or rather it's too much help. What's next?

Let's say you scan the first ten hits, and you see the *Association of College and Research Libraries Institute for Information Literacy* site and the *National Forum for Information Literacy* home page, for example. You see that each of these pages lists links to dozens of other pages. You've begun your quest, and you're using your information literacy skills to research information literacy.

Information literacy is defined as knowing *when* you need information, *where* to find it, *what* it means, *whether* it's accurate, and *how* to use it. Information literacy includes six components, as seen in Figure 3.2. Think about them as a step-by-step process as you begin working on your next paper or presentation.[26]

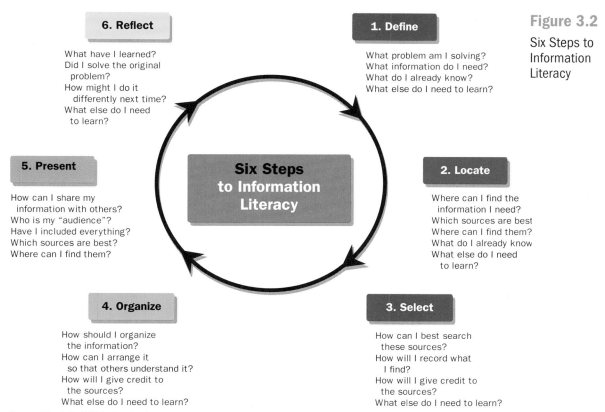

Figure 3.2

Six Steps to Information Literacy

6. Reflect
What have I learned?
Did I solve the original problem?
How might I do it differently next time?
What else do I need to learn?

1. Define
What problem am I solving?
What information do I need?
What do I already know?
What else do I need to learn?

5. Present
How can I share my information with others?
Who is my "audience"?
Have I included everything?
Which sources are best?
Where can I find them?

Six Steps to Information Literacy

2. Locate
Where can I find the information I need?
Which sources are best
Where can I find them?
What do I already know
What else do I need to learn?

4. Organize
How should I organize the information?
How can I arrange it so that others understand it?
How will I give credit to the sources?
What else do I need to learn?

3. Select
How can I best search these sources?
How will I record what I find?
How will I give credit to the sources?
What else do I need to learn?

Source: Wood, G. (2004, April 9). Academic original sin: Plagiarism, the Internet, and librarians. *The Journal of Academic Librarianship, 30*(3), 237–242.

CONTROL Your Learning

YOUR TOUGHEST CLASS

Identify a particular assignment in your most challenging class this term that will require you to use your information literacy skills. If your most challenging class does not include an assignment requiring you to use these particular skills, select another class in which a major project will challenge you to use them.

What is the specific assignment? For example, it could be "write a five-page paper in which you take a position on a controversial theme relating to our course topic." Now go through the six steps to information literacy as they relate to your assignment. What will you do to complete each step in order to do your best on your paper or presentation? Be as detailed as possible, answering the questions for each step.

1. DEFINE: _____
2. LOCATE: _____
    (a) Find three books on your topic, and list their titles, authors, publication dates, and publishers.
    (b) Find three articles from scholarly journals, and list their bibliographic information.
    (c) Work with one or more reference librarians, and list the librarian's name, and the day and time of your work session.
    (d) Find three relevant websites and list their URLs.
3. SELECT: _____
4. ORGANIZE: _____
5. PRESENT: _____
6. REFLECT: _____

Campus Resources: HELP Is Not a Four-Letter Word

CHALLENGE → REACTION

Challenge: List five campus resources you already know about that first-year students should take advantage of. Identify the building and room number for each one.

Reaction: 1. _____
2. _____
3. _____
4. _____
5. _____

No student is an island; no student stands alone. It's not uncommon for new college students to feel isolated from time to time, even at a small school. Everything about your college experience is new, and you're adjusting gradually. That's why getting connected to other students, your instructors, and the campus itself is essential to your success in college. In college, connections count.

Your college probably has an array of resources available to help you with almost anything that comes up. Perhaps you suffer from test anxiety, are terrorized by public speaking, freak out when your technology crashes, or wonder if you might have a learning disability. Whatever the problem, there's a place to go for help on campus. Even if your campus doesn't have the full array of support centers available on many huge campuses, student support professionals there can always direct you to services off campus.

Unfortunately, some students think that asking for help of any kind is a display of weakness or incompetence or somehow shameful. *I should be able to do this on my own!* they think, when actually, engaging in any new activity requires guidance. Here's an analogy: In 1979, Diana Nyad achieved the record for open-water swimming at 102.5 miles. But it took 51 other people to help her reach her goal (guides to check winds and currents, divers to look for sharks, and NASA nutrition experts to keep her from losing more than the 29 pounds she lost during that one swim).[27] Getting a college degree doesn't happen automatically or overnight. It takes a sustained academic investment, but you needn't go it alone. Your campus has all kinds of resources available for the taking. But you must take them. They won't come to you.

First-Year Students' FAQs

Take a look at some of the FAQs students often voice during their first term in college.

Social Connections

> *How can I meet other students?* Does your campus have a Student Center, Student Union, or University Center? Whatever it's called, it's where students tend to go between classes. Take advantage of favorite gathering spots on campus. To meet people, it helps to be where they are.

> *What student clubs and organizations are available?* If your campus has an active student government, it probably has an office somewhere on campus, most likely in the Student Center. The student newspaper and bulletin boards around campus are good sources of information about clubs, events, and activities. Some campuses have club booths set up at the beginning of the term so that it's easy to find the Young Democrats or Republicans, the Ski Club, or the chemistry honor society. Watch for an announcement about a Club Fair, or whatever your campus calls it.

> *What organizations are available to minority students?* If you're a member of an underrepresented population on campus, specific resources to connect you with other students may be available. Check with your Student Government Office to find out.

Academic Resources

> *How can I learn more about how I learn?* Check to see if your campus has a Learning Center, an office that helps with learning disabilities, or a place you can go to fill out a learning style instrument. Sometimes a modest fee is charged for diagnostic instruments, but the insights you gain may be well worth it. You can also find out for sure if you suspect

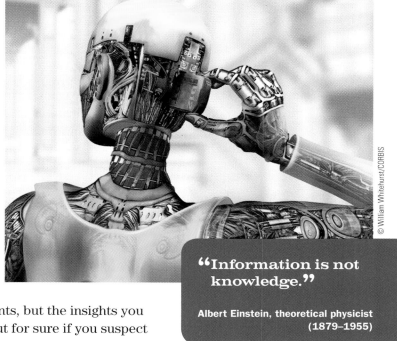

© William Whitehurst/CORBIS

"Information is not knowledge."

Albert Einstein, theoretical physicist (1879–1955)

you may have a learning disability. If you do, you can use the Learning Center to develop learning strategies to address your particular needs.

> *How can I become a better writer?* Your campus probably has a Writing Center to help you think through your writing assignments. Tutors there won't help you fix grammatical errors or proofread, but they will help you formulate a strong thesis statement. You'll be asked what you're trying to communicate and then be given help putting your thoughts into words.

> *How can I become a better speaker?* If the thought of standing up in front of multiple pairs of peering eyes leaves you in a cold sweat, you may be a good candidate for your campus's Oral Communication Center. If your campus has one of these, consider asking to be videotaped and critiqued while you do a dry run. If you want to become a better public speaker, there's nothing quite as motivating as watching your distracting habits, like swaying from side to side or jingling the change in your pocket. This kind of support can help you develop good speaking habits and build confidence.

> *What if I need help with a challenging course?* Many campuses have discipline-based support centers: a Science Learning Center or a Math Learning Center, for example. Or particular courses may offer what's called Supplemental Instruction, extra help beyond class sessions with basic principles or homework assignments. Work with the course's Teaching Assistant, or hire your own tutor. Check out whatever options are available to you, and use them, rather than struggle on your own if you're not getting results.

> *I'm not sure which classes to take next. Who can help me?* Academic advisors are the experts on campus who can help you decide on a major, choose classes, and locate many other resources. Use their expertise, rather than guessing or listening to another student who's not sure either.

> *I'm thinking of dropping a class. How do I do it?* The Office of the Registrar or Office of Admissions and Records is where to go. They also help with things like transferring credits and obtaining transcripts. Think about the ramifications of dropping a class thoroughly, however. Will doing so change your financial aid status, for example?

Adjustment

> *What if I need a counselor?* College is a time of accelerated personal development and wonderful discoveries. But it may also be a time when you face challenging issues, such as leaving the comfort zone of your family; breaking up or beginning a new romance; or dealing with feelings of anxiety, isolation, or depression. The Counseling Center on your campus can be a heartening resource to help you work through a variety of issues. And if you find yourself in the middle of a real crisis, call the campus hotline for immediate help.

"We are by nature observers and thereby learners. That is our permanent state."

Ralph Waldo Emerson,
American author (1803–1882)

> *Where can I attend church, join a religious group, or speak with a pastor, rabbi, or priest?* Check your local phonebook, look for postings in your Student Union, or ask other students. Some campuses even have a church or chapel of their own.

Finances

> *Where can I find information about financial aid?* Your campus Financial Aid Office can help with loans, scholarships, and grants to pay for college.

> *What if I run out of money?* If it's a real emergency—you lost the lease on an apartment, the residence halls are full, and you'll be living out of your car—help is available from the Red Cross or Salvation Army. If it's a matter of just blowing your budget, you can find advice, often free, from consumer credit agencies. Your campus may also offer free work-shops on managing your money through a Learning Center or Student Success Center.

Logistics

> *How can I find my way around?* Some universities are like small cities. Often you can download a campus map from the college's website that will help. Even though you will look like a tourist, carry it around to lower your stress level when you need to find something for the first time.

> *Who can help me decide where to live next year?* Is residence hall life a good thing? If you're attending a college far from home, having everything close by is convenient, and thankfully someone else will do the cooking! If you happen to live in the same town where you're going to school, it's an expensive option. But there is evidence that living on campus helps students feel connected. Other students may prefer living on their own or perhaps sharing an apartment off campus. Consider factors such as the importance of social connections, your financial situation, and your ability to focus, despite distractions. Besides your family (and your pock-etbook), your office of Residence Life or Student Housing can help with these decisions.

> *Can I work on campus?* Check with your Student Employment Office. Work-ing on campus is not only convenient, but it can also help you become a more successful student. Travel time to work is cut down and you learn things about how your campus works.

Technology

> *What if I have a technology meltdown?* The new version of the old "my dog ate my homework" story relates to numerous variations on a theme: technology crashing. Your campus may not have round-the-clock advice from techies, but the Computer Help Desk can often solve what sounds like a complicated problem with simple advice. Also, use the campus computer labs. You can make good use of short blocks of time—or long ones—between classes.

Health

> *Are health services available to students?* Many campuses have a Student Health Center where you can find a range of free or inexpensive services—everything from flu shots to strep throat tests to birth control advice if you're sexually active.

> *What if I need more exercise?* It's easy to find out if your campus has a recreation center, or whether there are gyms you can frequent nearby. Or join an intramural team, coach a children's soccer team, or devote a chunk of time to power walking each day.

Majors and Careers

> *What do I want to be when I grow up?* Thinking ahead to a career when you graduate from college is sometimes difficult when so much is going on at the moment. What do you like to do? What people skills do you have? Do you like to work with your hands or in your head? These questions may be difficult to answer if you haven't had experience in a real career field. But college is a great time to explore your options. Become an intern to try out a career or visit your campus's Career Center. Experts there can give you diagnostic tests to help you discover a major and career for which you are well-suited. They may be able to set you up with an internship off campus, put you in touch with alumni who work in a career field of interest to you, or help you apply for a competitive fellowship.

Et cetera

> *Is child care available?* Many campuses, particularly those with returning adult students, have inexpensive child care available. Being able to drop off a child in the morning right on campus and pick him up after your classes are over can be a real enabler.

> *Where can I buy my books?* Textbooks are a significant investment these days, and it's important to buy the right editions for your classes. Should you support your campus bookstore or order online? Buying books online may save you money, although you'll have to wait for shipment. The bookstore is a much quicker option, and it's a good idea to find out where it is, no matter where you buy your books. You'll most likely need it for other school supplies.

> *Where can I find community service opportunities?* Volunteerism is often a part of high school requirements or church-related activities, and you may wish to continue your community service in college. Check to see if your campus has a Service Learning or Community Center, or look for specific classes that offer service learning opportunities.

> *What if I'm in need of Campus Security?* If you feel unsafe walking to your car late at night or you need information about parking permits on campus, check with the Campus Security or Public Safety Office. They're there for your protection.

Get to know your campus and its full range of offerings—and take advantage of everything that's in place to help you be as academically successful as possible.

Finances, technology, and campus support—three resources that can help you or hinder you in college. Learning to master money management, use technology productively, and make time to reap the benefits of all the support systems your campus has to offer will help you not only as a first-year student, but throughout your time in college.

Exercise 3.5 VARK Activity

Complete the recommended activity for your preferred VARK learning modality. If you are multimodal, select more than one activity. Your instructor may ask you to (a) give an oral report on your results in class, (b) send your results to him or her via e-mail, (c) post them online, or (d) contribute to a class chat.

 Visual: To help you understand how your campus works, draw an organizational chart that identifies the top levels of the campus hierarchy. Who is at the top of the institution, and who runs the various units?

 Aural: Make use of campus resources by attending a public lecture. Give a three-minute presentation to your classmates summarizing what you heard.

 Read/Write: List the main points for each of the three sections in this chapter. After your three lists are complete, prioritize the points in each section as they related to you, and identify actions you need to take to help you be more successful in college.

 Kinesthetic: Go on a short field trip with a classmate to learn the locations of all the campus support centers that are available to you. As you walk, sketch out a rough map that you can show your classmates and instructor in class.

Ⓒ **CHALLENGE Yourself Quizzes** For more practice online, go to http://www.cengage.com/colsuccess/staleyconcise to take the Challenge Yourself online quizzes.

 NOW WHAT DO YOU THINK?

At the beginning of this chapter, Jessica Taylor, a frustrated student, faced a series of challenges as a new college student. Now after reading this chapter, would you respond differently to any of the questions you answered about the "FOCUS Challenge Case"?

REALITY CHECK

On a scale of 1 to 10, answer these questions now that you've completed this chapter.

1 = not very/not much/very little/low   10 = very/a lot/very much/high

In hindsight, how much did you *really* know about this subject matter before reading the chapter?

1   2   3   4   5   6   7   8   9   10

How much do you think this information might affect your college success?

1   2   3   4   5   6   7   8   9   10

How much do you think this information might affect your career success after college?

1   2   3   4   5   6   7   8   9   10

How long did it actually take you to complete this chapter (both the reading and writing tasks)? _____ Hour(s) _____ Minutes

Compare these answers to your answers from the "Readiness Check" at the beginning of this chapter. How might the gaps between what you thought before starting the chapter and what you now think affect how you approach the next chapter?

 To download mp3 format audio summaries of this chapter, go to http://www.cengage.com/colsuccess/staleyconcise.

4 Managing Your Time and Energy

YOU'RE ABOUT TO DISCOVER...

- Why time management alone doesn't work

- How time management differs from energy management

- How to calculate your study hours

- How to schedule your way to success

- How the P word can derail you

- How to realistically balance work, school, and personal life

READINESS CHECK

Before beginning this chapter, take a moment to answer these questions. Your answers will help you assess how ready you are to focus.

1 = not very/not much/very little/low   10 = very/a lot/very much/high

Based on reading the "You're about to discover..." list and skimming this chapter, how much do you think you probably already know about the subject matter?

1   2   3   4   5   6   7   8   9   10

How much do you think this information might affect your college success?

1   2   3   4   5   6   7   8   9   10

How much do you think this information might affect your career success after college?

1   2   3   4   5   6   7   8   9   10

In general, how motivated are you to learn the material in this chapter?

1   2   3   4   5   6   7   8   9   10

How ready are you to focus on this chapter—physically, intellectually, and emotionally? Circle a number for each aspect of your readiness to focus.

1   2   3   4   5   6   7   8   9   10

If any of your answers are below a 5, consider addressing the issue before reading. For example, if you're feeling scattered, take a few moments to settle down and focus.

Finally, how long do you think it will take you to complete this chapter? _____ Hour(s) _____ Minutes

Derek Johnson

As Derek Johnson walked out of his

World Civilizations class on Wednesday evening, he felt panicked. The professor had just assigned a twelve-page paper, due one month from today. *How could he?* Derek thought. *Doesn't he realize how busy most returning students are?* The syllabus had mentioned a paper, but twelve pages seemed downright excessive.

When Derek had decided to go back to college five years after he graduated from high school, he hadn't quite realized what a juggling act it would require. First, there was his family—his wife, Justine, his four-year-old daughter, Taura, and another baby due before winter break. Then there was his job, which was really quite demanding for an entry-level marketing position. He hoped that a degree in business would help him move into the management ranks, where the salaries were higher. Add to that singing in his church choir, coaching the youth soccer league, competing in cycling races, and working out every morning at the gym. Derek had been a high school athlete, and physical fitness was a priority for him.

His head began to swim as he thought about all his upcoming obligations: his mother's birthday next week, his dog's vet appointment, his brother who was coming to town for a visit, the training class he was required to attend for work. Something had to go, but he couldn't think of anything he was willing to sacrifice to make time for a twelve-page paper. Maybe he'd have to break down and buy one of those planners, but weren't most people who use those slightly, well … compulsive?

Still, the paper was to count as 25 percent of his final grade in the course. He decided he'd try and think of a topic for the paper on his way home. But then he remembered that his wife had asked him to stop at the store to pick up groceries. Somewhere on aisle 12, between the frozen pizza and the frozen yogurt, Derek's thoughts about his research paper vanished.

The following week, the professor asked the students in the class how their papers were coming along. Some students gave long soliloquies about their research progress, the wealth of sources they'd found, and the detailed outlines they'd put together. Derek didn't raise his hand.

A whole week has gone by, Derek thought on his way back to his car after class. *I have to get going!* Writing had never exactly

been Derek's strong suit. In fact, it was something he generally disliked doing. Through a great deal of hard work, he had managed to earn a 3.8 GPA in high school—a record he planned to continue. A course in World Civilizations—not even in his intended major—was *not* going to ruin things! The week had absolutely flown by, and there were plenty of good reasons why his paper was getting off to such a slow start.

It was true that Derek rarely wasted time, except for occasionally watching his favorite TV shows. But then again, with such a jam-packed schedule, he really felt the need to unwind once in a while. Regardless, he rarely missed his nightly study time from 11:00 p.m. to 1:00 a.m. Those two hours were reserved for homework, no matter what.

At the end of class two weeks later, Derek noticed that several students lined up to show the professor the first drafts of their papers. *That's it!* Derek thought to himself. *The paper is due next Wednesday. I'll spend Monday night, my only free night of the week, in the library. I can get there right after work and stay until 11:00 or so. That'll be five hours of concentrated time. I should be able to write it then.*

Despite his good intentions, Derek didn't arrive at the library until nearly 8:00 p.m., and his work session wasn't all that productive. As he sat in his library stall, he found himself obsessing about things that were bothering him at work. His boss was being difficult, and his team of coworkers couldn't come to an agreement on some important issues about their current project. Finally, when he glanced at his watch, he was shocked to see that it was already midnight! The library was closing, and he'd only written three pages. Where had the time gone?

On his way out to the car, his cell phone rang. It was Justine, wondering where he was. Taura was running a fever, and his boss had called about an emergency meeting at 7:00 a.m. *If one more thing goes wrong …* , Derek thought to himself. His twelve-page paper was due in two days.

WHAT DO YOU THINK?

Now that you've read about Derek Johnson, answer the following questions. You may not know all the answers yet, but you'll find out what you know and what you stand to gain by reading this chapter.

1. Describe Derek's time management strategies. Are they working? Is time management Derek's only problem?
2. How could calculating his study hours improve his productivity?
3. Describe the time-wasters that are a part of Derek's schedule. Do you think procrastination is an issue for Derek? What's behind his failure to make progress on his paper?
4. Identify three effective time management techniques Derek should begin to use.
5. Suggest three realistic ways for Derek to balance work, school, and personal life.
6. What aspects of Derek's situation can you relate to personally? What other time management issues are you experiencing in your life right now?

Time Management Isn't Enough

CHALLENGE → REACTION

Challenge: What is *time management* and how does it work?

Reaction: _____

_____

Before delving into the details of time management skills, let's clarify one important point. There's a sense in which the phrase *time management* is misleading. Let's say you decide to spend an hour reading an assigned short story for your literature class. You may sit in the library with your book propped open in front of you from 3:00 to 4:00 o'clock on the dot. But you may not digest a single word you're reading. You may be going through the motions, reading on autopilot. Have you managed your time? Technically, yes. Your planner says, "Library, short story for Lit 101, 3:00–4:00 p.m." But did you get results? Time management expert Jeffrey Mayer asks provocatively in the title of his book: *If You Haven't Got the Time to Do It Right, When Will You Find the Time to Do It Over?* (1991). Now that's a good question!

"Time management" is not just about managing your time, it's about managing your attention. Attention management is the ability to focus your attention, not just your time, toward a designated activity so that you produce a desired result. Time management may get you through reading a chapter of your textbook, but attention management will ensure that you understand what you're reading. It's about *focus*. If you manage your attention during that hour, then you've managed your time productively. Without attention management, time management is pointless.

Succeeding in school, at work, and in life is not just about what you do. It's about what gets done. You can argue about the effort you put into an academic endeavor all you want, but it's doubtful your professor will say, "You know what? You're right. You deserve an A just for staying up late last night working on this paper." Activity and accomplishment aren't the same thing. Neither are quantity and quality. Results count. So don't confuse being busy with being successful. Staying busy isn't much of a challenge; being successful is.

The activity versus accomplishment distinction holds true in today's workplace as well. In terms of pay, there's been a shift of emphasis from *position* to *performance*, and from *status* to *contribution*. You don't simply make more money because of your title or your prestige within the organization. You're rewarded for results. Demands in today's fast-paced workplace make time management more important than ever.[1]

Here's a list of preliminary academic time-saving tips. However, remember that these suggestions won't give you a surefire recipe for academic success. To manage your time, you must also manage yourself: your energy, your behavior, your attention, your attitudes, *you*. Once you know how to manage all that, managing your time begins to work.

> **"In truth, people can generally make time for what they choose to do; it is not really the time but the will that is lacking."**
>
> **Sir John Lubbock, British banker, politician, and archaeologist (1834–1913)**

> Have a plan for your study session; include time allotments for each topic or task.

> Keep track of what derails you. If you come to understand your patterns, you may be better able to control them.

> Turn off your phone or tell other people you live with that you don't want to be disturbed if a call comes in for you. Let them know what time they can tell callers to call you back.

> If you're working on your computer, work offline whenever possible. If you must be online to check sources frequently, don't give in to the temptation to check your social networking account or e-mail every ten minutes.

> Take two minutes to organize your workspace before beginning. Having the resources you need at your fingertips makes the session go much more smoothly, and you won't waste time searching for things you need.

> If you are in a study group, make sure everyone is clear about assigned tasks for the next session. Lack of clear communication about expectations is a big time-waster for study groups.

Digital Vision/Getty Images

"Don't confuse activity with accomplishment. 'Time = Success' is a myth."

Dr. Constance Staley, University of Colorado at Colorado Springs

> Learn to say no. Saying no to someone, especially someone you care about, can feel awkward at first, but people close to you will understand that you can't do everything.

> Focus. You can't do anything if you try to do everything. Multitasking may work for simple matters, such as scheduling a doctor's appointment while heating up a snack in the microwave. But when it comes to tasks that require brainpower, such as studying or writing, you need a single-minded focus.

> Slow down. As they say, "haste makes waste." Working at something a million miles a minute will most likely result in mistakes, superficial thinking, and poor decisions. Ironically, if you rush, you may run out of time and end up settling for less than your best.

> Don't make a habit of putting other people's priorities above your own. In other words, don't let their *lack* of planning affect your attempts to plan. At the same time, be prepared to shift your priorities as needed. Know the difference between legitimate interruptions and time-wasters, and act accordingly.

INSIGHT → ACTION

1. How would you evaluate your time management skills right now? Would you give yourself an A, B, C, or below? Why?

2. What actions must you take to become a more effective time-attention manager?

Energy, Our Most Precious Resource

CHALLENGE ⊖ REACTION

Challenge: What's the difference between *time* management and *energy* management?

Reaction: _____

_____

"We live in a digital time. Our rhythms are rushed, rapid-fire and relentless, our days carved up into bits and bytes. . . . We're wired up but we're melting down." So begins a bestselling book, *The Power of Full Engagement: Managing Energy, Not Time, Is the Key to High Performance and Personal Renewal* (2003). The authors, Jim Loehr and Tony Schwartz, have replaced the term *time management* with the term *energy management*. Their shift makes sense. Since most of us are operating in overdrive most of the time, energy is our most precious resource.

Energy management experts say you can't control time—everyone has a fixed amount—but you can manage your energy. And in fact, it's your responsibility to do so. Once a day is gone, it's gone. But your energy can be renewed.

It's clear that some things are energy *drains*, zapping your drive: bad news, illness, interpersonal conflict, bureaucratic hassles, a heavy meal, rainy days. Likewise, some things are energy *gains*, giving you a surge of fresh vitality: a new job, good friends, music, laughter, fruit, coffee. It's a good idea to recognize your own personal energy drains and gains so that you know how and when to replenish your supply.[2] Energy management experts say it's not just about *spending time*, it's about *expending energy*:

> physical energy

> emotional energy

> mental energy

> spiritual energy

Of the four dimensions of energy, let's take a closer look at the first two. To do your very best academically, it helps to be *physically* energized and *emotionally* connected. Physical energy is measured in terms of *quantity*. How much energy do you have—a lot or a little? Emotional energy, on the other hand, is measured by *quality*. What kind of energy do you have—positive or negative? If you put them together into a two-dimensional chart with *quantity* as the vertical axis and *quality* as the horizontal axis, you get something like Figure 4.1.

"Performance, health and happiness are grounded in the skillful management of energy."

Jim Loehr and Tony Schwartz, from *The Power of Full Engagement*

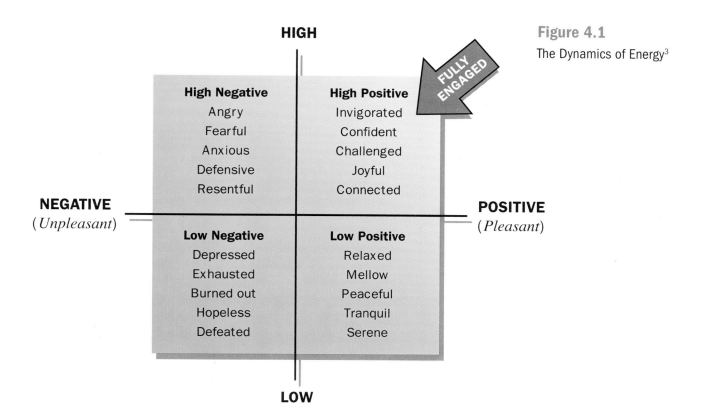

Figure 4.1
The Dynamics of Energy[3]

When you're operating in the upper right quadrant with high, positive energy, you're most productive, which makes sense. The question is: How do you get there? How do you make certain you're physically energized and emotionally connected so that you can do your best, academically?

Get Physically Energized

To make sure you're physically energized, try these suggestions.

1. **Go with the flow.** Have you noticed times of the day when it's easier to concentrate than others? Perhaps you regularly crash in the middle of the afternoon, for example. This is partly due to the patterns of electrical impulses in your brain, alpha rhythms that are unique to each individual. In other words, everyone has a biological clock. Paying attention to your body's natural rhythms is important. Plan to do activities that require you to be alert during your natural productivity peaks. That's better than plodding through a tough assignment when the energy just isn't there. Use low energy times to take care of mindless chores that require little to no brainpower.[4]

2. **Up and at 'em.** What about 8:00 a.m. classes? Don't use your body's natural rhythms as an excuse to sleep through class! ("I'm just not a morning person....") If you're truly not a morning person, don't sign up for early morning classes. Some freshmen get into the *social* habit of staying up late into the wee, small hours, and then they just can't get up in the morning. Sleeping through your obligations won't do much for your success—and you'll be playing a continual game of catch-up, which takes even more time.

3. **Sleep at night, study during the day.** Burning the midnight oil and pulling all-nighters aren't the best ideas, either. It only takes one all-nighter to help you realize that a lack of sleep translates into a plunge in performance. Without proper sleep, your ability to understand and remember course material is impaired. Research shows that the average adult requires seven to eight hours of sleep each night. If you can't get that much for whatever reason, take a short afternoon nap. Did you know that the Three Mile Island nuclear meltdown in Pennsylvania in 1979 and the Chernobyl disaster in the Ukraine in 1986 took place at 4 a.m. and 1:23 a.m., respectively? Experts believe it's no coincidence that both these events took place when workers would normally be sleeping.[5]

4. **"Prime the pump."** You've heard it before: Food is the fuel that makes us run. The better the fuel, the smoother we run. It's that simple. A solid diet of carbs—pizza, chips, and cookies—jammed into the fuel tank of your car would certainly gum up the works! When the demands on your energy are high, such as exam week, use premium fuel. If you don't believe it, take a look at how many of your classmates get sick during midterms and finals. Watch what they're eating and note how much sleep they're getting, and you'll get some clues about why they're hacking and coughing their way through exams—or in bed missing them altogether.

Get Emotionally Connected

Physical needs count, to be sure, but emotional connections are part of the picture, too. See if you agree with these suggestions.

1. **Communicate like it matters.** Sometimes we save our best communicating for people we think we have to impress: teachers, bosses, or clients, for example. But what about the people we care about most in our lives? Sometimes these people get the leftovers after all the "important" communicating has been done for the day. Sometimes we're so comfortable with these people that we think we can let it all hang out, even when doing so is *not* a pretty sight. Communicate as if everything you said would actually come true—"Just drop dead," for instance—and watch the difference! Communicating with people we care about is one of our primary vehicles for personal renewal.

2. **Choose how you renew.** Finish this analogy: junk food is to physical energy as _____ is to emotional energy. If you answered "TV," you're absolutely right. Most people use television as their primary form of emotional renewal, but, like junk food, it's not that nutritious and it's easy to consume too much. Try more engaging activities that affirm you: singing or reading or playing a sport.[6]

3. **Let others renew you.** Remember that people don't just make demands on your time, they can provide emotional renewal. There's pure joy in a child's laugh, a friend's smile, a father's pat on the back. These small pleasures in life are priceless—prize them!

We've focused on physical and emotional energy here, but remember that all four dimensions of energy—physical, emotional, mental, and spiritual—are interconnected. If you subtract one from the equation, you'll be firing on less than four cylinders. If you are fully engaged and living life to the fullest, all four dimensions of your energy equation will be in balance.

INSIGHT ➔ ACTION

1. How does your energy fluctuate throughout an average day? Describe your biological clock.

2. What actions can you take to regulate your physical and emotional energy for the sake of your own productivity?

"I'll Study in My Free Time" ... and When Is That?

CHALLENGE ➔ REACTION

Challenge: How do you spend your time?

Reaction: Complete this self-assessment, Where Did the Time Go?, to find out how you spend your time.

Fill in the number of hours you spend doing each of the following, then multiply your answer by the number given (7 or 5 to figure weekly amounts) where appropriate.

Number of hours per day

Sleeping: _____ × 7 = _____

Personal grooming (for example, showering, shaving, putting on makeup): _____ × 7 = _____

Eating (meals and snacks; include preparation or driving time): _____ × 7 = _____

Commuting during the week (to school and work): _____ × 5 = _____

Doing errands and chores: _____ × 7 = _____

Spending time with family (parents, children, or spouse): _____ × 7 = _____

Spending time with boyfriend or girlfriend _____ × 7 = _____

(continued)

Ask ten students when they study, and chances are at least eight will reply, "in my free time." The irony in this statement is that if you actually waited until you had free time to study, you probably never would. Truthfully, some students are amazed at how easily a day can race by without ever thinking about cracking a book. This is why you should actually *schedule* your study time, but to do that, you should first be aware of how you're currently spending those twenty-four hours of each day.

Notice that the "Challenge → Reaction" activity you just completed places studying at the bottom of the list, even though it's vital to your success in college. The exercise reflects a common attitude among college students, namely that studying is what takes place after everything else gets done. Where does schoolwork rank on *your* list of priorities?

If succeeding in college is a top priority for you, then make sure that you're devoting adequate time to schoolwork outside the classroom. Most instructors expect you to study two to three hours outside of class for every hour spent in class. If it's a particularly challenging class, you may need even more study

---

Box 4.1 Lame Excuses for Blowing Off Class

Do you find yourself skipping class at times in order to do something else: getting an oil change for your car, soaking up the sun's rays, or socializing with some friends you ran into on the way to class? If so, ask yourself this: Would you walk into a gas station, put a $20 bill down on the counter to prepay for a tank of gas, and then put in a dollar's worth and drive off? Absolutely not, you say?

Would you buy a $10 movie ticket and then just toss it in the trash because you decided there was something else you'd rather do on the spur of the moment? No way!

Why, then, would you purchase much more expensive "tickets" to class—the average cost of an hour in class is roughly upwards of $100—and then toss them in the trash by not attending? Don't you value your money more than that? More importantly, don't you value *yourself* more than that?

The next time you're tempted to opt out of your scheduled classes, ask yourself if you really want to throw away money, in addition to the opportunity. Check your priorities, then put one foot in front of the other and walk into that classroom. In the long run, it's the best investment in your own future.

time. You can use the following chart to calculate the total number of hours you ought to expect to study—effectively—each week:

Credit hours for less demanding classes: _____ × 2 hours = _____ hours

Credit hours for typical/average classes: _____ × 3 hours = _____ hours

Credit hours for more challenging classes: _____ × 4 hours = _____ hours

Expected total study time per week = _____ hours

Remember, just putting in the time won't guarantee that you'll truly *understand* what you're studying. You need to ensure that your study time is productive by focusing your attention and strategically selecting study techniques that work best for you.

C CULTIVATE Your Curiosity

ARE *YOU* CAUGHT IN THE NET?

It's noon. You decide to check your online life while you chow down a giant burrito. Three pokes and five new requests from potential friends. *Who are these people?* you wonder. You decide to start a new group called, the "Why do you want to be my friend when you don't even know me?" group. By 1:30 it has fifty-five members on campus. You ask yourself how you can get that interesting student who sits behind you in your biology class to poke you back. At 2:00, you decide on a whim to update your photo albums by uploading several shots from your weekend adventures. At 2:30 the response you've been waiting for finally pops up. The clock ticks away as you continue to poke around. You check your watch and are amazed to find that it's already 4:30. You realize that while you've made online contact with the object of your desire from your biology class, you've *missed* your real-life biology class. Four and a half hours have just vanished from your day.

Does this scenario sound uncomfortably familiar? A few stolen moments start a chain reaction that stretches out for several hours. You hate to admit it, but you're caught in the Net: a social networking epidemic that's sweeping the college scene everywhere.

Social networking has the potential to become a time-consuming addiction that can take over your life, "by far the biggest procrastination tool amongst college students" today.[7]

Are *you* addicted? Ask yourself these questions: Do you make a run for any idle computer on campus to log on between classes? Do you spend hours searching for people you've met whose names you can't remember? Do you inflate your friends list with people you don't know? Do you feel frustrated when you find out someone you'd really like to meet doesn't have an account yet? Do you spend more time with your online friends than your real friends? Do you check your account when you first wake up in the morning and right before you go to bed at night to see what's changed? If the answers to multiple questions in this paragraph are yes, are you ready to face the possibility of a social networking addiction?[8]

Don't get caught in the Net. Try these suggestions:

1. **Monitor your time online.** Estimate right now how much time you spend online per week. Then actually time yourself. Is your estimate accurate? Or are you way off base?

2. **Set limits.** Give yourself a hard-and-fast time limit, and stick to it.

3. **Shorten your social networking sessions.** Being online tends to distort time. You may think you've only been on for an hour when three hours have actually gone by. Set an old-fashioned timer, and when it goes off, get up and do something else.

4. **Separate work and play online.** It's easy to find yourself on a fun-seeking detour when you're supposed to be working on a research paper. When the two tasks are merged, it's easy to lose track of what's what. You end up wasting time because it feels as if you're doing something productive when you really aren't.

5. **Take a tech vacation.** Turn off your computer for a day, and then extend the time to a week or more. Use a computer lab on campus to complete your assignments, rather than tempting yourself to spend hours online in your room. Train yourself to withdraw, little by little.

6. **Get a life.** Take up yoga, chess, or swimming. Make some new friends, start a relationship, or join a club on campus. Occupy your time with real-time relationships and activities that are interesting and invigorating. Your real life might actually become more interesting if you open yourself up to other opportunities.

7. **Talk to people who care about you—a family member or a counselor on campus.** Recognizing the problem and admitting it are the first steps. Being one-sided isn't healthy, and secrecy and lies aren't a positive, productive way to live. There are experts and support groups available to help you overcome your addiction and make your real life more fulfilling.[9]

> **"The busier we are, the more important we seem to ourselves and, we imagine, to others."**
>
> **Wayne Muller, from *Sabbath: Restoring the Sacred Rhythm of Rest***

Schedule Your Way to Success

There is no one right way to schedule your time, but if you experiment with the system presented in this book, you'll be on the right path. Eventually, you can tweak the system to make it uniquely your own. Try these eight steps, and schedule your way to success!

STEP 1: Fill Out a "Term on a Page" Calendar. Right up front, create a "Term on a Page" calendar that shows the entire school term on one page. (See Exercise 4.1.) This calendar allows you to see the big picture. You will need to have the syllabus from each of your classes and your school's course schedule to do this step properly. The following items should be transferred onto your "Term on a Page" calendar:

> Holidays when your school is closed

> Exam and quiz dates from your syllabi

> Project or paper deadlines from your syllabi

> Relevant administrative deadlines (e.g., registration for the next term, drop dates)

> Birthdays and anniversaries to remember

> Important out-of-town travel

> Dates that pertain to other family members, such as days that your children's school is closed or that your spouse is out of town for a conference—anything that will impact your ability to attend classes or study

STEP 2: Invest in a Planner. While it's good to have the big picture, you must also develop an ongoing scheduling system that works for you. Using the "It's all right up here in my head" method is a surefire way to miss an important appointment, fly past the deadline for your term paper without a clue, or lose track of the time you have left to complete multiple projects.

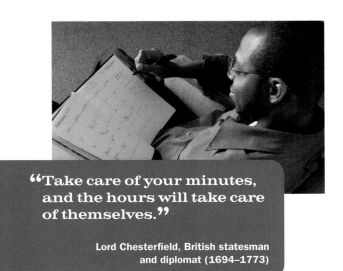

"Take care of your minutes, and the hours will take care of themselves."

Lord Chesterfield, British statesman and diplomat (1694–1773)

EXERCISE 4.1 Term on a Page

Take a few minutes right now to create your own Term on a Page using the charts in Figure 4.2.

Term _____ Year _____

Figure 4.2

Term on a Page

	Sunday	Monday	Tuesday	Wednesday	Thursday	Friday	Saturday
Month:							

	Sunday	Monday	Tuesday	Wednesday	Thursday	Friday	Saturday
Month:							

	Sunday	Monday	Tuesday	Wednesday	Thursday	Friday	Saturday
Month:							

	Sunday	Monday	Tuesday	Wednesday	Thursday	Friday	Saturday
Month:							

	Sunday	Monday	Tuesday	Wednesday	Thursday	Friday	Saturday
Month:							

Although your instructor will typically provide you with a class syllabus that lists test dates and assignment deadlines, trying to juggle multiple syllabi—not to mention your personal and work commitments—is enough to drive you crazy. You need *one* central clearinghouse for all of your important deadlines, appointments, and commitments. This central clearinghouse is a planner—a calendar book with space to write in each day. Derek Johnson in the "FOCUS Challenge Case" expressed his bias that planners are for nerds and neurotics. Not true! Most every successful person on the planet uses one.

When you go planner shopping, remember that you don't have to break the bank unless you want to. Many new college students find that an ordinary paper-and-pencil daily calendar from an office supply store works best. Having a full page for each day means you can write your daily to-do list right in your planner (more on to-do lists later), and that can be a huge help.

STEP 3: Transfer Important Dates. The next step is to transfer important dates for the whole term from your "Term on a Page" overview to the appropriate days in your planner. This may seem repetitious, but there's a method to the madness. While it's important to be able to view all of your due dates together to create a big picture, it's equally important to have these dates recorded in your actual planner because you will use it more regularly—as the final authority on your schedule.

STEP 4: Set Intermediate Deadlines. After recording the important dates for the entire academic term, look at the individual due dates for major projects or papers that are assigned. Then set intermediate stepping-stone goals that will ultimately help you accomplish your final goals. Working backward from the due date, choose and record deadlines for completing certain chunks of the work. For example, if you have a research paper due, you could set an interme-

---

FOCUS ON CAREERS: Judith Cara,
Community and Government
Relations Manager, Intel, Corporation

Q1: What do you do in your job? What are the main responsibilities?
In my position at Intel, I have four major responsibilities: Media Relations, Government Affairs, Education Manager, and Community Relations Manager. For Media Relations, I'm responsible for managing Intel's external image in the state media and am basically the "face of Intel" in our local communities. Often, I proactively approach the local media if there is specific information that we'd like them to have. At other times, I have to react to a call from a print media reporter or handle an on-camera interview with a television station. For Government Affairs, I handle relationships with elected officials at the federal, state, county, and city levels, monitor legislation to see if there are any proposed bills that would negatively impact Intel, and introduce legislation that would be in the best interests of other high-tech or manufacturing companies. As Education Manager, I am responsible for implementing Intel's science, technology, engineering and math K-20 educational programs. I am asked to speak at national educa-

tion conferences, have joined a couple of national education boards, and have even been on a panel with the U.S. Secretary of Education. As part of Community Relations, this area covers a number of diverse activities including neighbor relations, the annual United Way campaign, our volunteerism programs—called Intel Involved—and philanthropic grants to local non-profit or education organizations.

Q2: What are the three most important skills you need to do well in this career?
The field of public relations is all about relationships, so an outgoing personality, an ability to talk to strangers, and excellent networking skills are important. I often need to ask others for help, whether it's a city official who can assist me with a permitting issue or a newspaper reporter who has the ability to edit an article that may not be entirely favorable to the corporation. I don't want to give the impression that this is a one-way street. I also look for opportunities to assist these people with factory tours, an appointment to our Community Advisory Panel, or a silent auction item for a fundraising event.

diate deadline for completing all of your initial research and other deadlines for the pre-writing, writing, and rewriting steps for the paper.

STEP 5: Schedule Fixed Activities for the Entire Term. Next you'll want to schedule in all fixed activities throughout the entire term: class meeting times and reading assignments, religious services you regularly attend, club meetings, and regular co-curricular activities. It's also a great idea to schedule brief review sessions for your classes. Of course, sometimes you'll be going directly into another class, but ten-minute segments of time before and after each class to review your notes helps prepare you for any surprise quizzes and dramatically improve your understanding and retention of the material.

STEP 6: Check for Schedule Conflicts. Now, take a final look at your planner. Do you notice any major scheduling conflicts, such as a planned business trip smack dab in the middle of midterm exam week? Look for these conflicts now, when there's plenty of time to adjust your plans and talk with your instructor to see what you can work out.

STEP 7: Schedule Flextime. In all the scheduling of important dates, checking and double-checking, don't forget one thing. You do need personal time for eating, sleeping, exercising, and other regular activities that don't have a set time frame. Despite your planner, life will happen. If you get a toothache, you'll need to see a dentist right away. Several times each week, you can count on something coming up that will offer you a chance (or force you) to revise your schedule. The decision of how high the item ranks on your priority list rests with you, but the point is to leave some wiggle room in your schedule.

 CREATE a Career Outlook

PUBLIC RELATIONS SPECIALIST

Have you ever considered a career in public relations?

Facts to Consider[10]

Academic preparation required: a college degree in public relations, communication, journalism, or some related field, along with an internship in public relations or similar work experience

Future workforce demand: Employment in this field is expected to grow at greater than average rates, but competition for entry-level jobs will be high.

Work environment: Public relations or communication specialists focus on building and maintaining an organization's relationship with the public. They work with the media, community members, interest groups, government, and investors, for example. Public relations specialists often work forty-hour weeks, but they may occasionally need to work overtime or even around the clock during times of crisis.

Essential skills: creativity, initiative, communication, problem solving, and team working

Questions to Ponder

1. Do you have (or could you acquire) the skills this career requires?
2. Are you interested in a career like this? Why or why not?

For more career activities online, go to http://www.cengage.com/colsuccess/staleyconcise to do the Team Career exercises.

Q3: What is the most challenging time management issue in your job? How do you deal with it?
Public relations is definitely not a job for someone who wants to work 9 A.M. to 5 P.M. A school board meeting may require my presence until 11 P.M., or a telephone conference call with my counterparts in Asia can take place at 6 A.M. Of course, a 6 A.M. telephone call can be handled from my home and I still get a kick out of sitting at home in my pajamas, talking to my colleagues around the world, while my two dogs are sprawled across my feet!

Q4: What advice would you give college students who are interested in exploring a career in public relations?
If you are interested in pursuing a public relations career, find a public relations professional in your community and ask that person to spend a little time with you. Job shadowing is a very effective way to see firsthand what is involved. Most of us are extraverts so we're happy to mentor others who have an interest in our field.

STEP 8: Monitor Your Schedule Every Day. At this point, you've developed a working time management system. Now it's important to monitor your use of that system on a daily basis. Each night, take three minutes to review the day's activities. How well did you stick to your schedule? Did you accomplish the tasks you set out to do? Do you need to revise your schedule for the rest of the week based on something that happened—or didn't happen—today? This simple process will help you better schedule your time in the future and give you a sense of accomplishment—or of the need for more discipline—for tasks completed, hours worked, and classes attended.

To Do or Not to Do?
There *Is* No Question

Part of your personal time management system should be keeping an ongoing to-do list. While the concept of a to-do list sounds relatively simple, there are a few tricks of the trade.

Before the beginning of each school week, brainstorm all the things that you want or need to get done in the upcoming week. Using this random list of to-do items, assign a priority level next to each one. The A-B-C method is simple and easy to use:

A = must get this done; highest priority

B = very important, but not mandatory

C = would be nice to get done this week,
    but not necessary

The two factors to consider when assigning a priority level to a to-do item are *importance* and *urgency*, creating four time zones. Use Figure 4.3 as a guide.[11]

Figure 4.3
Time Zones

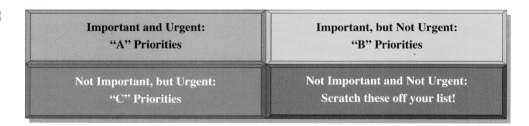

After you've assigned a time zone to each item, review your list of A and B priorities and ask yourself:

1. Do any of the items fit best with a particular day of the week? For example, donating blood may be a high priority task for you, yet you don't want to do it on a day when you have co-curricular sports planned. That might leave you with two available days in the upcoming week that you can donate blood.

2. Can any items be grouped together for easier execution? For example, you may have three errands to run downtown on your to-do list, so grouping them

together will save you from making three separate trips.

3. Do any A and B priorities qualify as floating tasks that can be completed anytime, anywhere? For example, perhaps you were assigned an extra long reading assignment for one of your classes. It's both important and urgent, an A priority item. Bring your book to read while waiting at the dentist's office for your semi-annual teeth cleaning appointment, a B priority. Planning ahead can really help save time.

4. Do any priorities need to be shifted? As the days pass, some of your B priorities will become A priorities due to the urgency factor increasing. Or maybe an A priority will become a C priority because something changed about the task. This is normal.

As for those not important and not urgent to-do items, scratch them off the list right now. Life is too short to waste time on unimportant tasks. Give yourself permission to focus on what's important. Since time is a limited resource, one of the best ways to guarantee a successful college experience is to use it wisely. If you don't already use these tools on a regular basis, give them a shot. What do you have to lose except time?

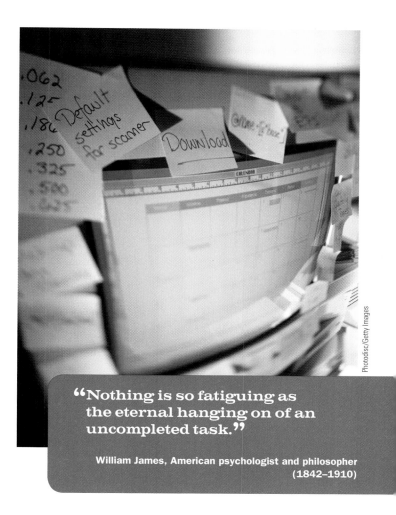

Photodisc/Getty Images

> **"Nothing is so fatiguing as the eternal hanging on of an uncompleted task."**
>
> **William James, American psychologist and philosopher (1842–1910)**

INSIGHT ⊖ ACTION

Look back at the Time Monitors you completed in an earlier "Challenge → Reaction" activity when answering the following questions:

1. How could the use of a schedule have improved the way you used your time on those two days?

2. How could the use of a to-do list have improved the way you used your time on those two days?

EXERCISE 4.2 So Much to Do—So Little Time

Assume this is your to-do list for today (Monday). Assign each item one of the four time zones described earlier: A, B, C (and strike through any items that are *not* urgent and *not* important). Finally, renumber the items to indicate which you would do first, which second, and so forth.

Start time: 9:00 a.m., Monday morning, during the second week of the fall term.

1. _____ Return Professor Jordan's call before class tomorrow. He left a message saying he wants to talk to you about some problems with your LIT 101 paper.

2. _____ Pick up your paycheck at McDonald's and get to the bank before it closes at 5:00 p.m. this afternoon.

(continued)

3. _____ Call the new love interest in your life and ask about going to the party together this weekend before someone else does.

4. _____ Visit the Speech Center to get critiqued on your first speech due Friday. It's closed evenings.

5. _____ Call your favorite aunt. She lives overseas in a time zone seven hours ahead of yours. Today is her fortieth birthday.

6. _____ Stop by the Health Center to take advantage of free meningitis vaccinations today only.

7. _____ Listen to the new CD you bought yesterday.

8. _____ Leave a note asking your roommate/sibling/child to please stop leaving messes everywhere. It's really aggravating.

9. _____ Read the two chapters in your History textbook for the in-class quiz on Wednesday.

10. _____ Watch the first episode of the new reality TV show you've been waiting for at 9 p.m. tonight.

11. _____ Write a rough draft of the essay due in your composition class on Thursday.

12. _____ Invite an out-of-town friend to spend the weekend.

13. _____ Return the three library books that are a week overdue.

14. _____ Call your math Teaching Assistant and leave a message asking for an appointment during her office hours to get help with the homework due on Wednesday. Nearly everyone is confused about the assignment.

15. _____ Go to the campus Athletic Banquet tonight at 6 p.m. to receive your award.

Outline the criteria you used for making your decisions.

How Time Flies!

CHALLENGE → REACTION

Challenge: What are the most common ways you waste time? What can be done about them?

Reaction: _____

_____

_____

According to efficiency expert Michael Fortino, in a lifetime, the average American will spend:

> Seven years in the bathroom

> Six years eating

> Five years waiting in line

> Three years in meetings

> Two years playing telephone tag

> Eight months opening junk mail

> And six months waiting at red lights[12]

What a waste of time! We can't do much about some of these items, but what *can* we do about other time-wasters? Plan—schedule—organize! Think about the issue of control in time management, and write in examples for the following:

1. Things you think you can't control, and you can't: _____

2. Things you think you can't control, but you can: _____

3. Things you think you can control, but you can't: _____

4. Things you think you can control, but you don't: _____

5. Things you think you can control, and you can: _____

Perhaps you wrote in something like *medical emergencies* for (1). You could have written in *family or friends barging into your room* for (2). For (4), maybe you could control your *addiction to social networking*, but you don't. And for (5), perhaps you wrote in *your attention*. You're absolutely right. But what about (3)? Did anything fit there? Are there things you think you can control, but you can't? Try and think of something that would fit into (3), and then think of creative ways you really could control this situation if you tried.[13]

INSIGHT ⟳ ACTION

Here is a list of some of the most common ways students waste time. As you read through the list, check off those that occur in your life most frequently.

☐ Unscheduled visitors   ☐ Lack of focus

☐ Telephone interruptions   ☐ Moving too quickly

☐ E-mail obsession   ☐ Procrastination

☐ Social networking   ☐ Bad choices

☐ Disorganized workspace/   ☐ Haphazard or, worse yet, a com-
  lost items   plete lack of scheduling

☐ Inability to say no   ☐ Other people's "emergencies"

If you think time management is a limiting concept, but you checked three or more boxes, perhaps the notion of scheduling is sounding more useful. What actions can you take to deal with the issues you marked?

The P Word. Read This Section *Now*! ... or Maybe Tomorrow ... or ...

CHALLENGE ⟳ REACTION

Challenge: What are the most common reasons you procrastinate?

Reaction: _____

Picture this: You sit down to work on a challenging homework assignment. After a few minutes, you think, *Man, I'm thirsty*, so you get up and get a soda. Then you sit back down to continue your work. A few minutes later, you decide that some chips would go nicely with your soda and you head to the kitchen. Again, you sit down to face the task before you, as you concentrate more on eating than on working. Ten minutes go by and a nagging thought starts taking over: *Must do laundry.* Up you go again and throw a load of clothes in the washer. Before long you're wondering where all the time went. Since you only have an hour left before your next class, you think, *Why bother getting started now? Doing this project will take much more time than that, so I'll just start it tomorrow.* Despite good intentions at the beginning of your work session, you've just succeeded in accomplishing zip, nada, nothing.

Congratulations! You—like thousands of other college students—have just successfully procrastinated! Researchers define procrastination as "needlessly delaying tasks to the point of experiencing subjective discomfort."[14] And according to researchers, 70 percent of college students admit to procrastinating on their assignments.[15]

You may be in the majority, but alas, in this case, there's no safety in numbers! Academic procrastination is a major threat to your ability to succeed in college. And procrastination in the working world can actually bring your job, and ultimately your career, to a screeching halt. Plenty of people try to rationalize their procrastination by claiming that they work better under pressure. However, the challenge in college is that during some weeks of the term, every single class will have an assignment or test due, all at once, and if you procrastinate, you'll not only generate tremendous anxiety for yourself, but you'll lower your chances of succeeding on any of them.

Blend Images/Getty Images

"Things which matter most should never be at the mercy of things which matter least."

Johann Wolfgang von Goethe, German writer and scholar (1749–1832)

Before you can control the procrastination monster in your life, it's important to understand *why* you procrastinate. Think about all the instances in which you don't procrastinate: meeting your friends for dinner, returning a phone call from a classmate, going to the store. Why are those things easy to do, but getting started on an assignment is difficult until you feel the jaws of a deadline closing down on you?[16] Procrastinators don't tend to be less smart or have a definitive psychological type. They do, however, tend to have lower self-confidence and get lost in their own thoughts.[17] The reasons for procrastinating vary from person to person, but once you know your own reasons for putting things off, you'll be in a better position to address the problem from its root cause.

The next time you find yourself procrastinating, ask yourself why. Procrastination is self-handicapping: "It's like running a full race with a knapsack full of bricks on your back. When you don't win, you can say it's not that you're not a good runner, it's just that you had this sack of bricks on your back."[18] In addition to understanding why you procrastinate, try these ten procrastination busters to help you kick the habit.

1. **Keep track (of your excuses).** Write them down consistently, and soon you'll be able to recognize them for what they are. Hold yourself accountable. Own your responsibilities—in school and in the rest of your life.

2. **Break down.** Break your project into its smaller components. A term paper, for example, can be broken down into the following smaller parts: prospectus, thesis, research, outline, small chunks of writing, and bibliography. Completing smaller tasks along the way is much easier than facing a daunting monster of a project.

3. **Trick yourself.** When you feel like procrastinating, pick some aspect of the project that's easy and that you would have to do anyway. If the thought of an entire paper is overwhelming you, for example, work on the bibliography to start. Starting with something—*anything*—will get you into the rhythm of the work.

4. **Resolve issues.** If something's gnawing at you, making it difficult to concentrate, take care of it. Sometimes you must deal with a bossy friend, your kids vying for your attention, or something equally intrusive. Then get down to work.

5. **Get real.** Set realistic goals for yourself. If you declare that you're going to finish a twelve-page paper in five hours, you're already doomed. Procrastinators are characteristically optimistic. They underestimate how much time something will take. Make it a habit to keep track of how long assignments take you in all your courses so that you can be increasingly realistic over time.

6. **Think positively.** Our imaginations can work for or against us. Don't let yours go haywire with thoughts that you're not up to the task or that your professor will hate your paper, so why bother. It has been said that the average person has 65,000 to 75,000 thoughts a day, and that many of these are negative. Don't imagine what can go wrong with your project. Imagine what can go right by getting it done on time and doing it well. Assume the best and you'll find it easier to get started.

7. **Make a deal with yourself.** Even if it's only spending fifteen minutes on a task that day, do it so that you can see progress.

8. **Overcome fear.** Many of the reasons for procrastinating have to do with our personal fears. We may fear not doing something perfectly, or failing completely—or even the responsibility that comes with success to keep succeeding. But as Susan Jeffers, author and lecturer states, "Feel the fear, and do it anyway!"

9. **Get tough.** Sometimes projects simply require discipline. The best way to complete a daunting task is to simply dig in. Become your own taskmaster, crack the proverbial whip, and force yourself to focus on those things that are high priorities, but perhaps not your idea of fun.

10. **Acknowledge accomplishment.** We're not talking major shopping sprees at Neiman Marcus here. We're talking reasonable, meaningful rewards commensurate with the action completed. Go buy yourself a small treat, call your best friend in another state, take a relaxing soak in the bathtub, or do something to celebrate your accomplishments—big and small—along the way. Acknowledgment, from yourself or others, is a great motivator for tackling future projects.

C CONTROL Your Learning

YOUR TOUGHEST CLASS

Does procrastination enter into the picture when it comes to your most challenging course this term? What impact does procrastination have on your potential success in this course? On your life as a student?

Examine this list of common reasons people procrastinate. Which ones apply to you in your most challenging course? Put a checkmark next to all the reasons that help explain your tendency to procrastinate. For each item with a checkmark, list one thing you can do to control your learning in this course.

[ ] Avoiding something you see as unpleasant

[ ] Wanting to do something perfectly

[ ] Feeling overwhelmed by all you have to do

[ ] Being intimidated by the task itself

[ ] Hoping to avoid responsibility

[ ] Fearing failure

[ ] Fearing success

[ ] Fearing new or added responsibilities

[ ] Not realizing how important the task is

[ ] Reacting to your own internal conflict

[ ] Protecting your self-esteem

[ ] Waiting for a last-minute adrenaline rush

[ ] Just plain not wanting to

Beyond Juggling: *Realistically* Manage Work, School, and Personal Life

CHALLENGE ⟳ REACTION

Challenge: How do successful people juggle work, school, and personal life?

Reaction: _____

_____

Your personal time management needs depend on who you are and how many obligations you have. Today's college students are more diverse than ever. Increasing numbers of college students are also parents, part-time employees, or full-time professionals, husbands or wives, community volunteers, soccer coaches, or Sunday school teachers. How on earth can you possibly juggle it all?

The answer? You can't. According to work-life balance expert Dawn Carlson, juggling is a knee-jerk coping mechanism—the default setting when time gets tight and it seems that nothing can be put on the back burner. If you, like millions of others, feel overworked, overcommitted, and exhausted at every turn, you may have already learned that you can't juggle your way to a balanced life. It's impossible.[19]

Now for the good news. Balance among work, school, and personal life is possible. All of us have three primary areas of our lives that should be in balance, ideally—meaningful work (including school), satisfying relationships, and a healthy lifestyle. In addition to work and relationships, we all need to take care of ourselves. See what you think of these five rebalancing strategies. The idea is you can't have it all, but you can have it better than you do now.

1. **Alternating.** If you use this strategy, your work-life balance comes in separate, concentrated doses. You may throw yourself into your career with abandon, and then cut back or quit work altogether and focus intensely on your family. You may give your job 110 percent during the week, but devote Saturdays to physical fitness or to your kids or running all the errands you've saved up during the week. Or you save Tuesdays and Thursdays for homework, and go to classes Mondays, Wednesdays, and Fridays. People who use this strategy alternate between important things, and it works for them. An alternator's motto is "I want to have it all, but just not all at once."

2. **Outsourcing.** An outsourcer's motto might be "I want to have it all, not do it all." This strategy helps you achieve work-life balance by giving someone else some of your responsibilities—usually in your personal life—to free up time for the tasks you care about most. If you have enough money, hire someone to clean the house or mow the lawn. If you don't, trade these jobs among family, friends, or neighbors who band together to help each other.

© Tetra Images/CORBIS

> **"The trouble with the rat race is that even if you win, you're still a rat."**
>
> **Lily Tomlin, comedian**

Of course, there are ways this strategy could be misused by college students. Don't even think about outsourcing your research papers by having someone else write them or downloading them from the Internet with a charge card! Warning: This practice will definitely be hazardous to your academic health! In fact, your college career may be over!

3. **Bundling.** This strategy helps you rebalance your life by killing two birds with one stone. Examine your busy life and look for areas in which you can double dip, such as combining exercising with socializing. If your social life is suffering because of time constraints, take walks with a friend so that you can talk along the way. A bundler's motto is "I want to get more mileage out of the things I do by combining activities." Bundling is efficient because it allows you to do two things at once.

4. **Techflexing.** Technology allows us to work from almost anywhere, anytime, using technology. If you telecommute from home several days a week for your job, you might get up early, spend some time on e-mail, go out for a run, have breakfast with your family, and then get back on your computer. In the office, you use instant messaging to stay connected to family members or a cell phone to call home while commuting to a business meeting. Chances are you can telecommute to your campus library and do research online, register for classes online, and pay all your bills online, including tuition. Use technology, and the flexibility it gives you, to your advantage to merge important aspects of your life.

5. **Simplifying.** People who use this strategy are ready to cry uncle. They've decided they don't want it all. They've reached a point where they make a permanent commitment to stop the craziness in their lives. The benefit of simplifying is greater freedom from details, stress, and the rat race. But there are trade-offs, of course. They may have to take a significant cut in pay in order to work fewer hours or at a less demanding job. But for them, it's worth it.[20]

These five strategies, used separately or in combination, have helped many people who are dealing with work, school, and family commitments at the same time. They all require certain trade-offs. None of these strategies is a magic solution.

But the alternative to rebalancing is more stress, more physical and emotional exhaustion, more frustration, and much less personal satisfaction. If you focus on rebalancing your life—making conscious choices and course corrections as you go—small changes can have a big impact. Work-life balance isn't an all-or-nothing proposition. It's an ever-changing journey. So take it one step at a time.

CHALLENGE Yourself Quizzes For more practice online, go to http://www.cengage .com/colsuccess/staleyconcise to take the Challenge Yourself online quizzes.

INSIGHT → ACTION

If you feel the need to rebalance your life due to the pressures of managing work, school, family, and friends at the same time, take some time to work through the following Rebalancing Plan worksheet.[21]

Why do I need to rebalance? _____

What rebalancing strategies will I use? _____

How will I do it? _____

How will I let go of _____? _____

Tasks that I should completely eliminate: _____

Tasks that I can outsource or give to others: _____

Expectations of others that affect me: _____

Time-consuming possessions or relationships that bring little value to me: _____

_____

EXERCISE 4.3 VARK Activity

Complete the recommended activity for your preferred VARK learning modality. If you are multimodal, select more than one activity. Your instructor may ask you to (a) give an oral report on your results in class, (b) send your results to him or her via e-mail, (c) post them online, or (d) contribute to a class chat.

 Visual: Buy a set of adhesive colored dots from a local office supply store. Go through your planner, putting red dots by A priority items, yellow dots by B priority items, and green dots by C priority items.

 Aural: Go to the National Public Radio website at www.npr.org and listen to a program that will increase your understanding of time management, workplace skills, or a related subject.

 Read/Write: Find a helpful library book on time management skills and summarize three pointers that don't appear in this chapter in a paragraph of your own.

 Kinesthetic: Visit a place of work and interview employees about the value of time management skills and specific techniques they use to prioritize their daily activities. Bring your findings to class.

 ## NOW WHAT DO YOU THINK?

At the beginning of this chapter, Derek Johnson, a frustrated and disgruntled student, faced a challenge. Now after reading this chapter, would you respond differently to any of the questions you answered about the "FOCUS Challenge Case"?

To download mp3 format audio summaries of this chapter, go to http://www.cengage.com/colsuccess/staleyconcise.

5 Thinking Critically and Creatively

YOU'RE ABOUT TO DISCOVER...

- How focused thinking, critical thinking, and creative thinking are defined

- How a four-part model of critical thinking works

- How to analyze arguments, assess assumptions, and consider claims

- How to avoid mistakes in reasoning

- What metacognition is and why it's important

- How to become a more creative thinker

READINESS CHECK

Before beginning this chapter, take a moment to answer these questions. Your answers will help you assess how ready you are to focus.

1 = not very/not much/very little/low   10 = very/a lot/very much/high

Based on reading the "You're about to discover..." list and skimming this chapter, how much do you think you probably already know about the subject matter?

1   2   3   4   5   6   7   8   9   10

How much do you think this information might affect your college success?

1   2   3   4   5   6   7   8   9   10

How much do you think this information might affect your career success after college?

1   2   3   4   5   6   7   8   9   10

In general, how motivated are you to learn the material in this chapter?

1   2   3   4   5   6   7   8   9   10

How ready are you to focus on this chapter—physically, intellectually, and emotionally? Circle a number for each aspect of your readiness to focus.

1   2   3   4   5   6   7   8   9   10

If any of your answers are below a 5, consider addressing the issue you're facing. For example, if you're feeling scattered, take a few moments to settle down and focus.

Finally, how long do you think it will take you to complete this chapter? _____ Hour(s) _____ Minutes

Annie Miller

Growing up in a big city was definitely a good

thing. So Annie Miller thought, anyway. Every day that went by, she missed L.A. more and more. She missed the fast pace, the diversity, the lifestyle. Why had she decided to go to a small college? She knew there had been reasons; it's just that she couldn't remember them from time to time. She guessed that it was probably because she wanted every aspect of her life at college to be different. She wanted to live on a different coast, have new friends, and study something exciting. Her huge high school had been amazing in its own way, but now she wanted a more personal education at a place where everyone knew everyone, like at the small liberal arts college she had chosen on the East Coast.

Her first semester of classes consisted of a college success course, an English composition class, Introduction to Poetry, and Philosophy 100. She was excited by the idea of learning in small classes with wise and learned professors. But Philosophy 100 had turned out to be a very challenging course. Professor Courtney had announced on the first day of class that he believed in the Socratic method of teaching. He taught by asking questions of students instead of lecturing. "Socrates, perhaps the greatest philosopher of all time," he announced the first day, "is the 'father' of critical thinking. In this class, you'll learn to think critically. *That* is what college is all about."

Professor Courtney began every class session with a hypothetical situation and always randomly chose a student to respond. His opening went something like this:

Assume it's Valentine's Day. A young man makes a trip to the biggest jewelry store in the mall to buy his fiancée a gift. He's saved up for a long time to afford 24 karat gold earrings and he's ready to choose the best money can buy. He finds the perfect pair and hands over his credit card. But when the salesclerk brings the receipt for him to sign, he notices that instead of $300, she has missed a digit, and the receipt reads $30. He now faces a dilemma: Does he sign and say nothing, or point out the error and pay the full amount? What should he do?

One student responded with, "He should sign his name and then take off quickly. This mistake was the clerk's, not his. If someone catches the mistake later, he can just claim he didn't notice. Maybe no one will ever figure it out, and he'll be $270 richer!"

Professor Courtney continued, "On what ethical principle do you base your response?" The student faltered, and the professor moved on to someone else, raising other points that hadn't been considered.

"But what if his fiancée decides to exchange the earrings for another pair? What if the clerk is fired for making a $270 mistake? What if the clerk were your sister or your best friend? What if the hero of a movie did what you're proposing? What if the clerk were you?" he continued. "What would Socrates say about what you should do? According to Socrates, no one errs intentionally. This means that whenever we do something wrong—including something *morally* wrong—it is out of ignorance rather than evil motives. If the young man decides to capitalize on the clerk's error, what are his motives—and are they evil? What would be the *right* thing to do?"

Professor Courtney continued putting students on the spot and raising questions posed by other philosophers they were studying. The questions seemed endless. Annie found herself listening more carefully than in her other classes so that she would be ready to jump in if called upon. And she silently thought through others' answers, too. Even though she had to admit that the learning environment was stimulating, speaking in front of other students made Annie nervous.

"There aren't always right answers," Professor Courtney told them. "What's important is thinking through the problem. The process of learning to think can be more important than the answer itself."

Frankly, that explanation didn't sit well with Annie. *If there aren't right answers, what am I doing in college? Things should be black and white, true or false, right or wrong. I'm paying tuition to hear what the professor thinks, not all the other students in class. He knows the right answers. Why doesn't he just tell us?*

Without fail, Annie always left Professor Courtney's class with a headache from thinking so hard. In fact, compared to Philosophy 100, all her other classes seemed effortless. She had to admit that she much preferred classes in which she could express herself creatively, like Introduction to Poetry.

WHAT DO **YOU** THINK?

Now that you've read about Annie Miller, answer the following questions. You may not know all the answers yet, but you'll find out what you know and what you stand to gain by reading this chapter.

1. How would the Socratic method of teaching used by Professor Courtney help first-year college students improve their critical thinking skills?

2. Do you agree with Professor Courtney's statement that "there aren't always right answers"? If that's true, why is getting a college education so important?

3. Even though Professor Courtney's teaching methods made her nervous, why did Annie find the learning environment in his class to be stimulating?

4. Annie says she prefers creative thinking to critical thinking. Are they two different things? Why or why not?

5. Identify three things Annie should do to get the most from Professor Courtney's class.

Rethinking Thinking

CHALLENGE → REACTION

Challenge: What's the difference between thinking and *critical* thinking?

Reaction: _____

Thinking is a natural, ongoing, everyday process we all engage in. In fact, we can't really turn it off, even if we try. We're always on. Everyone thinks all the time, right? It happens any time you talk to yourself, doesn't it? However, some experts say school teaches us how to regurgitate, not how to think.

In many ways, thinking is like speaking. But if you take a public speaking course, you're bound to be a better speaker by the end of it by knowing more about how to consciously direct your voice, gestures, and delivery. In a similar way, you can become a better thinker by learning how to direct your brain. *Focused thinking*—thinking critically and creatively—is what this chapter is about.

Picture this: You're in the library. It's late, and you're tired. You're supposed to be studying for your political science test, but instead of thinking about foreign policy, your mind begins drifting toward the vacation you took last summer, how tan you were when you returned, and how much fun it was to be with your friends.

Would the mental process you're engaging in while sitting in the library be called *thinking*? For our purposes in this chapter, the answer is no. Here thinking is defined as a focused cognitive activity you engage in purposefully. You direct your thoughts toward a particular topic. You're the *active* thinker, not the *passive* daydreamer who is the victim of a wandering mind. Focused thinking involves zeroing in and managing your attention. It's deliberate and intentional, not haphazard or accidental. You choose to do it for a reason.

Focused thinking is like a two-sided coin. Sometimes when you think, you *produce* ideas. That's what this chapter calls *creative thinking*, and that's something we'll deal with later. The other side of thinking requires you to *evaluate* ideas—your own or someone else's. That's *critical thinking*. The word *critical* comes from the Greek word for *critic* (*kritikos*), meaning "to question or analyze." You focus on something, sort through the information, and decide which ideas are most sensible, logical, or useful.

> **"'Knowledge is power.' Rather, knowledge is happiness. To have knowledge, deep broad knowledge, is to know truth from false and lofty things from low."**
>
> **Helen Keller, American author, activist, and lecturer (1880–1968)**

When you're thinking critically, you're asking questions, analyzing arguments, assessing assumptions, considering claims, avoiding mistakes in reasoning, problem solving, decision making, and all the while, thinking about your thinking.

What Is Critical Thinking?

Critical thinking is a particular kind of focused thinking. It is purposeful, reasoned, and goal-directed. It's thinking that aims to solve problems, calculate likelihood, weigh evidence, and make decisions.[1] In that sense, movie critics are critical thinkers because they look at a variety of standards (screenplay, acting, production quality, costumes, cinematography, and so forth) and then decide how a movie measures up. When you're thinking critically, you're not just fault-finding. You're being *discerning* of both faults and strengths. You're looking at how things measure up.[2]

Critical thinkers develop standards they can use to judge advertisements, political speeches, sales pitches, movies—you name it.[3] Critical thinking is not jumping to conclusions, buying arguments lock, stock, and barrel, accepting controversial ideas at face value, ignoring the facts, or disregarding the evidence.

Unfortunately, some people are noncritical thinkers. They may be biased or prejudiced or closed-minded. Other people are *selective* critical thinkers. When it comes to one particular subject, they shut down their minds. They can't explain their views, they're emotional about them, and they refuse to acknowledge any other position. Their particular positions may be right or wrong in your view, but the important issue is whether they are thinking critically about them. Why do they believe these things? Only if they understand the *why*, can they explain their views to someone else or defend them under fire. The importance of *why* can't be overstated. Some people, of course, have already thought through their beliefs, and they understand their positions and the reasons for them very well. Arriving at that point is the goal of aspiring critical thinkers.

Exercise 5.1 And Just Why Is Critical Thinking Important?

Here is a list of reasons why it's important to improve your critical thinking skills. Beside each entry, mark the degree to which you'd like to concentrate your efforts as a college student, soon ready for your career path. On a scale from 1 to 10 with 10 representing the highest degree, would you like to:

1. _____ **Become a more successful college student**? Most college courses require you to think critically (in answering essay questions, for example). In one study of

over 1,100 college students, higher scores on critical thinking skills tests correlated highly with better grades.[4] Critical thinkers, for example, can ask better questions in class. There's even evidence that interaction with other students in co-curricular activities can help you develop as a critical thinker.[5]

2. _____ **Become a better citizen**? Critical thinking is the foundation of a strong democracy. Voters must think critically about candidates' messages and their likelihood of keeping campaign promises. It's easy to talk about balancing the budget, or lowering taxes, but the truth is these highly complex tasks are very challenging to carry out. The American public must sift through information and examine the soundness of politicians' arguments in order to keep our democracy strong.

3. _____ **Become a better employee**? A workforce of critical—and creative—thinkers helps the American economy thrive and individuals become more successful. The U.S. Department of Labor reports that today's jobs require employees who can deal with complexity, learn and perform multiple tasks, analyze and deal with a wide variety of options, identify problems, perceive alternative approaches, and select the best approach.[6] Employers are "practically begging" for employees who can "think, collaborate, communicate, coordinate, and create."[7]

4. _____ **Become a more savvy consumer**? In today's marketplace, everyone wants your dollars. If you acted on every ad you read in magazines or watch on television, you'd run out of money very quickly. Critical thinking will help you evaluate offers, avoid slick come-ons, and buy responsibly.

5. _____ **Build stronger relationships**? Critical thinking helps us understand our own and others' actions and become more responsible communicators. Whether with friends or romantic partners, relationships take work. Sometimes you have to figure out what your partner really means or listen between the lines for important clues. Actually, critical thinking is at the heart of every relationship you care about.

6. _____ **Become a lifelong learner**? Your education doesn't end when you get your diploma. In many ways the real exams begin afterward when you put your classroom learning to the test. And in today's world you must continue to learn as you transition through jobs to give your life more meaning—personally and professionally. You'll need to keep expanding your skills, no matter what your career is.

INSIGHT ⮕ ACTION

1. Identify a time, subject, or event in which you used your critical thinking skills for your own benefit. Perhaps you investigated the salary range for a new job or read editorials on a particular subject to gain new perspectives. Explain what you did, how you went about it, and why.

2. Find a controversial headline in the newspaper. How would you advise others to investigate its truth or falsehood?

Exercise 5.2 Critical Searching on the Internet

One place where critical thinking is extremely important today is on the Internet. If you're like most students, you do some of your research for classes online; but some of what you see on screen may be bogus. You must cultivate your critical searching skills to weed out websites with inaccuracies and biases. Choose one of the following three assignments to complete.

Assignment 1: Create a list of ten websites that pertain to your intended major. (If you're not sure of your major right now, choose one to explore anyway.) Evaluate the websites to see which ones seem most useful to you as a student.

Assignment 2: Compare websites with contradictory information. Choose a controversial subject such as abortion, the death penalty, cohabitation, religion, politics, holistic healing, euthanasia, or some other subject of interest. Find four websites on your topic and compare them on these characteristics: (1) currency, (2) accuracy, (3) authority, (4) objectivity, and (5) coverage. Which of the four websites gets the highest marks? Why?

Assignment 3: Compare the content of an informational website on a particular subject with a print resource on the same subject. List the pros and cons of each source.

A Four-Part Model of Critical Thinking

CHALLENGE ⊖ REACTION

Challenge: Reasoning, problem solving, and decision making are all part of critical thinking. How are these three things related?

Reaction: _____

Now that we've defined critical thinking, let's ask an important related question: How do you do it? We'll look at the four primary components of critical thinking, and at the end of this chapter, we'll use a realistic news story, one that is relevant to many college campuses, to allow you to apply what you've learned and provide a memorable example.

Take a look at Figure 5.1 to preview the four-part model of critical thinking. You'll see right away that your reasoning skills underlie everything. They are the foundation upon which your problem-solving and decision-making skills rest, and your metacognitive skills, or thinking about your thinking, surround all the focused thinking you do.

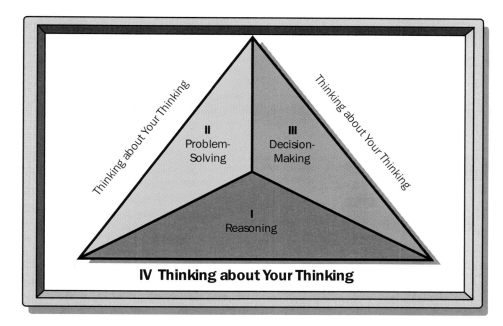

Figure 5.1

Critical Thinking Is Focused

"Few people think more than two or three times a year. I have made an international reputation for myself by thinking once or twice a week."

George Bernard Shaw, Irish literary critic, playwright, and essayist, 1925 Nobel Prize for Literature (1856–1950)

I. Reasoning: The Foundation of Critical Thinking

Reasoning, the foundation of critical thinking, is the ability to infer a conclusion from one or more arguments. A strong argument is convincing because it offers evidence to back up its claim. If no one would disagree with what you're saying, it's not an argument. It's self-evident. "Grass is green" is not an argument. But "Cows that are grass-fed make the best meat" (if supporting evidence is provided) is. Do you see the difference?

Think about your reasoning skills. How good are you at creating a sound argument? Let's say that you're trying to convince your friend to stop inviting people over while you're both studying for major exams. What evidence would you use to convince her? What's the likelihood of your success? How good are you at evaluating someone else's argument? For example, you're trying to decide whether an online discount is really a good deal. Would you take the advertiser's word for it or do some independent research to compare prices on your own?

Throughout the rest of this chapter, ask yourself: Are there ways I can improve my reasoning skills? As you critique your own skills, consider these reasoning nuts and bolts that are integral to creating and evaluating arguments.

Analyzing Arguments

CHALLENGE ⊖ REACTION

Challenge: What does the term *argument* have to do with critical thinking? How do you recognize a *sound* argument?

Reaction: _____

Have you ever seen the *Monty Python Flying Circus* "Argument Sketch"? In this bizarre skit a man comes to an "argument clinic" to buy an argument. The two arguers—"professional" and customer—engage in an interminably long, "yes, it is" "no, it isn't" squabble.

Critical thinking is about arguments. But when most of us think of an argument, that's the kind of bickering we think of. In the middle of the "Argument Clinic" sketch, however, the customer actually makes an important point. He protests that they're not really arguing; they're just contradicting each other. He continues, "An argument is a connected series of statements intended to establish a proposition." That's the kind of argument that's related to critical thinking.

Critical thinking is about an argument that *one* person puts forth. An op-ed piece in the newspaper contains an argument. (Op-ed stands for the page "opposite the editorial page" that features signed articles expressing personal viewpoints.) Both attorneys—prosecution and defense—put forth their closing arguments at the end of a trial. A politician puts forth an argument about where he stands on the issues. A professor puts forth an argument to persuade her class to learn important content in her discipline.

Arguments are said to be inductive or deductive. *Inductive* arguments go from specific observations to general conclusions. In criminal trials, the prosecution puts together individual pieces of evidence to prove that the defendant is guilty: eyewitnesses put him at the scene, the gun store salesman remembers selling him a pistol, and his fingerprints are on the weapon. Therefore, the prosecutor asserts that the defendant is guilty. Other arguments are said to be *deductive*, meaning they go from broad generalizations to specific conclusions. All serial killers have a particular psychological profile. The defendant has this psychological profile. Therefore the defendant is the killer.

What do arguments do? They propose a line of reasoning. They try to persuade. Arguments contain clear reasons to believe someone or something. Arguments say A plus B equals C. Once you understand what an argument is, you must also understand that arguments can be sound or unsound. If I tell you that two plus two equals four, chances are good that you'll believe me. If, on the other hand, I tell you two plus two equals five, you'll flatly deny it. If I say "Cats have fur." "Dogs have fur." "Therefore dogs are cats," you'll tell me I'm crazy—because it's an unsound argument.

The standard we use to test the soundness of arguments is logic, which is a fairly extensive topic. Let's just say for our purposes here that arguments are sound when the evidence to support the opinion they put forth is reasonable, more reasonable than the evidence supporting other opinions. The important point is that a sound argument provides at least one good reason to believe. Let's look at an example:

I don't see why all first-year students have to take Freshman Composition. It's a free country. Students shouldn't have to take courses they don't want to take.

Based on our definition, is this example an argument? Why or why not? Is the statement "It's a free country" relevant? What does living in a free country have to do with the curricula in colleges and universities? Nothing. *Relevancy* is a condition needed for a sound argument.

Now look at this example:

I don't see why all first-year students have to take Freshman Composition. Many students have cultivated good writing skills in high school, and their Verbal SAT scores are 600 or higher.

Is this second example an argument? Why or why not? The first example doesn't give you a good reason to believe the argument; the second example does. A true argument must contain at least one reason for you to believe it.

Here's another warning. Not everything that sounds like an argument is one. Look at this example:

Everyone taking Calculus 100 failed the test last Friday. I took the test last Friday. Therefore, I will probably get an F in the course.

Is that a sound argument—or is something missing? Even though all three statements may be true, they don't constitute a sound argument. What grade has this student earned on earlier calculus tests? How many tests remain in the course? What other assignments figure into students' grades? The information

> **"The aim of argument, or of discussion, should not be victory, but progress."**
>
> **Joseph Joubert, French moralist (1754–1824)**

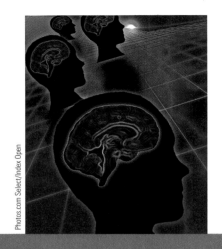

> **"Great minds discuss ideas. Average minds discuss events. Small minds discuss people."**
>
> **Eleanor Roosevelt, First Lady of the United States (1884–1962)**

present may not be adequate to predict an F in the course. *Adequacy* is another condition needed for a sound argument. This alternative, on the other hand, is a sound argument:

> *Everyone taking Calculus 100 failed the test last Friday. I took the test last Friday. Therefore, I earned an F on the test.*

When you're assessing the soundness of an argument, you must look for two things: *relevance* and *adequacy*.[8]

Not all arguments are sound. Have you ever heard this tale? A scientist decided to embark on a new study to find out what intoxicates people. He devised an experiment to proceed in an orderly, methodical way. On Monday night, he drank three tall glasses of scotch and water, mixed in equal proportions. The next morning, he recorded his results: intoxication. On Tuesday night, he drank three tall glasses of whiskey and water. On Wednesday night, he drank three tall glasses of rum and water. On Thursday night, he drank three tall glasses of vodka and water. Each morning, his recorded results were identical. He had become highly intoxicated. His erroneous conclusion? Water makes people drunk.

Not only is it important to be able to construct sound arguments, but it's also important to be able to recognize them. As a consumer in today's information society, you must know when to buy into an argument, and when not to.

Assessing Assumptions

When you're thinking critically, one of the most important kinds of questions you can ask is about the *assumptions* you or someone else is making, perhaps without even realizing it. Assumptions can limit our thinking. Consider this well-known puzzle, and afterward, examine how the assumptions you brought with you interfered with solving it.

> *One day Kerry celebrated her birthday. Two days later her older twin brother, Harry, celebrated his birthday. How could that be?*

You may have solved this puzzle if you were willing to question the underlying assumptions that were holding you back. (Answer is upside down at the bottom of this page.)

People reveal their underlying assumptions in what they say. If you listen carefully, you can uncover them. "Go on for a graduate degree after I finish college? No way! I'm out of here in four years, no matter what!" This student's underlying assumption is that college itself isn't as important as what comes afterward (like making money). This student may just tolerate her classes without getting engaged in the subject matter, and she checks off requirements as quickly as she can. Too bad.

Considering Claims

Evaluating claims is one of the most basic aspects of reasoning. A claim is a statement that can be true or false, but not both. This is different from a fact, which cannot be disputed. What's the difference between a *fact* and a *claim*? Facts can't be disputed; claims can be true or false, but they must be one or the other, not both.

Kerry and Harry are not twins. Harry and his brother are twins, and they are older than Kerry.

FACT: Ronald Reagan, George H. Bush, and Bill Clinton have been presidents of the United States during the last thirty years.

CLAIM: Bill Clinton was the most popular American president in the last thirty years.

The fact is obvious. The claim requires evidence to support it. As a critical thinker, it's important to use your reasoning skills to evaluate the accuracy and authenticity of evidence. Generally speaking, be wary of claims that

> - are supported by unidentified sources ("Experts claim…").
> - are made by interested parties who stand to gain ("Brought to you by the makers of…").
> - are put forth by a lone individual claiming his experience as the norm ("I tried it and it worked for me!").
> - use a bandwagon appeal ("Everybody's doing it.").
> - mislead with statistics ("over half" when it's really only 50.5 percent).

On the other hand, we must also keep an open mind and be flexible in our thinking. If you get good evidence to support a view that contradicts yours, be willing to modify your ideas. One way to evaluate the validity of claims is to use the Critical Thinking Pyramid below. Consider claims by asking these four key questions: "who?" "what?" "why?" and "how?" Figure 5.2 shows how the questions progress from level 1 to 3.

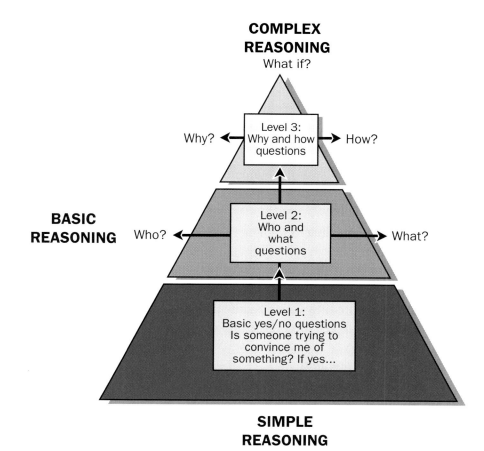

Figure 5.2

The Critical Thinking Pyramid

Source: Adapted from Hellyer, R., Robinson, C., & Sherwood, P. (1998). *Study skills for learning power.* New York: Houghton Mifflin, 18.

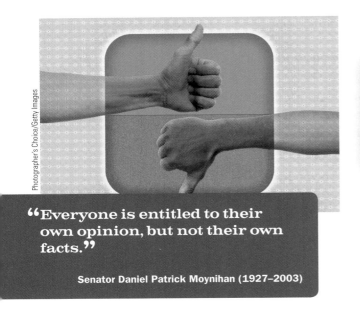

Photographer's Choice/Getty Images

"Everyone is entitled to their own opinion, but not their own facts."

Senator Daniel Patrick Moynihan (1927–2003)

Avoiding Faulty Reasoning

CHALLENGE → REACTION

Challenge: List as many reasoning mistakes as you can. Can you provide an example of one or two of them?

Reaction: _____

_____

Although we can certainly improve our critical-thinking skills, it's impossible to be a perfect critical thinker 100 percent of the time. As thinkers, we make mistakes, and sometimes others try to trick us with defective arguments. It's important to cultivate both types of critical thinking skills: your *productive* skills, which you use as a speaker and writer, and your *receptive* skills, which you use as a reader and listener. As responsible communicators, we must understand what a sound argument is and know how to construct one ourselves. We must also understand what a defective argument is in order to avoid getting sucked in when we shouldn't.

Here is a top-ten list of logical fallacies, or false logic strategies, we can slip into—or others can use against us—if we're not careful. For each of the ten types, read through the example and then see if you can come up with one of your own.

1. False cause and effect (assuming one cause for something when other causes are possible, too)

   I moved into my new dorm room last month. I've failed every exam I've taken since. Living in the residence hall is blowing my GPA!

2. Personal attack (reacting to a challenge by attacking the challenger)

   How could anyone believe Professor Courtney's views on ethics? We all know he's a very poor teacher.

3. Unwarranted assumption (taking too much for granted without evidence)

   You say universities give women equal opportunities. I say they don't. Reply: It's true. I read it on a website.

4. Emotional appeal (appealing to someone's feelings in order to gain acceptance of an argument)

   If you care about the institution that made you what you are today, you'll dig deep into your pockets and send a financial contribution now.

5. False authority (attributing your argument to someone else in a supposed position of power to get you off the hook)

   I'd really like to be able to change your grade, but my Department Chair frowns upon that.

6. Hasty conclusion (jumping to a conclusion when other conclusions are possible)

   I'm sure my roommate stole my textbook. He's too cheap to buy his own.

7. Straw man (attempting to "prove" an argument by overstating, exaggerating, or oversimplifying the arguments of the opposing side)

We should relax the entrance requirements to help attract more students. Reply: You actually want the quality of students here to take a nose dive? Oh, right, why don't we all just teach high school instead?

8. Shifting the burden of proof (shifting the responsibility of proving an assertion to someone else because you have no evidence for what you assert)

   The zero-tolerance policy on alcohol in the residence halls is working. Reply: No, it's not. Reply back: Oh yeah? Prove it.

9. Oversimplification/overgeneralization (reducing a complex issue to something very simple or stereotyping)

   College professors have it made. They teach a couple classes a week for a few hours, and then they have free time the rest of the week. That's the kind of job I want!

10. Either/or thinking (taking only an extreme position on an issue when other positions are possible)

    Either we ban alcohol on campus or we'll go bankrupt from lawsuits.

> **"To treat your facts with imagination is one thing, but to imagine your facts is another."**
>
> John Burroughs, writer on ecology
> (1837–1921)

Exercise 5.3 Rocky Mountain State University Case Study and Simulation

Great Bluffs Herald

Saturday, September 20, 2008

Cheap Beer + Fraternities = Recipe for Death

Great Bluffs, Colorado It's that time of year again. The fall semester began last month at Rocky Mountain State University, and again this year, a student died of alcohol poisoning within the first three weeks of classes. Clark Cameron of Valdosta, Georgia, a Gamma Beta Gamma pledge, was found dead yesterday morning in the GBG fraternity house on campus. The body of the collapsed student was found in a third-floor bedroom. An anonymous call to 9-1-1 came in at 6:15 a.m.: "We've got a guy here. We can't wake him, and we know he drank way too much last night." Cameron was pronounced dead on arrival at Great Bluffs General Hospital.

The incident represented RMSU's third death from alcohol poisoning in as many years. Roland Bishop, the University's new president, is said to deeply mourn the loss of another RMSU freshman. "No student should die during his first few weeks of college—what should be one of the most exciting times of his life. It's insane and very, very sad."

The national Gamma Beta Gamma office has suspended the RMSU chapter until fur-ther notice and banned its 83 members from participating in any Greek events.

Bishop will convene a cross-university panel of faculty, staff, and students to investigate the Greek system on campus and drinking privileges at all campus social functions, including athletic events. Professor Juan Cordova, Theology Department Chairperson, will head the new committee. A report with specific recommendations to President Bishop is expected by the end of the term.

Alcohol is to blame for the deaths of 1,400 college students per year, according to figures from the National Institute on Alcohol Abuse and Alcoholism. About 500,000 students between the ages of 18 and 24 are injured annually while under the influence of alcohol, more than 600,000 are assaulted by another student who has been drinking, and more than 70,000 students are victims of alcohol-related sexual assault or date rape.

Voted the number two party school in the nation, Rocky Mountain State University is known for its "party-hardy" social life. Away from home for the first time, many freshmen get swept up by the party scene. President Bishop's office indicates that moving "rush" further into the semester is one option under consideration. The president believes that students need more time to adjust to the transition from high school and get their academic careers underway. Being driven to drink, sometimes excessively, is often a "rite of passage" in sororities and fraternities, a spokesman for the President said in a telephone interview. The University will also explore creating several alcohol-free residence halls where students who want to buckle down academically can do so without fearing social pressure to party.

After this article appeared in the *Great Bluffs Herald*, many readers sent letters to the editor on September 21 and 22. Examine the following excerpts.

Trevor Ryan, RMSU Student, Denver, Colorado: "My first few weeks as a freshman at RMSU have been awesome. I knew I wanted to pledge GBG before I ever got here, and I have to say the "rush of rush" was totally cool—one of the highlights of my life so far. I'd do it all over again tomorrow. But I didn't want to join GBG just for the parties. It's an excellent organization with high academic standards. All the members say so."

Mitch Edgars, Father, Englewood, Colorado: "For me, college was a time of awakening. I had plenty of 'good times' and I want my son to do the same. You can't stop college kids from drinking. It's that simple. Sure, all college kids make mistakes. But if they're smart, they'll learn from them. I know my son pretty well, and he makes good decisions most of the time. I don't care what anybody says, experience is still the best teacher."

Carlos Cordova, RMSU Student, Brooklyn, New York: "This whole incident has been very hard on me. Clark was my roommate, and we were getting along great. I still can't believe this happened to him. Yeah, I was at the football game with him where he started drinking and then later at the frat party where he got totally wasted. But I lost him in the crowd, and I went back to the dorm around midnight. I wonder if I could have done something."

Evan Riley, RMSU Senior, Aspen, Colorado: "As president of the Interfraternity Council on campus, I feel fraternities and sororities across the country are being demonized by the press. We're not like that. We are service organizations and we participate in lots of community activities, like the Holiday Fundraiser in Great Bluffs. Last year GBG raised more money for the homeless than any other organization on campus. At a time like this, though, everybody forgets that. We become the bad guys. The University just wants someone to take the fall, and I know it's going to be us. It's unfortunate that a few irresponsible students ruin it for everyone. Ask anyone who's a member: overall, sororities and fraternities do much more good than bad. It's really not fair!"

Professor Ruby Pinnell, Biology Department, RMSU: "As a biologist, I see all the physiological damage today's college students are doing to themselves. The national study I spearheaded last year found that 31 percent of college students meet the clinical criteria for alcohol abuse, and 6 percent could be diagnosed as being alcohol-dependent. Young people don't realize that binge drinking could be risking serious damage to their brains now and actually cause increased memory loss later in adulthood. Many college males consume as many as 24 drinks in a row. These are very sad statistics."

Rufus Unser, Great Bluffs, Colorado, Citizen, Neighbor, and Voter: "I'm sick of my tax dollars going to fund institutions made up of immature college students who make bad decisions. A *Great Bluffs Herald* article published last year reported that neighbors living within one mile of college campuses are 135 percent more likely to suffer from public disturbances—also called "secondhand effects." My house is down the block from the GBG fraternity house, and sometimes the noise is so loud that I have to call the cops! Worse than that, I'm getting ready to sell my house and move into a retirement home next year. I'll bet my property values have dropped because of all the bad press! Higher education? That's a misnomer. 'Lower education' is more like it these days!"

Jim McArthur, Director, RMSU Residence Life: September is National Alcohol and Drug Addiction Recovery Month, and we're doing everything we can to help educate students about the risks of alcohol poisoning. The binge drinking problem at RMSU isn't unique, and it's not going to go away by itself. We offer weekly classes on drinking responsibly, but no one signs up for them. We put up posters about the dangers of alcohol all over campus, and we also train all of our RAs on alcohol abuse as part of their preparation for the job. They try to keep tabs on their freshmen, but to tell you the truth, I think some of the RAs drink a bit too much, too. This is society's problem, not just RMSU's."

Sergeant Rick Fuller, Great Bluffs Police Department: "I've worked in the Great Bluffs Police Department for 15 years now, and I've seen a dramatic rise in the number of arrests for alcohol possession by minors, arrests for selling alcohol to minors, and alcohol-related admissions to Great Bluffs General Hospital's ER. It's an epidemic, I'm afraid. I also know from my police work that alcohol abuse is a factor in 40 percent of violent crimes committed in the U.S."[9]

Now that you've read the story from the *Great Bluffs Herald* and the excerpts from letters to the editor, answer the following questions:

1. What are the facts relating to the alcohol problem at RMSU? How do you know they're *facts* and not *claims*?

2. Do you see logical fallacies in any of the eight letters to the editor of the *Great Bluffs Herald*? If so, which can you identify? What assumptions do the letter writers hold?

3. Identify an issue that has been generating debate on your campus, in your residence hall, or in a class. Make a list of the claims made on each side of the debate and consider each claim. Then, make a list of the arguments and evaluate each argument, looking at *relevancy* and *adequacy*. Next, list the assumptions that the arguments are based on. Finally, be creative and come up with a new approach to the issue. Is there another way to frame the debate? How can you look at the issue in an entirely different way?

II. Problem Solving: The Basic How-To's

When you have to solve a problem, your critical thinking skills should move front and center. Perhaps you need to find a way to earn more money. You run short each month, and the last few days before payday are nerve-racking. What should you do? Use a gunshot approach and try many different strategies at once or devise a more precise way to get the best results? See if the following steps make sense to you and seem like something you might actually do.

STEP 1: Define the problem. What is the exact nature of the problem you face? Defining the exact nature of the problem is something you must do if you hope to solve it. For example:

> Is it that you don't meter your spending and run out of money long before the next paycheck?

> Is it that you don't have a budget and you spend money randomly?

STEP 2: Brainstorm possible options. List all of the possible solutions you can come up with. For example:

> Eat all your meals in the residence hall instead of hitting the fast-food joints so often.

> Stop ordering in pizza four nights a week when you get the munchies at midnight.

> Ask your parents for more money. They told you to let them know when you need more.

> Look for a job that pays more. Tips at the Pancake House where you work don't really amount to much.

> Capitalize on your particular skills to earn extra money. If you're a whiz at math, you could sign on as a tutor at the Math Learning Center on campus.

STEP 3: Devise criteria to evaluate each option. For example:

> *Distance* is important. Your car isn't very reliable, so it would be good to find a job you can walk or ride your bike to.

> *Good pay* is important. In the past, you've always had low-paying jobs. You need whatever solution you arrive at to be worth your while.

> *Time* is important. You're taking a challenging load of classes, and you need to keep up your grades to keep your scholarship.

STEP 4: Evaluate each option you've proposed. For example:

> Eat all your meals in the residence hall. (This is a good idea because you've already paid for those meals, regardless of which solution you choose.)

> Stop ordering in pizza four nights a week. (This is also a good option because impromptu expenses like this can mount exponentially.)

> Ask your parents for more money. (You'd really like to avoid this option. You know they're already making sacrifices to help you through school.)

> Get a job that pays more. (Unfortunately, your campus is half an hour from the center of town where all the posh restaurants are.)

> Capitalize on your particular skills to earn extra money. (Tutors are paid more than minimum wage, and the Math Learning Center is across from your residence hall.)

STEP 5: Choose the best solution. In this case, it looks like the Math Learning Center fits the bill!

STEP 6: Plan how to achieve the best solution. When you call the Math Learning Center to find out how to apply, you discover that you need a letter of recommendation from a math professor. You e-mail your calculus professor and set up a meeting for later in the week. When the letter is ready, you call the Math Learning Center again to make an appointment to schedule an interview, and so forth.

STEP 7: Implement the solution and evaluate the results. A month or two after you take on the tutoring job, you evaluate if this solution is really the best one. You may need to request more hours or different days. Or you may find that this job leads to a better one as a Teaching Assistant for the math department. At any rate, you've used your critical thinking skills to solve a problem, systematically, logically, and effectively.

III. Decision Making: What's Your Style?

Arguments lead to decisions, and it's important to make good ones! After you've evaluated the arguments put forth, you must often do something about them. Before you know it, you'll be deciding on a major if you haven't already, a career field, a place to live, a romantic partner—you name it.

When you have an important decision to make, your critical thinking skills should kick into action. The more important the decision, chances are the more thoughtful the process of deciding should be. But people make decisions in different ways.

Alan J. Rowe and Richard O. Mason wrote a book about four basic decision-making styles used by managers. Although you may not be a manager now, think about what your style may be when you do have a position of responsibility. Here are the four styles they describe. See which one sounds as if it might describe you.

> **Directive.** This decision-making style emphasizes the here and now. Directives prefer structure and using practical data to make decisions. They look for speed, efficiency, and results, and focus on short-term fixes. Directive decision makers base their decisions on experience, facts, procedures, and rules, and they have energy and drive to get things done. On the down side, because they work quickly, they are sometimes satisfied with simplistic solutions.

> **Analytical.** This decision-making style emphasizes a logical approach. Analyticals search carefully for the best decision, and they sometimes get hung up with overanalyzing things and take too long to finally make a decision. They are sometimes considered to be impersonal because they may be more interested in the problem than in the people who have it. But they are good at working with data and doing careful analysis.

> **Conceptual.** This decision-making style emphasizes the big picture. Conceptuals are adaptable, insightful, and flexible, and they look for innovative solutions. They are sometimes too idealistic, but they take risks and are very creative.

> **Behavioral.** This decision-making style emphasizes people. Behaviorals enjoy people and the social aspects of work. They use their feelings to assess situations, communicate well, and are supportive of others. On the other hand, they are sometimes seen as wishy-washy or are criticized because they can't make hard decisions or can't say no.

Whether you're in college to prepare for a career field or retool for a new one, eventually, you will have to make important decisions on a daily basis. It's useful to begin thinking about your decision-making style now.

IV. Thinking about Your Thinking

One of the most important aspects of critical thinking is that it evaluates itself. As you're solving problems, for example, you're thinking about how you're thinking. You're assessing your progress as you go, analyzing the strengths and weaknesses in your thinking, and perhaps even coming up with better ways to do it. We call that metacognition, and that's one reason this book contains "Insight → Action" exercises—to give you opportunities to think about how you're thinking and make note of those thoughts.

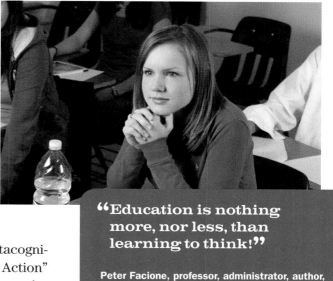

"Education is nothing more, nor less, than learning to think!"

Peter Facione, professor, administrator, author, consultant, and critical thinking expert

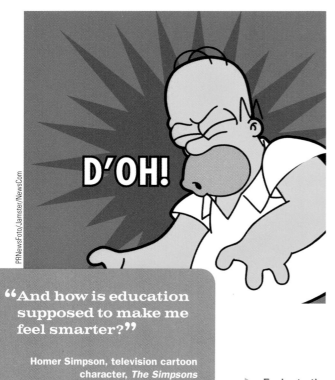

"And how is education supposed to make me feel smarter?"

Homer Simpson, television cartoon character, *The Simpsons*

Novice learners don't stop to evaluate their thinking and make revisions. Expert learners do. Actually, whenever you're faced with learning something new, metacognition involves three elements. Ultimately, these elements should become the foundation of all your learning experiences so that you improve your metacognitive skills as you go.

> Develop a plan of action. Ask yourself what you already know that can help you learn something new. What direction do you want to go in your thinking? What should be your first task? How much time should you give yourself? Talk through your plan with someone else.

> Monitor your plan. While you're working, ask yourself how you're doing. Are you staying on track? Are you moving in the right direction? Should you slow down or speed up? What should you do if you don't understand what you're doing? Keep track of what works for you and what doesn't. Assume responsibility for your own thinking and learning.

> Evaluate the plan. How well did you do? Did you do better than expected or not as well as you expected? What could you have done differently? Can you apply what you just did here to future tasks? Give yourself some feedback.[10]

Becoming a Better Critical Thinker

Sharpening your critical thinking skills is vital because these skills underlie all the others in your academic repertoire. If you think well, you will be a better writer, a better presenter, a better listener, and a better reader. You will be more likely to engage more fully in your academic tasks because you will question, probe, analyze, and monitor yourself as you learn. Here are some

---

FOCUS ON CAREERS: Harold "Hallie" Tyler, Federal Judge

Q1: What do judges do on a day-to-day basis? What are the main responsibilities of the job?
In the United States, there are a large number of judges; what they do on a daily basis can be very different. Appellate judges, for example, listen to arguments and write opinions and judgments. Trial judges do the same, but they do other things such as empanel and instruct jurors; sentence persons found guilty of criminal misconduct; and swear in new citizens (if they are trial judges in the federal system). The main responsibilities of a judge are to uphold the law, strive for fairness, and possess courage to make painful decisions based upon the law and the facts.

Q2: What are three important skills a person needs in order to be a judge?
The three most important skills of judges are: (1) the ability to critically analyze facts that are usually conflicting; (2) to write clearly but simply, and (3) to be timely in deciding cases.

Q3: How do you know you're arriving at "the truth"—or not?
The search for truth is difficult as always, but close observation of witnesses and counsel can lead to good results. Seldom is one completely satisfied that truth is forthcoming, but surprisingly, the experience of trial

suggestions for improving your skills. As you read them, think about how they pertain to you.

1. **Admit when you don't know.** If you don't know enough to think critically about something, admit it, and then find out more. With the volume of information available in today's world, we can't possibly know everything about anything. But the good news is that information is readily available. All you need to do is read, listen, point, and click to be well informed on many issues.

2. **Realize you have buttons that can be pushed.** We all have issues we're emotional about. That's normal. It's natural to feel strongly about some things, but it's also important to understand the reasons why so that you can articulate your views to someone else. And of course, realize that you're not the only one with buttons. Your teacher, roommate, significant other, boss, everyone else has them, too.

3. **Learn more about the opposition.** Many times, it's more comfortable to avoid what we don't agree with and selectively validate what we already believe. But part of being a well-educated person means learning about the history, backgrounds, values, and techniques of people you disagree with so that you can anticipate and deal with their arguments more effectively.

4. **Trust and verify.** During the cold war, President Ronald Reagan liked to quote an old Russian saying to his Soviet counterpart, Mikhail Gorbachev: "Doveryay, no proveryay," or "Trust, but verify." Being a good critical thinker means achieving a balance between blind faith and healthy skepticism.

5. **Remember that critical thinking is the cornerstone of all academic achievement.** There's nothing more important than learning to think critically. In college and in life, the skills discussed in this chapter will make you a better college student, a better citizen, a better employee, a savvier consumer, a better relational partner, and a better lifelong learner.

CREATE a Career Outlook

JUDGE

Have you ever considered a career as a judge, attorney, magistrate, or other legal professional?

Facts to Consider[11]

Academic preparation required: A bachelor's degree is required, but most workers in this career field have law degrees.

Future workforce demand: Prospects for new jobs will increase at an average rate in the future, although positions are competitive because of the status associated with serving on the bench.

Work environment: Judges apply the law in local, state, and federal courts, from minor traffic disputes to major corporate litigation. They work in law offices, law libraries, or courtrooms, directing juries on how to weigh the evidence, and then listening to their verdicts. Most judges work forty-hour weeks, but it is not uncommon to work longer hours.

Essential skills: reasoning, reading, writing, listening, researching, decision making

Questions to Ponder

1. Do you have (or could you acquire) the skills this career requires?
2. Are you interested in a career like this? Why or why not?

For more career activities online, go to http://www.cengage.com/colsuccess/staleyconcise to do the Team Career exercises.

judges enables them on occasion to discern truth from fiction because they see and hear the witnesses and the lawyers.

Q4: What advice would you give college students who are considering a legal career?
College students interested in a possible law career should be good readers, particularly of history; biographies of lawyers, judges, and statesmen; and the humanities. For my part, a course in the "dead languages," Latin and Greek, was helpful.

1. Provide real examples of critical thinking from any of your current classes. Are you being asked on exams to compare and contrast? To sort through evidence and make decisions? In class discussions are you encouraged to disagree with your instructor or classmates for the sake of a healthy, vigorous debate?

2. Can you describe your own intellectual progress as a critical thinker? Based on what you've read in this chapter, what can you do to strengthen your critical thinking skills?

Unleash Your Creativity!

Whether you're eighteen or eighty-one, it's safe to say that your life has been changed by an unending stream of new inventions. Which of the following have come into existence during your lifetime? PDAs? Microsoft Windows? PlayStation? DVDs? Microwavable mac and cheese? Cell phones? IMAX movies? The artificial heart? High-speed Internet? Side-impact air bags? Singer Bob Dylan crooned memorable words in 1964: "The times, they are a-changin'." He was right then, and it's still true now.

Creativity affects us all. It's true that some of these items haven't made a big impact. But other inventions affect you every single day. In his bestselling book, *The Rise of the Creative Class*, Richard Florida notes that in 1900, less than 10 percent of American workers were doing creative work. Farms and factories were most people's work sites. Eighty years later, the figure had only risen to 20 percent. But today, a full third of our working population engages in employment that gets their creative juices flowing, whether they're artists, designers, writers, analysts, musicians, or entrepreneurs. The creative sector of our economy accounts for nearly half of all wage and salary income—$1.7 trillion per year. Today's "no collar" workplace is fueled by creativity. And Florida says, we've barely scratched the surface. Human creativity is virtually limitless.[12]

Diversity in our surroundings is one thing that increases the potential for creativity. Creativity comes in all sizes, ethnicities, preferences, and genders. If you're around other open-minded, flexible, tolerant, forward-looking, innovative people, you're more likely to live up to your own creative potential. And in case you're wondering, you don't have to be an artist to be creative. Creativity simply means finding new and better ways to do things. In many ways, it's a choice you make; you *decide* to be creative.[13]

What does all this have to do with you as an entering college student? Florida says that the rise of the creative sector has also changed the way people work and their expectations. No longer are many Americans' aspirations to make a million dollars and buy the house of their dreams. It's about having enough money to be comfortable while doing enjoyable, interesting, and creative work. The best people in any field aren't motivated solely by money. They are motivated by passion for what they do.

> "If you have an apple and I have an apple and we exchange these apples, then you and I will still each have one apple. But if you have an idea and I have an idea and we exchange these ideas, then each of us will have two ideas."
>
> George Bernard Shaw, Irish literary critic, playwright, and essayist, 1925 Nobel Prize for Literature (1856–1950)

Creativity: "Thinking Outside the ... Book"

Do you believe this statement? *Everyone has creative potential.* It's true. Most of us deny it, however. "Me, creative? Nah!" We're often unaware of the untapped ability we have to think creatively. Try this experiment. Look at the following list of words, and divide the list into two (and only two) different categories, using any criteria you devise. Take a few moments and see what you come up with.

> **"A mind that is stretched to a new idea never returns to its original dimensions."**
>
> **Oliver Wendell Holmes, American poet (1809–1894)**

dog, salad, book, grasshopper, kettle, paper, garbage, candle

Whenever this experiment is tried, people always come up with very creative categories. They may divide the words into things that you buy at a store (dog, salad, kettle, paper, candle), things that move on their own (dog, grasshopper), things that have a distinct smell (dog, candle, garbage), words that have two consonants, and so forth. People never say it can't be done; they always *invent* categories. Interesting, isn't it? Our minds are hungry for the stimulation of a creative challenge.

The fact is that intelligence has more to do with coming up with the right answer, and creative thinking has more to do with coming up with multiple right answers. Often we get so focused on the *right* answer that we rush to find it instead of exploring all the possibilities. Creative thinking is thinking outside the box, or in terms of getting an education, perhaps we should call it thinking outside the book. Going beyond the obvious and exploring possibilities are important parts of becoming an educated person. Employers report that many college graduates today have specific skills, but that what they rarely see "is the ability to use the right-hand side of the brain—creativity, working in a team."[14]

In Figure 5.2 we looked at the Critical Thinking Pyramid. Creative thinking is at the top of the pyramid: What if? It goes beyond critical thinking. It is predictive and multidimensional. It asks "What if ...?" questions. Here are some interesting ones: "What if everyone was allowed to tell one lie per day?" "What if no one could perceive colors?" "What if universities didn't exist?" "If you looked up a word like *squallizmotex* in the dictionary, what might it mean?"[15]

According to creativity expert Alan Rowe, our creative intelligence demonstrates itself in four major styles. Each of us has aspects of all four styles of creativity.

> **Intuitive.** This creative style is best described as *resourceful.* If you are an Intuitive, you achieve goals, use common sense, and work to solve problems. You focus on results and rely on past experience to guide your actions. Managers, actors, and politicians are commonly Intuitives.

> **Innovative.** This creative style is best described as *curious.* Innovatives concentrate on problem solving, are systematic, and rely on data. They use original approaches, are willing to experiment, and focus on systematic inquiry. Scientists, engineers, and inventors typically demonstrate the Innovative creative style.

> **Imaginative.** This creative style is best described as *insightful.* Imaginatives are willing to take risks, have leaps of imagination, and are independent thinkers. They are able to visualize opportunities, are artistic, enjoy writing, and think outside the box. Artists, musicians, writers, and charismatic leaders are often Imaginatives.

> **Inspirational.** This creative style is best described as *visionary.* Inspirationals respond to societal needs, willingly give of themselves, and have the courage of their convictions. They focus on social change and the giving of themselves toward achieving it. They are often educators, motivational leaders, and writers.[16]

Which do you think is your predominant style? Think about how you can make the best use of your natural style. How will your creativity affect the major or career you choose? Most people have more than one creative style. Remember that motivation, not general intelligence, is the key to creativity. You must be willing to tap your creative potential and challenge yourself to show it.[17]

Ten Ways to Become a More Creative Thinker

Becoming a more creative thinker may mean you need to accept your creativity and cultivate it. Consider these suggestions on how to think more creatively.

1. **Find new eyes.** Find a new perspective on old issues. Here's an interesting example. Years ago, a group of Japanese schoolchildren devised a new way to solve conflicts and build empathy for others' positions, called the Pillow Method. Figure 5.3 is an adaptation of it, based on the fact that a pillow has four sides and a middle, just like most problems.

   The middle or *mu* is the Zen expression for "it doesn't really matter." There is truth in all four positions. Try it: take a conflict you're having difficulty with at the moment, and write down all four sides and a middle.[18]

2. **Accept your creativity.** Many mindsets block creative thinking: "It can't be done!" "I'm just not the creative type." "I might look stupid!" Many people don't see themselves as creative. This perception can become a major stumbling block. If creativity isn't part of your self-image, you may need to revamp your image. Everyone has creative potential. You may just have to learn how to tap into yours.

3. **Make your thoughts visible.** For many of us, things become clear when we can see them, either in our mind's eye or displayed for us. Even Einstein, a sci-

Figure 5.3

The Pillow Method

Position 1—I'm right and you're wrong.
Position 2—You're right and I'm wrong.
Position 3—We're both right.
Position 4—We're both wrong.

entist and mathematician, had a very visual mind. Sometimes if we write something down or sketch something out, we generate a new approach without really trying.

4. **Generate lots of ideas.** Thomas Edison held 1,093 patents, still the record. He gave himself idea quotients. The rule he set for himself was that he had to come up with a major invention every six months and a minor invention every ten days. Bach wrote a cantata every week, even if he was ill.

5. **Don't overcomplexify.** In hindsight, many of the most ingenious discoveries are embarrassingly simple. Biologist Thomas Huxley said, after reading Darwin's explanation of evolution: "How extremely stupid not to have thought of that!" But sometimes the most simple solution is the best one.[19]

6. **Capitalize on your mistakes.** Remember that Thomas Edison tried anything he could think of for a filament for the incandescent lamp, including a whisker from his best friend's beard. All in all, he tried about 1,800 things before finding the right one. Afterwards he said, "I've gained a lot of knowledge—I now know a thousand things that won't work."[20]

7. **Let it flow.** Mihaly Csikszentmihalyi, the author of *Flow: The Psychology of Optimal Experience* and many other books on creativity, discovered something interesting. For his doctoral thesis, he studied artists by taking pictures of them painting every three minutes. He was struck by how engaged they were in their work, so engaged that they seemed to forget everything around them. He began studying other "experts": rock climbers, chess players, dancers, musicians, surgeons. Regardless of the activity, these people forgot the time, themselves, and their problems. What did the activities have in common? Clear, high goals and immediate feedback. Athletes call it being in the zone. The zone is described as the ultimate human experience, where mind and body are united in purpose. Csikszentmihalyi's suggestions for achieving flow are these: Pick an enjoyable activity that is at or slightly above your ability level, screen out distractions, focus all your senses and emotions, and look for regular feedback on how you're doing.[21]

8. **Bounce ideas off others.** One good way to become more creative is to use your family or friends as sounding boards. Sometimes just verbalizing something helps you understand more about it. Each person who provides a critique will give you a new perspective, possibly worth considering.

9. **Stop searching for the "right" answer.** This advice doesn't pertain to your upcoming math exam. But it does to apply to situations in which there are many ways to solve a problem. There may be more than one acceptable solution. Fear of mistakes can be debilitating.

10. **Detach your self-concept.** For most of us, creativity is often linked to self-concept. An idea is your brainchild, and you want it to win approval. You've invested part of yourself in giving birth to it. But there's nothing like self-imposed judgment to shut down your creative juices. Your idea may not succeed on its own, but it may feed into someone else's idea and improve it. Or an idea you have about this problem may inform the next problem that challenges you. In the end, in addition to finding a workable solution, what's important is engaging in the creative process with others.

"A hunch is creativity trying to tell you something."

Frank Capra, Italian American film director (1897–1991)

1. Do you see yourself as a creative person? Instead of thinking about whether you're creative or not, ask yourself this question, "*How* am I creative?"

2. Select two of the ten ways to become a more creative thinker suggested in this chapter, and write a statement about future actions based on these recommendations.

EXERCISE 5.4 VARK Activity

Complete the recommended activity for your preferred VARK learning modality. If you are multimodal, select more than one activity. Your instructor may ask you to (a) give an oral report on your results in class, (b) send your results to him or her via e-mail, (c) post them online, or (d) contribute to a class chat.

 Visual: Use the white space in this chapter or sticky notes to record insights about how the chapter applies to you. Note which section of the chapter contains the most personal applications for you.

 Aural: Talk through this chapter with a classmate or friend or read through your notes on this chapter aloud.

 Read/Write: Read a newspaper article on a current controversy perhaps involving college students, such as alcohol poisoning, and summarize the article's main points.

 Kinesthetic: Ask a friend to help you videotape interviews with other students on campus. Ask individual students if they see themselves as creative and why or why not. Show your production in class.

Ⓒ CHALLENGE Yourself Quizzes For more practice online, go to http://www.cengage .com/colsuccess/staleyconcise to take the Challenge Yourself online quizzes.

 NOW WHAT DO YOU THINK?

At the beginning of this chapter, Annie Miller, a frustrated student, faced a challenge. Now after reading this chapter, would you respond differently to any of the questions you answered about the "FOCUS Challenge Case"?

REALITY CHECK

On a scale of 1 to 10, answer these questions now that you've completed this chapter.

1 = not very/not much/very little/low   10 = very/a lot/very much/high

In hindsight, how much did you *really* know about this subject matter before reading the chapter?

1   2   3   4   5   6   7   8   9   10

How much do you think this information might affect your college success?

1   2   3   4   5   6   7   8   9   10

How much do you think this information might affect your career success after college?

1   2   3   4   5   6   7   8   9   10

How long did it actually take you to complete this chapter (both the reading and writing tasks)? _____ Hour(s) _____ Minutes

Compare these answers to your answers from the "Readiness Check" at the beginning of this chapter. How might the gaps between what you thought before starting the chapter and what you now think affect how you approach the next chapter?

 To download mp3 format audio summaries of this chapter, go to http://www.cengage.com/colsuccess/staleyconcise.

6 Engaging, Listening, and Note-Taking in Class

YOU'RE ABOUT TO DISCOVER...

- How to get engaged in class

- How to listen with focus

- How to vary your listening styles according to lecture styles

- How to ask questions in class

- How to take good notes

- How to use your notes to achieve the best results

READINESS CHECK

Before beginning this chapter, take a moment to answer these questions. Your answers will help you assess how ready you are to focus.

1 = not very/not much/very little/low   10 = very/a lot/very much/high

Based on reading the "You're about to discover..." list and skimming this chapter, how much do you think you probably already know about the subject matter?

1   2   3   4   5   6   7   8   9   10

How much do you think this information might affect your college success?

1   2   3   4   5   6   7   8   9   10

How much do you think this information might affect your career success after college?

1   2   3   4   5   6   7   8   9   10

In general, how motivated are you to learn the material in this chapter?

1   2   3   4   5   6   7   8   9   10

How ready are you to focus on this chapter—physically, intellectually, and emotionally? Circle a number for each aspect of your readiness to focus.

1   2   3   4   5   6   7   8   9   10

If any of your answers are below a 5, consider addressing the issue before reading. For example, if you're feeling scattered, take a few moments to settle down and focus.

Finally, how long do you think it will take you to complete this chapter? _____ Hour(s) _____ Minutes

Lindsey Collier

It was Lindsey Collier's first trip

home since classes started. Thanksgiving! In addition to the family's traditional feast, she was eager to see her eight-year-old sister, her brother who was a sophomore in high school, and her parents. After she left home, she began to appreciate her family more than ever. What great people they are, she kept thinking. Still, she wondered: Will they be glad to see me? Will I fit back into the family? Will Mom have converted my bedroom into a guest room? Will Dad still want to watch our favorite TV shows together? A million questions were running through her mind. Even though they talked on the phone and sent e-mails and text messages nearly every day, actually seeing her family for the first time in three months was going to seem strange. She imagined that Max, the family's golden retriever, would be the first one to greet her. She expected to miss him, but not this much!

She knew one thing for sure: Her parents would ask questions about how her classes were going. *Pretty well*, she thought. She'd gotten a B+ on her English paper, a B on her first math exam, an A on her College Success "Academic Autobiography," and an A− on her philosophy paper. But then there was her computer science course. That was a different story.

Her computer science instructor was a graduate teaching assistant. This was his first experience teaching a college course, he had announced on the first day of class, and English was his second language. His lectures were jam-packed with information that went right over Lindsey's head. Take last Wednesday's lecture, for example:

The real beginning of modern computers goes back to the seventeenth century and intellectual giants such as Descartes, Pascal, Leibnitz, and Napier. In mathematics, particularly, tremendous progress was made in revolutionizing how people saw the world, and their calculations became so laborious that they needed a more sophisticated computing machine.

The development of logarithms by the Scottish mathematician John Napier in 1614 stimulated the invention of the various devices that substituted the addition of logarithms for multiplication. Napier published his great work of logarithms in the book called *Rabdologia*. This was a remarkable invention since it enabled people to transform multiplication and division into simple addition and subtraction. His logarithm tables soon

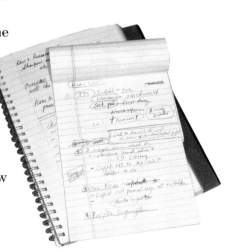

came into widespread use. Napier is often remembered more by another invention of his, nicknamed "Napier's Bones." This was a small instrument constructed of 10 rods, on which were engraved the multiplication tables. They are referred to as bones because the first set was made from ivory and resembled a set of bones. This simple device enabled people to carry out multiplication quickly if one of the numbers was only one digit (*i.e.*, $6 \times 6,742$).

The invention of logarithms led directly to the development of the slide rule. The first slide rule appeared in 1650 and was the result of the joint effort of two Englishmen, Edmund Gunter and the Reverend William Oughtred. The principle behind this device is one of two scales moving against each other. This invention was dormant until 1850 when a French Artillery officer, Amédée Mannheim, added the movable double-sided cursor, which gave it its appearance as we know it today. They gave it the name "astrolabe" because of its astronomical uses. The astrolabe was the true forerunner of the modern slide rule.[1]

Lindsey tried to pay attention to his words and copy down the writing scribbled all over the board, but no matter how hard she tried, her mind seemed to drift to the new guy she'd just met. Information seemed to fly out of her instructor's mouth at mach speed, and frankly, she used her instructor's accent as an excuse. Taking notes that quickly was just plain impossible. She tried giving him quizzical looks to communicate "Slow down, please," but he probably couldn't see her face in the back row.

Since nothing the professor said caught her interest, she knew that asking questions in class would only prove that she wasn't paying attention. Trying to read and take notes from the textbook chapters *before* class took more discipline than she could muster. Her usual strategy was to look like she was paying attention in class so that no one knew that her brain wasn't really there.

Lindsey had thought about trying to stop in during his office hours some morning, but she worked off-campus as a breakfast server at a local restaurant. She could try making an appointment with him, she thought, but was he really willing to meet with every single student who had a scheduling conflict? *That's why he has office hours*, she told herself. And after all, he was working hard at the same time to earn an advanced degree himself. Besides, did she really want to discuss how poorly she was doing? It was too late in the term to drop the class, and she needed the credits for financial aid. Still, she had to figure something out or computer science was going to blow her GPA and her parents' good opinion of her.

WHAT DO YOU THINK?

Now that you've read about Lindsey Collier, answer the following questions. You may not know all the answers yet, but you'll find out what you know and what you stand to gain by reading this chapter.

1. List five mistakes Lindsey is making.
2. Now list five things that Lindsey should do immediately to improve her computer science classroom experience.

Get Engaged in Class

CHALLENGE ⟶ REACTION

Challenge: What is *engagement*? Exactly what does it take to become engaged in class?

Reaction: _____

No, this chapter isn't about buying a ring and getting down on one knee. It's about your willingness to focus, listen, discuss, ask questions, take notes, and generally dive into your classes. It's about being a full participant in what you're learning, not just a spectator sitting on the sidelines. It's about not just memorizing information for exams and then forgetting it. You see, the secret to college success hinges on this one word: *engagement*.

Think about this analogy. How did you learn to swim? Did you read books about swimming? Did you get advice from your friends about swimming? No, you probably jumped in and got wet, right? The same thing is true with your college classes. The more willing you are to jump in and get wet, the more engaged you'll be in the learning process.

> **"What actually correlates with success are not grades, but 'engagement'—genuine involvement in courses and campus activities. Engagement leads to 'deep learning,' or learning for understanding. That's very different from just memorizing stuff for an exam, then forgetting it."**
>
> **John Merrow, reporter, *USA Today***

Dare to Prepare

If you want to get a head start on developing good academic habits in class, then start before you get there. Preparation separates students into two categories: those who excel at learning and those who don't. Although not all students see the value of preparation, do more than your classmates do—dare to prepare! Follow these suggestions and you'll find that it's easier to get engaged in class because you're ready.

1. Look ahead. By checking your course syllabus before class, you'll be prepared for the upcoming topic. You'll also avoid the "oops" factor of sitting down, looking around, and noticing that everyone else knows something you don't about what's supposed to happen today.

2. Do the assigned reading. If you have a reading assignment due for class, do it, and take notes as you read. Write in the margins of your textbook or on sticky notes. Question what you're reading and enter into a mental dialogue with the author. Having some background on the topic will allow you to listen more actively and participate more intelligently during any discussion: *Yes, I*

remember the chapter covering that topic, you'll think when the instructor begins talking about something you recognize. Instead of hearing it for the first time, you'll *reinforce* what you've already read. According to one study, as few as one-third of your classmates will have done the assigned reading prior to class. That factoid isn't a reason to excuse yourself from reading; instead it gives you insider information on how *you* can shine in class by comparison.[2]

3. Show up physically. Not only is attending class important for your overall understanding of the material, but it may move your grade up a few notches. Even if attendance isn't required by your instructor, require it of yourself. Research says that missing classes is definitely related to your academic performance. And once you give yourself permission to skip one single, solitary class, it becomes easier to do it the next time, and the time after that. Studies indicate that on any given day, approximately one-third of your classmates will miss class, and that most students think that several absences during a term is "the standard." Exercise good judgment, even if your classmates don't!

4. Show up mentally. Showing up means more than just occupying a seat in the classroom. It means assessing what you bring to the class as a learner on any particular day. Do a mental "Readiness Check" when you arrive in class. If you're not ready, what can you do to rally for the cause?

5. Choose your seat strategically. Imagine paying $150 for a concert ticket, just like everyone else, and then electing to sit in the nosebleed section as high up and far away from the action as you could get. Sitting in the back means you're more likely to let your mind wander and less likely to hear clearly. Sitting in the front means you'll keep yourself accountable by being in full view of the instructor and the rest of the class. What's the best spot for great

concentration? Front and center, literally—the "T zone"! In one study, students who sat at the back of a large auditorium were six times more likely to fail the course, even though the instructor had assigned seats randomly![3]

6. **Bring your tools.** Bring a writing utensil and notebook with you to every class. Your instructor may also ask you to bring your textbook, calculator, a blue book for an exam, or other necessary items. If so, do it. Question: how seriously would you take a carpenter who showed up to work without a hammer, nails, and screwdriver? Get the point?

7. **Don't sit by your best friend.** Resist the temptation to sit next to your best buddy in order to catch up during class. Of course, it's important to have friends, but class is hardly the best time to devote yourself to helping your friendship blossom.

8. **Posture counts!** Your parents may have told you more than once as a kid: "Sit up straight!" Sitting up straight in class will help you develop a healthy mind. It's hard to focus when you're slouched into a position that screams, "I could really use a power nap about now!" When your body says, "I'm ready to learn," your mind follows suit.

9. **Maintain your health.** Being sick can wreak havoc on your ability to concentrate, listen well, and participate. Take the preventative approach by getting enough sleep, eating well, and exercising. Remember, *energy management* is key to your ability to focus.

10. **Focus.** After sitting down in class each day, take a moment to clear your head of all daydreams, to-do's, and worries. Take a deep breath and remind yourself of the opportunity to learn that lies ahead. Think of yourself as a reporter at a press conference, listening intently because you'll be writing a story about what's going on. You *will* be writing a "story"—often in response to an essay question on an exam!

Follow the Rules of Engagement

Just as is the case with most places you can think of, college classrooms have rules about how to behave. You don't find people yelling in church or staring at other people in elevators or telling jokes at funerals. There are rules about how to behave in a variety of contexts, and college classrooms are no exception.

1. **Be aware that gab is not a gift.** In class, gabbing while others are speaking is inappropriate. And it's certainly not a gift—especially to your instructor. In fact, side conversations while your professor is lecturing or your classmates are contributing to the discussion is downright rude. If you're seated next to a gabber, don't get sucked in. Use body language to communicate that you're there to learn, not to gab. If that's not enough, politely say something like, "I really need to pay attention right now. Let's talk more later, okay?" Don't let other students cheat you out of learning.

2. **Control your hunger pangs.** If your class meets through a meal hour, get in the habit of eating before or after class. Crunching and munching in the classroom may get in the way of others' learning, not to mention the distraction caused

by enticing smells. Instructors differ on their preferences here. It's a good idea to find out what your instructors' preferences are, and then abide by them.

3. **Turn off your cell phone, please!** There's a reason why people are asked to turn off their cell phones before concerts, athletic events, or movies. Imagine being in a jam-packed theater trying to follow the film's plot with cell phones going off every few seconds. You've paid good money to see a film. The same thing goes for your college classes.

4. **Better late than never?** Students arriving late and leaving early are annoying, not only to your instructor, but to your classmates. To them, it looks like you don't value the other students or the class content. How would you like dinner guests to arrive an hour late, after you'd slaved over a hot stove all day? Your instructors have prepared for class, and they feel the same way. Build in time to find a parking place, hike to the building where class is held, or stop for a coffee. Do everything you can to avoid coming late and leaving early.

5. **Actively choose to engage, not disengage.** Engagement isn't something that just happens to you while you're not looking. It's a choice you make, and sometimes it's a difficult choice because the material isn't naturally appealing to you, or the course is a required one you didn't choose, or you're just plain out of sorts. Choose to engage, anyway. Instead of actively choosing to *dis*engage in class by sleeping through lectures, surfing the Internet, or instant messaging friends, choose to engage by leaning forward, processing information, finding your own ways to connect to the material, and formulating questions to ask.

"Politeness is the art of choosing among one's real thoughts."

Adlai Stevenson II, U.S. Presidential candidate (1900–1965)

INSIGHT → ACTION

1. Look over the ten Dare to Prepare suggestions. Which of the suggestions do you find most difficult to do? For which of your classes?

2. What can you do to increase your own engagement in the classroom?

Listening with Focus

CHALLENGE → REACTION

Challenge: What is *focused listening*? How can you achieve it?

Reaction: _____

Listening with focus is more than just physically hearing words as they stream by. It's actually a complicated process that's hard work.

"Easy Listening" Is for Elevators— Focused Listening Is for Classrooms

Stores, restaurants, and elevators are known for their programmed, background easy listening music. Chances are you hardly notice it's there. Listening in class, however, requires actual skill, and you'll be doing a great deal of it as a college student. Experts estimate that the average student spends 80 percent of class time listening to lectures.[4]

Many of us naively believe that listening is easy to do. If you happen to be around when there's something to listen to, you can't help but listen. Not so! Did you know that when you're listening at your best, your respiration rate, heartbeat, and body temperature all increase? Just as with aerobic exercise, your body works harder when you're engaging in focused listening. When all is said and done, listening is really about energy management. You can't listen well when your energy is zapped, when you've pulled the mother of all all-nighters, or when your stomach is growling with a vengeance. Focused listening means that you've cleared the deck for class, and you're focusing on engagement.

Here are some techniques for improving your listening skills in the classroom. Read through the list, then go back and check off the ones you're willing to try harder to do in class this week.

☐ **Calm yourself.** Take a few deep breaths with your eyes closed to help you put all those nagging distractions on the back burner during class time.

☐ **Be open.** Keep an open mind and view your class as yet another opportunity to strengthen your intellect and learn something new. Wisdom comes from a broad understanding of many things, rather than from a consistently limited focus on practical information.

☐ **Don't make snap judgments.** Remember, you don't have to like your instructor's wardrobe to respect his knowledge. Focus on the content he's offering you. You may not even agree with what he's saying, but he may be leading up to a point you can't predict and turn the argument around. Don't jump to conclusions about content *or* style.

☐ **Assume responsibility.** Speak up! Ask questions! Even if you have a professor with an accent who's difficult to understand, the burden of clarification rests with you. You will interact with people with all sorts of accents, voices, and speech patterns throughout your life. It's up to you to improve the situation.

☐ **Watch for gestures that communicate "Here comes something important!"** Some typical examples include raising an index finger, turning to face the class, leaning forward from behind the podium, walking up the aisle, or using specific facial expressions or gestures.

☐ **Listen for speech patterns that subtly communicate "Make sure you include this in your notes!"** For example, listen for changes in the rate, volume, or tone of speech, longer than usual pauses, or repeated information.

- ☐ **Uncover general themes or roadmaps for each lecture.** See if you can figure out where your instructor is taking you *while* he's taking you there. Always ask yourself, "Where's he going with this? What's he getting at? How does this relate to what was already said?"

- ☐ **Appreciate your instructor's prep time.** For every hour of lecture time, your teacher has worked for hours to prepare. Although she may make it look easy, her lecture has involved researching, organizing, creating a PowerPoint presentation, overheads, or a podcast, and preparing notes and handouts.

Listening Is More Than Hearing

Perhaps you've never thought about it, but, actually, listening and hearing aren't the same thing. Hearing—the physiological part—is only the first stage of a four-stage process. Listening is a much more complex process—especially *focused listening*, or listening at your best. The four stages of focused listening are:

1. Sensing: receiving the sounds through your auditory system. As you sit in class, sound waves enter your ears and register in your brain.

2. Interpreting: understanding the message. Sounds themselves don't mean anything until you assign meaning to them. Instead of just random noise, the instructor's message must mean something to you.

3. Evaluating: weighing evidence. You decide if something is true or important by sorting fact from opinion. Both interpretation and evaluation in class may involve asking questions to clarify things.

4. Responding: providing feedback or taking action. You respond by participating in the discussion, asking significant questions, and taking down clear, meaningful notes to study later.[5]

As you're listening in class, you must cycle through all four of these stages. You must *sense* the sound waves coming from your instructor, a classmate, or a guest speaker, *interpret* them, *evaluate* them, and *respond* by jumping into the discussion yourself, asking questions, and taking the best notes you can. If you're not focused, it's possible to skip a step or "listen out of order." You may take notes without really *interpreting* what you're hearing. You're operating on autopilot—you skip the interpretation step completely, and write down things you don't really understand. (And consequently, you can't interpret your notes later.) Or you may try and write down every word you hear without *evaluating* its importance, getting bogged down in insignificant detail.

Listen Hard!

It's estimated that college students spend ten hours per week listening to lectures.[6] Professors can speak 2,500–5,000 words during a fifty-minute lecture. That's a lot of words flying by at breakneck speed, so it's important to listen correctly. But what does *that* mean?

Think about the various situations in which you find yourself listening. You often listen to empty chit-chat on your way to class. "Hey, how's it going?" when you spot your best friend in the hallway is an example, right? Listening in this type of situation doesn't require a lot of brainpower. Although you wouldn't want to spend too much time on chit-chat, if you refused to engage in any at all, you'd probably be seen by others as odd, withdrawn, shy, or arrogant.

You also listen in challenging situations, some that are emotionally charged; for example, a friend needs to vent, relieve stress, or verbalize her anxieties. Most people who are blowing off steam aren't looking for you to fix their problems. They just want to be heard and to hear something from you like "I understand" or "That's too bad."

Listening to chit-chat and listening in emotionally charged situations require what are called soft listening skills. You must be accepting, sensitive, and nonjudgmental. You don't have to assess, analyze, or conclude. You just have to be there for someone else.

But these two types of listening situations don't describe all the kinds of listening you do. When you're listening to new information, as you do in your college classes, or when you're listening to someone trying to persuade you of something, you have to pay close attention, think critically, and ultimately make decisions about what you're hearing. Is something true or false? Right or wrong? How do you know? When you're listening to a person dispersing information or someone trying to persuade you, you need hard listening skills. In situations like these you must be discerning, analytical, and decisive.

One mistake many students make in class is listening the wrong way. They should be using their hard listening skills, rather than sitting back and letting information waft over them. Soft listening skills don't help you in class. You must listen intently, think critically, and analyze carefully what you're hearing. It's important to note that neither listening mode is better than the other. They are each simply better suited to different situations. But soft listening won't get you the results you want in your classes. You don't need to be there for your instructor; you need to be there for yourself.[7]

You may find many of your classes to be naturally fascinating learning experiences. But for others, you will need to be convinced. Even if you don't find Intro to Whatever to be the most engaging subject in the world, you may find yourself intrigued by your instructor. Most people are interested in other people. What makes him tick? Why was she drawn to this field? If you find it hard to get interested in the material, trick yourself by paying attention to the person delivering the message. Sometimes focusing on something about the speaker can help you focus on the subject matter, too. And you may just find out that you actually do find this class to be valuable. While tricking yourself isn't always a good idea, it *can* work if you know what you're doing and why.

Get Wired for Sound

Increasingly professors are providing podcasts and videocasts of their lectures so that you can *preview* the lecture in advance or *review* it after class. Some textbooks (like this one) offer chapter summaries you can listen to on the subway, in the gym, at home during a blizzard, or in bed while recovering from the flu via your computer or digital-audio player.

Regardless of your learning style, recorded lectures allow you to re-listen to difficult concepts as many times as needed. You can take part in the live action in class and take notes later while re-listening to the podcast. In one study, students who re-listened to a lecture one, two, or three times increased their lecture notes substantially each time.[8] Of course, recorded lectures aren't meant to excuse you from attending class, and in order to take advantage of them, you actually have to find time to listen to them. They're supplemental tools to *reinforce* learning for busy students on the go, which is virtually *everyone* these days.[9]

Identify Lecture Styles So You Can Modify Listening Styles

Regardless of how challenging it is to listen with focus, being successful in college will require you to do just that—focus—no matter what class or which professor. Sometimes your instructors are *facilitators*, who help you discover information on your own in new ways. Other times they are *orators*, who lecture as their primary means of delivering information. If you're not an aural learner, listening with focus to lectures will be a challenge for you.

> "The most basic and powerful way to connect to another person is to listen. Just listen. Perhaps the most important thing we ever give each other is our attention."
>
> **Rachel Naomi Remen, physician and author**

Chances are you won't be able to change your professors' lecturing styles. And even if you could, different students react differently to different lecture styles. But what you can do is expand your own skills as a listener—no matter what class or which instructor. Take a look at the lecture styles coming up and see if you recognize them.

> The Rapid-Fire Lecturer: You may have found yourself in a situation like Lindsey's with an instructor who lectures at breakneck speed. Listening and taking notes in a class like this are not easy. By the end of class your hand aches from gripping your pen and writing furiously. Since there'll be no time to relax, you'll need to make certain you're ready for this class by taking all the suggestions in this chapter to heart. Read ahead so that you recognize points the instructor makes. Also take advantage of whatever supplementary materials this teacher provides in the way of audio support, online lecture notes, or PowerPoint handouts.

> The Slow-Go Lecturer: Instead of rushing, some lecturers move very slowly. They contemplate, ruminate, and chew on every word before uttering it. This lecturer proceeds so slowly that there are pauses—seconds long—between phrases, while he paces back and forth, pontificating. Your attention tends to drift because you become impatient and stop listening. Instead, discipline yourself to use the extra time to your advantage by predicting what's coming next or by clarifying what's just been said in your own mind.

> The All-Over-the-Map Lecturer: Organization is not this lecturer's strong suit. While the lecture may be organized in the lecturer's mind, what comes out is difficult to follow. In this case, it will be up to you to organize the lecture content yourself.

> **The Content-Intensive Lecturer:** This lecturer is hardly aware that anyone else is in the room, intent on covering a certain amount of material in a particular amount of time. This teacher may use extensive discipline-specific jargon that you will need to learn rapidly to keep abreast. Prepare yourself for a potentially rich learning environment, but be sure to ask questions right away if you find yourself confused.

> **The Review-the-Text Lecturer:** This lecturer will follow the textbook closely, summarizing and highlighting important points. You may assume it's not important to attend class, but watch out for this trap! Receiving the same information in more than one format can be a great way to learn.

> **The Go-Beyond-the-Text Lecturer:** This lecturer will use class time to provide examples, tell stories, and bring in outside materials. Keeping up with reading in the text will be important so that you understand the additional information that you receive in class.

> **The Active-Learning Lecturer:** This lecturer may choose not to lecture at all or to intersperse short lectures with activities, role plays, or simulations. While you may find it easier to get engaged in class, and you'll most likely appreciate the teacher's creativity, remember that you are still responsible for connecting what happens in class to the course material itself. You will need to read, digest, and process the information on your own outside of class.

C CULTIVATE Your Curiosity

QUIET YOUR MIND!

Have you ever noticed there's a play-by-play commentary going on inside your head, just like an NFL announcer during a big game: "On third down with no timeouts left. And here's the snap ... rookie Davis Jones busts off tackle for an eight-yard gain! It's close to a first down...." Compare that to your own play-by-play observations: "And here he comes ... Matt's walking straight toward me. He's getting closer. Maybe this is my big chance."

It's normal to comment internally about what's going on around you, and it's perfectly human to think that your own internal dialogue is the most important thing on the planet. Most of us do. The question isn't whether or not you're engaged in constant conversation with yourself; it's whether that conversation is productive and useful, and if not, how to make it so.

Sometimes this incessant, internal chatter makes it's hard to be fully present in class because of three P's: **p**ressure, **p**reoccupation, and **p**riorities. While you're sitting there, you feel a rush of stress about your upcoming assignments; you worry about a sick relative you should attend to; and you obsess about whether you should tackle your calculus homework first tonight or start on your philosophy research paper. You feel overwhelmed.

Part of the problem you face trying to listen in class is fundamental to the listening process itself. People listen at a rate of 125–250 words per minute, but think at a rate of 1,000–3,000 words per minute. Where does your mind typically go during the extra time between listening and thinking?

In his book *Quiet Your Mind*, author John Selby reports that we can learn better control over our thoughts, and that the psychological and physiological benefits are well worth it.[10] Here are some tips to coach yourself to quiet your mind:

- **Choose where to focus your attention.** Instead of allowing your mind to run *you*, make a conscious decision to run *it*.
- **Spend your free time; don't squander it.** Ask yourself whether you use leisure-time activities as an escape. For example, do you watch television, exercise, or surf the Net to *avoid* what you see as unpleasant but necessary tasks, rather than to *revitalize*? Consider whether your free time is about *something* or about *nothing*.
- **Worry less; do more.** Worry is counterproductive; it drains us of the energy we need to get things done and keeps us from enjoying the present. Write down what's worrying you most, identify the worst that could possibly happen, and ask yourself if your fear is realistic.
- **Forgive and forget.** Some people obsess over the past. They should have done X; if only Y had happened instead. Life is full of ups and downs, but it's important to keep moving.
- **Be present.** Remember grade school? Your teachers would call roll every morning, and you'd answer "present" or "I'm here" when your name was called. Life coach Mark van Doren says, "There is one thing we can do, and the happiest people are those who can do it to the limit of their ability. We can be completely present. We can be all here. We can ... give all our attention to the opportunity before us."

YOUR TOUGHEST CLASS

Think about the courses you're taking this term. Use the following form to analyze your various professors' lecture styles. Be discrete as you listen and analyze their styles, of course, but after your chart is completed, decide what *you* can do as a listener to make adjustments in your toughest class. To get an idea of how to fill out the chart, look at what Lindsey's entries for her computer science class might have been. Filling out this chart for all your classes may give you some insights about why one particular class is your toughest and develop a set of actions that can help you become more successful.[11]

LECTURE STYLE ANALYSIS WORKSHEET					
COURSES	Example: *Computer Science 101*				
EMPHASIS Content, students, or both?	*Teacher emphasizes content, primarily. He lectures for the full class period with little student interaction.*				
ORGANIZATION Structured or unstructured	*Lectures seem unstructured with notes written all over the board.*				
PACE Fast, slow, or medium?	*Very fast*				
VISUAL AIDS Used? Useful?	*Board hard to see from the back of the room.*				
EXAMPLES Used? Useful?	*Few real examples are given that students can relate to.*				
LANGUAGE Terms defined? Vocabulary understandable?	*What is a logarithm, exactly? No, not defined.*				
DELIVERY Animated via body language?	*Delivery style isn't lively and interesting. Instructor doesn't notice when students are lost.*				
QUESTIONS Encouraged?	*He rarely pauses to take questions.*				
Proposed adjustments in my toughest class:	*Make special arrangements to meet with the professor outside his office hours.*				

Ask and You Shall Receive

Even if you listen carefully to every word your instructor utters, it's likely you won't understand them all. After all, your instructor is an expert in the subject you're studying, and you're a novice. At some point or other, you'll need clarification or elaboration, and the best way to get it will be to ask. Even though that makes sense, not all students ask questions in class. Why? See if you've excused yourself from asking questions for any of these reasons:

> I don't want to look stupid.

> I must be slow. Everyone else seems to be understanding.

> I'm too shy.

> I'll get the answer later from the textbook.

> I don't think my question is important enough.

> I don't want to derail the lecture. The instructor's on a roll.

> I'm sure the instructor knows what he's talking about. He must be right.

If any of these reasons for not asking questions in class applies to you, the good news is . . . you're in good company. Many students think this way. The bad news, of course, is that your question remains unasked, and therefore, unanswered.

The next time you find yourself in a situation where you don't understand something, consider these points.

1. **Remember that you're not in this alone.** Chances are you're probably not the only person in class who doesn't understand. Not only will you be doing yourself a favor by asking, but you'll also be helping someone else who's too shy to speak up.

2. **Ask academically relevant questions when the time is right.** As opposed to "Why do we need to know this?" or "Why did you make the test so hard?" ask questions to clarify information. Don't ask questions designed to take your instructor off

© Tomas Rodriguez/Solus-Veer/CORBIS

"He who is ashamed of asking is ashamed of learning."

Danish Proverb

on a tangent (to delay the impending quiz, for example). If you're really interested in something that's not directly related to the material being covered, the best time to raise the question would be during your instructor's office hours.

3. Save *personally* relevant questions for later. If your questions relate only to you (for example, you were ill and missed the last two classes), then don't ask in class. Set up an appointment with your instructor. You can also get answers by researching on your own, visiting or e-mailing your instructor, seeking out a teaching assistant or tutor, or working with a study group.

4. Build on others' questions. Listen to the questions other students ask. Use their questions to spark your own. Perhaps another student has a unique way of looking at the issue being discussed that will spark an idea for a follow-up question from you. Remember, to your instructor, good questions indicate *interest*, not *idiocy*.

Remember, your college education is an expensive investment. You've paid to learn, and asking questions is a natural part of that learning experience. Don't be shy—put that hand in the air!

EXERCISE 6.1 One-Way versus Two-Way Listening

To demonstrate the value of asking questions, try this in-class exercise. A student volunteer, or class "lecturer," will briefly replace the instructor to describe to the rest of the class two different, simple figures she draws herself. Each figure should take up a full piece of paper. The rest of the class must then replicate the drawings as accurately as possible on their own paper as the class "lecturer" describes each figure during two rounds. The point of the exercise is to replicate the two figures the class "lecturer" has drawn as accurately as possible from her description alone.

Round 1: The volunteer should turn her back to the group (to eliminate nonverbal cues), hiding her paper from view, and give the class instructions for drawing Figure 1. No questions from the group are allowed. Note the exact amount of time it takes for the rest of the class to listen to the instructions and complete the drawing.

Round 2: Next, the volunteer should now turn around and face the class, giving instructions for drawing Figure 2. Students may ask questions of the "lecturer" to clarify and elaborate as much as is necessary to get the drawing right. Again, note the exact amount of time taken.

After both rounds of the exercise are done, the "lecturer" should ask class members whether they think their drawings closely resemble the two originals and count the number of students who think they drew Figure 1 correctly and the number of students who think they drew Figure 2 correctly. Then the "lecturer" should show the two original figures as drawn, and count the number of students who actually drew Figure 1 and Figure 2 correctly. Finally, as a group, discuss the two rounds and the value of asking questions in lecture classes. Even though questions take more time, the results are usually much better.

Elapsed Time	# *Think* Correct	# *Actually* Correct
Round 1		
Round 2		

EXERCISE 6.2 How Well Do You Listen?

Now that you've read about focused listening, see which of the following statements apply to you. Check the box that most applies to what you usually do in the classroom. Use this self-assessment to develop a plan for improvement.

Listening Statements:	Always True of Me	Sometimes True of Me	Never True of Me
I stay awake during class.	☐	☐	☐
I maintain eye contact with the speaker.	☐	☐	☐
I don't *pretend* to be interested in the subject.	☐	☐	☐
I understand my instructor's questions.	☐	☐	☐
I try to summarize the information.	☐	☐	☐
I look for organizational patterns within material (*e.g.,* causes and effects, lists of items).	☐	☐	☐
I set a purpose for listening.	☐	☐	☐
I don't daydream during class.	☐	☐	☐
I try to predict what will come next.	☐	☐	☐
I take notes regularly.	☐	☐	☐
I ignore external distractions such as loud noises, late-arriving students, etc.	☐	☐	☐
I try to determine the speaker's purpose.	☐	☐	☐
I recognize that the speaker may be biased about the subject.	☐	☐	☐
I write down questions the instructor poses during class.	☐	☐	☐
I copy down items from the board or screen.	☐	☐	☐
Total check marks for each column:	☐	☐	☐

Add up the check marks in each column to learn the results of your analysis. Pay particular attention to the total in the "Always True of Me" column.

13–15 "Always True of Me": You're probably an excellent listener, both in the classroom and in other situations. Keep up the good work.

10–12 "Always True of Me": You are a good listener, but you need to fine-tune a few of your listening skills.

7–9 "Always True of Me": You need to change some behaviors so that you get more out of your classes.

6 or less "Always True of Me" or 7 or more "Never True of Me": You need to learn better listening skills if you want to achieve academic success in college.[12]

INSIGHT ⊖ ACTION

Which behaviors will you target in order to become a better listener? Select three of the items you marked in Exercise 6.2 as "Never True of Me" to focus on. Practice doing that behavior in class for several days.

Taking Lecture Notes:
Different Strokes for Different Folks

Riser/Getty Images

CHALLENGE ⊖ REACTION

Challenge: Does taking notes help students learn? Why or why not?

Reaction: _____

Listening in class is one thing. Taking notes is quite another. You must be a good listener to take good notes, but being a good listener alone doesn't automatically make you a good note-taker. Note-taking is a crucial and complex skill, and doing well on tests isn't based on luck. It's based on combining preparation and opportunity, in other words, knowing how to take useful notes in class that work for you.

Actually, one reason that note-taking is so important in the learning process is that it uses all four VARK categories: *visual* (you see your professor and the screen, if overheads or PowerPoint slides are being used), *aural* (you listen to the lecture), *read/write* (you write what you see and hear so that you can read it later to review), and *kinesthetic* (the physical act of writing opens up a pathway to the brain). Have you ever thought about it that way before?

> "Luck is what happens when preparation meets opportunity."
>
> **Darrell Royal, football coach**

According to one study, 99 percent of college students take notes during lectures, and 94 percent of students believe that note-taking is important.[13] These are good signs, but are these students taking notes correctly, as a result of focused listening? If 99 percent of college students are taking notes, why isn't nearly everyone getting straight A's? Here are some reasons:

> Students typically only record less than 40 percent of the lecture's main content ideas in their notes.[14]

> Only 47 percent of students actually review their notes later to see what they've written.

> Only 29 percent edit their notes later by adding, deleting, or reorganizing material.

> A full 12 percent do nothing other than recopy them verbatim.

> Some students never do anything with their notes once they leave class![15]

Does note-taking make a difference? Absolutely. During lectures, it serves two fundamental purposes: it helps you understand what you're learning at the time and it helps you preserve information to study later. In other words, both the *process* of note-taking (as you record information) and the *product* (your notes themselves) are important to learning. There is strong evidence that taking notes during a lecture leads to higher achievement than not taking notes, and working with your notes later increases your chances for academic achievement even more. Studies show that if you take notes, you have a 50 percent chance of recalling that information at test time versus a 15 percent chance of remembering the same information if you didn't take notes.[16]

But when it comes to note-taking, "different strokes for different folks" is literally true. Many different note-taking systems can work, and different systems work best for different learning styles.

Whichever strategy you choose to use, an important question to ask is: What constitutes *good* notes? The answer is: Writing down an *accurate, complete, organized* account of what you hear in class (or read in your textbook, which is discussed elsewhere in this book). How will you know if your notes are good? Show them to your instructor and get input, or assess your strategy after you see your results on the first exam. Your note-taking skills should steadily improve as you evolve as a student.[17]

The Cornell System

The Cornell format of note-taking, devised by educator Walter Pauk, suggests this. On each page of your notebook, draw a line from top to bottom about one and a half inches from the left edge of your paper. Take notes on the right side of the line. Leave the left side blank to fill in later with key words or questions you'd like answered. After class as you review your notes, put your hand over the right side and use the words or questions you've written on the left side as prompts.[18] By doing this to recall the lecture, you can get a good idea of how much of the information you've understood.

Let's go back to Lindsey, sitting in her computer science course listening to this lecture, and see what her notes might look like in the Cornell format shown in Figure 6.1.

Figure 6.1

"The History of Modern Computers": Cornell System Example

Origins	*Beginning of modern computers in 17th century. Descartes, Pascal, Leibnitz, and Napier revolutionized ancient view of world. Lots of progress made in math, and calculations difficult. More sophisticated computing machines needed.*
Logarithms	*Logarithms developed by the Scottish mathematician John Napier in 1614. Napier (clergyman, philosopher, and mathematician) played important role. Published his great work of logarithms in the book called Rabdologia. Enabled people to transform multiplication and division into simple addition and subtraction. Logarithm tables soon used by many people.*
Napier's Bones	*Napier is often remembered more by another invention of his, nicknamed "Napier's Bones." This was a small instrument constructed of 10 rods, on which were engraved the multiplication tables. They are referred to as bones because the first set was made from ivory and resembled a set of bones. This simple device enabled people to carry out multiplication in a fast manner provided one of the numbers was 1 digit only (i.e., 6 x 6,742).*
Slide Rule	*Invention of logarithms→development of slide rule. First slide rule in 1650 by two Englishmen, Edmund Gunter and the Reverend William Oughtred.*
Astrolabe	*Not used until 1850 when a French Artillery officer, Amédée Mannheim, added the movable double-sided cursor like today's. Called "astrolabe" because of astronomical uses. Forerunner of the modern slide rule.*

Mind Maps

An alternative to the Cornell system, or a way to expand on it, is to create mind maps. Mind maps use both sides of your brain: the logical, orderly left side and the visual, creative right side. Or think of the left side of your brain as the heavy-duty, brick-and-mortar content side and the right side as the artistic, designer side. What they're particularly good for is showing the relationship between ideas. Mind maps are a good note-taking method for visual learners, and just drawing one may help you remember the information, particularly if you're a kinesthetic learner. To give mind mapping a try, here are some useful suggestions:

1. Use extra wide paper (11 × 17 or legal size). You won't want to write vertically (which is hard to read) if you can help it.

2. Write the main concept of the lecture in the center of the page. Draw related concepts radiating out from the center.

3. Limit your labels to key words so that your mind map is visually clear.

4. Use colors, symbols, and images to make your mind map livelier and more memorable. Notice on the mind map in Figure 6.2 that names are in blue and terms are in red.

5. Use software such as MindManager, MindManuals, MindPlugs, Mindmapper, or MindGenius, which are all powerful brainstorming and organizing tools. As you type, these programs will intuit relationships and help you draw a mind map on screen.

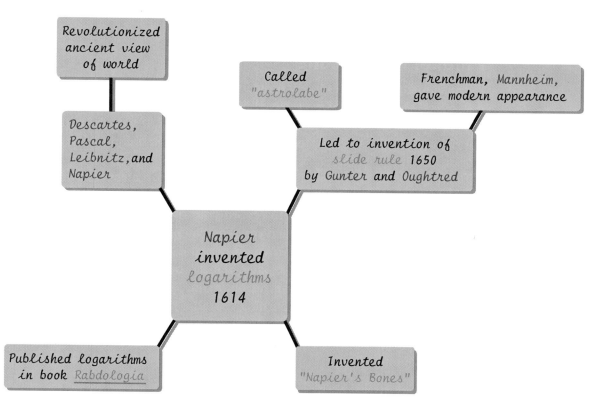

Figure 6.2

"The History of Modern Computers": Mind Map Software Example

PowerPoint Miniatures

Some instructors provide full-text lecture notes online or copies of their PowerPoint slides (three or six miniatures on a page), either as handouts in class or as e-mail attachments (see Figure 6.3). Tools such as these assure you that you have all the main lecture points on paper, and although it's helpful to have them available as a tool, you still need to take notes on your own to help you process the information you're listening to in class.

Figure 6.3

"The History of Modern Computers": PowerPoint Miniatures Example

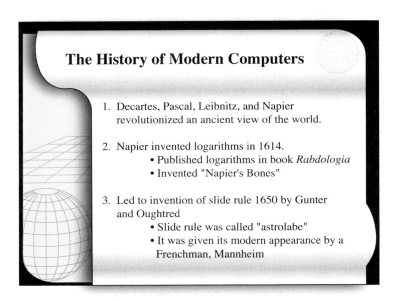

The History of Modern Computers

1. Decartes, Pascal, Leibnitz, and Napier revolutionized an ancient view of the world.

2. Napier invented logarithms in 1614.
   - Published logarithms in book *Rabdologia*
   - Invented "Napier's Bones"

3. Led to invention of slide rule 1650 by Gunter and Oughtred
   - Slide rule was called "astrolabe"
   - It was given its modern appearance by a Frenchman, Mannheim

Parallel Note-Taking

Because many professors today provide e-support for lectures, either through web notes, hard copies of onscreen slides, lecture outlines, or a full transcript, new note-taking strategies may be particularly useful, if you go about them in the right way. One such strategy is called parallel note-taking.[19] Here's how it works, ideally.

If they're available, print out lecture notes *before* class and bring them with you, preferably in a ring binder. As your instructor lectures, use the back (blank) side of each page to record your own notes as the notes from the ongoing, real-time lecture face you. You can parallel what you're hearing from your instructor with your own on-the-spot, self-recorded notes, using a Cornell format on each blank page. It's the best of both worlds! You're reading, writing, and listening at the same time, fully immersing yourself in immediate and longer-lasting learning. Parallel note-taking can work after the lecture as well, or while you re-listen to a podcast version of the lecture. Figure 6.4 illustrates how parallel note-taking might look for Lindsey in her computer science class.

> **"I make progress by having people around me who are smarter than I am and listening to them. And I assume that everyone is smarter about something than I am."**
>
> **Henry J. Kaiser, American industrialist (1882–1967)**

THE HISTORY OF MODERN COMPUTERS

Instructor's Lecture Notes

The real beginning of modern computers goes back to the 17th century. Having divorced themselves from all past speculations and authorities, such intellectual giants as Descartes, Pascal, Leibnitz, and Napier made a new beginning in philosophy, science, and mathematics, which was to revolutionize the ancient view of the world. In mathematics, particularly, such tremendous progress was made, and the attendant calculations became so laborious, that the need of more sophisticated computing machines became urgent. The development of logarithms by the Scottish mathematician John Napier (1550–1617) in 1614 stimulated the invention of various devices that substituted the addition of logarithms for multiplication. Napier played a key role in the history of computing.

THE HISTORY OF MODERN COMPUTERS

My In-Class Lecture Notes

Origins Beginning of modern computers in 17th century. Descartes, Pascal, Leibnitz, and Napier revolutionized ancient view of world. Lots of progress made in math, and calculations difficult. More sophisticated computing machines needed.

Figure 6.4

"The History of Modern Computers": Parallel Note-Taking Example

INSIGHT ⤏ ACTION

What are your strengths and weaknesses as a note-taker? Are you a good listener? Can you write quickly and legibly? Do you ask questions easily? Use this opportunity to critique yourself and identify some areas for improvement.

Using Lecture Notes

Taking good notes is only part of the equation. To get the most value from your notes, you must actually *use* them. As soon as possible after class, take a few minutes to review your notes. If you find sections that are unclear, take time to fill in the gaps while things are still fresh in your mind. One professor found that students who filled in any missing points right after class were able to increase the amount of lecture points they recorded by as much as 50 percent. And students who worked with another student to reconstruct the lecture immediately after class were able to increase their number of noted lecture points even more![20]

This part of the note-taking process is often overlooked, yet it is one of the most helpful steps for learning and recall. If you don't review your notes within twenty-four hours, there's good evidence that you'll end up *relearning* rather than *reviewing*. Reviewing helps you go beyond just writing to actually making sure you understand what you wrote. These three techniques help you get the best use of your notes: manipulating, paraphrasing, and summarizing.

> **Manipulating** involves working with your notes by typing them out later, for example. Some research indicates that it's not writing down information that's most important. Manipulating information is what counts. Work with your notes. Fill in charts, draw diagrams, create a matrix, underline, highlight, organize. Cut a copy of the professor's lecture notes up into paragraphs, mix them up, and then put the lecture back together. Copy your notes onto flash cards. Manipulating information helps develop your reasoning skills, reduces your stress level, and can produce a more complete set of notes to study later.[21]

> **Paraphrasing** is a process of putting your notes into your own words. Recopy your notes or your professor's prepared lecture notes, translating them into words you understand and examples that are meaningful to you. Paraphrasing is also a good way to self-test or to study with a classmate. If you can't find words of your own, perhaps you don't really understand the original notes. Sometimes students think they understand course material until the test proves otherwise, and then it's too late! Practice paraphrasing key concepts with a friend to see how well you both understand the material. Or ask yourself, if I had to explain this to someone who missed class, what words would I use?

> **Summarizing** is a process of writing a brief overview of all of your notes from one lecture. Imagine trying to take all your lecture notes from one class session and putting them on an index card. If you can do that, you've just written a summary. Research shows that students who use the summarizing technique have far greater recall of the material than those who don't.

Some students think that simply going over their notes is the best way to practice. Research shows that simply reading over your notes is a weak form of practice that does not transfer information into long-term memory.[22] You must actually *work with* the material, rearrange or reword it, or condense it to get the most academic bang for your buck. Active strategies always work better than more passive ones.

Manipulating, paraphrasing, and summarizing are more effective learning techniques.

EXERCISE 6.3 Note-Taking 4-M

Practice your note-taking skills by doing this. Immediately after class, or during the lecture if your instructor allows, compare notes with a classmate by following these four steps:[23]

1. <u>M</u>atching—look for content areas where your notes match those of your classmate's.

2. <u>M</u>issing—look for content areas where one of you has missed something important and fill in the gaps.

3. <u>M</u>eaning—talk about what this lecture means. Why was it included in the course? Do you both understand the lecture's main points?

4. <u>M</u>easuring—quiz each other. Measure how much you learned from the lecture. Give each other some sample test questions to see if you understand important concepts.

C CREATE a Career Outlook

JOURNALIST

Have you ever considered a career as a reporter?

Facts to Consider[24]

Academic preparation required: a college degree in mass communication or journalism, with experience writing for school newspapers or broadcasting stations, summer jobs, or internships

Future workforce demand: Jobs within large metropolitan areas will be highly competitive with growth projected to be slow between now and 2014. Jobs working for smaller outlets, freelancing, or jobs requiring specialized skills in new technologies or specialized knowledge about particular subject matter may be on the rise, however.

Work environment: Reporters (journalists) often have hectic work schedules. They follow the news story, when it happens, where it happens. Travel may be required, and deadlines often dictate their schedules. Working hours vary, depending on their medium: newspaper, television or radio, or magazine.

Essential skills: writing, technology, interpretation, accuracy, flexibility, working quickly under pressure, and overall communication skills

Questions to Ponder

1. Do you have (or could you acquire) the skills this career requires?

2. Are you interested in a career like this? Why or why not?

For more career activities online, go to http://www.cengage.com/colsuccess/staleyconcise to do the Team Career exercises.

Q4: What advice do you have for college students who are thinking about pursuing a journalism career?

Write for your college newspaper. Get summer internships at newspapers or magazines. You need to have published "clips" to get a journalism job. And college papers are a great place to get them, along with invaluable on-the-job experience. Summer internships are also a wonderful way to see how a news operation works, and for the news operation to see how you work, too. Get reporting and writing tips from the pros at the places you land internships. Journalists are usually quite generous and remember what it was like being in your shoes. One busy editor took me to lunch and showed me how she carefully outlined her stories before she wrote them. Check your career counseling office and your college newspaper office for lists of alumni with jobs in journalism. Then you can e-mail those folks and ask them who you ought to contact about internships where they work. Just try to get your foot in the door, and once it's there, don't let it out!

EXERCISE 6.4 VARK Activity

Complete the recommended activity for your preferred VARK learning modality. If you are multimodal, select more than one activity. Your instructor may ask you to (a) give an oral report on your results in class, (b) send your results to him or her via e-mail, (c) post them online, or (d) contribute to a class chat.

 Visual: Color-code a set of notes you've taken in one of your current classes to mark important themes (blue highlighter for main points, yellow highlighter for examples, etc.).

 Aural: Download a podcast from one of your most challenging classes this term. Re-listen to the lecture several times while filling in your notes from class, and compare the thoroughness and accuracy of your notes before and after your podcast experience. Alternatively, invite a classmate for coffee or a soft drink immediately after class to talk over the lecture you've just finished listening to. Make sure you actually talk about the lecture!

 Read/Write: Create a survey to hand out in one of your classes, asking students to identify their greatest note-taking challenges in one of their classes this term. Compile all the results and present them in the class for which you're using this textbook.

 Kinesthetic: Conduct on-the-spot fake television news interviews on campus with a friend. Choose a spot on campus for "person on the street" interviews. Act like a reporter copying down information. Ask students for the number one reason they have trouble taking notes. Bring your results to class and role play giving the news report on TV.

⟨C⟩ CHALLENGE Yourself Quizzes For more practice online, go to http://www.cengage .com/colsuccess/staleyconcise to take the Challenge Yourself online quizzes.

 NOW WHAT DO YOU THINK?

At the beginning of this chapter, Lindsey Collier, a frustrated student, faced a challenge. Now after reading this chapter, would you respond differently to any of the questions you answered about the "FOCUS Challenge Case"?

REALITY CHECK

On a scale of 1 to 10, answer these questions now that you've completed this chapter.

1 = not very/not much/very little/low   10 = very/a lot/very much/high

In hindsight, how much did you *really* know about this subject matter before reading the chapter?

1   2   3   4   5   6   7   8   9   10

How much do you think this information might affect your college success?

1   2   3   4   5   6   7   8   9   10

How much do you think this information might affect your career success after college?

1   2   3   4   5   6   7   8   9   10

How long did it actually take you to complete this chapter (both the reading and writing tasks)? _____ Hour(s) _____ Minutes

Compare these answers to your answers from the "Readiness Check" at the beginning of this chapter. How might the gaps between what you thought before starting the chapter and what you now think affect how you approach the next chapter?

 To download mp3 format audio summaries of this chapter, go to http://www.cengage.com/colsuccess/staleyconcise.

7 Developing Your Memory

YOU'RE ABOUT TO DISCOVER...

- Why memory is a process, not a thing
- How your memory works like a digital camera
- How to improve your memory using twenty different techniques
- How your memory can fail you

READINESS CHECK

Before beginning this chapter, take a moment to answer these questions. Your answers will help you assess how ready you are to focus.

1 = not very/not much/very little/low   10 = very/a lot/very much/high

Based on reading the "You're about to discover..." list and skimming this chapter, how much do you think you probably already know about the subject matter?

1   2   3   4   5   6   7   8   9   10

How much do you think this information might affect your college success?

1   2   3   4   5   6   7   8   9   10

How much do you think this information might affect your career success after college?

1   2   3   4   5   6   7   8   9   10

In general, how motivated are you to learn the material in this chapter?

1   2   3   4   5   6   7   8   9   10

How ready are you to focus on this chapter—physically, intellectually, and emotionally? Circle a number for each aspect of your readiness to focus.

1   2   3   4   5   6   7   8   9   10

If any of your answers are below a 5, consider addressing the issue before reading. For example, if you're feeling scattered, take a few moments to settle down and focus.

Finally, how long do you think it will take you to complete this chapter? _____ Hour(s) _____ Minutes

Kevin Baxter

As he got ready for work one morning,

it finally hit him. He took a long, close look at himself in the mirror, and frankly, he didn't like what he saw. Kevin Baxter was a forty-year-old father of three who was dissatisfied with his life. Yes, he earned a decent income as a construction foreman, and yes, his job allowed him to work outdoors. To Kevin, being cooped up in an office from eight to five every day held little appeal. Being outdoors, where you could see the sky, feel the sunshine, and breathe fresh air, was what made him feel alive. The world outside was where he wanted to be, yet at the same time, he knew the world inside his head was withering away. Kevin realized he hadn't really learned much since high school. *I feel brain-dead; that's the best way to describe it*, he frequently thought. *I've run out of options, and I'm stuck.*

Clearly, dropping out of college his first semester twenty-two years ago had been the wrong decision for him. But at the time, he'd convinced himself that he wasn't college material. Besides, college had seemed so expensive, and he desperately wanted to be on his own and begin a life with Carol, his high school sweetheart. Unfortunately, that hadn't worked out well, either. Now he was a single dad whose children lived out of state. He very rarely saw them. Nothing had quite turned out as he had planned.

But in a way, his divorce had jolted him into the midlife crisis he needed to change things, and going back to college to earn a degree in architecture was the right decision for him now. He was sure of it. Working in construction, he frequently saw flaws in the architects' plans, and he'd often come up with better ideas. *This is a chance to start over again*, he thought to himself, *and I'm going to do it right this time.* So at forty, he quit his construction job and enrolled in his hometown college. His first-term courses consisted of Introduction to Architecture, Introduction to Philosophy, Introduction to Rhetoric and Writing, and Introduction to Art Design. For Kevin, college would be an introduction to many new things. Underneath it all, he had to admit that he was proud of himself. *Going back to college at forty takes guts*, he congratulated himself.

But halfway into the term, Kevin's confidence was shaken. Although he'd been a construction foreman on huge projects, after he got his

first midterm exam back, he wondered, *Am I too old to learn new things? I keep up with the reading, come to every class, do my assignments conscientiously, and study until I'm blue in the face! But things just don't seem to stick.* His exam didn't reflect the time he was investing, and frankly, he was embarrassed. Younger students without his years of experience were outperforming him. *That* bothered him. Kevin was getting discouraged about school and his academic capabilities.

Without a doubt, his most challenging class was philosophy. How could anyone memorize schools of philosophical thought and all those names and terms? What did Socrates, Plato, Aristotle, Galileo, and Descartes have in common, and what separated them? Philosophy was unlike anything he had ever tried to learn. He'd read a chapter four, five, or six times, and feel sure he knew it, but when he faced the exam, it seemed as if he'd never studied at all. Of course, it didn't help that while he was trying to focus, his kids would call to talk about their problems or a telephone solicitor would interrupt his reading. He'd even bought a set of colored highlighters after watching a young student next to him, madly yellowing everything in his textbook right before class started, but that didn't seem to help either. He never had problems at work remembering details, like ordering materials and managing multiple construction teams, but trying to distinguish Plato, Aristotle, and Socrates was hard for him, and many of the new terms he was learning didn't really seem to have any relevance to his life. More than once on the exam, he just couldn't come up with a term that was on the tip of his tongue.

Kevin hated to admit it, but doubts were beginning to creep in. Maybe being a construction foreman was as far as he could ever go in life, and he should have left well enough alone. Maybe college was the last place he should be. Maybe he should have been satisfied with what he'd already achieved, instead of putting everything on the line for more.

WHAT DO **YOU** THINK?

Now that you've read about Kevin Baxter, answer the following questions. You may not know all the answers yet, but you'll find out what you know and what you stand to gain by reading this chapter.

1. Why is Kevin experiencing problems remembering course content in his philosophy class? List five reasons you identify from the case study.
2. Is Kevin too old to learn? Why or why not?
3. Identify three memory techniques that Kevin should use to help him memorize all the names and terms he needs to know.
4. If you were asked to explain how the memory process works and the scientific explanation behind his problems, what would you say?

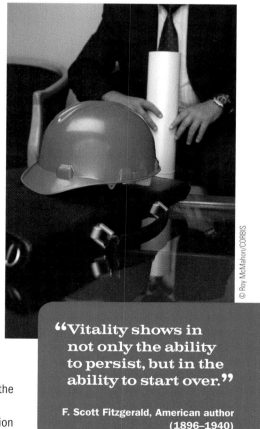

"Vitality shows in not only the ability to persist, but in the ability to start over."

F. Scott Fitzgerald, American author (1896–1940)

Memory: The *Long* and *Short* of It

Challenge: How good is your memory? Fill out Parts A and B to begin applying the information in this chapter to your own memory.

Reaction: Complete this Subjective Memory Test to find out how good your memory is.

How would you rate your memory overall?	Excellent			Good			Poor
	1	2	3	4	5	6	7

A. How often do the following *general* memory tasks present a problem for you?

	Never			Sometimes			Always
1. Names	1	2	3	4	5	6	7
2. Where I've put things	1	2	3	4	5	6	7
3. Phone numbers I've just checked	1	2	3	4	5	6	7
4. Words	1	2	3	4	5	6	7
5. Knowing if I've already told someone something	1	2	3	4	5	6	7
6. Forgetting things people tell me	1	2	3	4	5	6	7
7. Faces	1	2	3	4	5	6	7
8. Directions	1	2	3	4	5	6	7
9. Forgetting what I started to do	1	2	3	4	5	6	7
10. Forgetting what I was saying	1	2	3	4	5	6	7
11. Remembering what I've done (lock the door, etc.)	1	2	3	4	5	6	7

B. How often do the following *academic* memory tasks present a problem for you?

	Never			Sometimes			Always
12. What I've just been reading	1	2	3	4	5	6	7
13. What I read an hour ago	1	2	3	4	5	6	7
14. What I read last week	1	2	3	4	5	6	7
15. Assignment/Exam due dates	1	2	3	4	5	6	7
16. Appointments with instructors	1	2	3	4	5	6	7
17. Assignment details	1	2	3	4	5	6	7
18. Factual information for exams	1	2	3	4	5	6	7
19. Theoretical information for exams	1	2	3	4	5	6	7
20. Information from readings for exams	1	2	3	4	5	6	7
21. Information from in-class lectures for exams	1	2	3	4	5	6	7
22. Including everything I should study for exams	1	2	3	4	5	6	7

These informal assessments may help you understand your own perceptions of how well your memory works. The lower your score on each portion, the better you perceive your memory to be. Do your scores for Part A and Part B differ? The general tasks in Part A are presented in the order of concern reported by older adults cited in one study (with the top items perceived as most problematic).[1] Are your priorities similar? Did your numbers drop as you went down the list?

In one recent study in which college students were asked which aspects of memory they most wanted to improve among general and academic tasks, the top three items were improving schoolwork or study skills, remembering what was read, and remembering specific facts and details.[2] Understandably, the academic aspects of memory were those most personally valued. Is that true for you, too? Are the items in Part B generally higher priorities for you now as a college student?

Most of us may not even realize just how important memory is. We talk about our memories as if they were something we own. We say we have good memories or bad memories, just like we have a crooked smile or nice one. But no one would ever say, "Hey, that's one nice-looking memory you've got there!" in the same way they'd say, "Wow, you have a really nice smile!" Memory isn't a thing; it's a process. You can't see it or touch it or hold it. Even one specific memory has many different features: You can remember something by what you saw, smelled, heard, or felt. And even within one of these categories, individuals may differ in what they recall. You may be able to hum the movie's theme song, but your friend may remember conversations between the main characters almost verbatim.

Don't believe it when someone claims to have a one-size-fits-all, magic formula to help you unlock the secrets of your memory. It isn't that easy. Still, there are techniques which, when applied to the way you read your assignments or study for exams, can help you do your best academically. We can only begin to grasp the rich complexities of memory by understanding it as a process. However, it's important to recognize first that mastering memory depends on the answers to several questions like these:[3]

1. **Who is learning?** A calculus professor and a beginning calculus student would approach memorizing the main points of an article on math differently.

2. **What needs to be learned?** How you learn your lines for a play would differ from how you learn the Dutch masters' paintings for your art appreciation test.

3. **How will learning be tested?** Learning information to *recall* uses different memory techniques than learning information to *recognize*. Recognition requires that you select from several alternatives; recall requires that you come up with memorized information on your own.

4. **How long must the information be remembered?** Learning your multiplication tables as a child is something that must remain with you throughout your life. You use it on a daily basis to do routine things like figure how much it will cost you to fill up your gas tank. On the other hand, learning the date of the Battle of Hastings isn't quite as crucial to remember for the long haul.

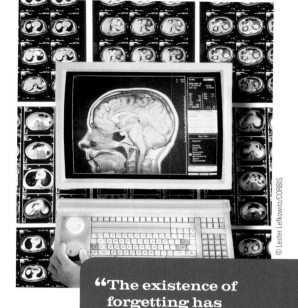

"The existence of forgetting has never been proved: We only know that some things don't come to mind when we want them."

Friedrich Nietzsche, German philosopher (1844–1900)

EXERCISE 7.1 Test Your Memory

For a more objective assessment of your memory, try this test. Study the following list of words for up to one minute. Then cover them with your hand and see how many you can remember and list them in the right-hand column.

theory   _____

rehearsal   _____

student   _____

bone   _____

frostbite   _____

camera   _____

rose   _____

calculus   _____

lecture   _____

How many words were you able to remember? Which words did you forget? Unfamiliar words? Words that had no relevance to your life? What memory techniques did you use to help you remember?

INSIGHT ➔ ACTION

1. From the list of items presented in Part B of the previous "Challenge → Reaction" activity, which ones do you find most challenging? Why are these memory issues problematic for you?

2. What, specifically, can you do to improve your memory in these areas?

Photodisc/Getty Images

The Three R's of Remembering: Record, Retain, Retrieve

CHALLENGE ➔ REACTION

Challenge: Think of three ways in which using your memory is like taking pictures with a digital camera.

Reaction: 1. _____

2. _____

3. _____

> **"I have a photographic memory but once in a while I forget to take off the lens cap."**
>
> **Milton Berle, comedian (1908–2002)**

Improving your memory is easier if you understand how it works. Memory consists of three parts: your *sensory memory*, your *working memory* (called short-term memory by some psychologists), and your *long-term memory*. These three parts of the memorization process are connected to these three memory tasks: *recording*, *retaining*, and *retrieving* memories—the "Three R's of Remembering."[4] We'll compare the three

R's of remembering to the process involved when taking pictures with a digital camera: record, retain, retrieve.

Your Sensory Memory: Focus

Before we discuss the first R of remembering—namely, *Record*—we have to talk first about focus. Before you even push the button to snap a picture, you have to focus on your subject. Most digital cameras today focus on things automatically, and unlike older cameras, you don't have to turn the focus knob until the image is clear. But you do need to decide what to focus *on*. What do you want to take a picture of? Where will you point the camera? When it comes to your college classes and the role your memory plays in your success, remember that focus doesn't come automatically. It requires consciously deciding where to direct your attention.

Imagine this: You're on your way to class. You walk through a student demonstration and get brushed by members of the crowd. Then you cross a busy intersection a little too slowly and get honked at by a speeding car. Finally, you see a billboard you've never noticed before: "I love you, Whitney. Will you marry me? Carl." *How romantic*, you think to yourself.

Three major sensations just passed through your *sensory memory* in this scenario, in this case, your *haptic* memory (touch, the crowd), your *echoic* memory (sounds, the car horn), and your *iconic* memory (sight, the billboard), all parts of your sensory memory. You have a different channel for each of these three senses. Most experts believe that your sensory memory retains an exact copy of what you've seen or heard—pure and unanalyzed—for less than a second.[5] Some of these images, or icons, will be transferred to your working memory.

To help you with attention management, consider the following suggestions:

1. **Slow down; you move too fast.** Imagine trying to take a photo of something on the way to class if you were running. Everything would be a blur; trying to take a picture would be futile. Focus requires your full attention aimed at one thing at a time. Turn down the music, turn off the television, shut down the six windows open on your browser, and focus.

2. **Deal with it.** If something is driving you to distraction, maybe you need to take care of it first so that you *can* focus.

3. **Notice where you go.** Wandering thoughts are normal. When *your* attention wanders off, where does it go? Knowing your mental tendencies helps you to recognize the pattern and work on changing it.

4. **Watch for signals.** As a college student, you'll probably take at least forty different courses from all sectors of your college and be exposed to literally thousands of facts. Not even a memory expert could master them all at once. You must be selective about focus. You're most likely to learn the subject material presented by your instructor and through your course readings. Your textbooks will guide you as you read by using bold fonts, different colors, charts, tables, and headings. Think of them as animated .jpegs on the page, calling out, "Hey, look at me!" In class, watch the instructor's body

language; listen to her inflection; notice what gets written on the board or which PowerPoint slides stay on the screen longer than others. Keep those handouts handy. Plenty of subtle signals exist, but you have to pay attention to them.

5. Get help if you need to. If you have been diagnosed with ADHD, your brain is wired somewhat differently, affecting your memory and your ability to concentrate.[6] If you've not been diagnosed with a learning disability, but your attention appears to be extremely challenging to harness and you're not sure why, seek help from a counselor or learning specialist on campus.

Your Working Memory: Record

After you've focused your camera on your subject, you're ready to take a picture, right? But with a digital camera, you don't just click and walk away. You actually click and then review the picture on the small viewing screen to decide whether you want to save it or delete it.

Similarly, *recording* sensory impressions involves an evaluation process that takes place in your short-term or *working memory*. Your working memory is like a review screen, where you review recently acquired sensory impressions, enhancing them with related information that you retrieve from your long-term memory. In fact, your working memory is often involved in the focus process. You give selected, focused attention to some of what you see and hear because it has personal meaning for you or relates to something in your past experience. In our example of you walking to class, which of these three specific sensations you just experienced are you likely to remember: the crowd, the car, or the billboard? To stay true to the analogy, which one would you take a picture of? It depends, right? You may remember the billboard because you plan to show it to someone else later, or the demonstration because you disagree with its cause, or the car horn because it scared you.

The problem with working memory is that the length of time it can hold information is limited. You probably don't remember what you ate for dinner

FOCUS ON CAREERS: Delanna Studi, Actress

Courtesy of DeLanna Studi

Q1: How did you decide on acting as a career, and what factors went into your decision?
I started seriously thinking about acting as a career when I was a freshman in college. I remember sitting down with my parents and asking for their advice about my future. My father told me to "do what you can live with." He wanted me to look back on life and my decision without wondering "what if." My parents sent me to L.A. to get my start. They gave me five days to find an apartment and one month to complete five goals. If I succeeded, they said I could stay and pursue acting. That was eight years ago.

Q2: Most people assume that actors learn their lines by rote, repeating them over and over. Is that what you do?
First, I learn the story. If I know the story I'm telling, the lines and dialogue come to me. True, the language may not be what I use in my daily

life, but I focus on that later. I find that if I can tell the story in my own words, I can act it. Then I start memorizing the lines, and yes, sometimes it is by rote. There is a reason why the writer has chosen the words that are on the page. My job is to make those words mine.

Q3: How do you go from memory to meaning? How do you make sure you mean what you're saying? How do actors make each performance unique so that their lines don't sound memorized and flat?
I understand the story, I try to make the language my own, and I lay the foundation for meaning while I am memorizing. I think the key element is visualizing the play or movie during the first read. This sets the first layer of meaning; however, the images I used in the first read-through may not be the ones in my head for the final performance. I will have discovered in rehearsal if those images (personalizations) work, and I will have either scrapped them or enhanced them. The key to making each

last Monday, do you? You'd have to reconstruct the memory based on other clues. Where was I? What was I doing? Who was I with?

The other problem with working memory is that it has limited capacity. It fills up quickly and then dumps what it doesn't need. If that weren't the case, our working memories would be cluttered with a chaotic array of useless information. If you look up a number in the campus directory, you can usually remember it long enough to walk over to the phone, right? A few minutes after you've dialed, however, the number is gone. Current estimates are that you can keep something in working memory for one to two minutes, giving your brain a chance to do a quick review, selecting what to save and what to delete.[7] Look at these letters and then close your eyes and try to repeat them back in order.

SAJANISMOELIHHEGNR

Can't do it? This task is virtually impossible because the string contains eighteen letters. Researchers believe that working memory can recall only seven pieces of information, plus or minus two.[8] (There's a reason why telephone numbers are prechunked for us.) Chunking these eighteen letters into five units helps considerably. Now look at the letters again and try to recall all eighteen.

SAJA NISM OELI HHEG NR

If we rearrange the letters into recognizable units, it becomes even easier, right?

AN IS MAJOR ENGLISH HE

And if the words are rearranged to make perfect sense, the task becomes simple.

HE IS AN ENGLISH MAJOR

The principle of chunking is also used to move information from your working memory to your long-term memory bank, and it's used in memorization techniques that we will describe later in this chapter.

---

performance unique is listening. It reminds me of playing catch. I know my partner is going to throw the ball to me, I just don't know what size ball or how he will throw it. If I pay attention, I can catch whatever he throws.

Q4: What advice do you have for first-year college students about acting as a career?
Acting is 85 percent work and 15 percent talent. I believe if you commit fully and practice, you will become a better actor. My advice is hard work and patience. There are rarely overnight successes. You have to love the craft because it's not as glamorous as the media might lead you to believe! If this is what you really want to do as a career, it is a tough journey, but well worth the adventure.

C CREATE a Career Outlook

ACTOR
Have you ever considered a career as an actor?

Facts to Consider[9]

Academic preparation required: highly variable; actors come from many different academic backgrounds, including degrees in theatre and performing arts

Future workforce demand: Competition is fierce for prize roles, and actors may find themselves unemployed at times, supplementing their income in other ways.

Work environment: Actors work under pressure, typically for relatively short periods of time, ranging from one day to several months. They work long, irregular hours on television or movie sets or on the stage live, so they must be devoted to their craft and enjoy entertaining others.

Essential skills: creativity, memory, ability to follow direction, stress management; singing or dancing skills may also be helpful

Questions to Ponder

1. Do you have (or could you acquire) the skills this career requires?
2. Are you interested in a career like this? Why or why not?

For more career activities online, go to http://www.cengage.com/colsuccess/staleyconcise to do the Team Career exercises.

Your Long-Term Memory: Retain and Retrieve

Let's go back to our camera analogy. Once your camera's memory card gets full, you probably transfer the photos to your computer, or you print them out and put them in photo albums or picture frames. However, before you do that, you generally review the photos, decide how to arrange them, where to put them, whether to print them, and so forth. In other words, you make the photos memorable by putting them into some kind of order or context.

Just as you must transfer photos from your camera's memory stick to a more permanent location with a larger capacity for storage, you must transfer information from short-term, or working, memory to long-term memory. You *retain* the information by transferring it, and this transfer is facilitated by reviewing and using it in a way that makes it memorable. It is this review process that we use when we study for a test. You transfer information to long-term memory by putting the information into a context that has meaning for you, linking new information to old information, creating stories or particular memory techniques, or organizing material so that it makes sense. You can frame it by putting a mental border around it, just as you put pictures into frames. Sometimes you need to frame information to keep it distinct and separate from other information.

Your long-term memory is the computer in which you store new knowledge until you need to use it. However, while the memories that reside in long-term memory aren't easily disturbed, they can be challenging to retrieve.[10] Ideally, you'd like your memories to be readily available when you wish to retrieve them, just like the pictures or digital images that you have transferred to your computer or put in a photo album. You can click on them to view them again,

Figure 7.1

Your Memory as a Digital Camera

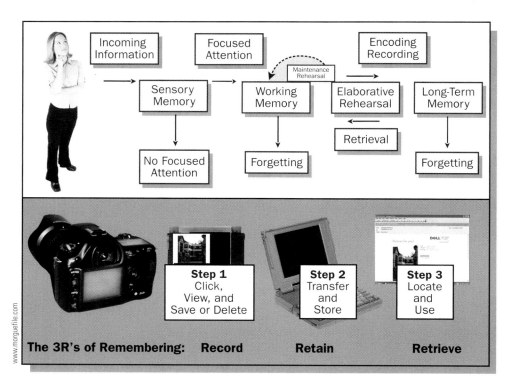

arrange them into a slideshow and publish them on the web, send them to your friends as e-mail attachments, or just review them yourself to recapture the earlier experience. If you just dump your photos onto your hard drive, or print them out and then put them into a box, with no organization or labeling system, how easy will it be to find a specific photo? Difficult, right? Retrieving information from your long-term memory can be equally challenging if you haven't organized your information, or created mental labels that will trigger data retrieval. Good recall often depends upon good storage techniques. The remainder of this chapter will be about how to *retain* information by transferring it from working memory into long-term memory and how to *retrieve* information when you need to.

> **"A memory is anything that happens and does not completely unhappen."**
>
> **Edward de Bono, creative thinking expert and author of *Lateral Thinking: Creativity Step by Step***

Twenty Ways to Master Your Memory

CHALLENGE → REACTION

Challenge: If you were actually tasked with learning the random list of words presented in Exercise 7.1 to test your memory, how would you proceed? Identify the precise method you believe would work best for you.

Reaction: _____

What can you do to sharpen your memory for the reading and test-taking you'll do in college? Try the following twenty techniques, grouped into five major categories (to help you remember them). These techniques are specifically designed to help you with the *retain* and *retrieve* parts of the memory process. As you consider each one, think about what you know about your own learning style.

Make It Stick

How do you actually move material from your working memory to your long-term memory? What will work best for you? Some techniques are more effective than others, but the following suggestions are a good start.[11]

Rehearse. Although it's not the most powerful memorization strategy available to you, especially by itself, repeating information helps. Nothing gets stored in your memory for long without practice. How did you learn those multiplication tables in fourth grade? Probably not by just reading it over once or twice.

Memory experts distinguish between *maintenance* (or shallow) rehearsal and *elaborative* rehearsal. Maintenance rehearsal helps you keep something in working memory for a short time. Repeating a phone number twenty times while you look for your cell phone might help you keep it there for several minutes, but will you remember it tomorrow when you need to call again? Shallow rehearsal didn't work for Kevin in the "FOCUS Challenge Case," who just

Figure 7.2

Which of these two pictures are you more likely to remember—the simple or the elaborate?

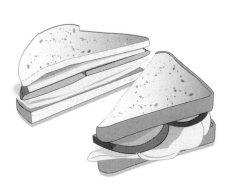

photolibrary.com pty. ltd./Index Open

kept rereading course material. Elaborative rehearsal—actually working with the information—helps transfer information to long-term memory more effectively. Most of the techniques described in this chapter will focus on elaborative rehearsal techniques. Typically, we remember the elaborate over the simple.

Overlearn. Overlearning helps you truly hardwire information, so that you can practically work in autopilot. When you think you've learned something, don't automatically assume it's time to move on. Keep working at it. The more you continue to work at it, the greater your degree of mastery.[12]

Space it out. Many studies show that studying for several hours at a time, as opposed to one long stretch, is much more effective. Clearing your entire day so that you can study calculus for six hours isn't the best idea. Your anxiety level would mount over that time, and fatigue would set in, keeping you from maximizing your memory. Instead, study in shorter spurts for several days leading up to the exam. Cramming may work in the short run, but your working memory will most likely dump what you think you've mastered right after the exam.

Separate it. When you're tasked with learning similar, yet distinct, information, bleeding can occur. One body of knowledge can spill over into another. Imagine the confusion you'd experience if you tried to learn Spanish, French, Russian, and Chinese at the same time.

Kevin from the "FOCUS Challenge Case" had trouble differentiating between Plato, Aristotle, and Socrates. He would have benefited from deliberately working to separate the three philosophers as he studied by making his own compare-and-contrast chart.

Interference presents a particular problem for college students because the subject matter in different courses often overlaps; one social science course may contain information that's similar to another's. Knowledge is interconnected; that's not the issue. It's the challenge of keeping knowledge bases separate for exams. If your sociology test is on Wednesday and your psychology test is on Friday, study sociology on Tuesday and psychology on Thursday. But if both tests are on Friday, separating the two bodies of information will be a challenge. Differentiate your study sessions as much as possible by studying for each test in a specific location or at a particular time of day, for example.[13]

Mind the middle. Perhaps you've heard of the serial-position effect. Research shows that we tend to remember what comes first because of the impression it makes on us, and what comes last because it's most recent. But what's in the middle sometimes tends to get lost.[14] That's an important principle for you to know. If you need to memorize a list of items, or a timeline, for example, pay particular attention to the middle.

Make It Meaningful

Sometimes we make the mistake of creating artificial distinctions between thoughts and feelings, when in fact, emotions and personal connections play an important role in learning.

Feel. Emotions and memories can team up in powerful ways. A piece of new information that makes you feel happy, angry, or sad lights up your amygdala, a small area of your brain that serves as your emotional center of operations. If a novel makes you cry or laugh or actually feel fear, you're likely to remember the story. If course content hooks into career goals you care about, you're likely to commit more of it to memory. Human beings care about other human beings and themselves, so the emotional side of new information (which you may have to create yourself) is a strong magnet for your memory.[15] All American adults remember where they were on September 11, 2001. Emotions enhance memory and recall.[16]

Connect. Create associations between what you're trying to commit to memory now and what you already know. That's why doing the reading assignment before class is so useful. During the lecture, you can think to yourself, *Oh, I remember that ... and that ... and that.* When you learn new information, it's almost as if you "file" it between other files already in place. If you know where to put it, instead of just stuffing it somewhere, that helps. Connecting it to previous knowledge also helps you retrieve the memory later.

Personalize. Find ways you can relate what you're memorizing to your own life. Okay, so you're thinking what do the plot and characters of *Pride and Prejudice*, a novel published by England's Jane Austen in 1813, possibly have to do with me now? Actually, there may be more similarities than you first think. Imagine the story taking place in your household. Do you have sisters? Does your mother worry about you marrying someone good enough for you? Do you have a close relationship with your father? Once you start actively searching for overlap, you may be surprised. This task is easier with some course content than others, but the very act of attempting to do this may be useful.

Make It Mnemonic

Some of the oldest ways to master your memory are through the use of mnemonic (pronounced *ne MON ik*) devices, verbal or visual memory aids, first used by Greek orators around 500 B.C. Imagine trying to remember a speech that goes on for hours; you'd need to devise specific ways to train your memory to keep working (without a teleprompter!). Although mnemonic devices can become complicated and aren't a solution to all memory challenges, for some students, these specialized elaborative rehearsal strategies can work well.

Spell. Acrostics and acronyms are the simplest type of mnemonic device, words you create by putting together the first letters of what you want to memorize. Let's say, for example, that you want to learn the first five items in the list of random words in Exercise 7.1: theory, rehearsal, student, bone, and frostbite. You could create a bizarre acrostic such as <u>T</u>en <u>r</u>abbits' <u>s</u>oup <u>b</u>owls <u>f</u>ell. If you had vowels to work with, you may also be able to create an acronym you can pronounce, such as RAM for Random Access Memory.

ACT ON YOUR MEMORY!

Have you ever watched a movie, wondering how *do* actors learn all those lines? Do they have superhuman memory powers? The average movie-goer assumes that actors simply repeat their lines over and over until they learn them. However, actors themselves say that's not all there is to it.[17]

Actually, what actors are most concerned with is convincing you that they're not playing a role. But actors' contracts require them to be absolutely precise in conforming to the script, so how do they do it? Four of the techniques used by actors may also be useful to you as you try to commit course material to memory. Maybe you've even tried some of these techniques.

Chunking: Actors chunk their material into beats. For example, an actor might divide a half page of dialogue into three beats: to flirt, to sweet-talk, and to convince. In other words, the character would first flirt with the other actor, then sweet-talk him to lower his

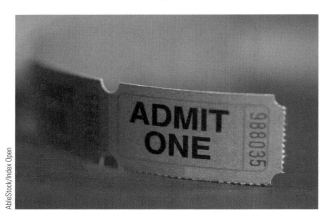

AbleStock/Index Open

guard, and then convince him to do something he might not want to do. The results? Three chunks to remember instead of twelve lines of double-spaced text.

Goal Setting: Notice that the chunks are based on goals, a strategy that also works well while you're studying. Actors ask themselves goal-oriented questions such as: "Should I be flirting with him here?" In the same way, you can ask yourself, "Am I trying to learn the underlying formula so that I can work other problem sets?" or "Should I be coming up with my own reasons for why the play is considered to be Shakespeare's best comedy?" When you ask yourself goal-oriented questions while you study, you steer your actions toward learning.

Moving: Going through the motions while rehearsing their lines helps actors memorize them. Imagine the hypothetical actor whose goals were to flirt, to sweet-talk, and to convince, glancing toward the other actor from across the room, moving closer and smiling, and then touching his arm while making the persuasive case. The actor must know the meanings behind the movements to give meaning to the lines. The meanings are tied to the movements, which are tied to the lines, and the lines become committed to memory. Likewise, when you study, moving around may help you learn. Even if you're not primarily a kinesthetic learner, pieces of information become tied to motions in ways that help you recall information.

Meaning: "Say what you mean" and "mean what you say" was Lewis Carroll's advice in *Alice's Adventures in Wonderland*. Researchers use the term *active experiencing* to refer to what actors do when they use all their physical, mental, and emotional channels to communicate the meaning of their lines to someone else, real or imagined. As you study course material, do the same thing. Imagine you need to communicate the information to someone you know who needs it.

Locate. The Loci (pronounced *LO si*) mnemonic system cues memory by using locations. Using the Loci system requires two steps. First, think of a familiar path, setting, or route. Perhaps you decide on the path from your residence hall room to the classroom where your exam will be given. On your way, you always pass distinct markers: the fountain in the quad, a tunnel that takes you beneath a busy street, the recreation center's pool, the Student Health Center, and the Humanities Building parking lot. Perhaps you want to use these five locations to cue your memory to produce the first five items on our random list: theory, rehearsal, student, bone, and frostbite. You might picture saying hello to your science professor, a foundation of knowledge who always espouses *theory* in class, in the quad. Then you might imagine conducting a *rehearsal* of the student philharmonic orchestra in the tunnel, which would be a ridiculous sight. Then you envision *students* on the swim team thrashing about in the pool during a competition. You know about a recent financial scandal involving the Student Health Center so you imagine skeletons (*bones*) in the closet. And finally, you think of how terrible it would be to lose your room key and get a case of *frostbite* from spending the night in your car in the parking lot. Now without looking back, try it and see if it works for you. Of course, the optimal way the Loci system works is if the locations are familiar to *you*. Its main benefits are that it uses cues, incorporates associations, and orders information into a sequence, all of which aid in memory transfer and storage.[18]

Link or narrate. Instead of a Loci system, you can create a linking mnemonic to help you memorize a list. To do this, you must connect item A to item B, item B to item C, and so forth. Consider again the list of words you were challenged to remember and write down: theory, rehearsal, student, bone, frostbite, camera, rose, calculus, and lecture. Your visual links might go like this: (1) (theory + rehearsal) You imagine a *theoretician* at a *rehearsal* dinner. (2) (rehearsal + student) The rehearsal dinner is attended by student friends of the bride and groom. (3) (student + bone) One student is in a leg cast because of a broken bone, and so forth.

Another way to use this method is to create a story that links each cue: A geeky theoretician went to a rehearsal dinner, where he sat next to a student from one of his classes who had a broken leg (bone). The student injured his leg in a hiking accident in which he suffered a fall and got frostbite from exposure, and so forth. Each item is linked to the item before, except for the first one. You must find a cue to remember it independently to get the chain started.

Peg. The Peg system uses rhyming syllables modified by England's John Sambrook in 1879.[19] Remember the old nursery rhyme, "One, two, buckle my shoe"? The Peg system uses these rhyming pairs:

one—bun	six—sticks
two—shoe	seven—heaven
three—tree	eight—gate
four—door	nine—wine
five—hive	ten—hen

To use the Peg system, create *specific* images for yourself: a big, fat hamburger *bun*, a stiletto-heeled *shoe*, a weeping willow *tree*, and so forth, and hang the items you're trying to memorize on these mental "pegs" in order. To continue with our example, you'd picture a *theoretical* treatise stuffed between the hamburger *bun*, an image of a teenage girl's *rehearsal* of how to walk in her first pair of stiletto high-heeled *shoes*, a *student* sprawled out studying under a weeping willow *tree*, and so forth. Other types of Peg systems have been devised, but the rhyming system is the most common.

Manipulate It

Although some of us tend to favor other modalities than kinesthetic learning, all of us can benefit from memory techniques with a kinesthetic basis. Actively doing something with information is a better way to commit it to memory than remaining passively disengaged. If you had three hours to study a textbook chapter that takes one hour to read, what should you do: read the chapter three times, or work with the material after reading it once? The second option is generally more effective. So what kinds of things should you *do*?

Mark it up. Be an active reader; interact with the text. People who are used to reading complex material—your instructors, for example—read slowly, chew on each word, and make copious notes in the margins, arguing, questioning, summarizing, or explaining. Take notes as you read, "talk" with the author, and write out your reactions. Highlighting can be somewhat helpful, but it's often not enough. It certainly wasn't for Kevin from the "FOCUS Challenge Case." Every time you reach for your highlighter, ask yourself why you want to highlight that passage. Why is it important? To commit information to memory, you must go beyond simply coloring.[20]

Mark it down. If you want to give yourself a break, don't bother committing something unimportant to memory. Just write it down. (Of course, you still have to remember where you put that piece of paper.) Writing something down is an obvious memory alternative; save your memory for more important tasks. If it's something you do want to remember, however, the physical act of writing itself can help. Unless the exam is open-book, however, actually bringing your notes with you at exam time could be hazardous to your academic health!

Organize. Arrange and rearrange the material you're trying to memorize. Outline it—putting concepts into hierarchical order can help you figure out important relationships. If you're trying to learn the responsibilities of the various branches of the government for your political science class, actually drawing a kind of written organizational chart is likely to help your essay answer flow better.

Picture. Drawings and mind maps can also be effective memory tools, particularly for visual learners. Think of drawing pictures to help you remember ridiculous visualizations or word associations. If you're trying to remember bones for your anatomy and physiology class, try Farsighted *Fibula*, Tempting *Tibia*, Party Girl *Patella*, Feathered *Femur*, and Pretty *Pelvis*. Any time you can engage in what's called dual coding, using more than one channel—verbal and visual—you'll likely reinforce what you're trying to memorize.[21]

Act. Consider putting motions to your memorizing. If you're trying to memorize a famous speech like Martin Luther King, Jr.'s "I Have a Dream," deliver it in front of a mirror. Write a short script and ask your roommate to play opposite you, if it helps you remember who said what to whom for an exam in history, or obviously, theater.

Produce. There's good evidence that putting things in your own words is highly beneficial to remembering.[22] Redeliver the professor's lecture. Can you explain the concepts he explained, or do you stop after a few minutes and puzzle? Producing information requires you to dig deeper into your memory and reconstruct information, a process that engages you more actively and benefits you and your memory beyond simple recognition tasks. One of the very best ways to produce is to teach something to someone else.

Test. Rather than assuming you remember something, test yourself. Create a multiple-choice, matching, or true-and-false test. Doing so requires you to ask: amidst this sea of information, what's important? Better yet, create essay questions that require you to organize and write what you know about a subject.

Make It Funny

Humor is an excellent memory-enhancing tool. Think about how easy it is to remember the plots of comedies you've seen at the movies or on television. For example, you may be able to remember conversations between *Friends* or *The Simpsons* cast members in shows you've watched once or twice, almost verbatim, just because they tickled your funny bone.

Mock it. Experts on learning and the brain believe that the optimal condition for learning is *relaxed alertness*. Sounds like an oxymoron, doesn't it? How can you be relaxed and alert at the same time? Actually, it is possible when the challenge is high, but the threat is low.[23] What better way to create those conditions than through humor? And what better way to engage your memory than to be a stand-up (or sit-down) comic?

Think back to some of the funniest TV or movie scenes you've ever seen. They're probably still vivid in your memory. Ask yourself how you could apply your own humor to the material you're attempting to trigger your memory to learn. If you're having trouble separating Socrates and Plato, draw a picture of a crate full of socks next to Socrates' name and a can of PlayDoh® next to Plato's.

Create a David Letterman–like top-ten list of the reasons why Shakespeare's ten tragedies are tragic. Or put Shakespeare's *Romeo and Juliet* into contemporary slang so that you can remember what it is about. Or if you can never remember which character is from the Montague family and which is a Capulet, write a silly limerick to help you remember:

There once was a girl named Cap

Who fell for a guy and was hap

But her family and his

Wouldn't stand for the biz

So they both ended up playing taps.

Set it to music. Be imaginative. We tend to remember what's bizarre, funny, or even obscene![24]

INSIGHT ➔ ACTION

1. Of the list of twenty ways to master your memory, which are your "regulars"? How well do they work for you, generally?

2. Which techniques have you never tried? Choose a specific technique for an upcoming exam, do it with gusto, and note your results afterward.

C CONTROL Your Learning

YOUR TOUGHEST CLASS

Think about your most challenging class this semester. What kind of information in this class is difficult for you to commit to memory: complex readings, formulas, lecture material? Answer the following questions to help you realize the role sharpening your memory can play in your success.

- So far in this class, have you been engaging in maintenance rehearsal or elaborate rehearsal? Now that you have read the chapter, what evidence do you have that this is true?
- How have you studied for quizzes or exams? Provide examples for each of the five principles discussed in this chapter:

Make the material stick.

Make it meaningful.

Make use of mnemonic devices.

Manipulate the material to help learn it.

Make it funny.

- How successful have your memory strategies been? What will you do differently now?

Send your instructor in this class an e-mail, if appropriate, indicating your efforts and detailing your progress.

How Our Memories (uh...hmmm...) Fail Us

Imagine this: You meet someone at a school reception who says, "Hey, I know you! Remember? We met a year ago—it was September—at that fraternity party, and we even went out a few times. I've never forgotten you." You rack your brain. This person doesn't even look familiar. You wonder, *Am I being confused with someone else? Am I crazy? I have no recollection at all!* Later, you comb through your calendar to reconstruct that month. You weren't even attending your current school then. It couldn't have been you.

Digital cameras can malfunction, files we've saved can become corrupted, and sometimes our memories fail us, too. We forget things or alter them in our thinking. Think of how many times you have had to e-mail someone for a password because you've forgotten your original one.

Here are seven ways our memories fail us from *The Seven Sins of Memory: How the Mind Forgets and Remembers*. See how many cause you to nod your head in recognition, and think about which ones particularly apply most to Kevin from the "FOCUS Challenge Case."

1. **Fading.** Memories are transient; they fade over time. You probably remember what you wore yesterday, but how about on October 5 a year ago? As time goes by, memories generally weaken.

2. **Absentmindedness.** Sometimes there's a disconnect between your focus and your memory. You were doing several things at one time—talking to the girl next to you after class and checking your cell phone while stuffing your backpack—and now you have no idea what you did with your history textbook. It's not that the information is lost over time; it probably never registered in the first place because your attention was elsewhere.

3. **Blocking.** It's right on the tip of your tongue, but you just can't quite retrieve it. You can see the face, but you can't conjure up the name. But later that day, without even trying, suddenly it comes to you. Psychologists call it TOT, the Tip of the Tongue phenomenon. You feel as if you're about to sneeze, but can't, and the word—whatever it is—just won't come to you.

4. **Misattribution.** You say to your friend, "Hey, that was an interesting story you told me about the new girl in our composition class." "What story?" your friend replies. Someone told you something, but you're wrong about who it was. Or you read a passage in one book, but think you've read it in another. Or you've dreamed about something for so long that the fantasy actually becomes real in your mind. Your memory deceives you by mistaking one source for another or tricks you by inventing a memory where none actually exists.

5. **Suggestibility.** Sometimes you retain bits of information that you think are memories, but they really aren't. Here's an example: perhaps your mother has told you the cute anecdote about yourself as a two-year-old toddler so many times that you can now envision it, and you think you remember it. You were actually too young to remember anything, but the event has become real at someone else's suggestion.

6. Bias. Sometimes we knowingly, or more often unknowingly, rewrite history. We insist on some detail that, if we had the ability to go back in time to verify it, is actually wrong. Perhaps someone has caught you in a trap in one of those instances by finding a piece of real evidence, and you've had to back down and admit that your memory is off a bit.

7. Persistence. Another way that memory plagues us is by nagging. You'd really like to forget something, but you just can't. You wake up in a cold sweat at 3 a.m., remembering the embarrassing thing you did at work or said in class. You'd like to be able to push the memory away, but it won't budge.

While these seven memory faults are aggravating and inconvenient at times, they also have value. Persistence may serve as a reminder to be more careful next time. Fading is the result of memory efficiency. Why waste time recalling outdated, insignificant details we no longer need? Chances are you can't recall something because you haven't needed to recently, and the memory connection has weakened. (This can happen if you don't keep up with your coursework. When it's exam time, and you haven't looked at your notes for weeks, the memory of what you'd studied long ago may have faded.) Generally, we remember what we need to remember in order to survive in the environment in which we live. We get the gist of things, and often the rest falls away. The point, however, is to take charge of the process of remembering![25]

INSIGHT ⇒ ACTION

1. Which of the seven memory faults is most problematic for you? How has reading this chapter informed you about why this memory problem persists?

2. Make a pledge to yourself to improve your memory in this area, and list the specific steps it will take.

Deepen Your Memory

The point of this chapter is this: In a classic study conducted in the mid-1970s, two Swedish scholars decided to find out the difference between effective and ineffective learners. They gave students this task: read an essay, summarize it, and solve a problem. Then they interviewed the students to find out how they had approached the task.

The interviews revealed two types of learners. One group of students said things like, "I just tried to remember as much as I could" or "I just memorized what I read." Other students said, "I tried to look for the main idea" or "I looked for the point of the article." The professors who conducted the study then characterized the difference between *surface-level processing*, looking at words and numbers alone, and *deep-level processing*, searching for underlying meaning.[26] To become a truly focused learner, you must process information as you go. Dig deep!

There is no doubt that memory is at the heart of learning. In the days before digital cameras, film had to be developed or processed. However, it's still important to remember those terms as they relate to your memory.

EXERCISE 7.2 VARK ACTIVITY

Complete the recommended activity for your preferred VARK learning modality. If you are multimodal, select more than one activity. Your instructor may ask you to (a) give an oral report on your results in class, (b) send your results to him or her via e-mail, (c) post them online, or (d) contribute to a class chat.

 Visual: Create a diagram that shows all of the steps a student should go through when committing challenging material to memory for an exam.

 Aural: Re-listen to one of your professor's lectures via podcast and stop periodically to repeat the information to yourself.

 Read/Write: Check out a library book on memory, and summarize a major section that's important to understanding memory as a process.

 Kinesthetic: Demonstrate three memory techniques that work for you in front of your classmates, and let them guess what you're trying to portray.

© CHALLENGE Yourself Quizzes For more practice online, go to http://www.cengage .com/colsuccess/staleyconcise to take the Challenge Yourself online quizzes.

FOCUS CHALLENGE CASE **NOW WHAT DO YOU THINK?**

At the beginning of this chapter, Kevin Baxter, a frustrated and discouraged returning adult student, faced a challenge. Now after reading this chapter, would you respond differently to any of the questions you answered about the "FOCUS Challenge Case"?

R E A L I T Y   C H E C K

On a scale of 1 to 10, answer these questions now that you've completed this chapter.

1 = not very/not much/very little/low   10 = very/a lot/very much/high

In hindsight, how much did you *really* know about this subject matter before reading the chapter?

1   2   3   4   5   6   7   8   9   10

How much do you think this information might affect your college success?

1   2   3   4   5   6   7   8   9   10

How much do you think this information might affect your career success after college?

1   2   3   4   5   6   7   8   9   10

How long did it actually take you to complete this chapter (both the reading and writing tasks)? _____ Hour(s) _____ Minutes

Compare these answers to your answers from the "Readiness Check" at the beginning of this chapter. How might the gaps between what you thought before starting the chapter and what you now think affect how you approach the next chapter?

 To download mp3 format audio summaries of this chapter, go to http://www.cengage.com/colsuccess/staleyconcise.

8 Reading and Studying

YOU'RE ABOUT TO DISCOVER...

- Why reading is important

- How to engage in focused reading

- How to tackle reading assignments as an ESL student

- What metacognition is and how it can help you

- How to become an intentional learner

- Why learning is greater than the sum of its parts

READINESS CHECK

Before beginning this chapter, take a moment to answer these questions. Your answers will help you assess how ready you are to focus.

1 = not very/not much/very little/low   10 = very/a lot/very much/high

Based on reading the "You're about to discover..." list and skimming this chapter, how much do you think you probably already know about the subject matter?

1   2   3   4   5   6   7   8   9   10

How much do you think this information might affect your college success?

1   2   3   4   5   6   7   8   9   10

How much do you think this information might affect your career success after college?

1   2   3   4   5   6   7   8   9   10

In general, how motivated are you to learn the material in this chapter?

1   2   3   4   5   6   7   8   9   10

How ready are you to focus on this chapter—physically, intellectually, and emotionally? Circle a number for each aspect of your readiness to focus.

1   2   3   4   5   6   7   8   9   10

If any of your answers are below a 5, consider addressing the issue before reading. For example, if you're feeling scattered, take a few moments to settle down and focus.

Finally, how long do you think it will take you to complete this chapter? _____ Hour(s) _____ Minutes

Katie Alexander

College would be a lot more fun if it weren't for all the reading and studying required. That was Katie Alexander's take on things. She wasn't much of a reader; she much preferred playing softball or volleyball with her friends to sitting in one spot with a book propped open in front of her. Reading for fun wasn't something she'd ever even consider doing. *Anyway, why read the book when you can just watch the movie?* she always asked. Katie was an energetic, active, outgoing person, and "doing" and "socializing" were her things. Reading and studying definitely weren't.

Actually, this was Katie's second attempt at college. She'd gone to a small liberal arts school right after high school, but the self-discipline required to read and study just wasn't there, so she dropped out. Working as a server for two years at a restaurant in her neighborhood helped her earn enough money to go back to school. "This time, *you* foot the bills," her parents had insisted. So now she was attending the local community college and determined to give it another go.

For Katie, reading and studying were hard work. She was smart enough to make it in college—she was sure of that—and this time around, she was more motivated. But reading was a labor-intensive activity that tried her patience, and after she'd read something, she was hard-pressed to summarize what it had been about. "In one eye and out the other" was the way she thought of her difficulties. Katie found it hard to focus, and things just didn't seem to stick. Before she knew it, she was off in some other world, thinking about her friends, or her schedule at work, or everything else she had to do.

Back in grade school, Katie had been labeled as a slow reader. She was never in the top reading group, and although she resented the label, she didn't quite know what do to about it. The last time reading had actually been a subject in school was sixth grade. Now, eight years later, she wondered if one of those speed-reading courses advertised online might be the answer.

Katie's roommate, Amanda, was an English major who loved to read. In fact, that's all she ever seemed to do. Her best friend, Brittney, however, had a different strategy. "There's so much required reading in all my classes that I don't even know where to start," Brittney admitted, "so I just don't do it. I go to class, listen to the lectures, and write down what the instructor has said on the essay tests. Learn to 'play the game'!"

But Brittney's strategy definitely wasn't going to work for Katie in Professor Harris-Black's Introduction to Ethnic Studies class. She'd assigned a shocking number of articles to read. The professor didn't even go over the readings in class, and her lectures were about all sorts of things, only some of which were related to the reading. Whenever she sat down to read an assignment, Katie found what to her were unfamiliar words and unnatural phrasing. The professor had suggested that students read with a dictionary at their sides, but who'd ever want to keep stopping to look up words? You'd never finish!

With a midterm exam coming up in her Ethnic Studies class next week, Katie was beginning to panic. She'd only read one of the nine articles assigned. In fact, she hadn't made it through the first article when she got discouraged and gave up. She knew the midterm essay test would be challenging. Winging it wouldn't work, and choosing to "watch the movie" instead of reading the book wasn't an option. Exactly what did Ethnic Studies have to do with anything, she puzzled, and why had her advisor suggested the course in the first place?

The night before the test, Katie decided to get serious. She sat down at her desk, armed with her yellow highlighter. As she began reading, however, she realized she didn't know exactly what to highlight since she didn't really understand what she was reading. Looking back at the page she had just finished, she saw that she had basically highlighted everything. Exasperated, Katie told herself that she couldn't go to bed until she'd finished reading everything, no matter when that was. She started with the second article, since she'd read the first one, and by morning, she'd be as ready as possible. Anyway, it wasn't up to her—it was up to Professor Harris-Black; she was the one making up the test.

Getting an A on her Introduction to Ethnic Studies midterm exam was probably out of the question, but if she could just manage to pass, Katie knew she would have to settle for that. On the other hand, she secretly hoped that maybe she'd just luck out.

WHAT DO YOU THINK?

Now that you've read about Katie Alexander, answer the following questions. You may not know all the answers yet, but you'll find out what you know and what you stand to gain by reading this chapter.

1. How would you characterize Katie as a student? Identify five specific problems described in this case study that could interfere with her college success.

2. Katie is probably an intelligent student, but she has decided that she dislikes reading and studying, so she avoids it. How important will these two skills be as she continues to pursue a college degree? Is she likely to succeed her second time around?

3. Is Katie like students you know? If so, in what ways, specifically?

4. Identify three specific things Katie should do to get her college career on track.

Who Needs to Read?

What's so important about reading? Teachers seem to think it's important, and parents consider it to be an admirable pastime, but times have changed, haven't they? Now you can just skim predigested information on websites, get a summary of the day's news from television, and watch movies for entertainment. Who needs to read? Look around the next time you're in a doctor or dentist's waiting room. You'll see some people staring at the TV screen mounted on the wall, others plugged into iPods, and still others working on their PDAs. A few may be skimming through magazines, but does anyone ever pick up a book to actually read it cover to cover anymore? Does it matter?

The answer, according to many experts, is a resounding yes, it does![1] Reading helped create civilization as we know it and taught us particular ways of thinking.

One fairly predictable result of doing anything less frequently is that eventually you may not do it as well. Practice keeps your skills from eroding. Even an Olympic athlete who doesn't stick with training gets rusty after a while. As students read less, their reading skills deteriorate and they don't enjoy doing it. Conversely, the better you get at reading, the more you may enjoy it. Falling down every ten minutes the first time you get on skis isn't all that much fun, but once you can zip down the mountain like a pro, you begin to appreciate the sport.

Like Katie from the "FOCUS Challenge Case," reading may not be your favorite pastime. You may feel about reading like many people do about eating cauliflower. You know it's good for you, but you'd prefer to avoid it. However, this chapter wouldn't be worth its weight in trees if it didn't try to convince you otherwise. One aspect of reading Katie particularly dislikes is that reading is not a social or physical activity. You can read with someone else in the room, of course, or talk about what you read afterward with friends, but basically, reading is something you do alone. It's a solitary activity that involves you, words on a page, an invisible author, and your brain. You need to do it with a minimum of physical movement. Reading while playing a game of volleyball would be tough to pull off.

If you enjoy reading, congratulations! When you settle in with an exciting novel, you can travel to the far corners of the Earth, turn back the clock to previous centuries, or fast-forward to a future that extends beyond your lifetime. Whether or not you enjoy reading, it will be one of the primary skills you need to cultivate in college. According to one study, 85 percent of the

Tom McCarthy/PhotoEdit

learning you'll do in college requires careful reading.[2] First-year students often need to read and comprehend 150–200 pages per week in order to complete their academic assignments.[3]

What's more, reading skills go hand in hand with writing skills, which makes them even more important. The better you get at reading, the more you raise your probability of academic success. Many of your classes will require intensive reading of complex material, including primary sources by original authors and scholarly research. If you complete reading assignments, and your classmates don't, think about how much ahead of the nonreaders *you* will be! But how do you become a better reader?

> "It matters, if individuals are to retain any capacity to form their own judgments and opinions, that they continue to read for themselves."
>
> Harold Bloom, literary critic

EXERCISE 8.1 What Is Your Reading Rate?

Before continuing, you'll need a stopwatch or a watch with a second hand. Keep track of how long it takes you to read the following article about getting a job. The object of the exercise isn't to race through; it's to read at your normal speed. After you read the article, you'll be asked to record your reading time and answer some questions to check your comprehension.

How Cool Is Your Job? Does It Even Matter?
By Adelle Waldman, Special to *The Wall Street Journal Online*

Dustin Goot has the kind of job that piques the interest of people he meets at parties, at least initially. The 27-year-old New Yorker is an associate editor of a glossy magazine aimed at young men, but his magazine—*Sync*—just launched last year, and many people haven't heard of it, which changes the dynamic.

"It seems like a cool job when you first say it," Mr. Goot says. But, "if you are at a magazine that not a lot of people have heard of, it's a bit of a letdown," he says. "People kind of shrug their shoulders." Mr. Goot may not be at a magazine with the name recognition of, say, *Sports Illustrated,* but in the complicated status hierarchy that emerges around the "coolness factor"—that is, how cool is your job?—Mr. Goot fares pretty well.

That's nothing to sneeze at. When we were in college, we all had the same job title—we were students. Sure, some schools are more prestigious than others, but at least among classmates at our own school, we were on pretty much equal ground. In a social setting, we might have bemoaned that we were judged on our appearances rather than our personalities, but it probably didn't occur to us that one day another basis for snap judgments would be added to the mix: the cachet of our jobs.

It's a biggie, and it's here to stay. For better or for worse, twentysomethings have to adjust to this new reality because for the rest of our lives, we can expect to be treated differently depending on the perceived prestige of our jobs.

So what happens if you love your job but it's not the kind of thing that commands instant respect at parties? Allison Predmore has been there. "When I tell people I am a social worker, they usually say something like, 'oh, that's nice, you must be a nice person,' and change the subject," says Ms. Predmore, who lives in Queens, N.Y., and turned 30 earlier this month.

Finding Your Own Niche

Her solution? She spends a lot of time with fellow social workers and others in the non-profit sector—that is, people who tend to be on her same page, socially as well as financially. "I'm really not used to being with people who have a lot of disposable money to spend on a day to day basis," she says.

(continued)

Besides, the fact that she really enjoys her work is more important to her than being treated like royalty at a party. That's something that many twentysomethings realize over the years, says Abby Wilner, co-author of "The Quarterlifer's Companion." We may be eternally judged by our jobs but that doesn't mean we'll always care quite so much if our title fails to bowl people over.

"When you are a senior in college or just a year or two out, a job is more conceptual or theoretical," Ms. Wilner says. That is, you don't have much else to gauge a job on other than how it sounds. But once the reality of working sets in—once you realize that work is not only a social signifier, but also the place where you'll spend about a third of your life—chances are, many other considerations, particularly how fulfilling the job is, tend to take precedence over the coolness factor, she says.

"After a couple years, you realize what's more important—the hours, who you are working with, what you are doing, possibilities for promotion," she says. "And you realize that while someone's job might sound cool, they might be miserable eight hours a day."

That doesn't mean that having a job that sounds glamorous isn't an added bonus, especially if it's an added bonus that comes on top of really liking the work, says Cathy Stocker, co-author with Ms. Wilner of "The Quarterlifer's Companion." "Glamour or coolness is just like another kind of compensation," Ms. Stocker says. Which is to say, it's one factor among many in evaluating a job, she says.

How Does Your Job Stack Up, Status-wise?

"In high school and college, there were set hoops to jump through," says Ms. Stocker. "You knew what the standards were and what being successful meant."

In the real world, it's not so clear. While investment bankers and management consultants rake in big bucks, money is far from the only factor in the complicated web of professional status. Some jobs are glamorous even if they're relatively low-paying—like, say, working in an entry-level position in fashion—while, to many people at least, doing things like the Peace Corps or Teach for America seem cool because they're considered exotic or admirable.

Hard to quantify as it is, you can measure your job status pretty easily. If you tell a stranger at a cocktail party what you do or where you work and, just like that, he or she seems to find you extremely smart and interesting and certainly worth talking to, then you have an impressive job. If that person instead reacts with a supercilious lack of interest and starts glancing around the room for other conversation partners, then your job is less glamorous (and the person you're talking to is unpardonably rude).

Some people seem to fare well in the brave new world of professional pecking orders, without ever breaking a sweat. It's just the nature of what they do.

Kevin Jasey didn't become an architect to impress people at parties, but he says it does the trick pretty well. Mr. Jasey, 29, is a project manager for a national architectural firm in Philadelphia. He has found that his chosen profession is creative and artsy enough to be interesting, but at the same time, it's seen as solid and professional. "It's pretty cool," he says. "It commands a certain type of respect."

And it counts even among people who make a lot more money, he says. Mr. Jasey's girlfriend is an investment banker, and he's often in crowds in which the majority of people are in a higher income bracket than he is.

But that doesn't mean they take him less seriously, he says. "They usually start asking my advice on their real estate holdings," he says. And more importantly, he really likes the work. "The profession is more important than the pay," he says.

Sometimes a particularly harrowing experience can also help us to put concerns with status in a better perspective. Huong Do had such an experience. The 28-year-old research assistant works in public health in New York City. Ms. Do, who has a master's degree in statistics, really enjoys her work, but knows that to really rise in her field, she should return to school for a Ph.D. But she's not in a hurry.

Nor is she worried that many of her friends are medical students and residents who, a few years down the line, will be full-fledged doctors, earning a lot more money than she does and treated with all the respect that our society affords physicians. "I used to be the overachiever who wanted to go off in a blaze of glory and discover the cure for cancer," she says. But when she was 23, she herself was diagnosed with cancer.

"That shifted my whole perspective," says Ms. Do, who is in remission. "I saw people who didn't make it, and I learned that it is important to do what makes you happy."

It's a key life lesson. After all, we spend a lot more time at our desks than we do making small talk at parties.

From "How Cool Is Your Job? And Does It Even Matter?" by Adelle Waldman, *Wall Street Journal* Online Edition, Oct. 24, 2005. Reprinted by permission, conveyed through Copyright Clearance Center, Inc.

Now let's see how you did.

Reading Speed: Stop! Look at your watch. Mark down how long it took you to read the article: _____ Minutes _____ Seconds. If you read this article in four to six minutes, your reading rate is average for a college student. (Note: Article contains 1,262 words. College students read 200–300 words per minute, on average.) If you read faster or slower than that, what does that mean? If it took longer than six minutes, but you answer the three questions in the "Reading Comprehension" that follows correctly, reading slowly may not be as much of a problem for you as you may think it is. Right about now, however, you may be thinking, *Hey, I don't have time to spare! I'm juggling several different courses, a job, family responsibilities—a dozen things.* That's the point! Read with focus so that you can record, retain, and retrieve information. If you don't understand what you read, it's difficult, if not impossible, to learn it. Reading without comprehension is just going through the motions.

Reading Comprehension: Answer the following questions without going back and rereading the article.

1. What was this article's main point? _____

2. What is the social worker's strategy to cope with how her job is perceived by others?
   _____

3. What was the profession of the interviewee who believes that his job is seen as very prestigious even though he doesn't earn a high salary? _____

Now go back and check the accuracy of your answers. Are you "reading right"?

Read Right!

CHALLENGE ⊝ REACTION

Challenge: Are there *right* ways to read? What have you learned about reading in college thus far? Provide as many suggestions about reading right as you can.

Reaction: _____

_____

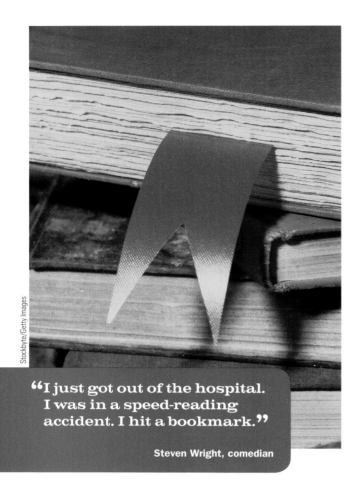

Stockbyte/Getty Images

"I just got out of the hospital. I was in a speed-reading accident. I hit a bookmark."

Steven Wright, comedian

What do we know about reading? How *should* you tackle your many reading assignments in college? Consider these twelve essential points:[4]

1. **Understand what being a good reader is all about.** Reading isn't a race. Remember the old children's story about the tortoise and the hare? The turtle actually won the race because he plodded along, slowly and steadily, while the rabbit zipped all over the place and lost focus. The moral of that story applies to reading, too. Reading is a process; understanding is the goal. The point isn't simply to make it through the reading assignment by turning pages every few minutes so that you can finish the chapter in a certain amount of time. When your instructors read difficult material, which they do regularly in their profession, they don't rush. They chew on the tough parts, reread sections, and make notes to themselves in the margins. Reading requires you to back up occasionally, just like when you back up a DVD to catch something you missed: "What did he say to her? I didn't get that."

   Students sometimes mistakenly think that good readers are speed-readers, when it's really about focus.[5] Science fiction writer Isaac Asimov once wrote, "I am not a speed reader. I am a speed understander."

2. **Take stock of your own reading challenges.** Which of the following are reading issues for you? Put a checkmark next to any that apply to you.[6]

___ boredom	___ vision	___ speed	___ comprehension	___ time
___ amount	___ interest	___ motivation	___ surroundings	___ fear
___ fluency	___ fatigue	___ level	___ retention	___ laziness

   Many people find reading challenging. You may have worked with an impatient teacher as a youngster, or you may have been taught using a method that didn't work well for you—factors that still cause you problems today. Reading involves visually recognizing symbols, transferring those visual cues to your brain, translating them into meaningful signals—recording, retaining and retrieving information (here's where your memory kicks in)—and finally using these meanings to think, write, or speak. Reading challenges can be caused by *physical factors* (your vision, for example) and *psychological factors* (your attitude). If you want to become a better reader in the future, it's a good idea to assess honestly what's most challenging about the process for you right now.[7]

3. **Adjust your reading style.** Reading requires versatility. Contrast these two situations: reading the menu on the wall at your local fast-food joint and poring over the menu at a fancy, high-end restaurant. You'd just scan the fast-food menu in a few seconds, wouldn't you? You wouldn't read word by word and

ask: "Is the beef in that burger from grass-fed cattle?" "What, exactly, is in the 'special sauce'?" If you did, the exasperated attendant would probably blurt out, "Look, are you going to order something or not?" That kind of situation requires quick skimming. But you'd take some time to study the menu at a pricy restaurant you might go to with friends and family to celebrate your college graduation. It's an entirely different situation, and the information is more complicated. And if it's a fancy French restaurant, you might even need to ask the definitions of some terms like *canard* (duck) or *cassoulet* (a rich, hearty stew). That kind of situation requires slow, considered study, word by word. You're going to pay for what you choose, and you want the best results on your investment. That's true about college, too. You're investing in your college degree, so reading right is important!

You'll face an enormous amount of reading in your combined college classes. The question is, what's fast food (to carry through with the analogy) and what's fine dining? According to research on reading, good readers know the difference and adjust their reading styles.[8]

Yes, some of the reading you'll do in college is fast food. You just need to skim to get the main points and then move on to the next homework item on your agenda. However, much of the reading you'll do in college is fine dining. That's why it's important to devote more time to reading and studying than you think you'll actually need. If you don't understand difficult material, go back and reread it, instead of assuming it will be explained by your instructor in class. Keep a dictionary at your side, and check unusual new terms. You'll be able to digest what you're reading much better.

4. **Converse with the author.** In every book you read, the author is trying to convince you of something. Take this book, for example. We have been engaged in a conversation all the way through. What do you know about me? What am I trying to persuade you to think about or do? Even though I'm not right in front of you in person on every page, you are forming impressions of me as you read, and I'm either convincing you to try the suggestions in this book or I'm not. As you read any book, argue with the author ("That's not how I see it!"), question her ("What makes you say that?"), agree with her ("Yes, right on!"), relate something she said earlier to something she's saying now ("But what about …?"). Instead of just coloring with your yellow highlighter, scribble comments in the margins, or keep a running commentary in a notebook. Make small ticks in the margins to mark words you'll look up in your dictionary at a good breaking point. Reading is an active process, not a passive one in which the words just float by you. In fact, mark up this page right now! How do you decide what's really important? One thing you can do is ask your instructor in this course to show you his or her mark-ups in this book, and see if the two of you agree on what's important.

5. **Dissect the text.** Whether you did it virtually online or physically in a real lab, cutting up those little critters in your biology class helped you figure out what was what. The ability to dissect text is important in reading. As you read and make notes in the margins, write what and why statements. Try it: beside each paragraph on this page, write a one-sentence summary statement: a what statement. Put the author's words into your own words.

READING WHEN ENGLISH IS YOUR SECOND LANGUAGE

Hints on Pronunciation for Foreigners

I take it you already know

Of laugh and bough and cough and dough?

Others may stumble but not you,

On hiccough, thorough, laugh and through.

Well done! And now you wish, perhaps,

To learn of less familiar traps?

Beware of heard, a dreadful word

That looks like beard and sounds like bird,

And dead: It's said like bed, not bead—

For goodness' sake don't call it "deed"!

Watch out for meat and great and threat

(They rhyme with suite and straight and debt.)

A moth is not a moth in mother

Nor both in bother, broth in brother

And here is not a match for there

Nor dear and fear for bear and pear,

And then there's dose and rose and lose—

Just look them up—and goose and choose,

And cork and work and card and ward,

And font and front and word and sword,

And do and go and thwart and cart—

Come, come, I've hardly made a start!

A dreadful language? Man alive.

I'd mastered it when I was five.

—T.S.W. (only initials of writer known) or possibly written by George Bernard Shaw

Go ahead. Try reading this poem aloud. Even if English is your first language, you probably had to pause and think about how to say a word occasionally. Most anyone would. English isn't exactly the easiest language in the world to learn, non-native English speakers say. It's filled with perplexing irregularities. Think about the raw courage it would take to pursue a college degree by reading and writing in a language other than your native tongue. If English is your first language, could *you* do

it in German or Arabic or Hindi? That being acknowledged, what strategies can ESL (English as a Second Language) students use to help with challenging reading assignments?

1. Remember that spoken English differs from the written English you'll find in textbooks and academic articles. In casual conversation, you'll hear, "And she's . . . like, 'wow!' and I'm . . . like, 'really?'" If you read that in a book, you'd have no idea what the speakers were communicating about. But if you're standing next to the conversationalists in the hallway, you have a chance of figuring it out. Learning to speak informally in conversation is very different from learning to read scholarly discourse. Address these questions to your instructor or study-group mates instead.

2. Ask your English-speaking friends and instructors to coach you. For example, ESL speakers sometimes struggle with the hundreds of idioms found in English. Idioms are groups of words with a particular, nonliteral meaning. For example, "I have a frog in my throat" means your voice is hoarse, not that you literally have swallowed a green amphibian. Idioms must be learned as a set of words in order to communicate their intended meaning. If you change one word ("I have a *toad* in my throat"), the idiom doesn't work. Considering how many idioms English has and how freely English speakers use them without consciously thinking about it, non-native speakers may find learning them all to be a challenge. You'll more likely hear idioms spoken, rather than read them. If you're an international student, ask about unique phrases that don't make sense to you.

3. Use the Internet or an online course to improve your language skills. According to one study, international students in an online course made significant gains in their language skills, compared with a control group of students who sat through the same course in a classroom. Online courses provide good exposure and practice in your reading and writing skills via e-mail, web searching, threaded discussions, and online postings.[9]

4. Try explaining what you're reading to someone else. Talking something through while you're reading, especially with a native English speaker, can help you clarify meanings on the spot—and may help the other student achieve better comprehension, too.

5. Mark up the textbook so that you can pursue difficult passages in greater detail later. Insert question marks in the margin. Read with your English–native tongue dictionary in front of you.

6. If you get completely stuck, find another book that may explain the concepts differently, or take a break and let your brain continue to decipher while you're doing something else.

Then write another sentence that focuses on why the paragraph is included. Does the paragraph contain *evidence* to make a point? Is it an *example* of something? Is it *counterevidence* the author will then refute? If you can tackle this recommendation, you'll do wonders for yourself when exam time rolls around.

Go back through the section of this chapter on reading that you just completed. Make notes to yourself in the margins (or on another sheet of paper) about *why* you underlined a word, phrase, or section. Why did you consider that part to be important? Knowing the answers to these questions is more important than the act of "coloring."[10]

6. **Make detailed notes.** You'll be much more likely to actually master a challenging reading assignment if you keep a notebook beside you and take full-blown notes as you read. Go back and forth, detailing main points and supporting evidence, so that you have a self-constructed outline by the time you've finished reading. If you're reading onscreen, open a new document and annotate there. The physical act of writing or typing can consolidate what you're reading and act as a form of rehearsal that helps you remember it later.

7. **Put things into context.** Reading requires a certain level of what's called cultural literacy, core knowledge that puts things into context and gives them meaning. Authors assume their readers have a common background. They refer to other books or current events, or historical milestones, and unless you know what they're referring to, what you're reading may not make sense to you. An example you might be familiar with is how the television show *Seinfeld* made real words that everyone now knows and uses out of fake ones: *yada yada yada*, for example. Those words are now part of our cultural literacy that have meaning for you and everyone you know, probably, but may not for people from another culture. They know the literacy of their own culture instead.

8. **Don't avoid the tough stuff.** Much of the reading you'll do in college includes complicated sentences that are difficult to navigate. When you try reading complex passages aloud, you may stumble because you don't immediately recognize how the words are linked into phrases. But practicing reading aloud is one way you can become more conversant with difficult language. Many instructors teach their first-year students a common approach to reading and studying called SQ3R:

> **Survey**—Skim to get the lay of the land quickly.
>
> **Question**—Ask yourself what, why, and how questions. What is this article or chapter about? Why is it included? How might I use this information?
>
> **Read** (1)—Go ahead now and read the entire assignment. Make notes in the margins or even create a study guide for yourself.
>
> **Recite** (2)—Stop every now and then and talk to yourself. See if you can put what you're reading into your own words.
>
> **Review** (3)—When you've finished, go back and summarize what you've learned.

"Force yourself to reflect on what you read, paragraph by paragraph."

Samuel Taylor Coleridge, British poet (1772–1834)

One expert suggests, however, that for scholarly articles, original published research, and complicated academic prose, you may need to add a few R's to make a new formula, SQ6R:

> **Reflect** (4)—You may need time to truly understand what you've read. Put it down and come back to it later—but definitely come back.

> **Rehash** (5)—Communicate your views to your study partners. They may be having trouble deciphering the language, too, and multiple heads may be better than one. You may gain some insights from them, and vice versa.

> **Rethink** (6)—Evaluate whether or not you understood the article on your own. Do you understand it better after rehashing it with other students? And finally, how will you use put the information you read to good use?[11]

9. **Learn the language.** Every discipline has its own perspective and its own vocabulary. In many of the introductory classes you take, you'll spend a good deal of time and effort learning terms to be used in classes you'll take later. In order to study *advanced* biology, everyone has to learn the same language in *introductory* biology. You can't be calling things whatever you want to call them. You call it a respiratory system, but your classmate calls it a reproductive system. In college you will learn about the humanities (philosophy, for example), the natural sciences (astrophysics, for example), and the social sciences (psychology, for example) as you take what are often called general education or core courses. It's important to get to know a discipline. Pay attention to its perspective, priorities, and practices as you read, study, and learn.

10. **Bring your reading to class.** Some of your instructors will infuse the outside course readings into their lectures. They may justify the readings in their course syllabus, preview the readings in class, talk about their importance, or create reading worksheets for use in small groups. If they don't, however,

---

FOCUS ON CAREERS: Barbara Swaby, Literacy Expert

Courtesy of Barbara Swaby

Q1: You're a national expert on reading. What attracted you to the field?
Literacy has always been a value in my family. Both my parents were educators and were vitally involved in literacy efforts. More critical to my decision, however, is the fact that I am a native of Jamaica in the West Indies. The illiteracy rates in my country of origin are high as are the poverty rates. I have long realized that the major weapon against poverty is education, which in my thinking is synonymous with literacy. These realities greatly formed my decision to work to develop literacy in young children.

Q2: What are some of the main challenges college readers face?
I believe that college students' literacy challenges begin with the sheer volume of reading they are expected to do (and rightly so) and the fact

that they have not been exposed to these expectations in the past. Many students go about reading their required texts in unproductive ways. Many do not allocate sufficient time to study. Many confuse the acts of reading and studying. Many are not reading with enough personal engagement and not connecting themselves to what they're reading or connecting what they're reading to the world itself.

Q3: What's your best advice for first-year college students? How can they become better readers and therefore more successful in their college careers?
First, you should allocate enough time for reading texts and for study. Remember that all college texts are not equally difficult and that reading difficult texts successfully requires more than one reading. Second, separate the act of reading from that of studying. Although reading and studying have some things in common, *purpose* differentiates them. You can read with one of several purposes: to prepare for

it's up to you to integrate them. Bring up the reading in class, ask questions about it, and find out how it relates to particular points in the lecture. Doing so is an important part of being responsible for your own learning.

11. **Be inventive!** Students who are the best readers invent strategies that work for them. Perhaps you're an auditory learner. Reading assignments aloud might drive your roommate or another family member to distraction (so find a place where you can be alone), but it might be the perfect way for you to learn. If you're a kinesthetic learner, you might make copies of particular passages from your textbook and lecture notes, and build your own scrapbook for a course. Or cut up the professor's lecture notes into small chunks and reassemble them. Using what you know about yourself as a learner is a big part of college success, so don't just do what everyone else does or even follow your instructor's advice verbatim, if it doesn't work for you. Figure out what does, and then do it!

12. **Make friends with your dictionary.** Okay, so it's annoying to stop every few minutes to look up a word. It's absolutely necessary, however. Yes, sometimes it's important to break your stride, stop, and look up a word or phrase because what follows in the reading is based on that particular definition. Other times, these strategies might be appropriate:

> Keep a stack of blank index cards next to you and write down the unknown word or phrase, the sentence it appears in, and the page number. Then when you have a sizable stack, or when you've scheduled a chunk of time, look up the whole stack.

> Try to guess the word's meaning from its context. Remember Lewis Carroll's "Jabberwocky"

class discussion, for example, or simply to be entertained. When you study, however, you have a single, predetermined purpose. You will be accountable to someone else for what you read. You must know what you will be expected to learn, prioritize the information accordingly, and read closely, stopping to fix breaks in comprehension. Third, always reflect on what you read. Stop often and think about what you have read. If you are unable to remember or reflect on the material, then reread the material and try again. Taking notes on the text material may help, too. Finally, if you feel that you have a reading problem that you are unable to solve by yourself, by all means, seek assistance from your advisor or from the learning center on your campus. They are available precisely for that purpose.

Brand X Pictures/Jupiter Images

> **"Outside of a dog, a book is man's best friend. Inside of a dog, it's too dark to read."**
>
> Groucho Marx, American comedian, actor, and singer (1890–1977)

poem from *Through the Looking-Glass*? Even though the poem contains fabricated words, when you read it, you infer that something was moving around sometime, somewhere, right?

> **'Twas brillig** ← ['twas usually indicates a time, as in 'twas daybreak],
>
> **and the slithy toves** ← [we don't know what *toves* are, but *slithy* sounds like a combination of slimy and slithering]

Often you can infer a word's meaning from how it's used or from other words around it, but not always. Many of your courses will require you to learn precise meanings for new terms. If you can't detect the meaning from the context, use your dictionary—and see it as a friend, rather than an enemy.

INSIGHT → ACTION

1. How would you characterize your reading skills, based on all your years of schooling and feedback you have received from teachers? Are you an above average, average, or below average reader? Why?

2. What are your particular strengths as a reader? For example, do you enjoy reading, comprehend what you're reading fairly quickly, find it easy to focus, and so on? What are your particular weaknesses? What can you do to improve your weaknesses?

C CONTROL Your Learning

YOUR TOUGHEST CLASS

Look back over the section of this chapter on reading and honestly assess the extent to which reading is part of what you find challenging about your toughest class.

1. Do you understand what being a good reader in this discipline is all about?
2. Do you understand, accept, and work to improve your reading skills in this course?
3. Do you adjust your reading style? If the reading required in this course is challenging, do you read more carefully and with more focus?
4. Do you converse with the author of the textbook for this course as you read?
5. Do you dissect the text, writing what and why statements in the margins of the textbook?

6. Do you make detailed notes?
7. Do you put things you read for this course into context? Is cultural literacy a part of the challenge you face?
8. Do you tackle the reading with gusto, even if it's tough stuff?
9. Are you learning the language of this discipline?
10. Do you bring up questions about the reading in class?
11. Do you invent your own reading strategies to help you?
12. Do you make regular use of your dictionary to help you understand what you're reading for this class?

Honestly assess the extent to which you do or don't practice these suggestions in your most challenging class this term. Make an action plan, citing which recommendations you'll put into effect immediately and how you'll do it. If it's appropriate, e-mail your plan to your instructor in this class.

To learn more about yourself and explore some new books, create your own reading profile. Open up your browser to the website of a major bookseller (amazon.com or barnesandnoble.com, for example). Search for six books whose titles communicate something about you: your likes and dislikes, hobbies and leisure-time activities, tastes and preferences, and so forth. Now, open up a PowerPoint or Word document, and copy and paste in the thumbnails of these six book covers. Line the pictures down the left side of the page, leaving yourself room beside each one to describe why you selected this book and something important the book's title communicates about you. Use these "You Are What You Read" sheets to learn more about your classmates—and commit to reading one of the books you've selected!

Meta-what? Metacognition, Reading, and Studying

CHALLENGE ⮕ REACTION

Challenge: What are your study habits like? To what extent do these ten statements apply to you? Write the number for each statement on the line preceeding it.

Never   Sometimes   Always

1   2   3   4   5   6   7

_____   1. I understand myself as a learner.

_____   2. When I'm studying something difficult, I realize when I'm stuck and ask for help.

_____   3. I make a study plan and stick to it in order to master class material.

_____   4. I do whatever I need to do in order to learn something.

_____   5. I talk through my problems, understanding things while I study.

_____   6. After I study something I think about how well it went.

_____   7. I know *when* I learn best: morning, afternoon, or evening, for example.

_____   8. I know *how* I study best: alone, with one other person, in a group, etc.

_____   9. I know *where* I study best: at home, in a library study carrel, at my computer, etc.

_____   10. I believe I'm in control of my own learning.

Reaction: Now tally your scores on this informal instrument. If you scored between 60 and 70 total points, you have excellent metacognitive skills. If you scored between 40 and 60 points, your skills are probably average. However, note any items you rated down in the 1 to 2 range, and then continue reading this section of the chapter carefully.

Talk about needing to use a dictionary! What does the word *metacognition* mean? *Meta* is an ancient Greek prefix that is often used to mean *about*. For example, metacommunication is communicating *about* the way you communicate. ("I feel humiliated when you tease me in front of other people. Can you *not* do that?")

Since cognition means thinking and learning, metacognition is thinking about your thinking and learning about your learning. It's about identifying your learning goals, monitoring your progress, backing up or getting help when you're stuck, forging ahead when you're in the groove, and evaluating your results. Metacognition is about knowing yourself as a learner and about your ability (and motivation) to control your own learning. Some things are easy for you to learn; others are hard. What do you know about yourself as a learner, and do you use that awareness *intentionally* to learn at your best?[14]

These questions may seem simple, but how do you know:

1. When you've finished a reading assignment?

2. When your paper is ready to turn in?

3. When you've finished studying for an exam?

When you're eating a meal, you know when you're full, right? But when it comes to academic work, how do you know when you're done?

Metacognition is about having an "awareness of [your] own cognitive machinery and how the machinery works."[15] It's about knowing the limits of your own learning and memory capabilities, knowing how much you can accomplish within a certain amount of time, and knowing what learning strategies work for you.[16] Know your limits, but at the same time, stretch.

Becoming an Intentional Learner: Make a Master Study Plan

What's your favorite class this term? Or let's turn the question around: what's your least favorite class? Becoming an educated person may well require you to study things you wouldn't *choose* to study. Considering all you have to do, including your most and least favorite classes, what would making a master study plan look like? You've been there, done that all through your schooling, but do you *really* know how to study?

To begin, think about what you have to think about. What's your goal? Is it to finish your English essay by 10:00 P.M. so that you can start your algebra homework? Or is it to write the best essay you can possibly write? If you've allowed yourself one hour to read this chapter, but after an hour, you're still not finished, you have three choices: keep reading, finish later, or give up entirely. What's in your best interest, honestly? See if you find the following planning strategies helpful.

1. **Make sure you understand your assignments.** Understanding is critical to making a master plan. You can actually waste a great deal of time trying to read your instructor's mind after the fact: "Did she want us to *analyze* the play or *summarize* it?" When you leave class, make sure you're clear on what's been assigned.

2. Schedule yourself to be three places at once. Making a master plan requires you to think simultaneously about three different time zones:

The past: Ask yourself what you already know. Is this a subject you've studied before? Have your study habits worked well for you in the past? How have you done your best work—in papers, on exams, on projects?

The present: Ask yourself what you need to learn now. How interested are you in this material? How motivated are you to learn it? How much time will you devote to it?

The future: Ask yourself how you'll go about learning it. Will you learn it using the strategies that work best for you? What learning factors will you control? Will you do what you can to change what's not working?[17]

3. Talk through your learning challenges. There's good evidence that talking to yourself while you're studying is a good thing. Researchers find it helps you figure things out: *Okay, I understand the difference between a neurosis and a psychosis, but I'm not sure I can provide examples on the test.* Once you've heard yourself admit that, you know where to focus your efforts next.[18]

4. Be a stickler. Have you ever thought about how important accuracy is? For example, an accuracy rate of 99 instead of 100 percent would mean:

   ➤ 500 airplanes in U.S. skies each day wouldn't be directed by air traffic controllers.[19] Disastrous!

As you read and study, remember this example. Be thorough. Read the entire assignment. Pay attention to details. Accuracy counts!

5. Take study breaks. The human attention span is limited, and according to some researchers, it's shrinking, rather than expanding.[20] Plan to take brief scheduled breaks to stretch, walk around, or grab a light snack every half hour during study sessions. Of course, it's important to sit down and get back to work again. Don't let a quick study break to get a snack multiply into several hours of television viewing that wasn't in the plan.

6. Mix it up. Put a little variety into your study sessions by switching from one subject to another, or from one mode of studying—for example, reading, self-quizzing, writing—to another. Variety helps you fight boredom and stay fresh.

7. Review, review, review! Review your course material often enough that you can retain and retrieve information at the level expected by your instructor. If you have to start fresh each time you come to class, trying to work from your memory of what was discussed during the last class, you'll always feel behind.

8. Find a study buddy. Find a classmate who also values studying, and commit to keeping one another focused during study sessions. Go beyond just studying together. Create quizzes and hypothetical test questions for each other, and use your study partner to keep you on track.

9. Estimate how long it will take. Before starting an assignment, estimate the amount of time you will need to complete that assignment (just as you do at the start of each chapter of this book), and then compare that estimate to the actual amount of time the assignment took to complete. Getting into this habit helps you develop realistic schedules for future projects.

10. Vary your study techniques by course content. When you study math, it's important to do more than read. Working problem sets helps you actually develop the skills you need. When you study history, you study differently. You might draw a timeline of the events leading up to World War I, for example.[21]

11. Study earlier, rather than later. Whenever possible, study during the daytime rather than waiting until evening. Research shows that each hour used for study during the day is equal to one and a half hours at night. Another major study showed that students who study between 6:00 P.M. and midnight are twice as likely to earn A's as students who put off their studying until after midnight.[22]

12. Create artificial deadlines for yourself. Even though your professors will have set deadlines for various assignments, create your own deadlines that precede the ones they set. Finish early, and you'll save yourself from any last minute emergencies that may come up, like crashed hard drives or empty printer cartridges.

13. Treat school as a job. If you consider the amount of study time you need to budget for each hour of class time, and you're taking 12–15 credits, then essentially you're working a 36–45 hour/week job on campus. Arrive at "work" early and get your tasks done during "business hours" so you have more leisure time in the evenings.

14. Show up. Once you've decided to sit down to read or study, really commit yourself to showing up—being present emotionally and intellectually, not just physically. If you're committed to getting a college education, then give it all you've got! Get help if you need it. If you have a diagnosed learning disability, or believe you might, find out where help is available on your campus. One of the best ways to compensate for a learning disability is by relying on metacognition. In other words, consciously controlling what isn't happening automatically is vital to your success.[23]

Sprinting to the Finish Line: When to Take Shortcuts

Let's be realistic. Planning is important, but there will be times when taking shortcuts will be the only way you can survive the onslaught of all you have to study. You'll need to prioritize your time and make decisions about what to study. When you do need to find a way to accomplish more than is humanly possible, try the following suggestions.

"Non scholae sed vitae discrimus. (We do not learn for school, but for life.)"

Lucius Annaeus Seneca, Roman philosopher and statesman (4 B.C.–A.D. 65)

1. **Triage.** With little time to spare, you must be efficient. Consider this analogy: If you're the physician on duty in the ER, and three patients come in at once, who will you take care of first: the fellow with strep throat, the woman with a sprained wrist, or the heart attack victim who needs CPR? It's called triage. Of all the material you need to study, ask what is most important, less important, and omittable. For example, if you are earning an A- in art history, a B + in world geography, and a C- in math, you know which course most needs your attention. Evaluate the material and ask yourself which topics have received the most attention in class and in the textbook. Then focus your study time on those topics, rather than trying to study everything.[24]

2. **Use every spare moment to study.** If flashcards work for you, take your flashcards with you everywhere, for example. Organize your essay answer in your head while you're filling up at the pump. It's surprising: small amounts of focused time do add up.

3. **Give it the old one-two-three-four punch.** Immerse *all* your senses in the precious little amount of time you have to study: *read, write, listen,* and *speak* the material.

4. **Get a grip on your gaps.** Honesty is the best policy. Rather than glossing over what you don't know, assess your knowledge as accurately as possible, and fill in the gaps.

5. **Cram, but only if it's warranted.** If you're ultra short on time due to a real emergency, and you have studying to do for several classes, focus on one class at a time. Be aware: If you learn new information that is similar to something you already know, the old information can interfere. So if you're studying for a psychology test that contains some overlap with your sociology test, separate the study sessions by a day. Studies also show that cramming up to one hour before sleeping can help to minimize interference.[25] Nevertheless, continually remind yourself: What's my goal here? Is it to just get through twenty-five pages or is it to truly understand?

A Final Word about Reading and Studying

Albert Einstein said this: "Never regard study as a duty, but as the enviable opportunity to learn to know the liberating influence of beauty in the realm of the spirit for your own personal joy and to the profit of the community to which your later work belongs." Reading and studying are what college is all about. Take his advice: consider the opportunities before you to become an expert thinker, an intentional learner, and a contributor to the community and world in which you live.

C CHALLENGE Yourself Quizzes For more practice online, go to http://www.cengage .com/colsuccess/staleyconcise to take the Challenge Yourself online quizzes.

EXERCISE 8.4 VARK Activity

Complete the recommended activity for your preferred VARK learning modality. If you are multimodal, select more than one activity. Your instructor may ask you to (a) give an oral report on your results in class, (b) send your results to him or her via e-mail, (c) post them online, or (d) contribute to a class chat.

 Visual: Make bar graphs that depict how much time you spend per day reading assignments for each of your classes. Label the X axis with the days of the week and the Y axis with increments of hours/minutes.

 Aural: Reread what you consider to be the most useful part of this chapter aloud. As you read, stop and ask questions or make comments (aloud) to make sure you comprehend what you are reading.

 Read/Write: Reread what you consider to be the most important part of this chapter. As you read, insert what and why statements beside each paragraph throughout in the margins.

 Kinesthetic: Make a copy of what you consider to be the most helpful part of this chapter. Also make copies of your notes from class or from your reading, and build a scrapbook to help you put everything together.

 FOCUS CHALLENGE CASE

NOW WHAT DO YOU THINK?

At the beginning of this chapter, Katie Alexander, a frustrated and disgruntled student, faced a challenge. Now after reading this chapter, would you respond differently to any of the questions you answered about the "FOCUS Challenge Case"?

R E A L I T Y C H E C K

On a scale of 1 to 10, answer these questions now that you've completed this chapter.

1 = not very/not much/very little/low   10 = very/a lot/very much/high

In hindsight, how much did you *really* know about this subject matter before reading the chapter?

1   2   3   4   5   6   7   8   9   10

How much do you think this information might affect your college success?

1   2   3   4   5   6   7   8   9   10

How much do you think this information might affect your career success after college?

1   2   3   4   5   6   7   8   9   10

How long did it actually take you to complete this chapter (both the reading and writing tasks)? _____ Hour(s) _____ Minutes

Compare these answers to your answers from the "Readiness Check" at the beginning of this chapter. How might the gaps between what you thought before starting the chapter and what you now think affect how you approach the next chapter?

 To download mp3 format audio summaries of this chapter, go to http://www.cengage.com/colsuccess/staleyconcise.

9 Taking Tests

YOU'RE ABOUT TO DISCOVER...

- Why you should change your thinking about tests
- What to do before, during, and after a test
- Why cramming doesn't always work
- What test anxiety is and what to do about it
- How to take different kinds of tests differently
- How cheating can hurt your chances for success

READINESS CHECK

Before beginning this chapter, take a moment to answer these questions. Your answers will help you assess how ready you are to focus.

1 = not very/not much/very little/low   10 = very/a lot/very much/high

Based on reading the "You're about to discover..." list and skimming this chapter, how much do you think you probably already know about the subject matter?

1 2 3 4 5 6 7 8 9 10

How much do you think this information might affect your college success?

1 2 3 4 5 6 7 8 9 10

How much do you think this information might affect your career success after college?

1 2 3 4 5 6 7 8 9 10

In general, how motivated are you to learn the material in this chapter?

1 2 3 4 5 6 7 8 9 10

How ready are you to focus on this chapter—physically, intellectually, and emotionally? Circle a number for each aspect of your readiness to focus.

1 2 3 4 5 6 7 8 9 10

If any of your answers are below a 5, consider addressing the issue before reading. For example, if you're feeling scattered, take a few moments to settle down and focus.

Finally, how long do you think it will take you to complete this chapter? _____ Hour(s) _____ Minutes

Joe Cloud

"Joe College," that's me, Joe Cloud kept thinking to himself. His long-awaited opportunity to leave his small rural community on the reservation had finally arrived. He was at college in the big city, where life was vastly different. He would be different, too, he had convinced himself—somehow more outgoing, more athletic, more popular, more successful—more of everything.

Growing up in his town of 1,000, he had been the basketball king, the after-school grocery store shelf stocker, and the smartest guy in his high school of thirty-five. He was leaving a trail of victories behind him, and everyone in town appeared to have a stake in his future success in college. As the end of the summer approached, whenever people saw him in the grocery store, they'd yell out, "Hey, Joe, when are you leaving for college?"

Much to his parents' delight, Joe had even won a scholarship that would pay for all of his expenses. The condition, of course, was that he would be successful, graduate, and return to the reservation to give back to the community in some capacity. Joe hoped to teach English and coach basketball at his own high school. Secretly, he wondered how much more stressful his life would be at college, competing with students from all over the country for the best grades.

Now that classes were in full swing and midterms were approaching, Joe was beginning to feel the stress. Generally, things were going well, except for his killer calculus course. There were 350 students in the lecture course, and Professor Buchanan was very businesslike and aloof. Joe was building up a great deal of anxiety over the course. Never before had he failed at anything, and if he didn't keep his grades up, he'd lose his scholarship.

The first week had been a review of what he had learned in his high school calculus class. But things became more challenging quickly. The pace quickened to the point that Joe found himself frantically trying to keep up. Math had never been his best subject, but by applying himself and hitting the books, he'd always been able to squeak by.

However, as the midterm exam approached, Joe began experiencing a funny sensation when he entered class each week. As he approached the door, his breathing became shallow and rapid, his heart was pounding, and he felt lightheaded when he sat in his seat. He finally had to get up and leave before passing out. Unfortunately, it was exam review day, too.

That evening at dinner, he talked over his experience with his friend, Chris. "I've been telling you to eat breakfast!" Chris said. "You have to start rolling out of bed earlier, man!" But deep within himself, Joe knew his problem was more than just skipping breakfast. His reaction to each class session had become progressively worse. *There's no way I'll pass this course,* he thought. *Not when my body is going to sabotage me like this.* So much was riding on his success, and so many people were pulling for him. How could he disappoint them?

Although he hated to admit it, calculus had become so distasteful that Joe hadn't cracked the textbook since the day he had to get up and leave. He knew cramming was a bad idea, but he also knew that he had given himself no choice. The night before the midterm, Joe figured he'd study all night and forget about everything else that was due the next day. As the clock ticked into the wee hours of the morning, he was making trips to the coffee machine every forty-five minutes. Chris offered him some pills to help him stay awake, but Joe knew better. It was hard to focus, but the test was tomorrow, and he figured he had to pull an all-nighter if he wanted to pass at all. Dr. Buchanan had said the test would consist of calculus problems with the answers in multiple-choice format, so Joe got out his highlighter and started reading the textbook chapters.

The morning of the exam, Joe woke up suddenly with a feeling of dread weighing him down. When he glanced at his alarm clock, he saw that he had overslept. The exam would start across campus in fifteen minutes. His palms were sweaty, and his heart was racing again. He leaped out of bed, threw on some clothes, and ran out the door. When he got to class, he noticed that he'd forgotten his watch and his book bag with his calculator in it. As he sat down in a random empty seat, a student next to him leaned over and whispered, "I am totally freaked out about this test, aren't you?" That didn't help.

Joe finally worked up the nerve to look at the first question and realized he couldn't answer it. Frantically, he paged through the rest of the exam. It all looked unfamiliar. He was so tired that he was having trouble focusing. His seat gave him a perfect view of another student's answer sheet one row down and over. He struggled with the temptation. It was the longest fifty minutes of his life, and when Dr. Buchanan called "time," Joe put down his pencil and slumped back into his chair.

The next week when the exams were handed back, Joe expected the worst—and he got it. What he stared at was the worst grade he'd ever gotten on any test in his entire life. Disgusted, he threw his exam in the trash can at the front of the lecture hall on his way out. *Why is there so much emphasis on exams in college, anyway? I'll never have to take a test again when I get out of here*, he muttered to himself. He was only halfway through his first term, and his scholarship was already on the line.

WHAT DO YOU THINK?

Now that you've read about Joe Cloud, answer the following questions. You may not know all the answers yet, but you'll find out what you know and what you stand to gain by reading this chapter.

1. What should Joe have done differently *before, during,* and *after* the exam?
2. Does Joe have test anxiety? Why or why not?
3. What's the *right* way to study for a multiple-choice exam in a calculus course?
4. Does cramming work? Why or why not?
5. If you were Joe, would you have cheated to save your scholarship? Why or why not?

Testing 1, 2, 3...*Show* What You *Know*

Let's face it, life would be very different without grades in college, or time clocks on the job, or performance reviews throughout your career, wouldn't it? You wouldn't have to show up at work if you didn't feel like it, and you'd get a paycheck anyway. You wouldn't have to do a good job because no one would care. And you wouldn't have to write papers, or give presentations, or take tests in college. Not only would you benefit by having more free time, but your instructors wouldn't have to forge their way through stacks of papers assigning grades, either. What a wonderful world that would be—or would it? Realistically, it would probably bring total chaos.

Life's not like that. Results count. Accountability is the bottom line. Achievement is taken seriously. Like Joe in the "FOCUS Challenge Case," you may be thinking, "I'll never have to take another test once I get out of here," but exams are actually realistic representations of life's requirements. The experience of taking a test is similar to running a critical meeting or giving a high-stakes presentation on the job. You'll need to walk into the room, ready to show what you know, and answer unanticipated questions. The anxiety you feel before taking a test isn't much different from the anxiety you might feel in stressful situations in your career. Exams ask you to demonstrate your knowledge on the spot at a particular juncture in your learning. They help you compare your progress to that of other students and to your professor's set of expectations about what all students should know.[1] On the job, every day will be a test of your skills and abilities, and you'll get your "grade" when your supervisor gives you an accounting of your performance over the last six months or year. Tests are inevitable; so rather than bemoan them, perhaps we should change the way we think about them.

The first step of test-taking, of course, is to make sure you're prepared. All of the information in this chapter is worthless if you haven't gone to class or read the textbook or taken good notes during lectures. Miracles, by their very definition, are in very short supply. Nothing can substitute for being conscientious about your work. Think about preparing for an exam as you would for an athletic event. Imagine running the 26 mile, 385 yard Boston Marathon. You'd have to work for months to develop the stamina you would need to finish successfully. You wouldn't want to just show up for kicks and wing it. If you did, at the very least, you'd probably pull a muscle. At the very worst, they'd carry you away on a stretcher.

The same principle holds true for exams in college. In order to have the stamina required and avoid the "injury" of not doing well, tests require this same kind

William B. Plowman/Getty Images

Christina Ripp wins the 2003 Boston Marathon Women's Wheelchair Division

of step-by-step, long-term preparation. Tests in your courses will usually ask you to do one or more of the following:

> *Remember* or *recognize* specific facts
> *Compare, contrast, synthesize,* or *interpret* information
> *Apply* theories and principles to recognizable or new problems
> *Predict* the outcomes to a set of variables
> *Evaluate* the usefulness of ideas, theories, or methods for a particular situation

Look at all those italicized verbs, and you begin to see the span of what will be required of you in all your courses.

Think about taking tests as a three-stage project with a beginning, middle, and end. What do you do *before* the test to get ready? What do you do *during* the test to do your best? What do you do *after* the test to ensure a productive learning experience you can use for future exams?

Before the Test: Prepare Carefully

CHALLENGE ⊖ REACTION

Challenge: List your five best specific ideas about how to prepare for tests. What works for you? Assume you are giving advice to a brand new student.

Reaction: 1. _____

2. _____

3. _____

4. _____

5. _____

As you read the upcoming sections about *before, during,* and *after* a test, evaluate how many of these suggestions apply to you. Put a plus sign (+) in front of each item you already do regularly and a (✓) in front of items you could start doing more regularly to improve your test-taking skills.

1. _____ Begin preparing for an exam on the first day of class. Nothing can replace consistent, regular study before and after each class. If you work along the way, then when it comes time for the exam, you will be much more ready and much less in need of heroic efforts. Keep up with the reading, even if there are things you'd rather be doing.

2. _____ Identify the days and times of all your exams for the whole term in your planner or PDA. At the beginning of the term, write in the days and times of all the exams in all your courses—even finals, which will seem very far off. You'll thank yourself many times over for completing this essential task.

3. _____ Find out exactly what the test will cover. There's nothing more terrifying than having a classmate next to you say something like this before the exam

begins, "I can't believe this test covers the entire first six chapters," when you thought it only covered the first four chapters. Clarify whether handouts will be included, previous quiz questions—anything you're not sure of. Phone or e-mail several other students, or better yet, ask your instructor questions like these: How long will the test be? What material will it cover? Which topics are most important? It's also a good idea to ask about criteria that will be used in grading. Do punctuation and grammar count? Will you be asked to turn in your notes or draft so that the instructor can see your work? Will there be an in-class review? All these questions are usually fair game.

4. _____ Understand that specific types of preparation are required for specific types of tests. As described in later sections in this chapter, objective and subjective tests should be approached differently. Online tests require that you know the answers to important questions up front. For example, will the test time out? Must you complete the exam once you start, or can you save your answers and come back to finish later? Should you compose essay answers elsewhere and paste them into the online exam so that you don't lose all your work in the case of a technology hiccup?

5. _____ Make a study schedule. How many days are left to study? What will you accomplish each day? Don't decide you'll use whatever time is left over to study for your test. Usually there isn't any time left over.

6. _____ Begin serious reviewing several days before the test. The best strategy is "tending" the class material, just as you take care of other things you care about, like your car or your dog, consistently and regularly. After each lecture, work with your notes, revising, organizing, or summarizing them. Then several days before the exam, step up your effort. Divide up the work by days or study blocks. Begin consolidating your lecture notes and reading notes. Make flashcards, outlines, charts, summaries, tables, diagrams, whatever works for your learning style and fits the material.

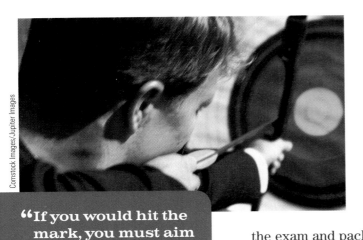

Comstock Images/Jupiter Images

"If you would hit the mark, you must aim a little above it."

Henry Wadsworth Longfellow, American poet (1807–1882)

7. _____ Maximize your memory. Research indicates that specific techniques help transfer information from short-term to long-term memory. Remember to "Make It Stick" (rehearse, overlearn, space it out, separate it, and mind the middle), "Make It Meaningful" (feel, connect, and personalize), "Make It Mnemonic" (spell, locate, link or narrate, and peg), "Manipulate It" (mark it up, mark it down, organize, picture, act, produce, and test), and "Make It Funny" (mock it).

8. _____ Get everything ready the night before. To calm your nerves, lay out your clothes the night before the exam and pack your book bag with things you'll need: several pencils, erasers, scrap paper, your calculator, and a watch that works. Remove as much hassle as you can from test day.

9. _____ Manage your energy so that you're ready to focus and work quickly. You've heard it before, but if you're exhausted or feverish, you're not as likely to

"show what you know" as you will if you're healthy and rested. Don't resort to artificial stimulants, like drinking excessive amounts of coffee to stay awake. "All-nighters" are a college ritual, but they catch up with you, and they're a bad habit to get into. According to one expert, "for every hour of sleep we lose, we drop one IQ point."[2] A series of all-nighters during mid-terms or final exams can seriously impair your intellectual performance.

10. _____ **Don't give in to a nonproductive, negative attitude.** Emotions are contagious. Stay away from other students who are freaked out or pessimistic about the exam. Think—and feel—for yourself. Make sure your selfcoaching is productive ("I've studied this section for an hour; if it's on the exam, I'll nail it."), rather than punishing ("I'm so stupid. Why didn't I keep up with the reading?").

11. _____ **Study with other students.** When you teach something to someone else, you must first learn it thoroughly yourself. Why not study with other students? You can take turns teaching one another, comparing class notes, and making practice exams for each other. For most of us, talking things through helps us figure them out as we go. But don't wait to be invited; take responsibility and start a study group yourself. And if you're concerned that a study group of several students may degenerate into a social club, study with just one other person—find a study buddy and commit to doing the work.

12. _____ **Remind yourself of your long-term goals.** Why are you going to college? All this sweat and toil is worth something or you wouldn't be doing it. Keep your sights on the finish line! Enjoy the feeling of accomplishing something now that contributes to your goal-oriented success later.

13. _____ **Arrive at the classroom early, but not too early.** Get there early enough to get a seat where the lighting is good and you won't be distracted by other students, but don't arrive so early that you build up excessive anxiety during a long wait.

14. _____ **Don't pop pills to stay awake.** You may know students who use Ritalin, Adderall, Vicodin, and OxyContin as study aids. This is a bad idea. When these drugs are used for the wrong reasons, they can help you stay awake for hours and enter a dreamy state. The potential side effects include insomnia, nausea or vomiting, dizziness, palpitations, headaches, tremors and muscle twitching, even seizures. With such horrible potential health risks staring you in the face, not to mention possible legal sanctions if you obtain these drugs without a prescription, why not make things simple? Just study.[3]

15. _____ **Don't let open-book or take-home tests lull you into a false sense of security.** What could be easier than an open-book test? What could be better than taking a test in the comfort of your own home? Actually, these two types of tests require substantial preparation. Time is the issue here. If you're unfamiliar with the material, flipping through pages of notes or skipping around in the textbook won't help. Create a reference guide for yourself so that you can find various topics in your notes or textbook and use your time efficiently.

16. _____ **Don't mess with success.** If you're doing well and earning the grades you deserve, don't discard what is working for you. Honestly assess the efficiency and effectiveness of your current practices, and then decide what ideas from this chapter you should add to your test-taking preparation repertoire.

Cramming: Does "All or Nothing" Really Work?

CHALLENGE ⊖ REACTION

Challenge: Why is cramming for tests a bad idea? List as many reasons as you can.

Reaction: _____

_____

Imagine yourself as the actor in the following scenarios. Compare these situations to cramming for tests.

> You haven't called your significant other since last year. Suddenly you appear at her door with candy, flowers, concert tickets, and dinner reservations at the most exclusive restaurant in town. You can't understand why she isn't happier to see you.

> You don't feed your dog for several months. When you finally bring him a plate loaded with ten T-bone steaks to make up for your neglect, you notice he's up and died on you. Oops!

Of course, these tongue-in-cheek, all-or-nothing situations are ridiculous, aren't they? How could anyone ever neglect such basic necessities of life? There's an important point to be made here. Many things in life require continuous tending. If you ignore them for a time, catching up is next to impossible. Your college courses should be added to the list.

Believe it or not, some students give themselves permission to follow this all-or-nothing principle of cramming in their academic work. They sail along without investing much time or energy in their studies, and then they try and make up for lost time right before an exam by cramming. The word *cram* provokes a distinct visual image, and rightly so. Picture yourself packing for spring break in a warm, sunny place and hardly being able to close your suitcase because it's crammed full. You can't decide what to bring so you bring everything you can think of.

The same holds for cramming for a test. You try to stuff your brain full of information, including things you won't need. Since you haven't taken the time to integrate the information and gather it into related chunks, you end up with random bits of unconnected data. Cramming is an attempt to overload information into your unreliable working memory. It's only available for a very short time. However, there are other reasons why cramming is a bad idea:

> Your anxiety level will surge.

> Your sleep will suffer.

> Your immune system may go haywire.

> You may oversleep and miss the exam altogether.

Despite the warnings here, most students cram at some time or other during their college careers, and doing so may even give them a temporary high and make them feel like they're suffering for a cause.[4] But generally, slow and steady wins the race.[5]

Test-Taking: High Anxiety?

CHALLENGE ⊖ REACTION

Challenge: What is *test anxiety*? What are the symptoms? Do you have it?

Reaction: Fill out the following informal survey to determine whether or not you may have test anxiety. For each of the twelve statements, rate your degree of agreement or disagreement.

1	2	3	4	5
Disagree Completely	Disagree Somewhat	Unsure	Agree Somewhat	Agree Completely

1. I cringe when I suddenly realize on the day of an exam that a test is coming up. _____

2. I obsess about the possibility of failing an upcoming exam. _____

3. I often experience disappointment, anger, embarrassment, or some other emotional reaction during an exam. _____

4. I think that instructors secretly get enjoyment from watching students squirm over exams. _____

5. I experience physical symptoms such as an upset stomach, faintness, hyperventilation, or nausea before an exam. _____

6. I tend to zone out during exams; my mind goes blank. _____

7. I feel extreme pressure to please others by doing well on exams. _____

8. If I'm honest, I'd have to admit that I really don't know how to study for tests. _____

9. I'd much rather write a paper or give a presentation than take an exam. _____

10. I usually fear that my exam grade will be lower than that of other students. _____

11. After taking an exam, I obsess on my performance, going over and over questions that I think I may have missed. _____

12. I convince myself that I'm not good at taking exams even though I often do fairly well on them. _____

If your score equals 49–60, you are a likely candidate for test anxiety. For suggestions on how to manage your anxiety, read on.

If you scored between 37 and 48, you have some signs of anxiety and may need help in managing your stress level.

If you scored 36 or below, you most likely experience a normal amount of anxiety and have already developed coping skills to help you.

Test anxiety—what is it? And, more importantly, does it affect you? While most people think of text anxiety as a negative, the truth is, it's natural to be anxious before, during, and even after an exam. Most everyone is. In fact, some anxiety is useful. The adrenaline rush that accompanies anxiety can keep you alert and focused.

But for some students, like Joe Cloud, test anxiety takes over and sabotages their efforts. They may say, "I knew it all before the test, but when I saw the questions, everything I knew vanished before my very eyes." These students experience fainting spells or even gastric distress that requires them to leave the testing room periodically. Some of them may be reacting to prior bad experiences with exams. Others may put intense pressure on themselves because they're perfectionists. Clearly, there's evidence from medical science that too much anxiety can work against you. Corticosterone, a hormone released during times of extreme stress, can actually impair your ability to retrieve information from long-term memory.[6] Regardless of the reason, the first part of the solution is understanding exactly what test anxiety is. It has four different, but related, components:[7]

> cognitive aspects—nonproductive thoughts that run through your head before, during, and after an exam ("I have to get an A on this test. If I don't, I'll flunk out of school.")

> emotional aspects—negative feelings you experience related to the exam (disappointment, frustration, sadness, and so on)

> behavioral aspects—observable indications of stress (fidgeting, drumming your fingers on the desk, walking quickly, and so on)

> physiological aspects—counterproductive physiological reactions (dry mouth, butterflies in your stomach, palpitations, a tension headache, lightheadedness, and so on)

Since you can't expect the tests you take in college to change for your sake—to alleviate your anxiety—the possibility for change must come from within *you*. Consider these suggestions as they relate to the four indicators of test anxiety.

Cognitive

> Understand your testing strengths and challenges, based on your learning style. Although research indicates that most students prefer multiple-choice tests over essay tests, you have your own strengths and preferences.[8]

> Don't catastrophize! Stop yourself from engaging in negative, unproductive self-talk. It's easy to imagine worst-case scenarios: "If I fail this exam, I'll lose my scholarship, and if I lose my scholarship, I won't be able to afford to go to college, and if I don't go to college, I'll probably end up as a homeless person, begging for change on the street." Negative thinking can

"Positive thinking will let you do everything better than negative thinking will."

Zig Ziglar, motivational speaker and author

easily spiral downward, and before you know it, you're thinking about major life catastrophes and the end of the world. Although some exams do have important outcomes, it's important to put things in perspective.

Emotional

> **Monitor your moods.** Your emotions fluctuate based on many factors; they vary by type, intensity, and timing.[9] If you eat well and get enough sleep before an exam, your moods are more likely to be even-keeled than if you skip meals, ride the carbohydrate roller coaster, and pull all-nighters. An eight-hour sleep debt will cause your mood to take a nosedive.[10]

> **"Park" your problems if you can.** When you go into a store, you leave your car outside in the parking lot and come back to it when you're finished shopping. Think about how that analogy relates to taking a test. Park your problems for a while. Focus on your work, and challenge yourself to do your best.

Behavioral

> **Relieve some stress with physical activity.** Expend some of that extra, pent-up energy before the exam. Sprint to class or take a walk to clear your head in the hour before the test begins.

> **"Step out of your life" by spending time outdoors.** Being in the outdoors is liberating. It's easy to forget that when you're spending large amounts of time in classrooms or at work.

Physiological

> **Teach yourself how to relax.** Relaxation training can be used to overcome test anxiety. As simple as it sounds, that may involve learning how to breathe. Watch a new baby sleep, and you'll see instinctive, deep, even breathing in which only the baby's stomach moves up and down. As adults, when we're anxious, we breathe rapidly and shallowly, which doesn't sufficiently oxygenate our brains.

> **Seek help from a professional.** An expert who works with anxiety-ridden college students can diagnose your problem and help you visualize success or take steps to overcome your fears.

INSIGHT → ACTION

1. Is test anxiety a problem for you? What are your reactions in each of the four areas to taking tests?

   - Cognitive
   - Behavioral
   - Emotional
   - Physiological

2. Which of the suggestions in this section will you focus on in the future? How are these changes likely to affect your reaction to taking tests?

REDUCE MATH ANXIETY AND INCREASE YOUR TEST SCORES!

Honestly, most people feel some twinge of anxiety about working a complex set of math problems on an exam. But if your level of anxiety interferes demonstrably with your test success, you may suffer from math anxiety. One expert estimates that roughly 20 to 25 percent of college students are in that category.[11] Some estimates are that as many as 85 percent of college students in introductory math classes experience some degree of math anxiety.[12]

According to one expert, "Math anxiety is an inability by an otherwise intelligent person to cope with quantification, and more generally mathematics."[13] If you're one of them, admitting the problem is the first step. Next, it's important to understand how math anxiety can work against you during exams so that you can do something about it. The most effective strategies to cope are direct and uncomplicated.[14]

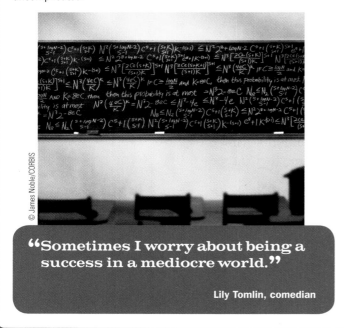

© James Noble/CORBIS

> **"Sometimes I worry about being a success in a mediocre world."**
>
> **Lily Tomlin, comedian**

Think back; perhaps you can speculate on the origin of your fear. It may have been a teacher or a class or a particular test. Perhaps your anxiety increased in junior high school, when social pressures began to mount.[15] Experts believe math anxiety is *learned*, and that learning can result in *rationalization* ("Who wouldn't be terrified? No one could learn this!"), *suppression* ("I know I shouldn't feel this way, so I'm not going to!"), or *denial* ("I don't have math anxiety; I just don't like it!").[16]

Why and how does math anxiety affect people? Try this experiment: multiply 86 × 7. To arrive at the answer, you must first multiply 6 × 7, make note of the 2, and carry the 4. Then you must multiply 7 × 8 and add the 4 to arrive at 602. Notice the steps involved in such a simple calculation. You have to keep certain numbers in your head while you continue to work on other computations, which is often the case with math. Your working memory allows you to pull it off.

Working memory is your short-term, temporary-storage, limited-capacity memory. It's the memory you use to hold certain pieces of information—your brain's scratchpad—keeping them accessible for you to manipulate and update.[17] A task like multiplying 639 × 924 would exceed the capacity of most people's working memories, but some people have more capacity than others. Here's the kicker: Math anxiety actually decreases your working memory.

Why? Managing anxiety takes up working memory space that could be used to solve math problems. When anxiety is reduced, working memory space is freed up to use in more productive ways. Math anxiety also causes people to take longer to complete mathematical operations and make more errors.[18]

It's not the case that you get caught up in overthinking the math problem in front of you; you think and think and think about how to work the problem to arrive at the right answer. Instead, you focus too little on the problem at hand. Your working memory is hijacked by negative thoughts, causing you to choke.[19]

The solution? Researchers suggest practicing for stressful exams under pressure. Set a timer, and tell yourself you must finish before it goes off. Make a game of it: for every question you miss on a practice exam, you must put a quarter in the kitty and pay off your friend, spouse, or mom. In other words, practicing in an equally stressful environment (or nearly so) can improve your performance.[20] Since math anxiety is a learned fear, it can be unlearned.

During the Test: Focus and Work Hard

CHALLENGE ➔ REACTION

Challenge: List five ways to focus and work hard during an exam that work for you. List one other technique you've never tried that you suspect would help you.

Reaction:
1. _____
2. _____
3. _____
4. _____
5. _____
   _____

During an exam, the heat is on! Do you use these strategies? If not, which ones can you incorporate to improve your performance? Put a plus sign (+) in front of each item you already do regularly and a (✓) in front of items you could start doing more regularly to improve your test-taking skills.

1. _____ Jot down what you don't want to forget right away. When you first receive your exam, turn it over and jot down everything you want to make sure you remember—mnemonic devices, charts you've created, acronyms—assuming, of course, that writing on the test is allowed. Some students treat the exam itself as if it were a sacred document, but marking up your exam is usually allowed. Circle key words and strike through answers you eliminate.

2. _____ Preview the exam. Just going through all the questions may help you review terms you know. And you'll notice which questions are easier and which are harder right away. It's also likely that reading sample questions will trigger your memory and help you come up with information you need. After the first few minutes, you may relax a bit, and answers will come to you more easily.

3. _____ Start with what you know. Make sure you get credit for answers you know; don't waste time early on struggling with the more difficult questions. This strategy will also boost your confidence and help you relax. Studies show that running up against extremely difficult test questions at the beginning of a test can actually negatively impact accuracy on simpler questions later on.[21]

4. _____ Weigh your answers. Allocate your time based on the relative weight of the questions. Don't wrestle with one question for ten minutes when it's only worth one point. Go on to a more heavily weighted one.

5. _____ Read directions thoroughly. Misreading or skipping the directions altogether can be a lethal mistake. Remember that your instructor can't read your mind. ("But that's not what I meant!") Slow down and make sure you understand what you're being asked to do.

6. _____ Read questions carefully. Sometimes skipping over a word in the sentence (or filling one in where none exists) will cause you to jump to a false conclusion. Don't let your eyes (or your brain) play tricks on you!

7. _____ If the test has a mixed format, complete the multiple-choice questions first. Often instructors create exams using both *objective* (multiple-choice, true-false) questions and *subjective* questions (fill in the blank, essay). Generally, objective questions ask you to *recognize* answers from several alternatives, and subjective questions ask you to *recall* answers from memory. A multiple-choice question may remind you of something you want to include in an essay. Keep a pad of paper nearby during the exam. Jot down ideas as you answer multiple-choice questions. You'll feel

"We all have ability. The difference is how we use it."

Stevie Wonder, singer and composer

more confident and do a better job if you keep a running list of ideas that occur to you as you go.

8. _____ **Explain your answer to an ambiguous question in the margin of your test.** You may point out a problem your instructor wasn't aware of or get partial credit.

9. _____ **Change your answers if you're convinced you're wrong.** Despite advice you've probably always received from teachers and classmates alike, changing answers when you're sure you've made a mistake is usually a good idea, not a bad one. In one study, less than 10 percent of students made changes that decreased their scores, while 74 percent made changes that increased their scores.[22]

10. _____ **Ask your instructor for clarification.** If the exam appears to have a typo or something seems askew, ask your instructor or proctor to clarify for you. Of course, if you ask for the definition of a word that is a clue, you probably won't get an answer, but if you have a technical question or a question about the test-taking process, don't be afraid to ask.

11. _____ **Pay attention to "aha" moments.** Don't let your "aha" moments turn into "oh, no" moments. If you remember something you couldn't think of earlier, go back to that question and finish it right away.

12. _____ **Don't give in to peer pressure.** If, while you're working away, you look around and see that many students are leaving because they're already finished, don't panic. Take as much of the allotted time as you need. Everyone works at a different rate.

13. _____ **Save time for review.** When you're finished, go back over all your answers. Make sure you've circled the right letter or filled in the correct bubble. Be certain you've made all the points you intended to make in your essay. Look at your work critically, as if you were the instructor. Careless errors can be costly!

FOCUS ON CAREERS: Beth Robinson, The College Board

Courtesy of Beth Robinson

Q1: What prepared you to work in an organization like The College Board?

I worked for fifteen years as an educator—eight of those years in a leadership role—first as a math teacher, then a school counselor, and then finally as a regional director of guidance. Over the years, I had a positive, ongoing relationship with The College Board, and when they had an opening, they invited me to join the organization and now I'm the Executive Director for the PSAT/NMSQT Program and College Planning Services.

Q2: What constitutes a good test?

I consulted my colleagues at ETS (Educational Testing Services), who are masters of test creation (the SAT, PSAT/NMSQT, and Advanced Placement tests for the College Board). A good test is one that fairly and consistently measures what it sets out to measure. A good test, therefore, always starts out with a clear sense of its intended purpose (to see if you know the rules of the road to obtain a driver's license, to see if you understand the main points covered in the chapter, and so forth.) After the purpose has been determined, a detailed set of specifications is agreed to. These specifications are the blueprint or recipe for the test. They say what material will be covered and in what proportion, the kinds of questions, and how hard the questions will be. Every test—standardized or not—should be constructed based on focus, content, difficulty level, and most importantly the "goal" of the test: what it is supposed to measure.

Q3: In your view, why do some students choke on exams?

Sometimes students choke on exams because they simply aren't prepared. They hope they can fake it through whatever they don't understand well. Preparing adequately, of course, is the cure. Other students may be obsessed with getting good grades. They have high self-expectations and usually high expectations imposed from home. They need to calm down, put tests and life in perspective, and develop a

14. _____ Be strategic about taking online tests. Often tests posted online are timed. If you're taking a distance education course or a classroom course with an online test component, watch for e-mail announcements that tests have been posted, and note particular instructions. When will the test expire and disappear? Can you reenter the test site and redo answers before you hit the submit button? Can you take tests collaboratively with other students? With online tests, of course, the other recommendations in this chapter for true-false or multiple-choice tests apply as well.

Taking Objective Tests

CHALLENGE → REACTION

Challenge: Are there specific ways to take objective tests? Identify five suggestions that apply to true-false and multiple-choice tests.

Reaction: 1. _____
2. _____
3. _____
4. _____
5. _____

Many of the exams you'll take in college will be objective, rather than subjective, tests. Let's examine the best strategies for taking objective tests.

healthy level of support. Other students do all the right things to prepare for tests, but they never really analyze what they're studying, thus their depth of understanding may not hold up under the scrutiny of well-written tests. They have a history of poor test results that doesn't reflect their time investment, and that leads to fear at the mere mention of testing. These students could benefit by joining study groups and talking with teachers about what they've learned. Still other students are nervous and insecure, often for reasons unrelated to their actual abilities. They prefer homework, projects, classroom presentations, or any other means of showing their level of learning, understanding, and achievement. For these students, practicing is important. They should take multiple practice tests, review their results, and get very familiar with test directions, test question types, test expectations, and timing. The point is to make the testing environment familiar and comfortable well ahead of time, so that test day is just like any other day. Finally, some students are anxious because of learning disabilities or language issues. They need to take advantage of campus resources to get the help they need to improve.

C CREATE a Career Outlook

MANAGER, NONPROFIT ORGANIZATION

Have you ever considered a career in the nonprofit, as opposed to the for-profit, sector of the economy?

Facts to Consider[23]

Academic preparation required: Completion of a bachelor's degree is required and variable backgrounds are accepted, depending on the specific type of nonprofit organization and its mission.

Future workforce demand: Because of relatively low wages and high turnover, job prospects for the future are excellent.

Work environment: Those involved in advocacy, grant making, and civic organizations—nonprofits—affect many areas of our lives: politics, health, arts, religion, education, and social causes, for example. Typically, nonprofits are run by a small core of paid staff, and whatever fees they charge for services (if any) must not exceed expenses. Most nonprofit employees work in a team environment (working with volunteers, for example) and have variable schedules. They believe in the causes for which their organizations stand, are challenged by the need to raise funds, and find their work rewarding.

Essential skills: communicating, fund-raising, being sensitive to social issues

Questions to Ponder

1. Do you have (or could you acquire) the skills this career requires?
2. Are you interested in a career like this? Why or why not?

For more career activities online, go to http://www.cengage.com/colsuccess/staleyconcise to do the Team Career exercises.

True-False: Truly a 50–50 Chance of Getting It Right?

Exam questions that test your recall are always more challenging than questions that test your recognition skills. T or F?

True-false tests may seem straightforward, but they can be tricky. You assume you have a 50–50 chance of answering correctly. But don't forget, you also have a 50–50 chance of answering incorrectly. Sometimes the wording of the statements makes the *process* of taking true-false tests more challenging than their *content*. Consider these helpful guidelines:

> Watch for parts of statements that make the entire statement false. The statement must be all true to be "true," and a few words may make an otherwise true statement "false." Here's an example:

> Derek Bok, who was president of Harvard University for thirty years, once said, "If you think education is expensive, try ignorance." T or F

> The main part of the statement is true; the quotation does belong to Derek Bok. Actually, however, Bok was president of Harvard from 1971 to 1991 (and returned to serve on an interim basis in 2006–2007), making the descriptive phrase about him, buried in the middle of the sentence, false. The entire statement, then, must be marked "false."

> Assume statements are true until you can prove them false. Statistically, exams usually contain more true answers than false ones. You have a better than 50 percent chance of being right if you guess "true." But teachers vary; yours may not follow the norm.

> Watch for *absolutes;* they often make a statement false. Words like *always*, *never*, and *entirely* often make otherwise true statements become false. "You can *always* get an A on an exam if you study for it." Unfortunately, no.

> Look for *qualifiers;* they often make a statement true. On the other hand, words like *sometimes*, *often*, and *ordinarily* often make statements true. "You can *sometimes* get an A on an exam if you study for it." Fortunately, yes.

> Remember that negatives can be confusing. Is this statement true or false? "Students who don't lack motivation are likely to excel." "Don't lack" really means "have," right?

Multiple *Choice* or Multiple *Guess*? Taking the Guess Work Out

Which of the following statements is (are) true?

a. Richard Greener, who became Harvard's first African American graduate in 1870, later became a lawyer, educator, and distinguished U.S. consul and diplomat.

b. Elizabeth Blackwell, who graduated from Geneva Medical College in New York, was the first woman in the United States to earn a medical degree.

c. Oberlin College was the first U.S. college to admit women and the last to admit African-American students on an equal footing with Caucasians.

d. a and b

e. a, b, and c

Are multiple-choice tests difficult for you? Often what's difficult about multiple-choice tests has more to do with the structure of the test than the content. Studying for these tests requires a particular approach, and if you master the approach, you'll find taking multiple-choice tests to be much easier. You can actually think of them as variants of true-false tests. [The correct answer to the question, by the way, is (d).]

> **Think of answers on your own before reading your choices.** You may get hung up on the wording of an answer. Answer it on your own so that you can recognize it, no matter how it's worded. You may want to do this by covering up the alternatives initially, and then proceeding after you know what you're looking for. Sometimes the alternatives will differ by only one or two words. It's easy to become confused.

> **Line up your test and answer sheet.** This sounds like a simple suggestion, but getting off a line can be very disruptive when you have to erase like crazy and start over!

> **Determine the TPI (time per item).** Divide the number of questions by the allotted time. If there are seventy-five questions to answer in an hour, you know that you'll need to work faster than one question per minute. Remember to save some time for review and revision at the end.

> **Don't decide answers based on the law of averages.** If you flip a coin three times, and it comes up "heads," most of us assume it's probably time for "tails" to come up next. Likewise, on exams, if you've answered (d) for three questions in a row, you may think it's time for an (a), (b), or (c). It may not be.

> **Using a process of elimination, guess if there's no penalty.** Some instructors subtract points for wrong answers, but if you do guess, guess wisely. And don't skip questions. Always mark something unless you're penalized for doing so. Take a look at this example:

Before you write an answer on an essay test, you should do all but the following:

a. Read all the questions.

b. Begin with the hardest question.

c. Look at what the questions are asking you to do, specifically.

d. Underline key words in the question.

You know that you should do (a). Reading all the questions before you start is a must. You know that option (d) makes sense, and so does (c). But you're not quite sure about option (b). You can eliminate (a), (c), and (d), so (b) must be the right answer based on a process of elimination. As you work, eliminate answers that you know are incorrect by marking through them ~~like this~~.

"I am easily satisfied with the very best."

Winston Churchill, Prime Minister of England (1874–1965)

© Image Source/CORBIS

> Look for highly similar pairs. Sometimes two options will differ by a single word or the order of words. Often one of these is the right choice.

> Look for contradictory answers. If two statements are complete opposites, one of them is often the right choice.

> Watch out for tricks intended to separate the prepared from the unprepared! For example, avoid answers that are true in and of themselves, but not true when attached to the sentence stem or question being asked. For example, imagine this question option on a multiple-choice exam:

Global warming is considered to be a serious issue among some scientists because:

    a. Former President Bill Clinton describes global warming as a greater threat to the world than terrorism.

While Clinton did espouse this view in a 2006 speech, it is not the reason for scientists' concern, so (a) isn't the correct answer.[24] Two other tips: generally, when numbers are in each alternative, choose numbers in the middle range. Choosing answers that are longer and more descriptive usually pays off, too.

> Consider each answer as an individual true-false question. Examine each option carefully, as if you had to decide if it were true or false, and use that analysis to make a decision about which option is correct.

> Be wary of "all of the above" or "none of the above" options. While instructors sometimes make these options the correct ones, it's also possible they resort to these options because making up enough plausible answers is challenging.

> Watch for terminology that has been emphasized. Look for key terms that appeared in your lecture notes and in chapters of the text. These words may provide links to the correct answer. Remember when taking multiple-choice tests that you are looking for the *best* answer, not simply the *right* one.[25]

Short-Answer, Fill in the Blank, and Matching Tests

Short-answer tests are like essay tests, which we'll discuss shortly, in many ways. You're required to come up with an organized, well-thought-through answer on your own. But instead of a long essay, you only need to write a paragraph or two. Is that easier? It may be, but sometimes it's just as hard or harder to condense what you have to say about difficult concepts into fewer words. Generally, however, the suggestions for essay tests hold.

For fill in the blank tests, first think the statement through. What does it mean? Try inserting different words. Which one sounds best? Which one was used during lectures or appeared in the textbook? If one word looks awkward, try another one. Although it's not a completely reliable hint, look at the number of words, placement of spaces, and length of the space. If you don't know the exact terminology the question is looking for, insert descriptive words of your own. You may earn partial credit.

Matching tests require particular strategies, too. First of all, you must determine whether items should be used only once or if they can be reused. If it's not clear from the test directions, ask for clarification. Match the items you're certain about first and cross them out if once only is the rule. If you mismatch an item early on, all your subsequent choices will be wrong, too.

INSIGHT → ACTION

Answer the following multiple-choice questions. Beneath each question, identify which of the principles of test-taking from this chapter you are using to identify the correct answer.

1. "I know of no more encouraging fact than the unquestionable ability of man to elevate his life by conscious endeavor." These words were said by:

   a. Bill Clinton

   b. Abraham Maslow

   c. Ronald Reagan

   d. Henry David Thoreau

2. Which of the following statements about the ACT test is not true?

   a. The ACT includes 215 multiple-choice questions.

   b. ACT results are accepted by virtually all U.S. colleges and universities.

   c. Students may take the ACT test as many times as they like.

   d. None of the above.

3. Which of the following suggestions about preparing for college is (are) true?

   a. Get involved in co-curricular activities in high school.

   b. Always take challenging courses that show your effort and ability.

   c. Involve your family in your decisions and preparation for college.

   d. Find a mentor, a teacher, or counselor who can give you good advice.

   e. All of the above.

[Answer key: (d), (d), (e)]

Taking Subjective Essay Tests

Essay Question: Please discuss the value of brain research in relation to our current knowledge of how learning takes place.

Essay questions are difficult for some students because details are required. Rather than being able to *recognize* the correct answer, you must be able to *recall* it totally from your own memory. Here are some recommendations you should consider:

> **Save enough time for essays.** If the test has a mixed format, it's important to save enough time to write well-thought-through essays. Often objective questions such as multiple choice or true-false only count a point or two, whereas essay questions often count into the double digits.

> **Read all the questions before you start.** To sharpen your focus and avoid overlap, give yourself an overview of all the questions before you start writing.

> **Make brief notes.** Somewhere on the exam or on scratch paper, write a brief plan for your responses to essay questions. A few minutes of planning may be time well spent. As you plan your answer, keep basic questions in mind—*who, what, when, where,* and *why*—as an organizing framework.

> **State your thesis up front.** How will you handle this question? What's your plan of attack? Your first paragraph should include your basic argument in a thesis statement.

> **Provide support for your thesis.** Writing an answer to an essay question requires you to make assertions. However, it's not enough that you assert things; you must try to prove that they are true. If your thesis asserts that college students cheat more today than they did when your parents went to college, you must present evidence—statistics, examples, or expert testimony—to demonstrate that what you're asserting is true.

> **Zero in on the verb.** The heart of an essay question is its verb. Take a look at this list and think about how each verb dictates what is required:

> Analyze—break into separate parts and examine or discuss each part
> Compare—examine two or more things, find the similarities and differences (usually you emphasize the similarities)
> Contrast—find the differences between two or more things
> Critique, criticize, or evaluate—make a judgment, describe the worth of something
> Define—provide the meaning (usually requires a short answer)
> Describe—give a detailed account, list characteristics or qualities
> Discuss—describe a cause/effect relationship, the significance of something, the pros and cons, or the role played by someone or something
> Enumerate—list qualities, characteristics, events, and so on
> Explain—similar to discuss
> Illustrate—give concrete examples
> Interpret—comment on, give examples, provide an explanation for, discuss
> Outline—describe the plot, main ideas, or organization of something
> Prove—support an argument with evidence from the text or class notes
> Relate—show the relationship or connection between two things
> State—explain in precise terms

Summarize—give a condensed account of key points, reduce to the essential components

Trace—describe a process or the development of something

> Use terminology from the course. Perhaps more than any other type of exam, an essay test allows you room to truly display your knowledge. Use the opportunity! Reflect new terms you have learned, and tie your answer directly to course content.

> Rifle your answer, don't shotgun. Here's an analogy: A shotgun fires many small metal pellets. A rifle fires a single bullet. When writing an essay answer, some students write down everything they know, hoping that something will be correct. You may actually lose points by doing this. It's better to target your answer and be precise.

> Generalize if you're unsure of small, exact details. You can't quite remember, was it 1884 or 1894? The best idea is to write, "Toward the end of the nineteenth century" instead of choosing one of the two and being wrong.

> Follow all the rules. When answering an essay question, it's important to be as concise yet thorough as possible. Enumerate your ideas ("There are *three* major…"). Avoid slang ("Wordsworth elaborated…" not "Wordsworth *jazzed up* the poem."). Refer to researchers or authors or noteworthy people by their last names ("Jung wrote…" not "Dr. Carl Jung wrote…").

> Watch your grammar. The reason why its important, to do this, is because many student's dont and there answers are marked wrong. They wish they would of done better afterwards. You get the point.

> Write an answer that corresponds to how much the question is worth. It's important to be concise, but generally, if one essay answer is worth 10 points and another is worth 25 points, your instructor will expect you to write more for the question that's worth more. A more detailed, thorough response is what is called for.

> Put down what you do know. If you see a question you didn't predict, don't panic. If you've studied, you know *something* that might help give you partial credit even if you don't know the answer in full.

> Proofread and make sure your handwriting is legible. While most instructors will count the number of points you covered and use specific standards, grading essays is a slightly subjective process. That means instructors must use their own judgment. A good essay answer is taken less seriously if it's littered with mistakes or a real mess to read. This is the real world; neatness counts. Anything you can do to create a positive impression may work in your favor.

> If you run out of time, jot down any remaining points in the time that's left. You may not get full credit, but partial credit is better than none.

> Include a summary statement at the end. Your essay answer should read like a real essay with an introduction, a body, and a conclusion. Don't just stop mid-sentence without wrapping things up.[26]

"Knowing is not enough; we must apply. Willing is not enough; we must do."

Johann Wolfgang von Goethe, German writer and scholar (1749–1832)

YOUR TOUGHEST CLASS

Think about your most challenging class this term. Identify one key challenge you face in this class that relates to this chapter. Now develop a step-by-step action plan to deal with this one challenge. For example, Joe's calculus class was his most challenging. His action plan might look like this:

    a. Reread the sections of the chapter on preparing for tests and test anxiety.

    b. Meet with my professor to discuss my problems in her class.

    c. Show her this action plan, and ask for her suggestions.

    d. Keep a journal of my progress to note improvement and meet with her four more times this term.

Now do the same for *your* most challenging class.

1. _____
_____

2. _____
_____

3. _____
_____

4. _____
_____

Don't Cheat Yourself!

What if you were in one of these situations? How would you respond?

> Many students in your math class get through the homework by sharing answers on their Facebook pages. The professor doesn't know, and the course isn't all that interesting anyway.

> A friend of yours stores all the names and dates she'll need to know for her history exams on her pocket PC. With just one click she can call up whatever information she needs. "Try it," she says. "Everyone else does it, and you'll feel cheated if you don't cheat. If you don't do what other students do, you'll graduate with mediocre grades, and you'll never be able to compete for the jobs you've always wanted. Besides getting away with it here just helps prepare you for the business world where things are *really* cutthroat!"

> You hear about an entrepreneurial student on a nearby campus who operates an underground ghostwriting service. For $20 a page, he will guarantee you the grade you want (based on the grade you already have going in the course so that your paper won't raise the professor's suspicions), and he "doctors" each sentence so that the source can't be found on the Internet. You have four papers, a presentation, and an exam all due the same week, and one or two ghostwritten papers would only run you around $150 to $200. That's not all that much considering the tips you make as a server. Hmm. . . .

How did you respond to these three scenarios? Are you aware of cheating schemes on your own campus? Could students you know be the ones these scenarios were written about? Notice that these students have practical-sounding reasons for what they are doing. If you want to cheat, it's not hard, and you can always blame someone else. What's the harm? You get better grades your teachers feel gratified, your school brags about the fine academic record of its students, and you pat yourself on your back for skillfully managing a very busy, demanding life. Everyone wins, right? Wrong.

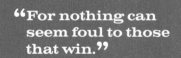

"For nothing can seem foul to those that win."

William Shakespeare, British poet and playwright (1564–1616)

© Vera Berger/zefa/CORBIS

According to some studies, fifty years ago, one in five college students admitted to cheating. Today's figures range from 75 to 90 percent. Here's some straight talk about cheating:[27]

1. **Remember that cheating snowballs.** What started as secretly pocketing some kid's CD or glancing at your neighbor's reading test in grade school turns into writing a math formula between your fingers or hiding the names of the constellations under your shirt cuff in middle school. Then these juvenile violations turn into full-fledged, sophisticated infractions as students "download their workload" in high school and knowingly violate their school's Academic Integrity Policy in college. Where does it stop? With corporate scandal and newspaper headlines?

2. **Instead of saving time, cheating can take time.** Everyone is busy. Many students are working at jobs for pay in addition to taking classes. How can anyone get everything done that needs to get done? But instead of devising elaborate cheating schemes, which take time to coordinate, why not just use that time to study?

3. **If you cheat now, you'll pay later.** Sooner or later, cheating will catch up with you. You may get past your history professor or your calculus instructor this time, and you may even get good grades on others' work you turn in as your own. But someday your boss will ask you to write something, or do some research, or use a skill a student is expected to have mastered in college, and you won't know where to start.

4. **If you do get caught, cheating may do you in.** Some students cheat because they know other students have gotten away with it. Cheating for them is a thrill, and not getting caught is akin to winning or beating the system. Roll the dice and see what happens, they say. But you should know that professors are in the know these days. Academic hallways are abuzz with faculty talk about cheating. If you do get caught, your academic career may come to an abrupt halt.

5. **Cheating is just plain wrong.** You may or may not agree with this point, but it deserves some serious consideration. How would you like to be cheated out of money that's owed you or days off that are due you? The Golden Rule may sound old-fashioned, but the fact that it's been around for a long time with roots in a wide range of world cultures tells you something. "Intellectual Property" and "Academic Integrity" may not be as tangible as money you deserve or eight hours of free time, but they are commodities that are increasingly protected by every college and university.

What are your personal ethical standards? Are you willing to cut corners? Would you cheat to achieve top grades in college? What kind of "devil's bargain" would you be willing to strike?

If you're tempted, remember this. Sooner or later, cheating costs you—big time! Don't cheat yourself out of learning what you need to learn in college. Learning is not all about product—the exams, papers, grades, and diplomas themselves—it's about process, too. The process involves gaining skills that will prepare you for life after college. That's a goal worth working toward.

You can't go through life devising elaborate schemes, or hiring someone else to do your work for you, or rationalizing about finding a way to beat the system because you're too busy to do your own work. Cheating in your college classes now just makes it that much easier to risk cheating your employer—and yourself—later on the job. Look through newspapers or watch the evening news to see who's been caught lately. It's a competitive world out there, but more and more companies find that having a good reputation, which comes from valuing integrity, is good business. Integrity starts now: *earn what you learn.*[28]

After the Test: Continue to Learn

CHALLENGE → REACTION

Challenge: What suggestions can you come up with for things to do after an exam—to help you remember the information, perhaps for a later exam or for another course, or do better next time?

Reaction: _____

After you finish an exam and get your results, you may be exhilarated or down-trodden. Regardless, exams can be excellent learning experiences if you take these steps. Put a plus sign (+) in front of each item you already do regularly and a (✓) in front of items you could start doing more regularly to improve your test-taking skills.

1. _____ Analyze your results. Conduct a thorough analysis of your test results. For example, an analysis like this one might tell you what kinds of questions are most problematic for you.

Type of Question	Points Earned/Right	Points Deducted/Wrong	Total
Multiple Choice	32	3	35
Fill in the Blank	15	2	17
True-False	20	8	28
Essay	10	10	20
Total	77	23	100

Or analyze your results by examining lecture questions versus textbook questions to find out where to concentrate your efforts on future tests. Or do an analysis by chapter content to tell you where to focus your time when studying for the final exam.

2. _____ Read your instructor's comments and take them to heart. After an exam, ask yourself: What was the instructor looking for? Was my writing ability critiqued? Does the test make more sense now than it did while I was taking it? Are there instructor's comments written on the test that I can learn from? What do the results of this exam teach me about preparing differently, perhaps, for the next test?

3. _____ Explain your grade to yourself. Where did you go wrong? Did you misread questions? Run out of time? Organize essay answers poorly? Does the grade reflect your effort? If not, why not? Did test anxiety get the better of you? On the other hand, if you studied hard and your grade reflects it, that's an explanation, too!

4. _____ Be honest. It's easy to get caught up in the blame game: "I would have gotten a better grade if the exam had been fairer, if the test had been shorter, if the material hadn't been so difficult, if I'd had more time to study...." Your instructors have heard every excuse in the book: "my dog ate my notes," "a relative died," "a family emergency made it impossible to study," "my hard drive crashed," you name it. Of course, sometimes crises do overtake events. But rather than pointing fingers elsewhere if you're disappointed with your results, be objective and look at what *you* can do differently next time.

> **"A man's errors are his portals of discovery."**
>
> James Joyce, Irish novelist
> (1882–1941)

5. _____ Make a specific plan for the next test. Most courses contain more than one exam. You'll probably have an opportunity to apply what you've learned and do better next time.

6. _____ Approach your instructor politely if you believe your exam has been mis-marked. Sometimes teachers make mistakes. Sometimes they're interrupted while grading and forget to finish reading an essay answer, or the answer key is wrong, or they miscalculate. Even if the scoring is correct, it may be a good idea to approach your instructor for help about how to improve your next test score.

7. _____ Reward yourself for good (study) behavior. After you've worked hard to prepare and the exam is over, reward yourself—take in a movie, go out with friends, do something to celebrate your hard work.[29]

INSIGHT ⟶ ACTION

Reflect on your own situation and answer the following questions. As you assessed your own test-taking strategies earlier in this chapter, how many checkmarks did you make for the suggestions on *before*, *during*, and *after* tests, indicating potential areas for improvement? Which of the suggestions from all three sections will you try to focus on in the future? What test-taking problems have you had in the past, and how will this information help you?

EXERCISE 9.1 VARK Activity

Complete the recommended activity for your preferred VARK learning modality. If you are multimodal, select more than one activity. Your instructor may ask you to (a) give an oral report on your results in class, (b) send your results to him or her via e-mail, (c) post them online, or (d) contribute to a class chat.

Visual: Make a flow chart to show how you will proceed *before*, *during*, and *after* the next test in one of your more challenging classes. Personalize the chart to show exactly what you will actually do.

 Aural: Talk to yourself as you study for an upcoming exam that will challenge your test-taking knowledge and skills. Ask yourself questions that you predict will appear on the exam and answer them aloud.

 Read/Write: Reduce the discussion of all the major topics that appear in this chapter into single-paragraph summaries.

 Kinesthetic: Construct a challenging practice test for an upcoming actual exam, and time yourself while taking it (to simulate the stress you'll face during the exam).

 # NOW WHAT DO YOU THINK?

At the beginning of this chapter, Joe Cloud, a frustrated and disgruntled student, faced a challenge. Now after reading this chapter, would you respond differently to any of the questions you answered about the "FOCUS Challenge Case"?

C CHALLENGE Yourself Quizzes For more practice online, go to http://www.cengage .com/colsuccess/staleyconcise to take the Challenge Yourself online quizzes.

REALITY CHECK

On a scale of 1 to 10, answer these questions now that you've completed this chapter.

1 = not very/not much/very little/low   10 = very/a lot/very much/high

In hindsight, how much did you *really* know about this subject matter before reading the chapter?

1 2 3 4 5 6 7 8 9 10

How much do you think this information might affect your college success?

1 2 3 4 5 6 7 8 9 10

How much do you think this information might affect your career success after college?

1 2 3 4 5 6 7 8 9 10

How long did it actually take you to complete this chapter (both the reading and writing tasks)? _____ Hour(s) _____ Minutes

Compare these answers to your answers from the "Readiness Check" at the beginning of this chapter. How might the gaps between what you thought before starting the chapter and what you now think affect how you approach the next chapter?

 To download mp3 format audio summaries of this chapter, go to http://www.cengage.com/colsuccess/staleyconcise.

10 Building Relationships

YOU'RE ABOUT TO DISCOVER...

- What emotional intelligence is

- How EI relates to leadership

- Whether your EI can be improved

- How communication is at the center of romantic relationships

- How to improve communication with people you care about

- What constitutes a "danger signal" in a relationship

READINESS CHECK

Before beginning this chapter, take a moment to answer these questions. Your answers will help you assess how ready you are to focus.

1 = not very/not much/very little/low   10 = very/a lot/very much/high

Based on reading the "You're about to discover..." list and skimming this chapter, how much do you think you probably already know about the subject matter?

1   2   3   4   5   6   7   8   9   10

How much do you think this information might affect your college success?

1   2   3   4   5   6   7   8   9   10

How much do you think this information might affect your career success after college?

1   2   3   4   5   6   7   8   9   10

In general, how motivated are you to learn the material in this chapter?

1   2   3   4   5   6   7   8   9   10

How ready are you to focus on this chapter—physically, intellectually, and emotionally? Circle a number for each aspect of your readiness to focus.

1   2   3   4   5   6   7   8   9   10

If any of your answers are below a 5, consider addressing the issue before reading. For example, if you're feeling scattered, take a few moments to settle down and focus.

Finally, how long do you think it will take you to complete this chapter? _____ Hour(s) _____ Minutes

Kia Washington

An emotional wreck. That's what Kia Washington was. Since she first arrived on campus, it seemed that everything had gone wrong. Her best friend, Alicia, had decided to go to a different school at the last minute, she was closed out of what probably would have been her favorite class—Introduction to Literature—and she hadn't been able to get into campus housing because of a computer mix-up. If she lived off campus now, the Housing Office told her they'd guarantee her a room next term. To top it off, she was questioning her choice of classes and wondering why she couldn't decide on a major that would lead to a good job.

The apartment she'd managed to find close to campus was run down and barely affordable. She bought an inexpensive microwave, a mattress, and some towels, but she really didn't have the money to fix it up. Feeling completely alone and isolated, she found herself in tears more than once those first few weeks. Home, for all its faults, was looking better than it had when she lived there.

For most of her teenage years, Kia had lived with her Mom, who worked two jobs to support her and her brother, William. Although they got along well, her Mom was always too tired to do anything, it seemed, so they rarely spent much time together. And she never saw her father anymore. He'd remarried after the divorce and moved to another state. All through school, her family life had been rocky. Kia's parents, who probably cared for each other deep down, just couldn't get along. As a child, Kia sometimes retreated to her bedroom to wait out the arguments. Their decision to divorce five years ago had actually come as a relief.

Despite trouble at home, Kia had been a very good student in high school. Perhaps because home was a difficult place, she threw herself into her studies. She liked to read anything she could get her hands on, and doing homework had been a good escape. In fact, Kia kept to herself a good deal of the time. Meeting new people was one aspect of college she'd never really looked forward to. She preferred to just do her own thing, like listen to music by herself with her earplugs in between classes. Visiting the University Center to meet people and get connected wasn't something that interested her at all.

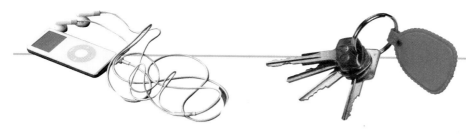

There really was only one other person that Kia cared about—Quentin. Throughout all of her high school years, Kia and Quentin had been inseparable. He'd chosen another college because her school didn't offer his major, but they spent most evenings on their cell phones, sometimes into the early morning hours. Quentin also happened to look like a movie star, and he was the funniest person Kia knew. No wonder every member of the female species was after him in high school. Luckily, he always told Kia that he wasn't in the market. But now that they were apart, she had to admit that she worried that he'd be in even greater demand in college. Holding onto him was her most important goal right now.

Most of the time, they got along really well, and fights were over quickly. Whenever a conflict came up, Kia exploded and Quentin just took it. He was the proverbial nice guy and she was—as her mother put it—moody. She often felt as if she was on an emotional roller coaster, and her temper got the best of her. Trying to communicate her way through a disagreement never seemed worth it to Kia. She'd spit out a few rude comments and then walk away or hang up. Fortunately, Quentin never seemed to hold a grudge.

But last Thursday, they'd had the worst fight ever on the phone over something silly; she couldn't even remember what. Suddenly she heard herself yelling into the phone, saying things she knew she'd regret. Quentin managed to get the words "control freak" out, and then this time *he* hung up. She hadn't heard from him since. He didn't return voicemails or e-mails, and his text messages abruptly stopped. She found herself obsessing about him, not able to sleep well or eat much over the weekend, and she couldn't face going to her classes on Monday or Tuesday. By Wednesday, she was so sick with worry that she couldn't drag herself out of bed.

Why does this have to be so hard? Kia kept asking herself. She'd decided to go to college to make a better *future* for herself. But right now the most important thing she had to do was get through the *present. My life is a soap opera*, she thought. And to anyone watching right now, she was right.

WHAT DO **YOU** THINK?

Now that you've read about Kia Washington, answer the following questions. You may not know all the answers yet, but you'll find out what you know and what you stand to gain by reading this chapter.

1. How would you characterize Kia's adjustment to college? Identify five specific problems described in this case study that could interfere with her college success.

2. To have done so well in school, Kia must be an intelligent person. But is her emotional quotient (EQ) different from her intelligence quotient (IQ)? Why or why not?

3. Kia's relationship with Quentin is the most important one in her life. What is she doing to contribute to the problems in the relationship? Will the relationship survive? If so, what would it take?

4. Identify three things Kia should do to get her college success and her life on track.

The Heart of College Success

CHALLENGE ⊖ REACTION

Challenge: How would you respond in the following situations?

Reaction: Read these five scenarios and identify your most likely reactions.[1]

1. You peer over a classmate's shoulder and notice she has copied your online response from a class chat and submitted it as her paper in the course, hoping the professor won't notice. What do you do?

   a. Tell the student off to set the record straight, right then and there.

   b. Tell the professor that someone has cheated.

   c. Ask the student where the research for the paper came from.

   d. Forget it. It's not worth the trouble. Cheaters lose in the end.

2. You're riding on a plane that hits a patch of extreme turbulence. What do you do?

   a. Grab hold of the person in the next seat and hold on for dear life.

   b. Close your eyes and wait it out.

   c. Read something or watch the movie to calm yourself until things improve.

   d. Panic and lose your composure.

3. You receive a paper back in your toughest course and decide that your grade is unacceptable. What do you do?

   a. Challenge the professor immediately after class to argue for a better grade.

   b. Question whether or not you're really college material.

   c. Reread the paper to honestly assess its quality and make a plan for improvement.

   d. Deemphasize this course and focus on others in which you are more successful.

4. While kidding around with your friends, you hear one of them tell an offensive, blatantly racial joke. What do you do?

   a. Decide to ignore the problem and thereby avoid being perceived as overly touchy.

   b. Report the behavior to your residence hall advisor or an instructor.

   c. Stop the group's conversation. Make the point that racial jokes can hurt and that it's important to be sensitive to others' reactions.

   d. Tell your joke-telling friend later that racial jokes offend you.

5. You and your romantic partner are in the middle of a heated argument, and tempers are flaring. What do you do?

   a. Stop, think about what you're trying to communicate, and say it as clearly and neutrally as possible.

   b. Keep at it because if the issue generated that much emotion, it must be important to get to the bottom of it.

   c. Take a twenty-minute time out and then continue your discussion.

   d. Suggest that both of you apologize immediately and move on.

College is a time of transition; it can be an emotionally turbulent time. Even if you're a returning student who's been on your own for years, college will require you to make some major adjustments in your life. Trying to do so without the internal resources you need may be overwhelming, as it was for Kia Washington in the "FOCUS Challenge Case." When it looked as if the relationship that was most important to her was falling apart, so did she.

Here's a fundamental truth: College isn't just about your head. Yes, academics are the reason you're in college, but your heart plays a critical role in your success, too. From friends to romantic partners, how you handle relationships can make or break you academically. Emotional reactions to troubling circumstances have the raw potential to stop you dead in your tracks. As may be the case for Kia Washington, who most likely has the *academic* skills required for success, *nonacademic* issues can interfere.

In college and in life, your EQ (emotional quotient), or *emotional intelligence*, can be just as important as your IQ (intelligence quotient). Studies show that first-year students often feel overwhelmed and lonely. Begin now to refine the emotional skills you'll need to face whatever challenges come your way.

Perhaps you've found yourself in settings such as those described in the "Challenge → Reaction" situations you just read. You might need more actual details to make the best choice in these five scenarios, but according to some experts, choice (c) is the most emotionally intelligent one in each case. Do you agree? How do *you* make decisions such as these? What constitutes an emotionally intelligent response?

What Is Emotional Intelligence?

Many experts believe that intelligence is multifaceted. Rather than a narrow definition of intelligence, they believe in Multiple Intelligences: Linguistic, Logical-Mathematical, Spatial, Kinesthetic, Musical, Interpersonal, Intrapersonal, and Naturalistic.[2] Emotional intelligence may well be a combination, at least in part, of *intrapersonal* and *interpersonal* intelligences.

Emotional intelligence is a set of skills that determines how well you cope with the demands and pressures you face every day. How well do you understand yourself, empathize with others, draw on your inner resources, and encourage the same qualities in people you care about? Emotional intelligence involves having people skills, a positive outlook, and the capacity to adapt to change. Emotional intelligence can propel you through difficult situations.

The bottom line? New research links emotional intelligence to college success, and learning about the impact of EI in the first year of college helps students stay in school.[3]

As you read about the five scales of emotional intelligence, begin assessing your own competence in these areas. As each scale is introduced, ask yourself whether you agree or disagree with the sample statement presented as it pertains to you.[4]

© William Whitehurst/CORBIS

"Managing your emotions is an inside job."

Doc Childre and Howard Martin,
performance experts

Intrapersonal Skills (Self-Awareness)

"It's hard for me to understand the way I feel." Agree or disagree?

To what extent are you in tune with your emotions? Do you fully realize when you're anxious, depressed, or elated? Or do you just generally feel up or down? Are you aware of layers of emotions? Sometimes we show *anger*, for instance, when what we really feel is *fear*. (For example, Kia was in the habit of screaming angrily at her boyfriend, Quentin, when she actually desperately feared losing him.) Are you emotionally self-reliant, rather than emotionally dependent on others? Do you realize that no one else can truly make you happy, that you are responsible for creating your own emotional states? Do you set goals that relate to things *you* value and work toward achieving them? How well do you understand yourself and what makes you tick?

Interpersonal Skills (Relating to Others)

"I'm sensitive to the feelings of others." Agree or disagree?

Are you aware of others' emotions and needs? Do you communicate with sensitivity and work to build positive relationships? Are you a good listener? Are you comfortable with others, and do you have confidence in your relationships with them?

Stress Management Skills

"I feel that it's hard for me to control my anxiety." Agree or disagree?

Can you productively manage your emotions so that they work *for* you and not *against* you? Can you control destructive emotions? Can you work well under pressure? Are you in control, even when things get tense and difficult?

Adaptability Skills

"When trying to solve a problem, I look at each possibility and then decide on the best way." Agree or disagree?

Are you flexible? Do you cope well when things *don't* go according to plan? Can you switch to a new plan when you need to? Do you manage change effectively? Can you anticipate problems and solve them as they come up? Do you rely on yourself and adapt well?

General Mood

"I generally expect things will turn out all right, despite setbacks from time to time." Agree or disagree?

Are you optimistic and positive most of the time? Do you feel happy and content with yourself, others, and your life in general? Are you energetic and self-motivated? Do people tell you you're pleasant to be around?

From EQ-e: Post Secondary version. Reprinted by permission.

Emotional intelligence and its effects reverberate throughout our lives. For example, researchers study related concepts: "hardiness," "resilience," and "learned optimism."[5] Some people are more resistant to stress and illness. Hardy, resilient, optimistic people are confident, committed to what they're doing, feel greater control over their lives, and see hurdles as challenges. Emotional intelligence is part of the reason why.

Looking back at the "FOCUS Challenge Case," we can see that Kia Washington probably lacks well-cultivated emotional intelligence. Her level of skill in these five areas may help explain her difficulty controlling her moods, communicating with Quentin, managing stress, adjusting to college, and being positive and optimistic about working through her problems. Will she be academically successful? What do you think?

Emotional intelligence and its five scales are important in all aspects of life, including your future career.[6] When *Harvard Business Review* first published an article on the topic in 1998, it attracted more readers than any article in the journal's previous forty years. When the CEO of Johnson & Johnson read it, he ordered copies for the company's 400 top executives worldwide.[7]

Why? Emotional intelligence is a characteristic of true leaders. Immediately after the first shock of the September 11, 2001, tragedy, the world tuned in to a press conference with New York's Mayor Rudy Giuliani. He was asked to estimate the number of people who had lost their lives in the World Trade Center collapse that day, and his reply was this: "We don't know the exact number yet, but whatever the number, it will be more than we can bear." In that one sentence, Giuliani demonstrated one of the most important principles of true leadership. Leaders inspire by touching the feelings of others.[8]

Can Emotional Intelligence Be Improved?

Everyone wants well-developed emotional intelligence, but how do you get it? Can EI be learned? While researchers admit that genes definitely play a role, most experts believe that emotional intelligence can be increased. One of the most convincing pieces of evidence is from a study that followed a cohort of students over seven years. Students assessed their emotional intelligence, selected particular competencies to strengthen, and then each created an individual plan to develop them. Seven years later, their competencies remained high.[9]

If you believe what this chapter says about the importance of emotional intelligence and college success, you're probably asking yourself what you can do about it. Are the skills related to emotional intelligence something *you* can work to improve?[10] And if so, how?

Seek honest input from others. It's hard to be objective about yourself. But it is possible to tap some of that necessary objectivity from those who interact with you regularly. How do they see you? Use other people as

"What's going on in the inside shows on the outside."

Earl Nightingale, success consultant

coaches to help you see which aspects of your emotional intelligence need strengthening.

Find an EI mentor. A mentor on the job is someone who's older and more experienced than you are and can help you navigate your way through tough problems and manage your career. Mentors help, and an EI mentor—someone with finely honed EI skills you admire—can provide you with invaluable advice about handling challenging emotional situations. Develop a personal relationship with someone whose wisdom you admire, be honest about your problems, and follow the guidance you get.

Complete an assessment tool. Other than just feeling up or down, or reflecting on how you handled problems when they came up, is there a way to know more about your own level of emotional intelligence? The oldest and most widely used instrument to measure emotional intelligence is the Emotional Quotient Inventory, the EQ-i, from which the sample statements for the five scales we have been discussing come. The instrument asks you to respond to various statements by indicating that they are "very seldom true of me" to "very often true of me," and the results provide you with a self-assessment of your emotional intelligence on each of the five major scales and further subscales.

As a part of the course for which you're using this textbook, you may have an opportunity to complete the EQ-i or an equivalent instrument. Check your campus's Counseling Center, too, to see if it offers EI assessment tools for students. You can also locate plenty of informal instruments online. They may not be valid, however, so be cautious about fully trusting their results.

Work with a counselor to learn more. Some areas of emotional intelligence may be too challenging to develop on your own. You may need some in-depth, one-on-one counseling to work on areas that need enrichment. Recognize that doing so isn't a stigma. Instead, you are taking advantage of the resources available on your campus and maximizing the potential for growth that can come during your college years.

Be patient with yourself. Learning to become more empathetic or more attuned to your partner's emotions in a close relationship aren't skills you can enhance overnight using cookbook techniques. Building emotional skills is a gradual process that involves awakening insights, acting on them, and noting the results over time.

Keep at it: Developing your emotional intelligence should be a long-term goal. It's safe to say that EI is something all of us can strengthen, if we're willing to work at it. Relationships that are important to us require the best of our emotional intelligence skills. In fact, studies show that the way in which we provide emotional support is strongly related to relationship satisfaction.[11]

INSIGHT ⊖ ACTION

1. Of the five EI scales, which do you experience as most challenging?

2. After reading this section of the chapter, what actions will you take to learn more about your EI and possibly work to improve it?

What Is This Thing Called Love?

Ah, romance.... Relationships—they're what make the world go 'round. Relationships count, and for many of us, romantic ones count as much or more than others.

Some experts say people are attracted to people with similar characteristics: "Birds of a feather flock together." An alternative theory is that "opposites attract." Which characteristics do you find attractive? Most of us have strong ideas about what we want in someone else: good looks, intelligence, or honesty, for example. But here's a puzzler: what do *you* have to offer? If your parents, a friend, or a previous partner were to write up a classified ad for the personals or put your profile on a matchmaking website, what would they say about you? What qualities do you bring to a relationship—loyalty, humor, caring?

In *Why We Love* (2004), anthropologist Helen Fisher defines love in ways you may not have thought about before: the psychological and physiological characteristics of love. Interestingly, Fisher found that neither age, gender, sexual orientation, religion, nor ethnic group made a difference. Love is love, she found. Participants in the study shared characteristics such as these five.[12]

1. *Extreme energy.* When you're in love, your heart pounds, you are breathless, you feel as if you could "leap over tall buildings with a single bound." Your brain is "hopped up" on chemicals, and you have energy to spare.

2. *Imagined betterment.* Although most people in love can easily point out faults in their romantic partners, they tend to persuade themselves that these characteristics are unimportant, unique, or perhaps even charming.

3. *Interfering thoughts.* People in love spend inordinate amounts of time thinking about their partners. No matter how hard they try to think about other things, their thoughts return to him or her. In some studies, participants report that they spend more than 85 percent of their waking hours thinking about their romantic partners.[13]

4. *Mood swings.* Lovers soar with ecstasy and sink to the depths of despair, based on their romantic partners' responses. "She loves me; she loves me not" is a realistic obsession.

5. *Hypersensitivity.* People in love continuously watch and wait for clues about how their romantic partners feel about them. They hover by the phone or computer, and search endlessly for a meaningful sign, reinterpret a facial expression, or translate a word or phrase into relational terms. Often lovers can't eat or sleep because they are so hyperactive in their diligence.

We may assume that characteristics such as age or gender or sexual orientation differentiate the way people view their romantic partners. Not so; love is love, Fisher claims. But not quite.

> "Eighty percent of life's satisfaction comes from meaningful relationships."
>
> **Brian Tracy, personal and career success author**

BUILD RELATIONSHIPS, ONE DROP AT A TIME

After the Korean War, the U.S. Army's chief psychiatrist studied the psychological warfare used against 1,000 American prisoners of war who had been kept at a North Korean camp. He made a startling discovery: negativity kills.[14]

The prisoners had not been treated cruelly. They were given food, water, and shelter. They hadn't been tortured, yet many American soldiers died in the camp. They weren't surrounded by barbed wire and armed guards, yet no one ever tried to escape. Instead, many of them turned against each other, formed relationships with their North Korean guards, and when they were finally freed, many didn't even bother to call home when given the opportunity to let their loved ones know they were alive.

Many of these men died of extreme hopelessness caused by a total removal of emotional support. Soldiers were rewarded for informing on one another and required to stand up in groups of their peers and tell all the bad things they had ever done, as well as the good things they should have done. All positive letters from home were withheld, but negative ones telling of relatives passing away or wives divorcing their husbands were delivered right away. Even notices of overdue bills from collection agencies were passed along. Eventually, many of these American prisoners simply gave up. They died of "give up-itis," as they called it, raising the overall death rate in the camp to 38 percent—the highest American POW death rate in U.S. history.

The record of what happened raised this fundamental question, described in the *New York Times* and *Wall Street Journal* bestseller *How Full Is Your Bucket?* If negativity can have such a devastating impact, what can positivity do? That's where the analogy of buckets and dippers begins. Most of us will never endure the kind of psychological warfare these soldiers did, but all of us can examine the negativity we inflict on others, and by contrast, the positivity we can bring to others' lives.

How Full Is Your Bucket? by Tom Rath and Donald Clifton claims that each of us has an invisible bucket; we function at our best when our buckets are full. We each also have an invisible dipper. In every interaction, we use our dipper to fill others' buckets *or* to dip from them. The principle of the book is simple; following its advice, however, is challenging.

How Full Is Your Bucket? makes these five recommendations:

1. **Dip less.** Get in the habit of listening to yourself. Are your words cynical, insensitive, or critical? If so, push the pause button and rephrase what you're trying to communicate. Keep track by scoring your interactions as positive or negative, and set a goal of five positive exchanges for every negative one.
2. **Bring out the best.** By filling others' buckets, we set off a chain reaction that comes back to us. Imagine a scenario in which something really annoys you about your romantic partner, and you find yourself being critical much more often than you should be. If you make a conscious decision to focus instead on all the good things instead of the one bad thing, you'll have a positive impact on the relationship, and your partner will begin responding more positively to you. Watch and see!
3. **Make more than one best friend.** Who ever said people are only allowed one best friend? High-quality relationships improve the quality of your life. Bucket filling from the start is the way to begin a new best friendship, and regular bucket filling is how to keep it.
4. **Fill a drop at a time.** Giving a small unexpected gift is a great way to fill someone else's bucket. It needn't be much: a token, a trinket, a compliment, or a thank you. Put your positive comments in an e-mail or a note to make them last. Make a habit of giving "drops."
5. **Apply the Golden Rule backwards.** Rather than "Do unto others as you would have them do unto you," try this: "Do unto others as *they would have you do unto them.*"

How full is your bucket? In your interactions, are you filling or dipping? Building a relationship is a process that occurs one drop at a time.

Physiologically, love differs by type and stage. When you're newly infatuated with someone, your brain has elevated levels of dopamine and norepinephrine, chemicals that result in focused attention, exhilaration, hyperactivity, and goal-directed behaviors. Scientists also hypothesize that lovers have lower levels of serotonin in their brains. These three chemicals—higher levels of dopamine and norepinephrine and lower levels of serotonin—appear to be the physiological basis for passionate, exhilarating, romantic love.

However, later in life, after years of marriage, perhaps, these chemicals are overtaken by others. None of us could tolerate a continuous rush of stimulating chemicals and their intense effects forever! Unbridled passion and wild ecstasy are replaced by feelings of contentment and security. However, many couples remain "in love" for twenty, thirty, fifty, or more years. They may even describe themselves as more in love than when they first met. In one remarkable study, couples married more than twenty years rated themselves higher on romantic love than couples married only five years. Researchers noted that their results looked like those of high school seniors![15]

The chemistry of love points to a truth worth noting: Love is not just an emotion. Chemicals wax and wane; emotions come and go. Commitment goes beyond attraction, beyond emotion. It's a *decision* to invest—and continually *reinvest*—in a relationship. As Fisher writes, "Don't assume the relationship will last forever; build it one day at a time. And never give up."

Communicating in Relationships

CHALLENGE ➔ REACTION

Challenge: Are you are involved in an intimate relationship right now? If so, which of these ten statements describe it? Put a checkmark in the "yes" or "no" column for each one.

Reaction: Put a checkmark in the "yes" or "no" column for each one.

	Yes	No
1. My partner is a very good listener.	___	___
2. My partner does not understand how I feel.	___	___
3. We have a good balance of leisure time spent together and separately.	___	___
4. We find it easy to think of things to do together.	___	___
5. I am very satisfied with how we talk to each other.	___	___
6. We are creative in how we handle our differences.	___	___
7. Making financial decisions is not difficult.	___	___
8. Our sexual relationship is satisfying and fulfilling.	___	___
9. We are both equally willing to make adjustments in the relationship.	___	___
10. I can share feelings and ideas with my partner during disagreements.	___	___

Now continue your reading to find out how other couples responded in a national study.

It's not easy to know exactly what characterizes a healthy relationship. What does it take? A study of 21,501 couples across the country compared the answers of the happiest couples to those of the unhappiest.[16] The areas of maximum difference between the two groups were found on responses like the following.

	Happy Couples	Unhappy Couples
1. My partner is a very good listener.	83%	18%
2. My partner does not understand how I feel.	13%	79%
3. We have a good balance of leisure time spent together and separately.	71%	17%
4. We find it easy to think of things to do together.	86%	28%
5. I am very satisfied with how we talk to each other.	90%	15%
6. We are creative in how we handle our differences.	78%	15%
7. Making financial decisions is not difficult.	80%	32%
8. Our sexual relationship is satisfying and fulfilling.	85%	29%
9. We are both equally willing to make adjustments in the relationship.	87%	46%
10. I can share feelings and ideas with my partner during disagreements.	85%	22%

[Note: numbers do not total 100 percent because of the study's design.]

Piglet sidled up to Pooh from behind. "Pooh!" he whispered." "Yes, Piglet?" "Nothing," said Piglet, taking Pooh's paw. "I just wanted to be sure of you."

A. A. Milne, British author (1882–1956)

Look at the highest percentages in the "Happy Couples" column. These results point to an all-important truth: Communication is at the heart of every quality relationship.

In relationships we sometimes communicate in ways that aren't productive. The work of communication specialist Deborah Tannen focuses on miscommunication between men and women. Remember the *Seinfeld* episode in which George's date asks him if he'd like to come up to her apartment for coffee when he takes her home? George completely misses the point and replies that he never drinks coffee late at night. She meant, "Would you like to continue our date?" but he took the question at face value. Later he kicked himself for being so slow-witted. Trying to "listen between the lines" in romantic relationships is a challenge. We say one thing and mean another, or we hope a partner can read our minds and then resent it when they do.

The classic work of psychiatrist Dr. George Bach and others can help relational partners communicate more openly and honestly and meet conflict head on. He described types of "crazymaking" that cause communication breakdowns and, at their worst, relationship failures. See if you recognize people you know—romantic partners or even friends—in these six types of crazymakers.[17]

> The TRAPPER: *Trappers* play an especially dirty trick by requesting a desired behavior from the other person and then attacking when the request is met.

> The BLAMER: *Blamers* are more interested in whose fault the problem is than they are in solving it.

> The MINDREADER: *Mindreaders* try to solve the problem by telling their partners what they're *really* thinking.

> The GUNNYSACKER: *Gunnysackers* save grudges. They fill up proverbial gunnysacks, and then dump all the contents on their partners at some "opportune" moment.

> The HIT AND RUN FIGHTER: *Hit and run fighters* attack and then leave the scene quickly without giving their partners a chance to explain or defend themselves.

> The "BENEDICT ARNOLD": *Benedict Arnolds* like to stir up trouble behind the scenes by playing "let's you and someone else fight."

YOUR TOUGHEST CLASS

Over the course of your college career, you'll take classes from excellent teachers, mediocre ones, and less preferable ones. What role does the relationship you have (or don't have) with your instructor play in your toughest class? Relationships with teachers have different power dynamics than other relationships in your life. Unlike your friends or romantic partners, instructors give grades (although students *earn* them) that can have long-term, high-stakes impact. Is the relationship you have with the instructor in your most challenging class as productive as it could be? Perhaps it is, but if not, try doing something about it.

Relationships of any kind have two participants. The only person you can control is yourself; however, your choices can affect the other person's actions. What can you do to make the relationship as productive as possible? Ask yourself these questions:

1. What behaviors or habits do I exhibit in this class that might be adversely affecting my relationship with my instructor?
2. What could I do instead to draw a more positive reaction?
3. If I were an instructor, what kinds of behaviors would I expect from students?
4. Can students help instructors become better teachers?
5. Can I make changes in my behavior that might improve my own learning?

Try a new set of behaviors in this class for a month, and then come back to this exercise and note the results you have observed.[18]

If you think you're a victim of crazymaking communication, what should you do about it? Try these five suggestions:

1. **Step back and try to figure out the situation.** Is the crazymaker making a request of you (to be more open, reliable, or responsible, for example)? If so, is the request reasonable, and are you willing?

2. **Become aware of the feelings behind the crazymaking.** Is your partner feeling powerless or vulnerable, for example?

3. **Try not to respond with anger, even though it's difficult.** Piling more wood on the fire certainly won't help to put it out.

4. **Check out your assumptions with the other person.** Ask, "Are you feeling frustrated? Is that what this is about? What would you like me to do?"

5. **Try and reach a mutually agreeable solution by changing communication patterns that aren't productive.**

Once you've identified any unproductive communication habits, you can work on improving your communication skills as well as your relationships. The following five suggestions are a place to start. Several of these recommendations work for any type of close relationship—friends or romantic partners.

> Choose wisely. When it comes to selecting someone you may want to build a future with, don't settle. Seek someone who shares your values, whose background is compatible, but who is different enough to make life interesting. Choose someone who values productive communication as much as you do.

> Let go of unrealistic expectations. Remember that although people live happily ever after in movies, in truth, all relationships have ups and downs. We're human; we make mistakes as communicators. Metaphorically speaking, one blip on the screen doesn't necessarily indicate that the

whole program should be scrapped. Conversely, working on problems together strengthens your relationship.

> **Engage in preventative maintenance.** You take your car in for a checkup every so many thousand miles to prevent major breakdowns; it's a good idea to do the same with relationships you care about. Keep the channels of communication open, and talk about small issues before they escalate into colossal ones. Make deposits into a positive "memory bank." Experts say that doing interesting new things together—going on a vacation, for example—can trigger renewed romantic love.[19]

> **Monitor your own communication.** You can't change your partner, but you can change your own communication: "Although it takes two to have a relationship; it takes only one to change its quality."[20] Eliminate an annoying behavior or modify your conflict style. Be more tolerant of your partner's communication faults, too. Communicate your needs; relationships aren't guessing games. Check, don't assume. Remember that listening is one of the highest compliments you can pay someone.

> **Take the high road.** Don't give in to momentary temptations that may lead to regret and possibly the end of a relationship with great potential. Without trust as the bedrock of your communication, little else matters. If you've promised yourself to someone, keep your promise.[21]

INSIGHT ⊖ ACTION

Do you agree with the suggestions for effective communication in this section? Which one do you think is most important? Why? Give an example of its importance from your own experience.

Breaking Up Is Hard to Do

Research documents the far-reaching effects of bad relationships. They can hurt your job performance, your finances, your physical and mental health—even your life span.[22] Conflict with romantic partners, friends, or with anyone you're in close proximity to can bring on major stress that affects your academic performance, not to mention your overall happiness.[23]

Unfortunately, movies and television often communicate—subtly or not so subtly—that conflict can be resolved by the end of the show. Just lighten up or settle down and you can resolve almost any problem. And if you can't, just swallow, take a deep breath, and move on. But life isn't like that, nor should it be. Managing the conflict in your life takes time, energy, and persistence. It requires understanding your natural tendencies, considering why you communicate as you do, and making productive choices as a communicator.

If you've ever monitored yourself during a particularly heated conflict, you may remember doing something like this: yelling in anger at someone at the top of your lungs, being interrupted by a phone call and suddenly communicating calmly and quietly to the caller, and then returning to the original shouting match after you hang up.

Why? We make *choices* as communicators. Sometimes our choices are productive ones, and sometimes they aren't. It's important to remember that we *do* choose what we say and how we behave. Our choices affect both the *process*—how things go during the conflict—and the *product*—how it turns out in the end. Negative choices produce destructive conflict that includes personal attacks, name calling, an unwillingness to listen, or the crazymaking strategies described earlier in this chapter. Positive choices are much more likely to bring productive conflict that helps us learn more about ourselves, our partners, and our relationships.

Just like healthy relationships, unhealthy ones have identifying characteristics, too. While every relationship can teach us something important about future ones, some red flags are worth our attention. Here are three to think about.[24] If you see these danger signals, it may be time to end the relationship or to devote more time and energy toward improving it.

Danger signal 1: "All we ever do is fight!" This point seems obvious, but sometimes it's so obvious it's overlooked. All some couples talk about is how much they disagree or how wrong things are between them. As a general rule, if 50 percent or more of what you talk about is devoted to managing conflict, sit up and take notice. But when so much of your time is spent walking on eggshells to avoid conflict, airing your differences during conflict, or smoothing things over afterward, there's little time or energy left for other topics.

Danger signal 2: "Let's dig in deeper!" Can you imagine anyone saying something like this: "We've been going out for two years now, but we're just not getting along. I think if we got engaged, we'd both be more committed." Or consider a couple who is unhappily married, who say, "Maybe we should have a baby. That would bring us closer together." Whoa! Statements such as these are danger signals. Relationships should escalate (or reach the next level of commitment) when we're satisfied with them, when we find them fulfilling, and when we are ready to take the next step together. Trying to force intimacy doesn't work. While this point makes sense intuitively, it's surprising how many couples fall into this trap.

Danger signal 3: "This relationship just isn't worth it!" From two unique individuals, a third entity—a unique relationship—is born. The relationship you create with one person is unlike the one you'll create with anyone else. Not only are *you* different in many ways, but *your relationship* with each of these individuals is unique, too. Relationships, like individuals, have their own attitudes, values, and sensitivities.

"The difference between friendship and love is how much you can hurt each other."

Ashleigh Brilliant, author and cartoonist

At some point, you may decide that a relationship just isn't worth it anymore. The costs outweigh the rewards. The relationship is suffocating or lifeless, and you find yourself thinking about having a relationship with someone else, or you're actually on the lookout for a new one. It may be best to face this realization squarely and end the dissatisfying relationship honestly, rather than allowing another one to develop in secret. When relationships end, the quality and quantity of communication between the two participants change. But as the golden oldie goes, "Breaking Up Is Hard to Do," and applying all the emotional intelligence you can muster will help you through it.

Diversity Makes a Difference

CHALLENGE → REACTION

Challenge: What are your views on diversity?

Reaction: Look at the following ten statements and indicate the extent to which you agree or disagree.

Strongly Agree	Agree	Not sure	Disagree	Strongly Disagree
1	2	3	4	5

1. Race is still a factor in hiring decisions today.

2. Multiculturalism implies that all cultures have equally valid viewpoints.

3. Workforce diversity improves the quality of work.

4. The number of male versus female corporate CEOs is nearing the halfway mark in the United States.

5. In some situations, sexual orientation is a justifiable basis for discrimination.

6. All cultures tend to see the rest of the world through their own cultural lens.

7. Feminism is a set of beliefs held by females.

8. A global perspective ensures objectivity.

FOCUS ON CAREERS: Linda Holtzman, Diversity Trainer

Q1: You're a corporate trainer. Are you an internal trainer, working within the Human Resources department of an organization, or are you an external trainer who works with a variety of companies as a consultant?

I am a university professor who teaches courses about diversity, and I conduct diversity training for corporations, nonprofit organizations, other colleges and universities, and school districts. Organizations hire me when they realize how important diversity is to their organization's goals, or when conflicts erupt and they believe diversity training will help.

Q2: How did you become interested in diversity training? What prepared you to do what you do?

I have a strong commitment to equity and social justice. I work to help individuals and institutions change. When that happens, people see and treat each other with greater respect, personally and professionally. I've studied diversity both formally and informally through my graduate degrees, my participation in national organizations, my research and writing, and the way I choose to live my life. I believe it's important to have an understanding of the deep culture of many diverse groups.

9. Religious persecution is a thing of the past.

10. There is less racism in the United States today than there was ten years ago.

As you continue reading this section of the chapter, search for points relating to these topics. Also, your instructor may wish to use these ten items to begin a discussion in class.

These ten statements are intentionally provocative to stimulate your thinking. They relate to diversity: the differences between human beings based on gender, race, ethnicity, age, culture, physical features and abilities, mental capability, socioeconomic status, religion, politics, sexuality, gender identity, and points of view. Throughout your life, you've had relationships with all types of people and you always will. It's important to think about the richness diversity adds to our lives by providing for potential relationships with people who are unlike you.

If you conducted a survey on your campus to find out if discrimination exists, you might be surprised at the results. Research continues to show that minority students experience discrimination at higher rates than majority students. Many of us downplay the prejudice all human beings harbor to one extent or another. Our brains are "programmed" to group like entities and standardize our views about these groups, resulting in stereotypes.

But refraining from stereotyping groups of people and appreciating individuals for what they are could drastically alter the way we think and act. Perhaps you've always assumed that all nerds are A, all athletes are B, and all sorority women are C. What if you switched the labels around? Are the results ludicrous? When labels come to us easily, they are probably negative, and it's likely they apply to groups *other than* the ones *we* belong to. However, when you liberate yourself to think differently, you're not bogged down by tired, old labels. If you open up your thinking to new possibilities, all kinds of new options present themselves.

C CREATE a Career Outlook

HUMAN RESOURCES
Have you ever considered a career in Human Resources?

Facts to Consider[25]

Academic preparation required: a college degree in human resources, liberal arts, and often a business background or internship

Future workforce demand: Competition for entry-level jobs will be high.

Work environment: Human Resources departments, particularly in large organizations, fulfill many employee-oriented functions: training and development; recruiting, interviewing, and hiring; employee relations; and compensation and benefits (health insurance and pension plans). Increasingly, employers realize the value of training employees to improve their skills, build company loyalty, and increase business results through on-the-job training, classroom training, and e-learning.

Essential skills: speaking, writing, teamwork, and problem solving

Questions to Ponder

1. Do you have (or could you acquire) the skills this career requires?

2. Are you interested in a career like this? Why or why not?

For more career activities online, go to http://www.cengage.com/colsuccess/staleyconcise to do the Team Career exercises.

Q3: Describe a typical diversity training session. What types of skills do you teach employees? Does it work?
I have conducted training that is anywhere from three hours to six-day in-residence institutes. I approach diversity training in three different ways: from the *head*, from the *heart*, and with the *hand*. The *head* refers to the theories, concepts, and history. The *heart* refers to the emotional dimension of learning about diversity. My co-trainers and I spend a great deal of time in this realm since many of us have strong experiences, feelings, and fears about issues related to diversity. The *hand* refers to what participants can do to develop specific personal and organizational goals and strategies. My overall goal as a trainer is to bring about change. When I see that beginning to happen, I know I'm doing something very important as a trainer.

Appreciate the American Mosaic

Kin Wah Lam/Time Inc./Time & Life Picture/Getty Images

Take a good look at this woman. She was created by a computer from a mix of several races. What you see is a remarkable preview of . . .

THE NEW FACE OF AMERICA
How Immigrants Are Shaping the World's First Multicultural Society

"We have become not a melting pot, but a beautiful mosaic. Different people, different beliefs, different yearnings, different hopes, different dreams."

Jimmy Carter, thirty-ninth president of the United States

This November 18, 1993, *Time Magazine* cover featured a multiracial, computer-generated woman's face. The blended features were intended to show that increasingly Americans are a composite: the "New Face of America," the magazine called it. It's becoming more and more impossible to draw clear lines between what separates us physically. Tiger Woods tells people he's "Cablinasian," a term he created to reflect his Caucasian, Black, Indian, and Asian ancestry. Keanu Reeves is Hawaiian, Chinese, and Caucasian; Mariah Carey is Black, Venezuelan, and Caucasian; and Johnny Depp is Cherokee and Caucasian.[26] Most of us are a blend, but diversity is about more than physical appearance. Each of us is a unique human being.

Actually, college is a perfect time to immerse yourself in diversity—in the classroom and beyond it. Classrooms are becoming more diversely populated; it's true. By the standard definition, only 27 percent of today's college students are "traditional" (meaning a high school graduate who immediately goes on to college, depends on parents fully for financial support, and doesn't work or works only part-time). Most traditional students today don't fit the traditional definition of "traditional."[27] Adult nontraditional learners have varied backgrounds, interests, and approaches to getting an education. Often they try to work their way through systems that are designed around the needs of younger students.[28] Today, twice as many minority students are enrolled in college than were enrolled twenty years ago, and the number of Hispanic college students has tripled since 1980.[29] Diversity in higher education gives you an opportunity to expand your world view and develop empathy for others who have vastly different experiences.

Diversity makes a difference, and as educator Adela A. Allen once wrote, "We should acknowledge differences, we should greet differences, until difference makes no difference anymore." What can we do about it? Some campuses have launched programs in Sustained Dialogue, used in the past to deal with international tensions. This structured approach brings together students with different backgrounds for a year of deep conversation in small groups. Other colleges have developed similar programs to allow students to dialogue about deeply rooted prejudices—sometimes buried to an extent that they are not even realized—to discuss commonalities, and to recognize the potential for conflict—and change.[30] Raising awareness is a first step on the road to recognizing the reality and the richness of diversity.

INSIGHT ⊖ ACTION

Have you traveled outside the United States? If so, have those experiences broadened your worldview? How? If not, how might you do so even without the opportunity to travel and see differences firsthand?

Box 10.1 Service-Learning: Learning by Serving

One of the best ways to learn about diversity in college is by serving others. Instead of spending all your time in a classroom, imagine a class on aging in which you team up with an elder in your community and work together on a term project. You might help a senior write her memoirs, for example, or help an elderly man create a family tree for the next generation. You might be wondering, *How would that work? What could we possibly have in common—an 18-year-old teamed up with an 88-year-old?* You might be surprised.

Campus Compact, a national organization with 950 member colleges, estimates that college student volunteering was worth $4.45 billion to the communities they served in 2004. They report that more than 30 percent of college students regularly do community service for approximately four hours per week.[31]

Beyond the dollars calculated, college students' community service provides invaluable support. Literally thousands of college students volunteered to help with Hurricane Katrina and Rita relief efforts in 2005, for example, to help displaced victims of one of the country's worst natural disasters ever.

However, here's an important point: *community service* and *service-learning* aren't quite the same thing.[32] Service-learning is specifically about the learning. It's a learning experience in which you connect what you're learning in the classroom for credit with what you're learning in the community. You're applying what you're learning, which in turn solidifies—and modifies—your perspective. "Service, combined with learning, adds value to each and transforms both."[33] While you're engaged in a service-learning experience, you'll also be engaged in critical reflection. Critical reflection is like critical thinking, recalling or looking back at the service experience and writing about what you're learning in a *continuous, connected, challenging,* and *contextualized* way.[34] That's not the same thing as donating your time for a good cause, as important as that is, in terms of you and your own personal development and the lives of the people you help.

The average number of college professors who include service-learning in their courses nearly tripled between 2000 and 2005. Search out these opportunities to enhance your own learning and your appreciation for diversity by serving other people.[35]

Brand X Pictures/Getty Images

> "We make a living by what we get, but we make a life by what we give."
>
> **Winston Churchill, Prime Minister of England (1874–1965)**

EXERCISE 10.1 VARK Activity

Complete the recommended activity for your preferred VARK learning modality. If you are multimodal, select more than one activity. Your instructor may ask you to (a) give an oral report on your results in class, (b) send your results to him or her via e-mail, (c) post them online, or (d) contribute to a class chat.

 Visual: Make a chart of the five scales of emotional intelligence and select representative artwork or graphics for each scale to help you remember its meaning and importance.

 Aural: Ask a friend or classmate to describe a real, model relationship they know or have been a part of. Following their description, discuss the specific qualities that make this relationship work.

 Read/Write: Write a case study about a real relationship using fictitious names that demonstrates some of the principles of crazymaking described in this chapter.

 Kinesthetic: Interview three international students on your campus about how college life differs between what they experience on your campus and what they might experience at colleges in their home country.

NOW WHAT DO YOU THINK?

At the beginning of this chapter, Kia Washington faced a series of challenges as a new college student. Now after reading this chapter, would you respond differently to any of the questions you answered about the "FOCUS Challenge Case"?

C CHALLENGE Yourself Quizzes For more practice online, go to http://www.cengage.com/colsuccess/staleyconcise to take the Challenge Yourself online quizzes.

REALITY CHECK

On a scale of 1 to 10, answer these questions now that you've completed this chapter.

1 = not very/not much/very little/low   10 = very/a lot/very much/high

In hindsight, how much did you *really* know about this subject matter before reading the chapter?

1   2   3   4   5   6   7   8   9   10

How much do you think this information might affect your college success?

1   2   3   4   5   6   7   8   9   10

How much do you think this information might affect your career success after college?

1   2   3   4   5   6   7   8   9   10

How long did it actually take you to complete this chapter (both the reading and writing tasks)? _____ Hour(s) _____ Minutes

Compare these answers to your answers from the "Readiness Check" at the beginning of this chapter. How might the gaps between what you thought before starting the chapter and what you now think affect how you approach the next chapter?

 To download mp3 format audio summaries of this chapter, go to http://www.cengage.com/colsuccess/staleyconcise.

11 Choosing a College Major and Career

YOU'RE ABOUT TO DISCOVER...

- Why "College in a Box" isn't an accurate view of coursework

- How the disciplines connect in the Circle of Learning

- How to choose a major and a career

- What a SWOT analysis is

- How to launch a career

- How internships, co-ops, and service-learning can give you experience

READINESS CHECK

Before beginning this chapter, take a moment to answer these questions. Your answers will help you assess how ready you are to focus.

1 = not very/not much/very little/low   10 = very/a lot/very much/high

Based on reading the "You're about to discover..." list and skimming this chapter, how much do you think you probably already know about the subject matter?

1   2   3   4   5   6   7   8   9   10

How much do you think this information might affect your college success?

1   2   3   4   5   6   7   8   9   10

How much do you think this information might affect your career success after college?

1   2   3   4   5   6   7   8   9   10

In general, how motivated are you to learn the material in this chapter?

1   2   3   4   5   6   7   8   9   10

How ready are you to focus on this chapter—physically, intellectually, and emotionally? Circle a number for each aspect of your readiness to focus.

1   2   3   4   5   6   7   8   9   10

If any of your answers are below a 5, consider addressing the issue before reading. For example, if you're feeling scattered, take a few moments to settle down and focus.

Finally, how long do you think it will take you to complete this chapter? _____ Hour(s) _____ Minutes

Ethan Cole

One thing was certain: Ethan

Cole was unsure. Unsure of his abilities, unsure of which major to choose, unsure of what he wanted to do with his life, unsure of himself. Unsure of almost everything.

Ethan came from a good family, and his parents were actually his best friends. They had been very successful, and they wanted to share the wealth—literally—with their three children. They supported Ethan, no matter what. When he ended up in the principal's office time after time in grade school, they defended him. When he totaled his car in high school, they bought him another one. When he wanted to take a term off to travel and "find himself," they said yes without raising one, single eyebrow. And now that he was thinking of dropping out of college, they said he could move back home, so long as he agreed to a few ground rules and promised to take back his old chores, like mowing the yard. That seemed only fair to him.

The only thing Ethan was sure of was that skateboarding was his life right now. It's all he wanted to do and all he ever thought about. He'd look at a curve on a window frame or an arc in a picture and imagine what skating on it would feel like. All his friends were skateboarders, too, and he read skateboarder magazines and dreamed of the day he might even go pro. He realized not many people make a living at it, but a few really talented athletes did, and maybe—just maybe—he'd be one of them. Recently, he'd found out about the largest concrete skatepark on the globe, Black Pearl in the Grand Cayman Islands—62,000 square feet! He'd made a promise to himself to skate there someday. *Life couldn't get much better than that*, he thought.

But school...that was a different story. Schoolwork had never captured his attention. In primary school, his physician had diagnosed Attention Deficit Disorder (ADD), and in middle school, a learning specialist had discovered that Ethan was dyslexic. *No wonder I don't like school*, he remembered thinking then. But finally knowing why he couldn't focus didn't change his attitude. He still hated sitting in a classroom.

Despite these challenges, his parents had always told him he was smart. "You can do anything you want to do," they'd said. "Look at you: you're a good-

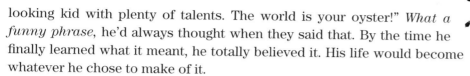

looking kid with plenty of talents. The world is your oyster!" *What a funny phrase*, he'd always thought when they said that. By the time he finally learned what it meant, he totally believed it. His life would become whatever he chose to make of it.

The problem was there were too many choices. How could anyone decide what he wanted to be when he was only nineteen? Ethan remembered liking geometry, he was good at creative writing, he played the drums like a real jazz musician, and he was an incredible artist. *But what do you do with* that *combination of skills?* he'd asked himself more than once. What possible college major and career would really fit him?

He'd managed to pull decent grades his first term—a B average—at the arts college close to home. He'd taken Freshman Composition, Introduction to Communication, Drawing 101, and Study Skills, and while he'd done well, none of the course material really sparked a genuine interest. His professors didn't take much of an interest in him, either. His Study Skills instructor was friendly and tried to interest him in the course, but Ethan had been hearing that information repeated in school for years now. He claimed he already had all those skills; he just wasn't motivated to apply them. Instead, he skateboarded every minute he could.

The more he thought about it, the more he thought it was a good idea to take a year off from college. He could get a job delivering pizzas, think about his life, and try to figure it all out. He'd have nobody to tell him what to do, nobody to hold him accountable, nobody to pressure him to study, nobody to force him into making decisions—and plenty of free time to skateboard.

WHAT DO **YOU** THINK?

Now that you've read about Ethan Cole, answer the following questions. You may not know all the answers yet, but you'll find out what you know and what you stand to gain by reading this chapter.

1. In your view, what will become of Ethan? What are his prospects for the future? Do you think he'll decide on a major and finish college? Why or why not?

2. Why is Ethan experiencing problems? Are these problems serious? Should they hold him back? List all the problems you can identify.

3. Which majors and careers might Ethan be well suited for? If you were an academic advisor, what advice would you give him?

4. Who would you send Ethan to on your campus for help? What are his options? What do you think he should do at this point?

What's the Connection?

CHALLENGE → REACTION

Challenge: Is there a connection between what you study in art, psychology, engineering, and chemistry? If so, how would you try to explain the relationships?

Reaction: _____

College is about becoming an educated person, learning how to think, solve problems, and make decisions. College is much more than the "sum of its tests." It's about developing yourself as a person and becoming well-educated. What does it mean to be well-educated? Simply put: Being well-educated is about the pursuit of human excellence.[1]

Colleges and universities help societies *preserve the past* and *create the future*. Studying the history of the U.S. Constitution in a political science course as opposed to studying potential cures for cancer in a cell biology course are concrete examples. Colleges and universities help us look back (preserve the past) and look ahead (create the future).

College in a Box?

Have you ever thought about the fact that college courses appear to exist in discrete "boxes"? Schools tend to place courses in academic departments, and your class schedule reflects these divisions. For example, your schedule this term might look something like the one in Figure 11.1.

This organizing system helps you keep things straight in your head, and it also helps your school organize a complex institution. Professors normally work in one department or another. And classes are categorized into particular academic disciplines.

Figure 11.1

Most Schools Compartmentalize Learning

	M	T	W	Th	F
9–10	ENG			SOC	
10–11		PHY			
11–12			PSCI		PSCI

But something first-year students often wonder about is how to connect the dots. What's the big picture? Knowledge isn't quite as neat as departments and boxes; it's messy. It overlaps and converges. Despite the convenient institutional compartmentalization of knowledge on a college campus, you might be able to take a somewhat similar course in visual art from the art department, the computer science department, or the communication department. You've probably noticed that you sometimes hear something discussed in one of your classes that's also being discussed in another one. Knowledge is interconnected. College in a Box isn't an accurate way of looking at things.

Even though each discipline has its own history and identity and way of asking questions and finding answers, the disciplines aren't as distinct as your class schedule might lead you to believe.

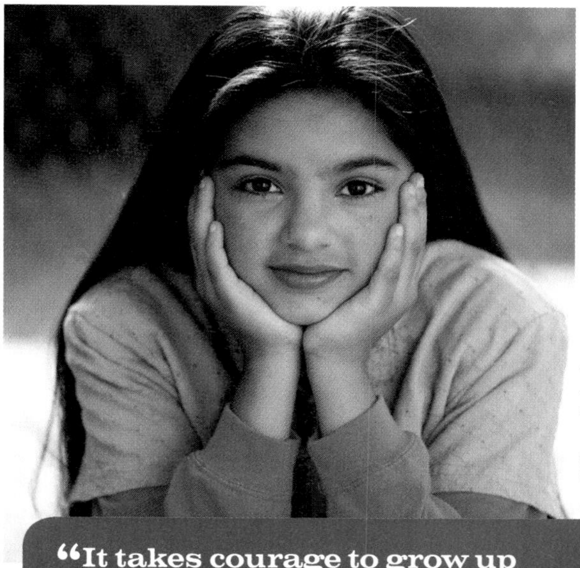

Brand X Pictures/Jupiter Images

"It takes courage to grow up and become who you really are."

e. e. cummings, American poet (1894–1962)

How Do the Disciplines Connect?

The Circle of Learning (see Figure 11.2) illustrates the interconnectedness of knowledge. Although this circle could be drawn in many different ways, using many different traditional academic disciplines, here is an example to get you thinking.[2]

It works like this. Let's start at the top of the circle with *math*, which is a basic "language" with rules and conventions, just like spoken language. You manipulate numbers and operations and functions, just as you manipulate sounds and words and sentences. Now, move clockwise around the circle.

Math is the fundamental language of *physics*, the study of atomic and subatomic particles. When atoms combine into elements, such as carbon

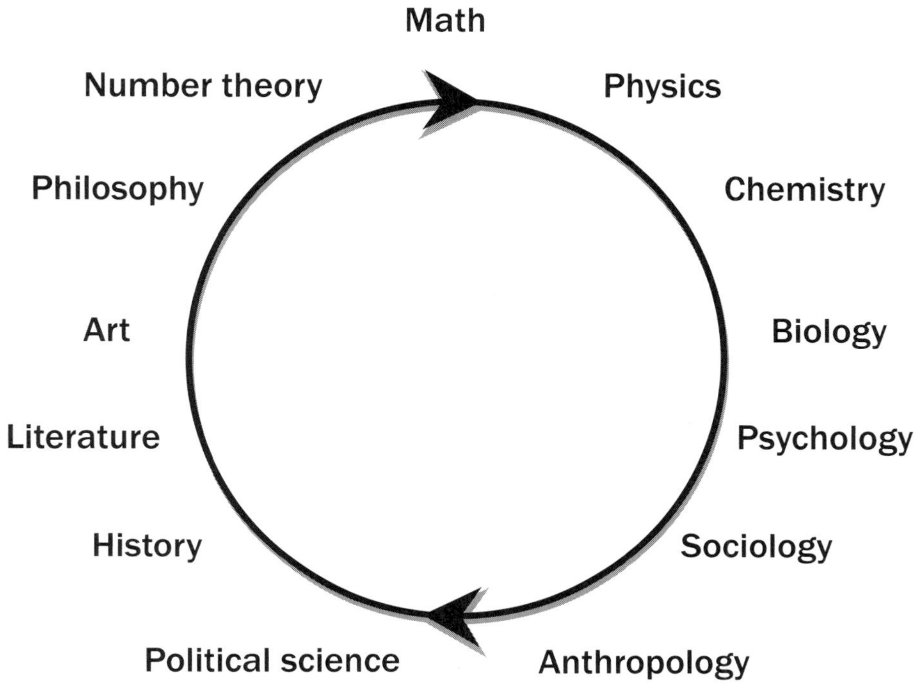
Math
Physics
Chemistry
Biology
Psychology
Sociology
Anthropology
Political science
History
Literature
Art
Philosophy
Number theory

Figure 11.2
The Circle of Learning

> **"Never mistake knowledge for wisdom. One helps you make a living; the other helps you make a life."**
>
> Sandra Carey, consultant and lobbyist

and oxygen, the academic discipline is called *chemistry*. Chemicals combine to create living organisms studied in *biology* courses. Living organisms don't just exist, they think and behave, leading to the study of *psychology*. They also interact in groups, families, and organizations, which you study in *sociology*. You can also study units of living beings throughout time and across cultures in the discipline of *anthropology*. These units—people—who live and work together are typically governed or govern themselves, leading to *political science*. Let's keep going.

When an account of peoples and countries and their rulers is recorded, you study *history*. These written accounts, sometimes factual or sometimes fictional (for pleasure or intrigue) comprise the study of *literature*. Literature is one way to record impressions and provoke reactions—poetry is a good example—through the use of words. But images and symbols can do the same things—enter *art*. A particular question artists ask is "What is beauty?" otherwise known as *aesthetics*, which is also a particular topic of study in *philosophy*. Philosophy also includes another subspecialty called *number theory*, one of the earliest branches of pure mathematics. And now we're all the way around the Circle of Learning, arriving right back at *math*.

That's a quick rundown. Of course, many academic disciplines don't appear on this chart, but they could and should. A philosophy major might see her discipline at the center of the circle, or a geography major might say, "Hey, where's geography on this chart?" The circle, as it appears here, is representative. The point isn't which disciplines are represented. Instead, the Circle of Learning demonstrates that academic disciplines are interconnected because knowledge itself is interconnected. *Anthropology* (understanding people throughout time and across cultures) can provide an important foundation for *political science* (how people are governed or govern themselves), and *history* (a record of peoples and countries and rulers) can easily be the basis for *literature*. Capitalizing on what you're learning in one discipline can lead to deeper understanding in another.

In your career, you'll need to use knowledge without necessarily remembering in which course you learned it. You'll be thinking critically and creatively, solving problems, and calling upon all the skills you're cultivating in all the courses you're studying in college. The bottom line is that connections count. Recognize them, use them, and strengthen them to reinforce your learning.

INSIGHT → ACTION

What "boxes" are you studying this term? Do they seem distinct or connected? Why? How?

YOUR TOUGHEST CLASS

Think about your most challenging class this semester. Is it a general education course or one required for your major? If it's a general education course, make a list of all the ways this course can help you either to further your career or to become a well-educated person.

If this course is one in your major, ask yourself why the challenge is so great. Do you understand the course content? Do you keep up with readings and assignments? Can you follow your professor's teaching style? Send your instructor in this class an e-mail indicating your specific efforts to do your best and detailing your progress.

How to Choose a Major and a Career

Like many students, you probably put value in how well college prepares you for a profession.[3] Choosing a college major and directing yourself toward a prospective career can be stressful. Many students feel pressure to make the right decision—and make it right now! You might hear conflicting advice from family members that put a high priority on financial success above other important factors, and feel overwhelmed by the number of possibilities from which to choose.[4] You may know what you want to do with the rest of your life right now, but many of your classmates don't, and even if they *say* they do, they may well change their minds several times. Yes, these decisions are important. But where do you start? The decision-making process should involve these critical steps. If you're still deciding, or even if you think you already have, consider how they apply to you.

Step 1: Follow Your Bliss

In an ideal world, which major and career would you choose? Don't think about anything except the actual content you'd be studying. Don't consider career opportunities, requirements, difficulty, or anything else that might keep you from making these choices in an ideal world. What are you passionate about? If it's skateboarding, think about which majors might apply. Majoring in physics would help you understand skateboard ascent versus decent, trajectories, spin, and angles. Majoring in landscape architecture would allow you to design skateparks. Majoring in journalism would put you in a good position to write for a skateboarding magazine.

Like Ethan Cole from the "FOCUS Challenge Case," you may be wondering what to do with your life. Perhaps the *idealist* in you has one potential career in mind and the *realist* in you has another. The $300,000 salary you'd earn as a surgeon may look very compelling until you consider the years of medical school required after college, the time invested in an internship and residency, and the still further years of necessary specialization. It takes long-term diligence, commitment, dedication, and resources—yours or borrowed ones—to make that dream come true. Do these factors lessen the appeal?

Perhaps there's conflict between your *idealism* and your family's *pragmatism*. Comedian Robin Williams once said, "When I told my father I was going to be an actor, he said, 'Fine, but study welding just in case.'"

photolibrary.com pty. ltd/Index Open

"The self is not something that one finds. It's something one creates."

Thomas Szasz, Professor Emeritus in Psychiatry, State University of New York Health Science Center, Syracuse

FOCUS YOUR I'S!

The huge printing presses of a major Chicago newspaper began malfunctioning on the Saturday before Christmas, putting all the revenue for advertising that was to appear in the Sunday paper in jeopardy. None of the technicians could track down the problem. Finally, a frantic call was made to the retired printer who had worked with these presses for over forty years. "We'll pay anything; just come in and fix them," he was told.

When he arrived, he walked around for a few minutes, surveying the presses; then he approached one of the control panels and opened it. He removed a dime from his pocket, turned a screw ¼ of a turn, and said, "The presses will now work correctly." After being profusely thanked, he was told to submit a bill for his work.

The bill arrived a few days later, for $10,000.00! Not wanting to pay such a huge amount for so little work, the printer was told to please itemize his charges, with the hope that he would reduce the amount once he had to identify his services. The revised bill arrived: $1.00 for turning the screw; $9,999.00 for knowing which screw to turn. (Anonymous)

So what does it take? After forty years on the job, the retired printer knew many things, including one elusive but critical piece of knowledge—which screw to turn. But perhaps you're just starting out, and experience is something you don't have yet. Or perhaps you're an adult returning to school to boost your career or shift to a new one. No matter where you are on your journey, how will you achieve life and career success?

Mel Levine, author of *Ready or Not, Here Life Comes,* says, "We are in the midst of an epidemic of work-life unreadiness because an alarming number of emerging adults are unable to find a good fit between their minds and their career directions.... Because they are not finding their way, they may feel as if they are going nowhere and have nowhere to go."[5]

How can anyone have nowhere to go with more than 12,000 different occupations or careers to choose from with 8,000 alternative job titles—for a total of over 20,000 options?[6] Some students, like Ethan, start college and become overwhelmed. Sometime during the first year, or possibly later, they take a step back and announce in so many words, "There are too many choices. I refuse to choose at all."[7]

Here's another tough issue many college graduates face when entering the world of work. Many of them have already categorized work as boring because their part-time jobs in high school and col-

lege *were* boring. They don't want to climb the ladder of success. They'd like to skip the bottom and start somewhere closer to the top rung. But every job involves some element of grunt work, even those at the top. No job is round-the-clock fun, and in every new job, eventually the honeymoon is over, and the tough challenges begin. The simple truth is this: building a career takes time, persistence, dedication, and focus. Seemingly overnight successes like J. K. Rowling of *Harry Potter* fame are rare; steady progress toward a goal is the norm.[8]

So what does it take to launch your career successfully? You'll need to focus your I's on four things: **I**nner direction, **I**nterpretation, **I**nstrumentation, and **I**nteraction—the four I's of career-life readiness. Here's what they mean.[9]

- **Inner direction**. You've lived with yourself for some time now, but how well do you know yourself? How accurate is your view of yourself? Can you honestly and accurately appraise your potential? Do you know where are you headed and why? Are you well suited for your major and career destinations? You must first understand the inner you before you can direct it toward a career that fits.

- **Interpretation**. Memorization isn't the most important skill you'll need in most careers. On the job there's more required than repeating back what the boss has told you. You must interpret the information and apply it in your own way, which will demonstrate whether you do (or don't) understand what you're doing.

- **Instrumentation**. In your career, you'll need a toolkit filled with an array of abilities—engaging in high-level thinking, brainstorming, problem solving, making decisions, tapping your creativity, and cultivating both hard (technical) and soft (interpersonal) skills. And not only must you know *how* to use each of these tools, but you'll need to know *when* and *why*.

- **Interaction**. Business (or any profession) isn't just about facts and figures. It's about people, sensitivities, values, and relationships—not products, not machines, not words in a report. While these things are important, too, chances are that people will be what help you build your career. Without people to buy, sell, trade, consume, or produce, there is no business.

These four I's are keys to your future. The more you focus your I's, the better prepared you'll be for the challenges ahead.

And perhaps you just don't know yet. If that's the case, don't panic. Despite the increased pressure these days to choose the right major because of rising tuition and a changeable economy, Ethan Cole is right: it's hard to have it all figured out from the start.[10]

One thing is certain: you'll be a happier, more productive person if you do what *you* want to do *and* pursue it vigorously. When it comes to success, ability (*Can* you do it?) and effort (Are you *willing* to invest what it takes?) go hand in hand. Whatever your motivation, remember this. It's unusual for people to become truly successful halfheartedly. There are undeniable emotional and psychological components involved in success. Wayne Gretzky, called the greatest player in the history of hockey, once said, "God gave me a special talent to play the game . . . maybe he didn't give me a talent, he gave me a *passion*."

Having said that, what if your "bliss" just isn't feasible? You'd give anything to play for the NBA, but you're five foot two and female. You dream of being a rock star, but you can't carry a tune. Then it may be time to set aside the idealism and resurrect the realism in you. Maybe then it's time to translate—or shift—your dreams into goals.

Can Ethan translate his dreams into goals and become a professional skateboarder? How many professional skateboarders are there—especially compared to other professionals such as teachers, architects, and physicians? When the statistics are against you, achieving success isn't impossible, but it might take more than expert skill. It might also take some luck, very specific planning, and perseverance.

Step 2: Conduct Preliminary Research

Has it ever occurred to you that you may not have all the facts—accurate ones—about your ideal major? Do you know what it *really* takes? Have you gotten your information from qualified sources—or are you basing your opinion on your friend's reaction to one course he took in the major or on the campus grapevine?

Try an experiment. Choose three majors you're considering, one of which is your ideal major, and send yourself on a fact-finding mission. To find out if you're on target, obtain the answers to the following ten questions for each of the three possibilities. Go to the physical location (department) where each major is housed, and interview a professor. The experiment requires legwork; don't just let your fingers do the clicking.

1. What is the major?

2. Who is the interviewee?

3. What is the name of the academic department where this major is housed? Where are the department offices physically located on campus?

4. Which introductory courses in this major would inform you about your interests and abilities?

5. Which upper-level courses in this major interest you? (List three.)

6. What are the department's entry requirements to become a major?

7. How many students major in this discipline on your campus?

8. Which required course in the major do students usually find most challenging? Which is most engaging? Which is most valued? Why?

9. How would the interviewee describe the reputation of this department on campus? What is it known for?

10. From the interviewee's perspective, why should a student major in this discipline?

After you complete your interviews, review the facts. Did you change any of your opinions, based on what you learned?[11]

> "The privilege of a lifetime is being who you are."
>
> **Joseph Campbell, American professor and writer (1904–1987)**

Step 3: Take a Good Look at Yourself

CHALLENGE ⊖ REACTION

Challenge: Take a good look at yourself and answer the following questions about how you prefer to work.

Reaction: Rank each item 1 or 2 based on your general preference. While many careers, if not most, require both, your task is to decide which of the two you prefer.

I prefer to work at a job:

1. Alone	_____	With other people	_____
2. Indoors	_____	Outdoors	_____
3. With people	_____	With equipment or materials	_____
4. Directing/leading others	_____	Being directed/led by others	_____
5. Producing information	_____	Managing information	_____
6. In an organized, step-by-step way	_____	In a big-idea, holistic way	_____
7. Starting things	_____	Completing things	_____
8. Involving a product	_____	Involving a service	_____
9. Solving challenging problems	_____	Generating creative ideas	_____
10. Finding information	_____	Applying information	_____
11. Teaching/training others in groups	_____	Advising/coaching others one-on-one	_____

Now look at your eleven first choices. Identify several career fields that come to mind that would allow you to achieve as many of them as possible.

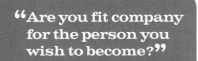

> **"Are you fit company for the person you wish to become?"**
>
> **Anonymous**

Here's a bottom-line question: For you—as Dr. Bernie Siegel would say—what *is* the "right wall" to lean your ladder of success on? How do you know? Many first-year college students don't know. They don't have enough experience under their belts to plan for a lifetime. They're in college to *discover*. It all comes down to questions this book has been asking you all along: Who are you? And what do you want? If you're unsure of how to proceed in your decision making, follow these recommendations to see if they help you bring your future into focus.

Send in the SWOT Team!

A SWOT analysis is an excellent way to begin taking a good look at yourself in relation to your future. SWOT stands for Strengths, Weaknesses, Opportunities, and Threats. SWOT analyses are typically used in business, but creating one for yourself may be useful when it comes to deciding on a college major and a career. Make a matrix with four quadrants, label each one, and fill them in as objectively as you can.

> **Strengths** are traits that give you a leg up. These are talents you can capitalize on and qualities you can develop.

> **Weaknesses** are traits that currently work against you. You can, however, work to reduce or eliminate them.

> **Opportunities** are conditions or circumstances that work in your favor, like a strong forecast for your prospective career's future.

> **Threats** are conditions that could have adverse effects. Some of these factors are beyond your control; however, sometimes you can successfully lessen their potential effects.

As you create the matrix begin with two basic questions:

What kinds of forces will impact your potential career?

Internal—forces inside you, such as motivation and skill

External—forces outside you that may affect your success: the job market or economy, for example

What kind of influence can these forces exert?

Positive—some forces will give you a boost toward your goals

Negative—other forces will work against you[12]

Let's complete a SWOT analysis for Ethan and his dream of becoming a professional skateboarder. Of course, you might say that, technically, he doesn't need an academic degree for that particular career. But if he wants to pursue related, more traditional careers—design a new skatepark or write for a skateboard magazine, for example—he would need an array of knowledge and enhanced skills from writing and design to finance and marketing. Besides, college isn't just about jobs, it's about living a fuller life as a well-educated person.

Look back at the "FOCUS Challenge Case," and see if you agree with the basic SWOT analysis shown in Figure 11.3.

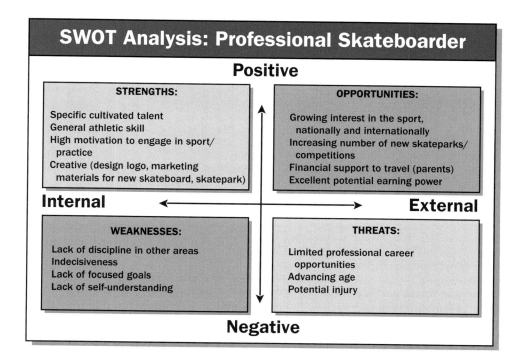

SWOT Analysis: Professional Skateboarder

Positive

STRENGTHS:
Specific cultivated talent
General athletic skill
High motivation to engage in sport/ practice
Creative (design logo, marketing materials for new skateboard, skatepark)

OPPORTUNITIES:
Growing interest in the sport, nationally and internationally
Increasing number of new skateparks/ competitions
Financial support to travel (parents)
Excellent potential earning power

Internal ← → **External**

WEAKNESSES:
Lack of discipline in other areas
Indecisiveness
Lack of focused goals
Lack of self-understanding

THREATS:
Limited professional career opportunities
Advancing age
Potential injury

Negative

Figure 11.3
SWOT Analysis

Looking at his SWOT analysis, what would you conclude? Is professional skateboarding a good career option for him? In your view, do the opportunities outweigh the threats? For example, does the potential earning power of a professional skateboarder outweigh the risks associated with possible incapacitating injuries? Do his well-cultivated athletic skills compensate for his lack of discipline in other areas? If not, might he gravitate toward other potential careers, perhaps those that also involve skateboarding? "Ethan remembered liking geometry, he was good at creative writing, he played the drums like a real jazz musician, and he was an incredible artist." Do you see potential majors for him in college? Sports management? Kinesiology? Architecture? Journalism? Jazz studies? Creative writing? What should Ethan do?

EXERCISE 11.1 Group Résumé

Your instructor will provide a sheet of newsprint and several markers per team of three to four students. Your job is to work on the floor, desktops, or somewhere with sufficient space to create a group résumé, highlighting the characteristics you bring with you that can help you succeed in college. Your collective qualifications may look like this:

Qualifications:

- 16 combined years of high school success
- average incoming GPA of 3.4
- familiarity with Word, PowerPoint, Photoshop, and Excel
- Internet savvy with specialization in academic resources
- eager to learn
- well-developed time management skills
- interest in co-curricular activities

After each team has completed the task, hang the newsprint sheets on the walls to create a gallery and present your résumé to the rest of the class.[13]

Box 11.1 Five Ways to Open the Door (or Close It) during an Interview

By the time you graduate from college, you will have been interviewed many times to get a new job or to be admitted to graduate school, for example. And after you graduate, you'll go through a series of interviews on the path to the dream job you really want.

Often interviewers aren't particularly skilled at asking questions. They haven't been trained on how to interview prospective employees, so they just ask whatever questions come to them. And often, interviewees don't quite know what they're doing either.

Of course, you should always be honest, but there are various ways to communicate the same information. Telling an interviewer you "like to work alone" sounds antisocial.

But if you say you "like to really focus on what you're doing without distractions," you've shown dedication to your work ethic. You also need to be aware of real pitfalls to avoid. See what you think of these suggestions.

1. **"You've got to ac-centuate the positive; e-liminate the negative."** To resurrect an old Bing Crosby song here, remember this piece of obvious advice. A trap question interviewers sometimes ask is, "What's your worst fault?" While you may be tempted to say the first thing that comes to mind, that could be a big mistake. "Umm . . . sleeping too much! I really like to sleep in. Sometimes I sleep half the day away."

Not good. But some faults you could identify might actually be construed as strengths: "I have a little too much nervous energy. I'm always on the go. I like to stay busy."

2. **Stay focused.** "Tell me about yourself" is a common question interviewers ask. How much time do you have? Most of us like to talk about ourselves, but it's important to stay on track. Think possible questions through in advance, and construct some hypothetical answers. When we're put on the spot, we can get tongue-tied. Keep your answers job-focused: what you liked about your last job, why you liked those aspects of it, what your long-term career goals are, and how this job can help you prepare. You don't need to go into your family background or your personal problems. And it's always a bad idea to bash a previous job or former boss. The interviewer may worry that you'll bring whatever didn't work there with you to this new job.

3. **Don't just give answers, get some.** A job interview is like a first date. Find out what you need to know. If the job is one you're interested in long-term, ask questions such as these three key ones:

   - **What does this company value?** Listen to the answer. Hard work? Achievement? Innovation? Communication skills? Doing things by the book? The answer will tell you about the personality of the company.
   - **What's a typical day like for you?** Ask the interviewer. An answer such as "I get up at 5:00 a.m., get here at 6:30 a.m., and go home around 7:00 p.m.—and then I do paperwork all evening" tells you something. This may—or may not—be the job or the company for you.
   - **What happened to the last person in this job?** If you find out he was promoted, that's one thing. But if you learn he was fired or quit, see if you can find out why. Maybe he had job performance problems, or maybe this is an impossible job that no one could do well.

Remember, too, that interviews are conversations with give and take, not just one person doing all the giving and the other doing all the taking. Listen to the interviewer. She may be looking for an opportunity to tell you things she thinks are important, too.

4. **Watch for questions out of left field.** Some companies like to get creative with their interviewing. Microsoft, for example, is known for asking problem-solving questions, such as "If you could remove any of the fifty states, which would it be? Be prepared to give specific reasons why you chose the state you did." There is no right or wrong answer, although some answers are better than others. ("We should just nuke state X. I had a bad experience there once" would probably furrow some brows, and naming Washington state, where Microsoft is located, might be an inadvisable choice.) The interviewer just wants to hear how you think. Well-received answers "talk" an interviewer through underlying reasoning and present additional questions posed by the hypothetical situation.[14] Beware the interviewer with off-the-wall techniques: "I know most interviewers ask questions, but I don't. I consider the interview to be a time for *you* to ask *me* questions. What questions about this job or this company do you have?" "Uh ..." isn't an impressive answer. Read up on what to expect and good ways to respond before the big day. Remember: Today's interviewers are looking for more than technical skills; they're looking for critical thinking skills, problem-solving skills, and creativity.[15]

5. **Don't start off with salary questions.** Make sure the first question out of your mouth isn't, "So tell me about the salary, again? Any way to notch that up a bit?" The last thing you want to do is give the interviewer the idea you're just in it for the money. Of course, you are, but not just for that. More importantly, in every job you have, you'll gain experience and knowledge that will always better prepare you for the *next* job to come.

Step 4: Consider Your Major versus Your Career

CHALLENGE ⊖ REACTION

Challenge: What is the relationship between choosing a major and choosing a career?

Reaction: _____

Which comes first, the chicken or the egg? The major or the career? Silly question? The obvious answer, of course, is that you must first major in something in college before you can build a career on it. But the question isn't as straightforward as it seems.

Should you choose a major based on an intended career? Perhaps you know you want to be a science teacher, first and foremost. You don't know whether to major in one of the sciences or in education. You like all sciences, but teaching is your real interest. If you major in science, which one should it be (see Figure 11.4)?

Figure 11.4

Which Science Should a Science Teacher Major In?

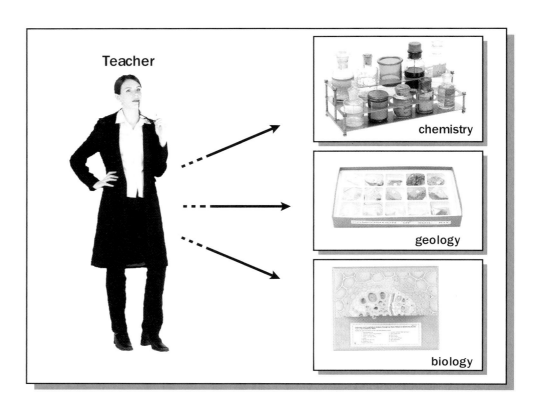

FOCUS ON CAREERS: Tanya Sexton, Associate Partner, Lucas Group Consulting Firm

Q1: What was your major in college? How does it relate to your current career field? How did you get from your college degree to where you are today?

I was an accounting major in college, and now I am a recruiter with a specialty in the accounting and finance fields, so it's a perfect fit. As a former accountant, I am able to earn credibility quickly with my hiring authorities and job candidates. I understand the responsibilities of the positions, structure of departments, and complexities of the profession. I started my career as a staff accountant for a local men's retailer in Chicago, became the Accounting Manager for a widely known Chicago-based service company, and eventually moved into a hybrid accounting/operations position that required me to travel.

When I began traveling to where I work now, which was part of my territory, I knew that's where I belonged. And when I began a new job as a recruiter in 1999, I knew this was the career field for me. The rest is history.

Q2: What do you and your colleagues do on a day-to-day basis?

Honestly, every day is different. We continually recruit talent and market the talent to hiring authorities. We spend lots of time on the telephone, screening candidates, matching them to the right jobs, presenting them to clients, briefing and debriefing them for interviews, and negotiating job offers.

Q3: What are employers looking for in the best college graduates today?

Employers look for a myriad of things. Internships add marketability to a college degree. Employers look at grade point averages overall and

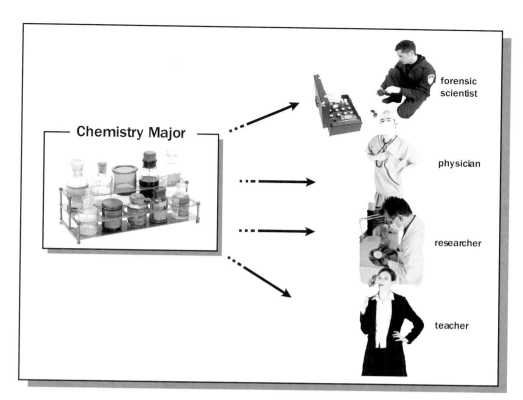

Figure 11.5

Which Career Should a Chemistry Major Choose?

Chemistry Major

forensic scientist

physician

researcher

teacher

Or instead, should you choose a major first, and then decide on a career? Say you made a firm decision to major in chemistry when your favorite science teacher did "mad scientist" experiments for the class in eighth grade. But at this point, you're not certain of the professional direction you'd like to pursue. Chemistry is your passion, but should you apply your chemistry degree as a forensic scientist, a physician, a researcher, or a teacher (see Figure 11.5)?

in graduates' majors. They look for strong verbal, written, and interpersonal communication skills. More and more, we hear that you can teach responsibilities of the job on the job, but the "soft skills," the "people skills," are not easily taught.

Q4: If employers were asked to identify which skills are in need of further development in today's college graduates, which skills would those be?
Work ethic. Employers say more recent graduates sometimes expect to automatically progress through the ranks without necessarily putting in the time to "earn their stripes."

C CREATE a Career Outlook

RECRUITER

Have you ever considered a career as a recruiter, placement, or employment specialist?

Facts to Consider[16]

Academic preparation required: A college degree in business, human resources, management, or communication would be good preparation.

Future workforce demand: Competition may be stiff because of plentiful numbers of qualified college graduates.

Work environment: Recruiters can either work inside a specific company's human resources department in its personnel office, or as a third-party agent, possibly within a consulting firm, that helps individual organizations find the best candidates for particular types of positions.

Essential skills: interviewing, speaking, writing, decision-making, and technology skills (using the Internet for job searches, etc.)

Questions to Ponder

1. Do you have (or could you acquire) the skills this career requires?
2. Are you interested in a career like this? Why or why not?

For more career activities online, go to http://www.cengage.com/colsuccess/staleyconcise to do the Team Career exercises.

A few schools don't actually use the word *major*, preferring the term *concentration*, and some schools encourage *interdisciplinary studies*, a tailor-made system in which you create your own major with guidance from advisors and faculty. Other schools may even encourage double majors, which can make sense, particularly some combinations (international business and Chinese language, for example). But by and large, the concept of having a major (and sometimes a minor) in college is the norm.

So which comes first—major or career? It depends.[17] The answer sounds ambivalent, and it's meant to. Although some professional degree programs put you into a particular track right away (nursing or engineering, for example), generally either direction can work well. Doors will open and close for you, and as you gain more knowledge and experience, you'll narrow your focus. As you learn more about your chosen major, you'll also learn about its specific career tracks. But it's important to remember that a major doesn't have to lock you into one specific career. And you can always narrow or refocus your area of emphasis in graduate school after you earn your undergraduate degree.[18]

What's Your Academic Anatomy?

Thinking about your academic anatomy is a simple way to begin to get a handle on what you find fulfilling. If you had to rank order the four parts of you listed in Figure 11.6, what would you put in first place? Second, third, and last? To get yourself thinking, ask these questions:

1. Do you find fulfillment by using your *head*? Do you enjoy solving complex problems or thinking through difficult situations? Do you like to reason things out, weigh evidence, and think critically? A philosophy major who

Figure 11.6
What's Your Academic Anatomy?

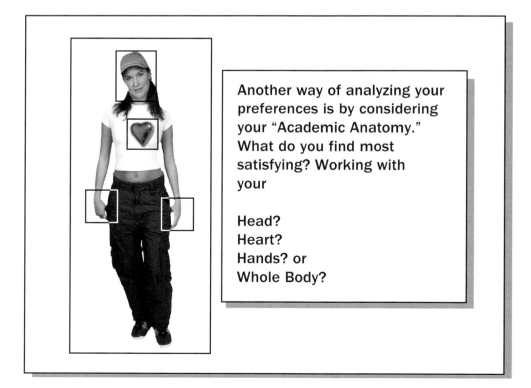

Another way of analyzing your preferences is by considering your "Academic Anatomy." What do you find most satisfying? Working with your

Head?
Heart?
Hands? or
Whole Body?

continues on to a career in law might be what students with this preference choose, for example.

2. Do you find it satisfying to work with matters of the *heart*? Are you the kind of person others come to with problems because you listen and care? Does trying to make others happy make you happy? A psychology major who pursues a counseling career might be what students with this preference choose, for example.

3. Do you like to create things with your *hands*? Do you enjoy making art? Doing hands-on projects? Building things out of other things? An architecture major who designs and builds models might be what students with this preference choose, for example.

4. Do you excel at physical activities that involve your *whole body*? Are you athletic? Do you like to stay active, no matter what you're doing? A physical therapy major who goes on to work in a rehabilitation facility helping stroke victims relearn to walk might be what students with this preference choose, for example.

Now look at your academic anatomy rankings. Of course, the truth is that "all of you" is involved in everything you do. And achieving balance is important. But what are your priorities? This type of simple analysis can be one way of informing you about who you are and where you should be headed.

However, no system for choosing a major is perfect. In fact, most are imperfect at best. Here are four things to consider.

1. Sometimes students who don't select a likely major based on their "anatomical preferences" can still be successful. A whole-body person (like Ethan Cole probably is) may decide to major in art (using his hands). But he'll have to find other ways to meet his whole-body needs unless he becomes a sculptor involved in creating large constructed projects.

2. You may intentionally choose an unlikely major. Perhaps art (using your hands) comes so naturally to you that you decide to major in astrophysics (using your head). You need the challenge to stay fully involved in getting your education. While it may sound unlikely, it's been known to happen.

3. You may choose an unlikely major because one particular course turns you on. You had no idea majoring in this subject was even possible, and you didn't know what it entailed. But you find studying it fascinating—so you shift gears to focus all your attention on it.

4. You may be equally engaged, no matter what. You love subjects that require using your head, hands, heart, and whole body. The anatomy of learning is less important to you than other factors—a teacher whose enthusiasm is contagious, for example.[19]

Ethan's rankings would probably go something like this: (1) whole body, (2) hands, (3) heart, and (4) head. And just because "head" is in last place for him doesn't mean he's doomed in college. A career as a financial analyst sitting behind a desk probably wouldn't be his cup of tea, for example. But it may well be yours. Whatever major and career he's thinking about—or you do—you may want to consider whether it's "anatomically correct."

INSIGHT ➔ ACTION

1. Do a SWOT analysis on yourself. Describe your strengths, weaknesses, opportunities, and threats as they relate to a particular major you may be interested in. Describe the insights you gain from the process.

2. Describe your academic anatomy. Is this something you've thought about before? What majors and careers might be "anatomically correct" for you?

EXERCISE 11.2 Get a Job!

Bring an employment ad from a newspaper or Internet website to class, perhaps for a job that's related to your prospective career. After carefully considering your individual ads in small groups of three or four, create an employment ad for the "job" of college student. For example, "_____ College/University seeks applicants with excellent skills in oral and written communication, problem solving, time management, and technology for positions as professional students preparing for a variety of future opportunities. . . ." Your ad should list particular job requirements, benefits, information about your institution, and so on, and be as much like a real ad as possible. When your group is finished constructing its ad, present it to the entire class.[20]

How to Launch a Career

CHALLENGE ➔ REACTION

Challenge: Assume you have $100,000 to spend on the following items. In a few minutes, your instructor will begin a real-live auction, putting one item at a time up for auction.

Reaction: Before the auction begins, budget your money in the first column. You may select as many items as you wish to bid on, but you may *not* place all your money on any single item. As the group auction proceeds, fill in the appropriate amounts that are actually spent by members of the class for each item.

	BUDGETED AMOUNT	WINNING BID
1. Becoming the CEO of a leading Fortune 500 company	_____	_____
2. Being a top earner in your career field	_____	_____
3. Being the number one expert in your profession	_____	_____
4. Having good friends on the job	_____	_____
5. Being your own boss	_____	_____
6. Creating a good balance between productive work and a happy family life	_____	_____
7. Having opportunities for travel and adventure in your job	_____	_____
8. Doing work you find fully satisfying	_____	_____
9. Working in a beautiful setting	_____	_____
10. Being a lifelong learner so that your career can develop and change over time	_____	_____

After you graduate from college, it'll be time to launch your career, right? What do you really want from a career? What's important to you? Even though your views may change over time, it's important to start thinking about them now. Item 7, "Having opportunities for travel and adventure in your job," may be a top priority now, but item 6, "Creating a good balance between productive work and a happy family life," may be more appealing a few years down the road if you have several young children to parent.

Interestingly, according to research, the most important factor in job satisfaction isn't any of these ten items. The number one contributor to job satisfaction, statistically speaking, is the quality of your relationship with your boss.[21]

If all your jobs thus far have been just that—*jobs*—to help you pay the bills, how do you know what you want in a *career*? Your career is something you haven't launched yet. Exactly how do you do that? You have to start somewhere, so perhaps you'd go online or open the want ads. You'd be likely to read this: *"Opening in . . . (anything). Experience required."* Isn't that the way it always goes? You have to *have* experience in order to get a job that will *give* you experience. So how do you launch a career?

This problem is one many college graduates face. Sure, they have experience. It's just not the right kind. They've bagged fries, mowed yards, bussed tables, and chauffeured pizzas to help pay for college expenses. If that's not the kind of experience the posted opening is looking for, how do you get the right kind? Try a job on for size.

> **Internships:** One way to gain experience is by trying things out. An internship, for example, is an opportunity for you to work alongside a professional in a career field of interest to you, and to learn from him or her. Your supervisor will mentor you, and you'll get a clearer picture of what the career field is like.

> **A Co-op Program:** Some schools have co-op programs that allow you to take classes and then apply what you've learned on the job, either alternatively or concurrently. You may take classes for a term and then work full-time for a term. A potential employer can get a sense of your potential, and you can gain practical experience.

© Jose Luis Pelaez, Inc./CORBIS

"You can be just like me. Don't just pussy foot around and sit on your assets. Unleash your ferocity upon an unsuspecting world."

Bette Midler, singer

> Service-Learning: An experience in which you volunteer your time, but not just as community "charity work," or classes with a service-learning component built right into the syllabus can give you valuable, practical experience. In these situations, your goal is to connect what you learn in your service work with what you're learning in class. The emphasis is on hands-on learning.

These experiences help you in two ways. First, they allow you to test a potential career field. The actual day-to-day work may be exactly what you expected, or not. They show you whether or not that particular career field is one you'd really be interested in. *I had no idea this field was so cutthroat, hectic, dull . . . exciting, stimulating, invigorating. . . .* A thumbs-down can be just as informative as a thumbs-up. At least you can eliminate one option from your list. Second, internships, co-ops, and service-learning opportunities give you experience to list on your résumé. That's invaluable!

Sometimes internships are offered through your academic major department, or through a central office on campus, or sometimes you can pursue one on your own through the Internet or personal connections. If you want to major in journalism, for example, you might try contacting your local newspaper, a business magazine that focuses on your city, or some other published outlet to find out if they're willing to sponsor you. *I'm a journalism major at X university, and I'm looking for an internship opportunity. I'm particularly interested in working at the* Daily Planet, *especially on the Education Beat, because I'm trying to learn more about this city and its school system.* If you receive pay, it may be a modest amount. You're in a learning mode, and you don't have experience, after all. If you land the internship through your school, you may receive course credit instead of pay.

The key to successful "trial" experiences such as internships is the relationship between you and your sponsor in the host organization. If you're not being given enough to do, or not allowed to test your competence in a particular area, speak up. The answer may be put in terms of "company policy," your "not quite ready for prime time" skills, or your supervisor's unwillingness to experiment in high-stakes areas. Nevertheless, the two of you must communicate about these kinds of important issues. No one can read your mind!

As you work your way toward launching your career, keep up with the latest information. Read up on interviewing (see Box 11.1), résumé writing (see Box 11.2), networking, hot career fields, and the latest employment trends. As you continue studying in your college courses, apply what you're learning—in your major and in your general education courses—to your future career. You'll be the winner!

INSIGHT ⊖ ACTION

1. What might keep you from choosing a major and career focus that you're actually interested in? Are these areas attractive enough for you to try to work out whatever might deter you?

2. What kinds of internship, co-op, or service-learning opportunities have you participated in? What did you learn from these experiences? If you've not participated, what opportunities are available on campus?

Box 11.2 A Model Résumé

In today's competitive world, when literally hundreds of people may be applying for one choice position, how should a résumé be written? Can a résumé be appealing, but not flashy? Solid, but not stuffy? Professional, but still personal? Thorough, but brief? Take a look at Jennifer's and see what you think.

> This résumé uses a skills approach, rather than a chronological approach. A chronological approach works best if you have a career underway and can list various relevant positions that prepared you for this one.

> Center your name, and use a standard résumé format. Many companies now scan résumés so that they can be read conveniently from one source. Skip the neon pink paper. Go for a highly professional look.

JENNIFER DANIELS

Current Address	Permanent Address:
Evelyn Edwin Living-Learning Center	1234 Aspen Way
Rocky Mountain State University	Vail, CO 81657
Great Bluffs, CO 89898	(101) 555-9128
(100) 555-6543 or jdaniels@rmsu.edu	

> Provide both your temporary address, if you're attending college away from home, and your actual home address. The employer may save your résumé and call you later, over the summer for example, if the current opening is filled by someone else.

> Build your career objective according to the position's advertised needs. "One size fits all" doesn't work when it comes to résumés.

CAREER OBJECTIVE

To obtain a position as a communications specialist in a large company, designing web pages, creating internal e-newsletters, and planning corporate events.

EDUCATION

> Provide numbers whenever you can. Text can be glossed over, but numbers stand out and make your accomplishments more quantifiable.

Rocky Mountain State University, Great Bluffs, CO
Bachelor of Arts, Communication Major, 2008 (Minor: Spanish)
GPA 3.6/4.0
Personally financed 80% of college tuition through employment and athletic scholarship

HONORS

Secretary, RMSU Freshman Honor Society
Vail "Invest in the Future" League Soccer Scholarship (4 years, chosen from 150 applicants)

SUMMARY OF BEST ACADEMIC COURSEWORK

> Select coursework that applies directly to the advertised position.

Organizational Communication	Advanced Composition
Business and Professional Communication	Emerging Technologies
Principles of Web Design	Event Planning

SKILLS

Technology

> Technology is important in today's workplace. Don't underrate your competence. Many senior employees don't know as much as you do!

Part-time work, web-page design
Proficient in Word, PowerPoint, Excel, Access, Macromedia Flash, Adobe Acrobat, and Photoshop

Event Planning

RMSU Freshman Honor Society, planned campus ceremonies for 1,000 guests (2 years)
Student Government, Campus Life Committee Chair (1 year)
Soccer Fundraising Events, Planning Committee Chair (3 years)

Writing

1st place winner, campus creative writing competition, 2007

EMPLOYMENT HISTORY

> If you're able, show that you have worked all throughout college to demonstrate your commitment to your goal.

Intern, Peak Industries, Human Resources Department, fall 2007
Student Assistant, Office of the Dean, Arts and Sciences, spring 2006
Residence Life, Floor Supervisor (2 years)
Hostess, Pancake Heaven, summers, 2006-2007

REFERENCES (available on request)

> Always obtain preapproval from your references, even if you don't list their names. You may be asked to provide them on a moment's notice.

EXERCISE 11.3 VARK Activity

Complete the recommended activity for your preferred VARK learning modality. If you are multimodal, select more than one activity. Your instructor may ask you to (a) give an oral report on your results in class, (b) send your results to him or her via e-mail, (c) post them online, or (d) contribute to a class chat.

 Visual: Select a quotation from this chapter that was particularly memorable to you. Create a poster of the quote, using large font and graphics, to hang on a wall in your room.

 Aural: Talk through the Circle of Learning aloud to help you remember the connections between academic disciplines.

 Read/Write: Find a book that extends the ideas presented in this chapter. Select a passage that impresses you from the book to share with your classmates.

 Kinesthetic: Go on a "field trip" to the Career Center on your campus. Collect resources you find there and bring them to class.

© CHALLENGE Yourself Quizzes For more practice online, go to http://www.cengage .com/colsuccess/staleyconcise to take the Challenge Yourself online quizzes.

 NOW WHAT DO YOU THINK?

At the beginning of this chapter, Ethan Cole, a confused and discouraged student, faced a challenge. Now after reading this chapter, would you respond differently to any of the questions you answered about the "FOCUS Challenge Case"?

R E A L I T Y   C H E C K

On a scale of 1 to 10, answer these questions now that you've completed this chapter.

1 = not very/not much/very little/low   10 = very/a lot/very much/high

In hindsight, how much did you *really* know about this subject matter before reading the chapter?

1   2   3   4   5   6   7   8   9   10

How much do you think this information might affect your career success after college?

1   2   3   4   5   6   7   8   9   10

How much do you think this information might affect your college success?

1   2   3   4   5   6   7   8   9   10

How long did it actually take you to complete this chapter (both the reading and writing tasks)? _____ Hour(s) _____ Minutes

Compare these answers to your answers from the "Readiness Check" at the beginning of this chapter. How might the gaps between what you thought before starting the chapter and what you now think affect how you approach the next chapter?

 To download mp3 format audio summaries of this chapter, go to http://www.cengage.com/colsuccess/staleyconcise.

FOCUS EXIT INTERVIEW

Although you have not quite completed your first term as a college student, we're interested in your reactions to college so far: how you have spent your time, what challenges you've experienced, and your general views about what college has been like. Please answer thoughtfully.

INFORMATION ABOUT YOU

Name _____

Student Number _____   Course/Section _____

Instructor _____

Gender _____   Age _____

INFORMATION ABOUT YOUR COLLEGE EXPERIENCE

1. **How did you find you learned best in college? (Check all that apply.)**

   _____ by looking at charts, maps, graphs   _____ by reading books

   _____ by looking at color-coded information   _____ by writing papers

   _____ by looking at symbols and graphics   _____ by taking notes

   _____ by listening to instructors' lectures   _____ by going on field trips

   _____ by listening to other students during an in-class discussion   _____ by engaging in activities

   _____ by talking about course content with friends or roommates   _____ by actually doing things

2. **For each of the following pairs of descriptors, which set sounds most like you based on what you've learned about yourself this term? (Please choose between the two options on each line and place a checkmark by your choice.)**

   _____ Extraverted and outgoing   or   _____ Introverted and quiet

   _____ Detail-oriented and practical   or   _____ Big-picture and future-oriented

   _____ Rational and truthful   or   _____ People-oriented and tactful

   _____ Organized and self-disciplined or   _____ Spontaneous and flexible

3. *FOCUS* **is about 11 different aspects of college life. Which did you find most interesting person-ally? Which contained information that you found to be most challenging to apply in your own life? (Check all that apply.)**

Most interested in	Most challenging to apply to myself		Most interested in	Most challenging to apply to myself	
_____	_____	Building dreams, setting goals	_____	_____	Engaging, listening, and note-taking in class
_____	_____	Learning to learn	_____	_____	Developing your memory
_____	_____	Using resources: finances, technology, and campus support	_____	_____	Reading and studying
_____	_____	Managing time and energy	_____	_____	Taking tests
_____	_____	Thinking critically and creatively	_____	_____	Building relationships
			_____	_____	Choosing a major and career

4. **Which one of your classes was most challenging this term and why?**

   Which class? (course title *or* department and course number) _____

   Why? _____

   Did you succeed in this class? _____ yes _____ no

   Somewhat (please explain): _____

   _____

5. **How many total hours per week did you spend outside of class studying for your college courses this term?**

___ 0–5	___ 16–20	___ 31–35
___ 6–10	___ 21–25	___ 36–40
___ 11–15	___ 26–30	___ 40+

6. **Which of the following on-campus resources did you use once or more this term? (Please check all that apply.)**

___ library

___ campus learning centers (whatever is available on your campus, such as a Writing Center, Math Learning Center, etc.)

___ computer labs

___ the Student Success Center or New Student Center, if one is available

___ the Counseling Center, if one is available

___ professors' office hours for individual meetings/conferences/help

___ student clubs or organizations

___ none

7. **For the following sets of opposite descriptive phrases, please put a checkmark on the line between the two that best represents your response.**

My first term of college:

challenged me academically	___ ___ ___ ___ ___	was easy
was very different from high school	___ ___ ___ ___ ___	was a lot like high school
was exciting	___ ___ ___ ___ ___	was dull
was interesting	___ ___ ___ ___ ___	was uninteresting
motivated me to continue	___ ___ ___ ___ ___	discouraged me
was fun	___ ___ ___ ___ ___	was boring
helped me feel a part of this campus	___ ___ ___ ___ ___	made me feel alienated

8. **Please mark your *top three areas of concern* relating to your first term of college by placing 1, 2, and 3 next to the items you choose.**

___ I did not fit in.

___ I did have difficulty making friends.

___ I was not academically successful.

___ My performance disappointed my family.

___ My personal life interfered with my studies.

___ My studies interfered with my personal life.

___ I had financial difficulties.

___ My job(s) interfered with my studies.

___ My studies interfered with my job.

___ My social life interfered with my studies.

___ My studies interfered with my social life.

___ My professors did not care about me as an individual.

___ I may not finish my degree.

___ I missed the company of my friends.

___ I missed the company of my family.

___ I did not manage my time well.

___ I was bored in my classes.

___ I felt intimidated by my professors.

___ I was overwhelmed by all I had to do.

___ other (please explain) _____

9. **Have you changed your thinking about selecting a major since entering college? Broadly speaking, now which area do you expect to major in?**

___ Arts & Sciences	___ Nursing/Health Sciences
___ Education	___ Business
___ Engineering	___ other (please explain)

10. **How certain are you now of a chosen major (1 = totally sure, 5 = totally unsure)** ___

11. **How certain are you now that you will complete your degree? (1 = totally sure, 5 = totally unsure)** ___

12. **How certain are you now that you will complete your degree at this school? (1 = totally sure, 5 = totally unsure)** ___

13. **How certain are you now of your intended career choice? (1 = totally sure, 5 = totally unsure)** ___

14. **How certain are you now about whether you'll obtain an advanced degree after you finish college? (1 = totally sure, 5 = totally unsure)** ___

15. What will your grade point average to be at the end of your first term of college?

____ A+   ____ B+   ____ C+   ____ D or lower

____ A   ____ B   ____ C

____ A−   ____ B−   ____ C−

16. Which of the following sources of information about college turned out to be most accurate? (Mark your top three information sources with 1, 2, and 3.)

____ TV and movies

____ friends/siblings who have already gone to college

____ discussions with teachers/counselors in high school

____ information I received from colleges in the mail

____ talks with my parents

____ talks with my friends who are also now freshmen

____ the Internet

____ other (please explain) _____

17. How confident are you in yourself in each of the following areas now? (1 = very confident, 5 = not at all confident)

____ overall academic ability   ____ technology skills

____ mathematical skills   ____ physical well being

____ leadership ability   ____ writing skills

____ reading skills   ____ social skills

____ public speaking skills   ____ emotional well being

____ study skills   ____ teamwork skills

18. Why did you decide to go to college? Now that you've experienced your first term of college, how would you respond? (Check all that apply)

____ because I want to build a better life for myself.

____ because I want to build a better life for my family.

____ because I want to be very well off financially in the future.

____ because I need a college education to achieve my dreams.

____ because my friends were going to college.

____ because my family encouraged me to go.

____ because it was expected of me.

____ because I was recruited for athletics.

____ because I want to continue learning.

____ because the career I am pursuing requires a degree.

____ because I was unsure of what I might do instead.

____ other (please explain) _____

19. Looking ahead, how satisfied do you expect to be with your decision to attend this school?

____ very satisfied   ____ somewhat dissatisfied

____ satisfied   ____ very dissatisfied

____ not sure

20. Which of the following statements best reflects your educational intention?

____ I plan to stay at this school until I complete my degree.

____ I plan to transfer to another institution (please identify which one _____)

____ I plan to stop out of college for awhile (to work, for example) and then return to this school.

____ I plan to drop out of college.

21. If you are thinking about transferring to another institution, why are you thinking of doing so?

____ This school does not offer my intended major (which is _____).

____ This school is too small.

____ This school is too large.

____ This school is too expensive.

____ I don't feel I fit in.

____ I want to go to a school closer to home.

_____ I want to go to a school further from home.

_____ I want to be closer to my boy/girlfriend.

_____ I want to be closer to my friends.

_____ I will change job locations.

_____ I want to transfer from a two-year to a four-year institution.

_____ I want to transfer from a four-year to a two-year institution.

_____ other (please explain) _____

22. **Did you achieve the outcomes you were hoping to achieve at the beginning of this term? Why or why not?** _____

_____

23. **What was the biggest difference between what you thought college would be like and what it was actually like for you?** _____

_____

NOTES

Chapter 1

1. Multi-tasking adversely affects brain's learning, UCLA psychologists report. (2006, July 26). *ScienceDaily*. Available: http://www.sciencedaily.com/releases/2006/07/060726083302.htm.

2. Spielberg finally to graduate. (2002, May 15). BBC News. Available at http://news.bbc.co.uk/2/hi/entertainment/1988770.stm.

3. Cranton, P. (1994). *Understanding and promoting transformative learning: A guide for educators of adults*. San Francisco: Jossey-Bass.

4. Davis, J. R. (1993). *Better teaching, more learning*. Phoenix, AZ: Oryx Press.

5. French, B. F., & Oakes, W. (2003). Measuring academic intrinsic motivation in the first year of college: Reliability and validity evidence for a new instrument. *Journal of the First-Year Experience*, *15*(1), 83–102; French, B. F. Executive summary of instruments utilized with systemwide first-year seminars. Policy Center on the First Year of College.; French, B. F., Immerkus, J. C., & Oakes, W. C. (2005). An examination of indicators of engineering students' success and persistence. *Journal of Engineering Education*, *94*(4), 419–425.

6. For more information, see U.S. Department of Labor, Bureau of Labor Statistics, *Occupational Outlook Handbook, 2006–2007 Edition*. Also available at http://www.bls.gov/oco/ocos056.htm.

7. Based on Harrell, K. (2003). *Attitude is everything: 10 life-changing steps to turning attitude into action*. New York: HarperBusiness.

8. Dweck, C. S. (2000). *Self-theories: Their role in motivation, personality, and development*. New York: Psychology Press, p. 1.

9. Berglas, S. & Jones, E. E. (1978). Drug choice as a self-handicapping strategy in response to noncontingent success. *Journal of Personality and Social Psychology*, *36*, 405–417; Jones, E. E. & Berglas, S. (1978). Control of attributions about the self through self-handicapping strategies: The appeal of alcohol and the role of underachievement. *Personality and Social Psychology Bulletin*, *4*, 200–206; Dweck, C. S. (2006). *Mindset: The new psychology of success*. New York: Random House.

10. Dweck, C. S. (2000). *Self-theories: Their role in motivation, personality, and development*. New York: Psychology Press; Dweck, *Mindset*.

11. Robins, R. W., & Pals, J. (1998). *Implicit self-theories of ability in the academic domain: A test of Dweck's model*. Unpublished manuscript.

12. Mangels, J. A., Butterfield, B., Lamb, J., Good, C. D., & Dweck, C. S. (2006). Why do beliefs about intelligence influence learning success? A social cognitive neuroscience model. *Social Cognitive and Affective Neuroscience, 1*(2), 75–86.

13. Bauer, A. R., Grant, H., & Dweck, C. S. (2006). *Personal goals predict the level and impact of dysphoria.* Unpublished manuscript.

14. Hoover, E. (2006, February 24). Study finds school-college "disconnect" in curricula. *The Chronicle of Higher Education, 52*(25), A1.

15. Omara-Otunnu, E. (2006, July 24). Conference examines transition from high school to college. University of Connecticut *Advance.* Available at http://advance.uconn.edu/2006/060724/06072407 .htm.

16. Data show value of college degree. (2005, April 8). *The Chronicle of Higher Education, 51*(31), A22.

17. Pascarella, E. T., & Terenzini, P. T. (2005). *How college affects students: A third decade of research.* San Francisco: Jossey-Bass, p. 403.

Chapter 2

1. Leamnson, R. (1999). *Thinking about teaching and learning: Developing habits of learning with first year college and university students.* Sterling, VA: Stylus.

2. Caine, R. N., & Caine, G. (1994). *Making connections: Teaching and the human brain.* Menlo Park, CA: Addison Wesley.

3. Livermore, B. (1992, September-October). Build a bet-ter brain. *Psychology Today.* Available at http://www.psychologytoday.com/articles/pto-19920901-000024.html.

4. Jozefowicz, C. (2004, May-June). Sweating makes you smart. *Psychology Today.* Available at http://psychologytoday.com/articles/pto-20040514-000004.html; Wu, A., Ying, Z., & Gomez-Pinilla, F. (2004). Dietary omega-3 fatty acids normalize BDNF levels, reduce oxidative damage, and counteract learning disability after traumatic brain injury in rats. *Journal of Neurotrauma, 21,* 1457–1467; PT Staff. (1998, March-April). Brain Boosters. *Psychology Today*; Alzheimer's Association. (2004). Think about your future. Maintain your brain. Available at http://www.alz.org/we_can_help_brain_health_ maintain_your_brain.asp.

5. Associated Press. (2005, June 21). Brain exercise is key to healthy mind. Available at http://www .thirdage.com/news/articles/DAI/05/07/01/050701-01.html.

6. Springer, M. V., McIntosh, A. R., Winocur, G., & Grady, C. L. (2005). The relation between brain activity during memory tasks and years of education in young and older adults. *Neuropsychology, 19*(2), 181–192.

7. Csikszentmihalyi, M. (2006). *Flow: The psychology of optimal experience.* New York: Academic Internet Publishers; Csikszentmihalyi, M. (1997). *Creativity: Flow and the psychology of discovery and invention.* New York: Harper Perennial; Gross, R. (1999). *Peak learning.* New York: Tarcher.

8. Caine & Caine, *Making connections*; Jensen, E. (2000). *Different brains, different learners.* San Diego: The Brain Store.

9. Brandt, R. (1998). *Powerful learning.* Alexandria, VA: Association for Supervision and Curriculum Development, p. 29.

10. Campbell, B. (1992). Multiple intelligences in action. *Childhood Education, 68*(4), 197–201; Gardner, H., & Hatch, T. (1989). Multiple intelligences go to school: Educational implications of the theory of multiple intelligences. *Educational Researcher, 18*(8)., 4–9; Gardner, H. (1983). *Frames of Mind: The Theory of Multiple Intelligences.* New York: Basic Books.

11. Armstrong, T. (2000). *MI and cognitive skills.* Available at http://www.ascd.orged_topics/ 2000armstrong/ chapter12.html.

12. Law of Supply and Demand. Wikipedia. Available at http://en.wikipedia.org/wiki/Supply_and_ demand.

13. Davis, B. (1993). *Tools for teaching.* San Francisco: Jossey-Bass, p. 185.

14. Fleming, N. D. (1995). I'm different; not dumb: Modes of presentation (VARK) in the tertiary class-room. In A. Zeimer (Ed.), *Research and Development in Higher Education, Proceedings of the 1995 Annual Conference of the Higher Education and Research Development Society of Austral-asia (HERDSA), HERDSA, 18,* 308–313; Fleming, N. D., & Mills, C. (1992). Not another inventory, rather a catalyst for reflection. *To Improve the Academy, 11,* 137–149. Available at http://www.ntlf .com/html/lib/suppmat/74fleming.htm.

15. Fleming, I'm different; not dumb.

16. Also available at http://www.bls.gov/oco/ocos066.htm.

17. Fleming, N. D. (2005). *Teaching and learning styles: VARK strategies.* Christchurch, NZ: Microfilm Limited.

CHAPTER 3

1. Leonhardt, D. (2005, May 24). The college dropout boom. *The New York Times,* p. A1, column 1.

2. Irvine, M. (22 January, 2007). Polls say wealth important to youth. Associated Press. Available at: http://www.eons.com/love/feature/kids/polls-say-wealth-important-to-youth/12850

3. Farrell, E. F. (2005, February 4). More students plan to work to help pay for college. *The Chronicle of Higher Education, 51*(22), A1. Available online at http://chronicle.com/weekly/v51/i22/22a00101 .htm.

4. Clark, K. (2005, 12 December). Econ 101: College is time to budget. *U.S. News & World Report, 139*(22), 62–63.

5. Kendrick, E. (1999). Give 'em credit: When is it right for students? *Austin Business Journal, 19*(25), 26.

6. Joo, S. G., Grable, J. E., & Bagwell, D. C. (2003). Credit card attitudes and behaviors of college students. *College Student Journal, 37*(3), 405–420.

7. The Associated Press. (2005, May 24). College students carrying fewer credit cards. Available at http://www.msnbc.msn.com/id/7968677/.

8. Ibid.

9. Financial literacy statistics. Young Americans: Center for Financial Education. Available at http://www.yacenter.org/index.cfm?fuseAction=financialLiteracyStatistics.financialLiteracyStatistics.

10. See http://www.costofwedding.com/?gclid=CI-59NquhIoCFQLYYgodkjakRQ.

11. See http://www.motortrend.com/features/news/112_news030430_ave/.

12. See http://usgovinfo.about.com/od/consumerawareness/a/avghomeprice04.htm.

13. Kantrowitz, M. (2007). FAQs about financial aid. FinAid: The Smart Student Guide to Financial Aid. Available at http://www.finaid.org/questions/faq.phtml.

14. Norvilitis, J. M., & Santa Maria, P. (2002). Credit card debt on college campuses: Causes, consequences, and solutions. *College Student Journal, 36*(3), 356–364.

15. Kantrowitz, M. (2007). Defaulting on student loans. FinAid: The Smart Student Guide to Financial Aid. Available at http://www.finaid.org/loans/default.phtml.

16. Repaying student loans held by the U.S. Department of Education. Federal Student Aid. Available at http://www.ed.gov/offices/OSFAP/DCS/repaying.html.

17. Bollet, R. M., & Fallon, S. (2002). Personalizing e-learning. *Educational Media International, 39*(1), 39–45; Thompson, G. (2001–2002). Overcoming your resistance to distance learning. *E-Learning Magazine*; Online student induction package. Available at http://www2.tafe.sa.edu.au/lsrsc/oes/induct/.

18. Roach, R. (2004). Survey unveils high-tech ownership profile of American college students. *Black Issues in Higher Education, 21*(16), 37.

19. Jones, S., & Madden, M. (2002). The Internet goes to college: How students are living in the future with today's technology. Pew Internet. Available at http://www.pewinternet.org/PPF/r/71/report_display.asp.

20. stats.com. Available at http://www.internetworldstats.com/stats.htm.

21. Available at http://www.bls.gov/oco/ocos042.htm and http://www.bls.gov/oco/cg/cgs033.htm.

22. Simon, H. A. (1996). *Observations on the sciences of science learning.* Paper prepared for the Committee on Developments in the Science of Learning for the Sciences of Science Learning: An Interdisciplinary Discussion. Department of Psychology, Carnegie Mellon University.

23. Wood, G. (2004, 9 April). Academic original sin: Plagiarism, the Internet, and librarians. *The Journal of Academic Librarianship, 30*(3), 237–242.

24. Loppatto, E. (2007, 6 February). Porn viewed by almost half of kids, often mistakenly. *Bloomberg.com.* Available at http://www.bloomberg.com/apps/news?pid=20601103&sid=ap3R1lomUalk&refer=us.

25. Nathan, R. (2005). *My freshman year: What a professor learned by becoming a student.* Ithaca, NY: Cornell University Press.

26. Fitzgerald, M. A. (2004). Making the leap from high school to college. *Knowledge Quest, 32*(4), 19–24; Ehrmann, S. (2004). Beyond computer literacy: Implications of technology for the content of a college education. *Liberal Education.* Available at http://www.aacu.org/liberaleducation/le-fa04/le-fa04feature1.cfm.

27. Dweck, C. S. (2006). *Mindset: The new psychology of success.* New York: Random House. pp. 104–105.

CHAPTER 4

1. Cooper, R. K. (1991). *The performance edge.* Boston: Houghton Mifflin, p. 53.

2. Eade, D. M. (1998). Energy and success: Time management. *Clinician News,* July/August. Available at http://www.adv-leadership-grp.com/articles/energy.htm.

3. Loehr, J., & Schwartz, T. (2003). *The power of full engagement: Managing energy, not time, is the key to high performance and personal renewal.* New York: Free Press

4. Bittel, L. R. (1991). *Right on time! The complete guide for time-pressured managers.* New York: McGraw-Hill, p. 16.

5. Bittel, Right on time! p. 16.

6. Loehr, The power of full engagement.

7. Soumaré, F. (2006, February 24). The dangers of facebook addiction. *The Sophian.* Available at http://media.www.smithsophian.com/media/storage/paper587/news/2006/02/24/Opinions/The-Dangers.Of.Facebook.Addiction-1637444.shtml; Withall, R. (2005, November 18). Facing the facts about facebook. *The Villanovan.* Available at http://www.villanovan.com/media/paper581/news/2005/11/18/verge/facing.the.facts.about.facebook-1108785.shtml

8. Greene, L. (2006, March 8). You might be a Facebook stalker if. . . . *Winonan.* Available at http://www.winona.edu/winonan/S2006/3-8-06/YoumightbeaFacebookstalkerif....htm; Hollister, L. (2005, October 5). Facebook addiction is needless, yet compelling. *The Volante Online.* Available at http://media.www.volanteonline.com/media/storage/paper468/news/2005/10/05/Opinion/Facebook.Addiction.Is.Needless.Yet.Compelling-1008873.shtml.

9. Greenfield, D. N. (1999). *Virtual addiction.* Oakland, CA: New Harbinger Publications; Yair, E., & Hamburger, A. (2005). *The social net.* Oxford: Oxford University Press; Young, K. S. (1998). *Caught in the net.* New York: John Wiley.

10. Also available at http://www.bls.gov/oco/ocos086.htm.

11. Based on Covey, S. R., Merrill, A. R., & Merrill, R. R. (1996). *First things first: To live, to love, to learn, to leave a legacy.* New York: Free Press, 37.

12. Fortino, M. (2001). *E-mergency.* Groveland, CA: Omni Publishing.

13. Hobbs, C. R. (1987). *Time power.* New York: Harper & Row, pp. 9–10.

14. Solomon, L. J., & Rothblum, E. D. (1984). Academic procrastination: Frequency and cognitive-behavioral correlates. *Journal of Counseling Psychology, 31,* 503–509.

15. Hoover, E. (2005, December 9). Tomorrow I love ya! *The Chronicle of Higher Education, 52*(16), A30–32.

16. Ferrari, J. R., McCown, W. G., & Johnson, J. (2002). *Procrastination and task avoidance: Theory, research, and treatment.* New York: Springer Publishing.

17. Schouwenburg, H. C., Lay, C. H., Pychyl, T. A., & Ferrari, J. R. (Eds.). (2004). *Counseling the procrastinator in academic settings.* Washington DC: American Psychological Association.

18. Hoover, Tomorrow I love ya!.

19. Sandholtz, K., Derr, B., Buckner, K., & Carlson, D. (2002). *Beyond juggling: Rebalancing your busy life.* San Francisco: Berrett-Koehler Publishers.

20. Adapted from Sandholtz et al., *Beyond juggling.*

21. Ibid.

Chapter 5

1. Halx, M. D., & Reybold, E. (2005). A pedagogy of force: Faculty perspective of critical thinking capacity in undergraduate students. *The Journal of General Education, 54*(4), 293–315.

2. Walkner, P., & Finney, N. (1999). Skill development and critical thinking in higher education. *Teaching in Higher Education, 4*(4), 531–548.

3. Diestler, S. (2001). *Becoming a critical thinker: A user friendly manual.* Upper Saddle River, NJ: Prentice Hall.

4. Falcione, P. A. (1998). *Critical thinking: What it is and why it counts.* Millbrae, CA: California Academic Press.

5. Twale, D., & Sanders, C. S. (1999). Impact of non-classroom experiences on critical thinking ability. *NASPA Journal, 36*(2), 133–146.

6. Thomas, C., & Smoot, G. (1994, February/March). Critical thinking: A vital work skill. *Trust for Educational Leadership, 23*, 34-38.

7. Kaplan-Leiserson, E. (2004). Workforce of tomorrow: How can we prepare *all* youth for future work success? *Training & Development, 58*(4), 12–14. 13. Based in part on Brookfield, S. D. (1987). *Developing critical thinkers: Challenging adults to explore alternative ways of thinking and acting.* San Francisco: Jossey-Bass.

8. Van den Brink-Budgen, R. (2000). *Critical thinking for students.* (3rd ed.). Oxford: How to Books; Ruggiero, V. R. (2001). *Becoming a critical thinker.* (4th ed.). Boston: Houghton Mifflin.

9. Although the case in this story is fictitious, it is representative of the drinking problems on many college campuses. Facts were taken from College binge drinking issues. About.com. Available at http://alcoholism.about.com/od/college/, and ideas were suggested by Students' initiation with booze. (2004, October 3). *Denver Post*, p. 2E.

10. Blakey, E., & Spence, S. (1990). Developing metacognition. ERIC Clearinghouse on Information Resources, Syracuse NY. Available at http://www.vtaide.com/png/ERIC/Metacognition.htm.

11. Also available at http://www.bls.gov/oco/ocos272.htm.

12. Florida, R. (2002). The rise of the creative class: And how it's transforming work, leisure, community and everyday life. New York: Basic Books, xii.

13. Sternberg. R. J. (2004). Teaching college students that creativity is a decision. *Guidance & Counseling, 19*(4), 196–200.

14. Vance, E. (2007, February 2). College graduates lack key skills, report says. *The Chronicle of Higher Education, 53*(22), A30.

15. Kurtz, J. R. (1998). It's all in your mind! Creative thinking essential in times of change. *Outlook, 66*(3), 5.

16. Rowe, A. J. (2004). *Creative intelligences: discovering the innovative potential in ourselves and others.* Upper Saddle, NJ: Pearson Education, pp. 3–6, 34.

17. Michalko, M. (2001). *Cracking creativity: The secrets of creative genius.* Berkeley, CA: Ten Speed Press.

18. Adapted from Adler, R., & Towne, N. (1987). *Looking out/Looking in.* (5th ed.) New York: Holt, Rinehart, and Winston, pp. 99–100.

19. Douglas, J. H. (1977). The genius of everyman (2): Learning creativity. *Science News, 111*(8), 284–288.

20. Harris, R. (1998). Introduction to creative thinking. VirtualSalt. Available at http://www.virtualsalt .com/crebook1.htm.

21. Eby, D. Creativity and flow psychology. Talent Development Resources. Available at http://talent develop.com/articles/Page8.html.

Chapter 6

1. Based on http://www-sop.inria.fr/acacia/personnel/Fabien.Gandon/lecture/uk1999/history/.

2. Burchfield, C. M., & Sappington, J. (2000). Compliance with required reading assignments. *Teaching of Psychology, 27*(1), 58–60; Hobson, E. H. (2004). *Getting students to read: Fourteen tips.* IDEA Paper No. 40, Manhattan, KS: Kansas State University, Center for Faculty Evaluation and Development; Maleki, R. B., & Heerman, C. E. (1992). *Improving student reading.* IDEA Paper No. 26, Manhattan, KS: Kansas State University, Center for Faculty Evaluation and Development. Most Idea Center papers available at http://www.idea.ksu.edu/

3. Perkins, K. K., & Wieman, C. E. (2005). The surprising impact of seat location on student performance. *The Physics Teacher, 43*(1), 30–33. Available: http://scitation.aip.org/journals/doc/ PHTEAH-ft/vol_43/iss_1/30_1.html.

4. Armbruster, B. B. (2000). Taking notes from lectures. In R. F. Flippo & D. C. Caverly (Eds.), *Handbook of college reading and study strategy research* (pp. 175–199). Mahwah, NJ: Erlbaum.

5. Staley, C. C., & Staley, R. S. (1992). *Communicating in business and the professions: The inside word.* Belmont, CA: Wadsworth, p. 223.

6. Hughes, C. A., & Suritsky, S. K. (1993). Notetaking skills and strategies for students with learning disabilities. *Preventing School Failure, 38*(1).

7. Staley & Staley, *Communicating in business and the professions*, pp. 229–236.

8. Kiewra, K. A., Mayer, R. E., Christensen, M., Kim, S., & Risch, N. (1991). Effects of repetition on recall and note-taking: Strategies for learning from lectures. *Journal of Educational Psychology, 83*, 120–123.

9. Brock, R. (2005, October 28). Lectures on the go. *The Chronicle of Higher Education, 52*(10), A39–42; French, D. P. (2006). iPods: Informative or invasive? *Journal of College Science Teaching, 36*(1), 58–59; Hallett, V. (2005, October 17). Teaching with tech. *U.S. News & World Report, 139*(14), 54–58; *The Horizon Report.* (2006). Stanford, CA: The New Media Consortium.

10. Selby, J. (2004). *Quiet your mind.* Makawao, Maui, HI: Inner Ocean Publishing.

11. Based on Staley, C. (2003). *50 ways to leave your lectern.* Belmont, CA: Wadsworth, pp. 80–81.

12. Adapted from *Effective listening skills.* Elmhurst College Learning Center. Available at http://www .elmhurst.edu/library/learningcenter/Listening/listening_behaviors_survey.htm.

13. Palmatier, R. A., & Bennett, J. M. (1974). Note-taking habits of college students. *Journal of Reading, 18*, 215–218; Dunkel, P., & Davy, S. (1989). The heuristic of lecture notetaking: Perceptions of American and international students regarding the value and practices of notetaking. *English for Specific Purposes, 8*, 33–50.

14. Armbruster, *Handbook of college reading and study strategy research.*

15. Van Meter, P., Yokoi, L., & Pressley, M. (1994). College students' theory of note-taking derived from their perceptions of note-taking. *Journal of Educational Psychology, 86*, 323–338.

16. Davis, M., & Hult, R. (1997). Effects of writing summaries as a generative learning activity during note taking. *Teaching of Psychology 24*(1), 47–49; Boyle, J. R., & Weishaar, M. (2001). The effects of strategic notetaking on the recall and comprehension of lecture information for high school students with learning disabilities. *Learning Disabilities Research & Practice 16*(3); Kiewra, K. A. (2002). How classroom teachers can help students learn and teach them how to learn. *Theory into Practice 41*(2), 71–81; Kiewra, How classroom teachers can help students learn and teach them how to learn; Aiken, E. G., Thomas, G. S., & Shennum, W. A. (1975). Memory for a lecture: Effects of notes, lecture rate and informational density. *Journal of Educational Psychology, 67*, 439–444; Hughes, C. A., & Suritsky, S. K. (1994). Note-taking skills of university students with and without learning disabilities. *Journal of Learning Disabilities, 27*, 20–24.

17. Bonner, J. M., & Holliday, W. G. (2006). How college science students engage in note-taking strategies. *Journal of Research in Science Teaching, 43*(8), 786–818.

18. Pauk, W. (2000). *How to study in college.* Boston: Houghton Mifflin.

19. Pardini, E. A., Domizi, D. P., Forbes, D. A., & Pettis, G. V. (2005). Parallel note-taking: A strategy for effective use of Webnotes. *Journal of College Reading and Learning, 35*(2), 38–55. Available at http://www.biology.wustl.edu/pardini/TeachingMaterials/JCRL_spring2005_pardini.pdf.

20. Kiewra, How classroom teachers can help students learn and teach them how to learn.

21. Porte, L. K. (2001). Cut and paste 101. *Teaching Excep-tional Children, 34*(2), 14–20.

22. Craik, F. I. M., & Watkins, M. J. (1973). The role of rehearsal in short-term memory. *Journal of Verbal Learning and Verbal Behavior, 12*, 599–607.

23. Adapted from Staley, *50 Ways to Leave Your Lectern*, p. 116.

24. Also available at http://www.bls.gov/oco/ocos272.htm.

CHAPTER 7

1. Bolla, K. I., Lindgren, K. N., Bonaccorsy, C., & Bleecker, M. L. (1991). Memory complaints in older adults: Fact or fiction? *Archives of Neurology, 48*, 61–64.

2. Higbee, K. L. (2004). What aspects of their memories do college students most want to improve? *College Student Journal, 38*(4), 552–556.

3. Higbee, K. L. (1988). *Your memory: How it works and how to improve it* (2nd ed.). New York: Prentice Hall.

4. Ibid.

5. Nairine, J. S. (2006). *Psychology: The adaptive mind.* Belmont, CA: Wadsworth/Thomson Learning.

6. Klingberg et al., Computerized training of working memory in children with ADHD.

7. Nairine, *Psychology.*

8. Miller, G. A. (1956). The magical number seven plus or minus two: Some limits on our capacity for processing information. *Psychological Review, 63,* 81–97.

9. Also available at http://www.bls.gov/oco/ocos093.htm.

10. The neurological scratchpad: what is working memory? (2004, July 7). Brain Connection.com. Available at http://www.brainconnection.com/topics/?main=fa/working-memory2; Kotbagi, H. (1997). Human memory. Human-Computer Interface. Available at http://www.cc.gatech.edu/classes/cs6751_97_winter/Topics/human-cap/memory.html; Memory. Dr. Brown's Psychology 1501 Home Page. Available at http://www.gpc.edu/~bbrown/psyc1501/memory/stm.htm; Clark, D. Memory: The three memory storage systems. Available at http://www.nwlink.com/~donclark/hrd/learning/memory.html; Kerry, S. (1999–2002). Memory and retention time. Education Reform.net. Available at http://www.education-reform.net/memory.htm; Goodhead, J. (1999). The difference between short-term and long-term memory [On-line].

11. Rozakis, L. (2003). *Test-taking strategies and study skills for the utterly confused.* New York: McGraw Hill; Meyers, J. N. (2000). *The secrets of taking any test.* New York: Learning Express; Ehren, B. J. Mnemonic devices. Available at http://itc.gsu.edu/academymodules/a304/support/xpages/a304b0_20600.html; Lloyd, G. (1998–2004). Study skills: Memorize with mnemonics. Available at http://www.back2college.com/memorize.htm.

12. Willingham, D. T. (2004). Practice makes perfect—but only if you practice beyond the point of perfection. *American Educator.* Available at http://www.aft.org/pubs-reports/american_educator/spring2004/cogsci.html.

13. Tigner, R. B. (1999). Putting memory research to good use: Hints from cognitive psychology. *College Teaching, 47*(4), 149–152.

14. Murdock, B. B., Jr. (1960). The distinctiveness of stimuli. *Psychological Reports, 67,* 16–31; Neath, I. (1993). Distinctiveness and serial position effects in recognition. *Memory & Cognition, 21,* 689–698.

15. Cahill, L. (2003). Similar neural mechanisms for emotion-induced memory impairment and enhancement. *Proceedings of the National Academy of Sciences, 100*(23), 13123–13124. Available at http://www.pnas.org/cgi/content/full/100/23/13123.

16. Dingfelder, S. F. (2005). Feelings' sway over memory. *Monitor on Psychology, 26*(8). Available at APA Online at http://www.apa.org/monitor/sep05/feelings.html.

17. Noice, H., & Noice, T. (2006). What studies of actors and acting can tell us about memory and cognitive functioning. *Current Directions in Psychological Science, 15*(1), 14–18.

18. Higbee, *Your memory.*

19. Ibid.

20. Bean, J. (1996). *Engaging ideas.* San Francisco: Jossey-Bass.

21. Tigner, Putting memory research to good use.

22. Higbee, *Your memory.*

23. Caine, R. N., & Caine, G. (1997). *Education on the edge of possibility.* Alexandria, VA: Association for Supervision and Curriculum Development.

24. Berk, R. A. (2002). *Humor as an instructional defibrillator.* Sterling, VA: Stylus; Berk, R. A. (2003). *Professors are from Mars®, students are from Snickers®.* Sterling, VA: Stylus.

25. Schacter, D. L. (2001). *The seven sins of memory: How the mind forgets and remembers.* Boston: Houghton Mifflin; Murray, B. (2003). The seven sins of memory. *Monitor on Psychology.* Available at APA Online at http://www.apa.org/monitor/oct03/sins.html.

26. Tagg, J. (2004, March-April). Why learn? What we may really be teaching students. *About Campus,* 2–10; Marton, F., & Säljö, R. On qualitative differences in learning: I-Outcome and process. (1976). *British Journal of Educational Psychology, 46,* 4–11.

CHAPTER 8

1. Rogers, M. (2007, March-April). Is reading obsolete? *The Futurist,* 26–27; Waters, L. (2007, February 9). Time for reading. *The Chronicle of Higher Education, 53*(23), 1B6.

2. Caverly, D. C., Nicholson, S. A., & Radcliffe, R. (2004). The effectiveness of strategic reading instruction for college developmental readers. *Journal of College Reading and Learning, 35*(1), 25–49; Simpson, M. L., & Nist, S. L. (1997). Perspectives on learning history: A case study. *Journal of Literacy Research, 29*(3), 363–395.

3. Caverly, Nicholson, & Radcliffe, The effectiveness of strategic reading instruction for college developmental readers; Burrell, K. I., Tao, L., Simpson, M. L., & Mendez-Berrueta, H. (1997). How do we know what we are preparing students for? A reality check of one university's academic literacy demands. *Research & Teaching in Developmental Education, 13,* 15–70.

4. Bean, J. C. (1996). *Engaging ideas: The professor's guide to integrating writing, critical thinking, and active learning in the classroom.* San Francisco: Jossey-Bass; Wood, N. V. (1997). College reading instruction as reflected by current reading textbooks. *Journal of College Reading and Learning, 27*(3). 79–95.

5. Saumell, L., Hughes, M. T., & Lopate, K. (1999). Under-prepared college students' perceptions of reading: Are their perceptions different than other students? *Journal of College Reading and Learning, 29*(2), 123–125.

6. Buzan, T. (1983). *Use both sides of your brain.* New York: E. P. Dutton.

7. Ibid.

8. Sternberg, R. J. (1987). Teaching intelligence: The application of cognitive psychology to the improvement of intellectual skills. In J. B. Baron & R. J. Sternberg (Eds.), *Teaching thinking skills: Theory and practice.* New York: Freeman. pp. 182–218

9. Al-Jarf, R. S. (2002). Effect of online learning on struggling ESL college writers. San Antonio, TX: National Educational Computing Conference. Available at http://scholar.google.com/scholar?hl=en&lr=lang_en&q=cache:nUFnaTizpjgJ:dwc.hct.ac.ae/elearning/Research/SaudiResearchESL.pdf+ESL+college+success+recommendations.

10. Based on Bean, *Engaging ideas.*

11. Based partly on Williams, S. (2005). Guiding students through the jungle of research-based literature. *College Teaching, 53*(4), 137–139.

12. Also available at http://www.bls.gov/oco/ocos069.htm.

13. Staley, C. (2003). *50 ways to leave your lectern.* Belmont, CA: Wadsworth, 49–50.

14. Soldner, L. B. (1997). Self-assessment and the reflective reader. *Journal of College Reading and Learning*, *28*(1), 5–11.

15. Melchenbaum, D., Burland, S., Gruson, L., & Cameron, R. (1985). Metacognitive assessment. In S. Yussen (Ed.), *The growth of reflection in children*. Orlando, FL: Academic Press. p. 5

16. Hall, C. W. (2001). A measure of executive processing skills in college students. *College Student Journal*, *35*(3), 442–450; Taylor, S. (1999). Better learning through better thinking: Developing students' metacognitive abilities. *Journal of College Reading and Learning*, *30*(1), 34–45.

17. Learning to learn. Study Guides and Strategies. Available at http://www.studygs.net/metacognition.htm.

18. Simpson, M. L. (1994/1995). Talk throughs: A strategy for encouraging active learning across the content areas. *Journal of Reading*, *38*(4), 296–304.

19. How Air Traffic Control Works. Available at http://travel.howstuffworks.com/air-traffic-control.htm.

20. Elias, M. (2004, April 5). Frequent TV watching shortens kids' attention spans. *USA Today*. Available at http://www.usatoday.com/news/health/2004-04-05-tv-kids-attention-usat_x.htm.

21. Bol, L., Warkentin, R. W., Nunnery, J. A., & O'Connell, A. A. (1999). College students' study activities and their relationship to study context, reference course, and achievement. *College Student Journal*, *33*(4). 608–622.

22. When students study makes a difference too. (2005, November). Recruitment & Retention. Available at http://www.magnapubs.com/pub/magnapubs_rr/19_11/news/598079-1.html.

23. Trainin, G., & Swanson, H. L. (2005). Cognition, meta-cognition, and achievement of college students with learning disabilities. *Learning Disability Quarterly*, *28*, 261–272.

24. Cramming bites. Study Skills for College. Available at http://www.bmb.psu.edu/courses/psu16/troyan/studyskills/cramming.htm; Final exams and cramming.Eastern Illinois University. Available at http://www.eiu.edu/~lrnasst/finals.htm.

25. Meyers, D. (2001). *Psychology* (6th ed.). New York: Worth Publishers.

CHAPTER 9

1. Petress, K. (2004). What do college examinations accomplish? *College Student Journal*, *38*(4), 521–522.

2. Coren, S. (1996). *Sleep thieves*. New York: Free Press; Cox, K. (2004, October 14). The lights are on, but nobody's home. *The Oxford Student*. Available at http://www.oxfordstudent.com/mt2004wk1/Features/the_lights_are_on,_but_nobody's_home.

3. Grant, K. B. (2003, September 4). Popping pills and taking tests. *The Ithacan Online*. Available at http://www.ithaca.edu/ithacan/articles/0309/04/news/2popping_pill.htm.

4. Brinthaupt, T. M., & Shin, C. M. (2001). The relationship of academic cramming to flow experience. *College Student Journal*, *35*(3), 457–472.

5. Tigner, R. B. (1999). Putting memory research to good use: Hints from cognitive psychology. *Journal of College Teaching*, *47*(4), 149–152.

6. Small, G. (2002). *The memory bible*. New York: Hyperion.

7. Counseling and Career Services. (2004). Do you have test anxiety? *Glendale Community College*. Available at http://www.gc.maricopa.edu/ccs/test.html.

8. Tozoglu, D., Tozoglu, M. D., Gurses, A., & Dogar, C. (2004). The students' perceptions: Essay versus multiple-choice type exams. *Journal of Baltic Science Education*, *2*(6), 52–59.

9. Schutz, P. A., & Davis, H. A. (2000). Emotions and self-regulation during test taking. *Educational Psychologist*, *35*(4), 243–256.

10. Coren, *Sleep thieves*.

11. Perina, K. (2002). Sum of all fears. *Psychology Today*. Available at http://www.psychologytoday.com/articles/pto-20021108-000001.html.

12. Perry, A. B. (2004). Decreasing math anxiety in college students. *College Student Journal*, *38*(2), 321–324.

13. Krantz, S. G. (1999). *How to teach mathematics*. Providence, RI: American Mathematical Society.

14. Perry, Decreasing math anxiety in college students.

15. Perina, Sum of all fears.

16. Coping with math anxiety. (1997–2006). Platonic Realms MiniTexts. Avaiable at http://www.mathacademy.com/pr/minitext/anxiety/index.asp.

17. Jonides, J., Lacey, S. C., & Nee, D. E. (2005). Processes of working memory in mind and brain. *Current Directions in Psychological Science*, *14*(1), 2–5.

18. Ashcraft, M. H., & Kirk, E. P. (2001). The relationships among working memory, math anxiety, and performance. *Journal of Experimental Psychology: General*. *130*(2), 224–237.

19. Beilock, S. L., Kulp, C. A., Holt, L. E., & Carr, T. H. (2004). More on the fragility of performance: Choking under pressure in mathematical problem solving. *Journal of Experimental Psychology: General*, *133*(4), 584–600.

20. Mundell, Test pressure toughest on smartest.

21. Firmin, M., Hwang, C., Copella, M., & Clark, S. (2004). Learned helplessness: The effect of failure on test-taking. *Education*, *124*(4), 688–693.

22. Heidenberg, A. J., & Layne, B. H. (2000). Answer changing: A conditional argument. *College Student Journal*, *34*(3), 440–451.

23. Also available at http://www.bls.gov/oco/cg/cgs054.htm.

24. See http://news.bbc.co.uk/2/hi/uk_news/scotland/glasgow_and_west/4755297.stm.

25. Preparing for multiple choice exams. (2006). York University. Available at http:www.yorku.ca/cdc/lsp/eponline/exam4.htm.

26. Taking exams. Brockport High School. Available at http://www.frontiernet.net/~jlkeefer/takgexm.html. Adapted from Penn State University; On taking exams. University of New Mexico. Available at http://www.unm.edu/~quadl/college_learning/taking_exams.html; Lawrence, J. (2006). Tips for taking examinations. Lawrence Lab Homepage. Available at http://cobamide2.bio.pitt.edu/testtips.htm; The multiple choice exam. (2003). Counselling Services, University of Victoria. Available at http://www.coun.uvic.ca/learning/exams/multiple-choice.html; General strategies for taking essay tests. GWired. Available at http://gwired.gwu.edu/counsel/asc/index.gw/Site_ID/46/Page_ID/14565;

Test taking tips: Guidelines for answering multiple-choice questions. Arizona State University. Available at http://neuer101.asu.edu/additionaltestingtips.htm; Landsberger, J. (2007). True/false tests. Study Guides and Strategies. Available at http://www.studygs.net/tsttak2.htm; Landsberger, J. (2007). Multiple choice tests. Study Guides and Strategies. Available at http://www.studygs.net/tsttak3.htm; Landsberger, J. (2007). The essay exam. Study Guides and Strategies. Available at http://www.studygs.net/tsttak4.htm; Landsberger, J. (2007). Short answer tests. Study Guides and Strategies. Available at http://www.studygs.net/tsttak5.htm; Landsberger, J. (2007). Open book tests. Study Guides and Strategies. Available at http://www.studygs.net/tsttak7.htm; Rogers, T., & Kline, D. Test-taking advice: Especially for the multiple-choice challenged. University of Calgary. Available at http://www.psych.ucalgary.ca/undergraduate/current-students/student-support#tta; Rozakis, L. (2003). *Test-taking strategies and study skills for the utterly confused.* New York: McGraw-Hill; Meyers, J. N. (2000). *The secrets of taking any test.* New York: Learning Express; Robinson, A. (1993). *What smart students know.* New York: Crown Trade Paperbacks.

27. Plagiarism.org. Available at http://www.plagiarism.org/facts.html; A cheating crisis in America's schools. (2007, 17 April). ABC News. Available at http://abcnews.go.com/Primetime/print?id=132376.

28. Caught cheating. (2004, April 29). *Primetime Live*, ABC News Transcript. Interview of college students by Charles Gibson; Zernike, K. (2002, November 2). With student cheating on the rise, more colleges are turning to honor codes. *The New York Times*, p. Q10, column 1, National Desk; Warren, R. (2003, October 20). Cheating: An easy way to cheat yourself. The Voyager via U-Wire. University Wire (www.uwire.com); Thomson, S. C. (2004, February 13). Amid wave of cheating, universities push "academic integrity." Knight Ridder/Tribune News Service. Available at http://www.highbeam.com/doc/1G1-113209265.html; Heyboer, K. (2003, August 23). Nearly half of college students say Internet plagiarism isn't cheating. *The Star-Ledger Newark, New Jersey.*; Kleiner, C., & Lord, M. (1999). The cheating game. *U.S. News & World Report.* Available at http://www.usnews.com/usnews/culture/articles/991122/archive_002427_8.htm.

29. Standardized tests. Mapping Your Future. Available at http://mapping-your-future.org/selecting/standard.htm; Grant, K. B. (2003). Popping pills and taking tests. The Ithacan Online. Available at http://www.ithaca.edu/ithacan/articles/0309/04/news/2popping_pill.htm; Survival strategies for taking tests. (2003). Indiana State University. Available at http://www.indstate.edu/isucceed/tests.htm; Cummins, C. (2004, May 14); Rogers & Kline, Test-taking advice; Rozakis, *Test-taking strategies and study skills for the utterly confused*; Meyers, *The secrets of taking any test.*

Chapter 10

1. Some situation topics suggested at Emotional Intelligence. Scottish Further Education Unit EI. http://www.sfeu.ac.uk/projects/emotional_intelligence.

2. Gardner, H. (1993). Multiple intelligences: The theory in practice. New York: Basic Books; Checkley, K. (1997). The first seven . . . and the eighth: A conversation with Howard Gardner. Expanded Academic ASAP (online database). Original Publication: Education, 116.

3. Parker, J. D. A., Duffy, J. M., Wood, L. M., Bond, B. J., & Hogan, M. J. (2005). Academic achievement and emotional intelligence: Predicting the successful transition from high school to university. *Journal of the First Year Experience & Students in Transition 17*(1), 67–78; Schutte, N. S., & Malouff, J. (2002). Incorporating emotional skills content in a college transition course enhances student retention. *Journal of the First Year Experience & Students in Transition 14*(1), 7–21.

4. EQ-i:S™ Post Secondary, Multi-Health Systems, Inc. North Tonawanda, NY. Available at http://www .mhs.com/index.htm. Used with permission.

5. Turning lemons into lemonade: Hardiness helps people turn stressful circumstances into opportunities. (2003, December 22). *Psychology Matters.* Available at APA Online at http://www.psychology matters.org/hardiness.html; Marano, H. E. (2003). The art of resilience. *Psychology Today.* Available at http://www.psychologytoday.com/articles/pto-20030527-000009.html; Fischman, J. (1987). Getting tough: Can people learn to have disease-resistant personalities? *Psychology Today,* 21, 26–28; Friborg, O., Barlaug, D., Martinussen, M., Rosenvinge, J. H., & Hjemdal, O. (2005). Resilience in relation to personality and intelligence. *International Journal of Methods in Psychiatric Research,* *14*(1), 29–42; Schulman, P. (1995). Explanatory style and achievement in school and work. In G. M. Buchanan & M. E. P. Seligman (Eds.), *Explanatory style* (pp. 159–171). Hillsdale, NJ: Lawrence Erlbaum; American Psychological Association. (1997). Learned optimism yields health benefits. *Discovery Health.* Available at http://health.discovery.com/centers/mental/articles/optimism/ optimism.html.

6. Maher, K. (2004) Emotional intelligence is a factor in promotions. *CollegeJournal from the Wall Street Journal.* Available at http://www.collegejournal.com/columnists/thejungle/20040322-maher .html.

7. Cherniss, C. (2000). *Emotional Intelligence: What it is and why it matters.* Paper presented at the Annual Meeting of the Society for Industrial and Organizational Psychology, New Orleans, LA. Available at http://www.eiconsortium.org/research/what_is_emotional_intelligence.htm.

8. Goleman, Could you be a leader? p. 4.

9. Boyatzis, R. E., Cowan, S. S., & Kolb, D. A. (1995). *Innovations in professional education: Steps on a journey from teaching to learning.* San Francisco: Jossey-Bass.

10. Saxbe, D. (2004, November/December). The socially savvy. *Psychology Today.* Available at http:// www.psychologytoday.com/articles/pto-3636.html.

11. Cramer, D. (2004). Satisfaction with a romantic relationship, depression, support and conflict. *Psychology and Psychotherapy: Theory, Research and Practice,* *77*(4), 449–461.

12. Fisher, H. (2004). *Why we love.* New York: Henry Holt.

13. Beach, S. R. H., & Tesser, A. (1988). Love in marriage; a cognitive account. In R. J. Sternberg & M. L. Barnes (Eds.), *The Psychology of Love.* 330–355 New Haven, CT: Yale University Press; Hatfield, E., & Walster, G. W. (1978). *A new look at love.* Lanham, MD: University Press of America.

14. Rath, T., & Clifton, D. O. (2004). *How full is your bucket?* New York: Gallup Press.

15. Knox, D. H. (1970). Conceptions of love at three developmental levels. *The Family Coordinator,* *19*(2), 151–157; Fisher, *Why we love.*

16. Schwartz, P. (2003, May-June). Love is not all you need. *Psychology Today.* Available at http://www .psychologytoday.com/articles/pto-20030213-000002.html.

17. Bach, G. R., & Goldberg, H. (1974). *Creative aggression: The art of assertive living.* Garden City, NJ: Doubleday; Bach, G. R, & Wyden, P. (1972). *The intimate enemy: How to fight fair in love and marriage.* New York: Avon; Bach, G. R., Deutsch, R. M., (1985). *Stop! You're driving me crazy.* New York: Berkley Publishing Group; Tucker-Ladd, C. E. (1996–2006); *Driving each other crazy.* Psychological self-help. Available at http://psychologicalselfhelp.org/Chapter9/chap9_90.html.

18. Based on Walter, T. L. (2003). Turn a negative student-to-instructor relationship into a positive relationship. In C. Staley, *50 Ways to leave your lectern* (pp. 146–149). Belmont, CA: Wadsworth.

19. Fisher, *Why we love.*

20. Fisher, R., & Brown, S. (1988). *Getting together: Building a relationship that gets to yes.* Boston: Houghton Mifflin, p. xi.

21. Based in part on Marano, H. (2002). Relationship rules. *Psychology Today.* Available at http://www .psychologytoday.com/articles/

22. (2006, March 3). Study: Bad relationships bad for heart. *CBS News.* Available at http://www.cbsnews .com/stories/2006/03/03/earlyshow/contributors/emilysenay/main1364889.shtml; (2005, December 5) Unhappy marriage: bad for your health. *WebMD.* Available at http://www.webmd.com/sex relationships/news/20051205/unhappy-marriage-bad-for-your-health. Based on Keicolt-Glaser, J. (2005). *Archives of general psychiatry, 62,* 1377–1384.

23. Dusselier, L., Dunn, B., Wang, Y., Shelley, M. C., & Whalen, D. F. (2005). Personal, health, academic, and environmental predictors of stress for residence hall students. *Journal of American College Health, 54*(1), 15–24; Hardigg, V., & Nobile, C. (1995). Living with a stranger. *U.S. News & World Report, 119*(12), 90–91. Available at http://www.usnews.com/usnews/edu/articles/950925/archive_ 032964_print.htm; Nankin, J. (2005). Rules for roomies. *Careers & Colleges, 25*(4), 29.

24. Miller, G. R., & Steinberg, M. (1975). *Between people: A new analysis of interpersonal communication.* Chicago: Science Research Associates.

25. Also available at http://www.bls.gov/oco/print/ocos021.htm.

26. Bucher, R. D. (2004). *Diversity consciousness: Opening our minds to people, cultures, and opportunities* (2nd ed.). Upper Saddle River, NJ: Pearson Education.

27. Moore, D. G. (2003, November 14). Toward a single definition of college. *The Chronicle of Higher Education, 50*(12), B7.

28. Pusser, B., Breneman, D. W., Gansneder, B. M., Kohl, K. J., Levin, J. S., Milam, J. H., & Turner, S. E. (2007). *Returning to learning: Adults' success in college is key to America's future.* Lumina Foundation. Available at http://www.luminafoundation.org/publications/ReturntolearningApril2007.pdf.

29. Gomstyn, A. (2003, October 17). Minority enrollment in colleges more than doubled in past 20 years, study finds. *The Chronicle of Higher Education, 50*(8), A25; Schmidt, P. (2003, 28 November). Academe's Hispanic future. *The Chronicle of Higher Education, 50*(14), A8.

30. Parker, P. N. (2006, March-April). Sustained dialogue: How students are changing their own racial climate. *About Campus,* 17–34.

31. Farrell, E. F. (2005, August 5). Student volunteers are worth billions. *The Chronicle of Higher Education, 51*(48), A33.

32. Zlotkowski, E. (1999). Pedagogy and engagement. In R. G. Bringle, R. Games, & E. A. Malloy (Eds.). (1999). *Colleges and Universities as Citizens* (pp. 96–120). Needham Heights, MA: Allyn & Bacon.

33. Honnet, E. P., & Poulsen, S. J. (1989). *Principles of good practice for combining service and learning: A Wingspread special report.* Racine, WI: The Johnson Foundation. Available at http://www .servicelearning.org/resources/online_documents/service-learning_standards/principles_of_good_ practice_for_combining_service_and_learning_a_wingspread_special_report/index.php.

34. Eyler, J., Giles, Jr., D. E., & Schmiede, A. (1996). *A practitioner's guide to reflection in service-learning: Student voices and reflections.* Nashville, TN: Vanderbilt University Press.

35. Farrell, Student volunteers are worth billions.

CHAPTER 11

1. Gregory, M. (2003, September 12). A liberal education is not a luxury. *The Chronicle of Higher Education, 50*(3), B16.

2. Staley, R. S., II. (2003). In C. Staley, *50 ways to leave your lectern* (pp. 70–74). Belmont, CA: Wadsworth.

3. Farrell, E. F. (2006, December 12). Freshmen put high value on how well college prepares them for a profession, survey finds. *The Chronicle of Higher Education.* Available at http://chronicle.com/daily/2006/12/2006121202n.htm; Farrell, E. F. (2007, January 5). Report says freshmen put career prep first. *The Chronicle of Higher Education, 53*(18), A32.

4. Irvine, M. (2007, January 22). Polls say wealth important to youth. SFGate.com. Available at http://www.sfgate.com/cgi-bin/article.cgi?file=/n/a/2007/01/22/national/a111238S28.DTL; Schwartz, B. (2004, January 23). The tyranny of choice. *The Chronicle of Higher Education, 50*(20), B6.

5. Levine, M. (2005). *Ready or not, here life comes.* New York: Simon & Schuster, p. 4; Levine, M. (2005, February 18). College graduates aren't ready for the real world. *The Chronicle of Higher Education, 51*(24), B11.

6. *Dictionary of occupational titles.* (1991). Washington, DC: Bureau of Labor Statistics. Or see O*Net Online (Occupational Information Network) at http://online.onetcenter.org/find/.

7. Based on Schwartz, The tyranny of choice.

8. See J. K. Rowling Biography at http://www.biography.com/search/article.jsp?aid=9465815&page=2&search=.

9. Levine, *Ready or not, here life comes.*

10. Koeppel, D. (2004, December 5). Choosing a college major: For love or for the money? *The New York Times,* section 10, p. 1, column 4. Available at http://www.nytimes.com/2004/12/05/jobs/05jmar.html?ex=1259989200&en=51dcc14fa52a65e7&ei=5090&partner=rssuserland; Dunham, K. J. (2004, March 2). No ivory tower: College students focus on career. *Wall Street Journal* (Eastern Edition), pp. B1, B8. Available at http://online.wsj.com/article/SB107818521697943524.html.

11. Based in part on Gordon, V. N., & Sears, S. J. (2004). *Selecting a college major: Exploration and decision making, 5th edition.* Upper Saddle River, NJ: Pearson Education.

12. Based on Hansen, R. S., & Hansen, K. *Using a SWOT analysis in your career planning.* Quintessential Careers. Available at http://www.quintcareers.com/SWOT_Analysis.html.

13. Staley, *50 ways to leave your lectern,* p. 33. Based on "Group Resume." (1995). In M. Silberman, *101 ways to make training active* (pp. 49–50). Johannesburg: Pfeiffer.

14. *Job interviews get creative.* (2003, August 22). NPR. Available at http://www.npr.org/templates/story/story.php?storyId=1405340.

15. Vance, E. (2007, February 2). College graduates lack key skills, report says. *The Chronicle of Higher Education, 53*(22), A30.

16. Also available at http://www.bls.gov/oco/ocos021.htm; Recruiter. Wikipedia. Available at http://en.wikipedia.org/wiki/Recruiter.

17. Rowh, M. (2003, February-March). Choosing a major. *Career World, 31*(5), 21–23.

18. Ezarik, M. M. (2007, April-May). A major decision. *Career World, 35*(6), 20–22.

19. Rask & Bailey, Are faculty role models?

20. Based on Staley, *50 ways to leave your lectern*, p. 82.

21. Goldhaber, G. M. (1986). *Organizational communication* (4th ed.). Dubuque, IA: Wm. C. Brown, p. 236. In Staley, R. S., II, & Staley, C. C. (1992). *Communicating in business and the professions: The inside word*. Belmont, CA: Wadsworth.

TEXT CREDITS

This page constitutes an extension of the copyright page. We have made every effort to trace the ownership of all copyrighted material and to secure permission from copyright holders. In the event of any question arising as to the use of any material, we will be pleased to make the necessary corrections in future printings. Thanks are due to the following authors, publishers, and agents for permission to use the material indicated.

Chapter 1. 7: Based on J. Bransford, et al. (2000). How People Learn: Brain, Mind, Experience, and School. Washington, DC: National Academy Press. **11:** French, B.F., & Oakes, W. (2003). Measuring academic intrinsic motivation in the first year of college: Reliability and validity evidence for a new instrument. Journal of the First Year Experience 15(1), 83–102.

Chapter 2. 42: N. Fleming. (2001–2007). VARK, a Guide to Learning Styles. Version 7.0. Available at http://www.vark-learn.com/english/page.asp?p=questionnaire. Used with permission from Neil Fleming.

Chapter 3. 65: Companion, M. (2006). Victoria Tymmyns Ispy.com. Used with permission.

Chapter 4. 98: Adapted from Sandholtz, K., Derr, B., Buckner, K., & Carlson, D. (2002). Beyond juggling: Rebalancing your busy life. San Francisco: Berrett-Koehler Publishing.

Chapter 8. 173: From "How Cool Is Your Job? And Does It Even Matter?" by Adelle Waldman, Wall Street Journal Online Edition, Oct. 24, 2005. Reprinted by permission.

Chapter 10. 220: From EQ-e:S Post Secondary version. Reprinted by permission.

PHOTO CREDITS

All student cast photographs not credited are the work of © Larry Harwood Photography and the property of Cengage Learning.

All credits for images not cited on the following pages are as follows:

Chapter 1, p. 3 L to R: ©Photodisc/Getty Images; ©Hemera Photo Objects; ©Brand X/Jupiter Images; ©Cengage Learning; ©Cengage Learning/Heinle Image Resource Bank **p. 4 L to R:** ©FogStock LLC/Index Open; ©PhotoObjects.net/Jupiter Images **p. 12:** Courtesy of Eric Sween **p. 15:** ©Denis Scott/CORBIS **p. 19:** ©Patrick Giardino/CORBIS **p. 20:** ©Digital Vision/Getty Images **p. 23:** ©Photodisc/Getty Images

Chapter 2, p. 29 L to R: ©Photodisc/Getty Images; ©Photodisc/Getty Images; ©Cengage Learning; ©Cengage Learning **p. 33:** ©Colin Anderson/Blend Images/CORBIS **p. 42:** ©Holger Winkler/zefa/CORBIS **p. 44:** Courtesy of Neil Fleming

Chapter 3, p. 51 L to R: ©Cengage Learning; ©Photodisc/Getty Images; ©Brand X Pictures/Jupiter Images; ©Brand X Pictures/Jupiter Images; ©Comstock/Jupiter Images **p. 52:** ©Hot Ideas/Index Open **p. 57:** ©Susan Van Etten/PhotoEdit **p. 59:** ©Brand X Pictures/Jupiter Images **p. 60:** ©Tom & Dee Ann McCarthy/CORBIS **p. 62:** Courtesy of John M. Hearn Jr. **p. 64:** ©PhotoAlto/Getty Images **p. 65:** Companion, M. (2006). Victoria Tymmyns Ispy.com. Used with permission. **p. 69:** ©William Whitehurst/CORBIS

Chapter 4, p. 77 L to R: ©VStock LLC/Index Open; ©Photodisc/Getty Images; ©Photodisc/Getty Images; ©Photodisc/Getty Images **p. 79:** ©Digital Vision/Getty Images **p. 88:** Courtesy of Judith Cara **p. 91:** ©Photodisc/Getty Images **p. 94:** ©Shalom Ormsby/Blend Images/Getty Images **p. 97:** ©Tetra Images/CORBIS

Chapter 5, p. 103 L to R: ©North Wind Picture Archives; ©Siede Preis/Photodisc/Getty Images; www.morguefile.com; ©Cengage Learning **p. 108:** ©John Lund/CORBIS **p. 110:** ©Photos.com Select/Index Open **p. 112:** ©Jac Depczyk/Photographer's Choice/Getty Images **p. 118:** ©PRNewsFoto/Jamster/NewsCom **p. 123:** ©William Whitehurst/CORBIS

Chapter 6, p. 126: ©Photodisc/Getty Images **p. 127 L to R:** Courtesy of author; ©Steve Cole/Photodisc/Getty Images; ©Brand X Pictures/Jupiter Images; ©Cengage Learning **p. 138:** ©Tomas Rodriguez/Solus-Veer/CORBIS **p. 141:** ©Marc Romanelli/Riser/Getty Images **p. 146:** Courtesy of Karen Springen

Chapter 7, p. 151 L to R: ©North Wind Picture Archives; ©North Wind Picture Archives; ©North Wind Picture Archives; ©Brand X Pictures/Jupiter Images; ©Roy McMahon/CORBIS **p. 153:** ©Lester Lefkowitz/CORBIS **p. 154:** ©C Squared Studios/Photodisc/Getty Images **p. 156:** Courtesy of Delanna Studi **p. 158:** bottom four photos: www.morguefile.com **p. 160:** ©photolibrary.com pty. ltd./Index Open **p. 162:** ©AbleStock/Index Open

Chapter 8, p. 171 L to R: ©Photodisc/Getty Images; ©Photodisc/Getty Images; ©Ablestock/Index Open; ©Photodisc/Getty Images **p. 172:** ©Tom McCarthy/PhotoEdit **p. 176:** ©Stockbyte/Getty Images **p. 180:** Courtesy of Barbara Swaby **p. 182:** ©Brand X Pictures/Jupiter Images

Chapter 9, p. 191 L to R: ©Cengage Learning; ©Eyewire/Getty Images; ©Eyewire/Getty Images; ©Photodisc/Getty Images **p. 192:** ©William B. Plowman/Getty Images **p. 194:** ©Comstock Images/Jupiter Images **p. 198:** ©Photodisc/Getty Images **p. 200:** ©James Noble/CORBIS **p. 202:** Courtesy of Beth Robinson **p. 205:** ©Image Source/CORBIS **p. 210:** ©Vera Berger/zefa/CORBIS

Chapter 10, p. 217 L to R: ©Cengage Learning; ©Comstock/Jupiter Images; ©Photodisc/Getty Images; ©Photodisc/Getty Images **p. 219:** ©William Whitehurst/CORBIS **p. 220:** ©Hemera Photo Objects **p. 221:** ©Robert Recker/zefa/CORBIS **p. 226:** ©Everett Collection **p. 232:** ©Ted Thai, computer morphed face by Kin Wah Lam/Time Inc. /Time & Life Pictures/Getty Images **p. 233:** ©Brand X Pictures/Getty Images

Chapter 11, p. 237 L to R: ©Comstock/Jupiter Images; ©Eyewire/Getty Images; ©Artville/Getty Images; ©Photodisc/Getty Images **p. 239:** ©Brand X Pictures/Jupiter Images **p. 240:** ©Photodisc/Getty Images **p. 241:** ©photolibrary.com pty. ltd/Index Open **p. 248 L to R:** Courtesy of Tanya Sexton; ©Hemera Photo Objects; ©Hemera Photo Objects; ©Hemera Photo Objects; ©Hemera Photo Objects **p. 249 all:** ©Hemera Photo Objects **p. 253:** ©Jose Luis Pelaez, Inc./CORBIS

INDEX